On the Philoso
Chapters Histor

By William Whewell

To the History of the Inductive Sciences are appended two Indexes (in Vol. 1.), an Index of Proper Names, and an Index of Technical Terms. These Indexes, and the Tables of Contents of the other works, will enable the reader to refer to any person or event included in this series.

PREFACE

The two works which I entitled The History of the Inductive Sciences, and The Philosophy of the Inductive Sciences, were intended to present to the reader a view of the steps by which those portions of human knowledge which are held to be most certain and stable have been acquired, and of the philosophical principles which are involved in those steps. Each of these steps was a scientific Discovery, in which a new conception was applied in order to bind together observed facts. And though the conjunction of the observed facts was in each case an example of logical Induction, it was not the inductive process merely, but the novelty of the result in each case which gave its peculiar character to the History; and the Philosophy at which I aimed was not the Philosophy of Induction, but the Philosophy of Discovery. In the present edition I have described this as my object in my Title.

A great part of the present volume consists of chapters which composed the twelfth Book of the Philosophy in former editions, which Book was then described as a 'Review of Opinions on the nature of Knowledge and the Method of seeking it.' I have added to this part several new chapters, on Plato, Aristotle, the Arabian Philosophers, Francis Bacon, Mr. Mill, Mr. Mansel, the late Sir William Hamilton, and the German philosophers Kant, Fichte, Schelling and Hegel. I might, if time had allowed, have added a new chapter on Roger Bacon, founded on his Opus Minus and other works, recently published for the first time under the direction of the Master of the Rolls; a valuable contribution to the history of philosophy. But the review of this work would not materially alter the estimate of Roger Bacon which I had derived from the Opus Majus.

But besides these historical and critical surveys of the philosophy of others, I have ventured to introduce some new views of my own; namely, views which bear upon the philosophy of religion. I have done so under the conviction that no philosophy of the universe can satisfy the minds of thoughtful men which does not deal with such questions as inevitably force themselves on our notice, respecting the Author and the Object of the universe; and also under the conviction that every philosophy of thevi universe which has any consistency must suggest answers, at least conjectural, to such questions. No Cosmos is complete from which the question of Deity is excluded; and all Cosmology has a side turned towards Theology. Though I am aware therefore how easy it is, on this subject, to give offence and to incur obloquy, I have not thought it right to abstain from following out my philosophical principles to their results in this department of speculation. The results do not differ materially from those at which many pious and thoughtful speculators have arrived in previous ages of the world; though they have here, as seems to me, something of novelty in their connection with the philosophy of science. But this point I willingly leave to the calm decision of competent judges.

I have added in an Appendix various Essays, previously published at different times, which may serve perhaps to illustrate some points of the history and philosophy of science.

Trinity Lodge,
February 8, 1856.

CHAPTER I.
INTRODUCTION.

By the examination of the elements of human thought in which I have been engaged, and by a consideration of the history of the most clear and certain parts of our knowledge, I have been led to doctrines respecting the progress of that exact and systematic knowledge which we call Science; and these doctrines I have endeavoured to lay before the reader in the History of the Sciences and of Scientific Ideas. The questions on which I have thus ventured to pronounce have had a strong interest for man from the earliest period of his intellectual progress, and have been the subjects of lively discussion and bold speculation in every age. I conceive that in the doctrines to which these researches have conducted us, we have a far better hope that we possess a body of permanent truths than the earlier essays on the same subjects could furnish. For we have not taken our examples of knowledge at hazard, as earlier speculators did, and were almost compelled to do; but have drawn our materials from the vast store of unquestioned truths which modern science offers to us: and we have formed our judgment concerning the nature and progress of knowledge by considering what such science is, and how it has reached its present condition. But though we have thus pursued our speculations concerning knowledge with advantages which earlier writers did not possess, it is still both interesting and instructive for us to regard the opinions upon this subject which have been delivered by the philosophers of past times. It is especially interesting to see some of the truths which we have endeavoured to expound, gradually dawning in men's minds, and assuming the4 clear and permanent form in which we can now contemplate them. I shall therefore, in the ensuing chapters, pass in review many of the opinions of the writers of various ages concerning the mode by which man best acquires the truest knowledge; and I shall endeavour, as we proceed, to appreciate the real value of such judgments, and their place in the progress of sound philosophy.

In this estimate of the opinions of others, I shall be guided by those general doctrines which I have, as I trust, established in the histories already published. And without attempting here to give any summary of these doctrines, I may remark that there are two main principles by which speculations on such subjects in all ages are connected and related to each other; namely, the opposition of Ideas and Sensations, and the distinction of practical and speculative knowledge. The opposition of Ideas and Sensations is exhibited to us in the antithesis of Theory and Fact, which are necessarily considered as distinct and of opposite natures, and yet necessarily identical, and constituting Science by their identity. In like manner, although practical knowledge is in substance identical with speculative, (for all knowledge is speculation,) there is a

2

distinction between the two in their history, and in the subjects by which they are exemplified, which distinction is quite essential in judging of the philosophical views of the ancients. The alternatives of identity and diversity, in these two antitheses,—the successive separation, opposition, and reunion of principles which thus arise,—have produced, (as they may easily be imagined capable of doing,) a long and varied series of systems concerning the nature of knowledge; among which we shall have to guide our course by the aid of the views already presented.

I am far from undertaking, or wishing, to review the whole series of opinions which thus come under our notice; and I do not even attempt to examine all the principal authors who have written on such subjects. I merely wish to select some of the most con5iderable forms which, such opinions have assumed, and to point out in some measure the progress of truth from age to age. In doing this, I can only endeavour to seize some of the most prominent features of each time and of each step, and I must pass rapidly from classical antiquity to those which we have called the dark ages, and from them to modern times. At each of these periods the modifications of opinion, and the speculations with which they were connected, formed a vast and tangled maze, the byways of which our plan does not allow us to enter. We shall esteem ourselves but too fortunate, if we can discover the single track by which ancient led to modern philosophy.

I must also repeat that my survey of philosophical writers is here confined to this one point,—their opinions on the nature of knowledge and the method of science. I with some effort avoid entering upon other parts of the philosophy of those authors of whom I speak; I knowingly pass by those portions of their speculations which are in many cases the most interesting and celebrated;—their opinions concerning the human soul, the Divine Governor of the world, the foundations or leading doctrines of politics, religion, and general philosophy. I am desirous that my reader should bear this in mind, since he must otherwise be offended with the scanty and partial view which I give in this place of the philosophers whom I enumerate.

6

CHAPTER II.
Plato.

There would be small advantage in beginning our examination earlier than the period of the Socratic School at Athens; for although the spirit of inquiry on such subjects had awakened in Greece at an earlier period, and although the peculiar aptitude of the Grecian mind for such researches had shown itself repeatedly in subtle distinctions and acute reasonings, all the positive results of these early efforts were contained in a more definite form in the reasonings of the Platonic age. Before that time, the Greeks did not possess plain and familiar examples of exact knowledge, such as the truths of Arithmetic, Geometry, Astronomy and Optics became in the school of Plato; nor were the antitheses of which we spoke above, so distinctly and fully unfolded as we find them in Plato's works.

The question which hinges upon one of these antitheses, occupies a prominent place in several of the Platonic dialogues; namely, whether our knowledge be obtained by

3

means of Sensation or of Ideas. One of the doctrines which Plato most earnestly inculcated upon his countrymen was, that we do not know concerning sensible objects, but concerning ideas. The first attempts of the Greeks at metaphysical analysis had given rise to a school which maintained that material objects are the only realities. In opposition to this, arose another school, which taught that material objects have no permanent reality, but are ever waxing and waning, constantly changing their substance. "And hence," as Aristotle says1, "arose the doctrine of ideas which the Platonists held. For they7 assented to the opinion of Heraclitus, that all sensible objects are in a constant state of flux. So that if there is to be any knowledge and science, it must be concerning some permanent natures, different from the sensible natures of objects; for there can be no permanent science respecting that which is perpetually changing. It happened that Socrates turned his speculations to the moral virtues, and was the first philosopher who endeavoured to give universal definitions of such matters. He wished to reason systematically, and therefore he tried to establish definitions, for definitions are the basis of systematic reasoning. There are two things which may justly be looked upon as steps in philosophy due to Socrates; inductive reasonings, and universal definitions;—both of them steps which belong to the foundations of science. Socrates, however, did not make universals, or definitions separable from the objects; but his followers separated them, and these essences they termed Ideas." And the same account is given by other writers[2]. "Some existences are sensible, some intelligible: and according to Plato, if we wish to understand the principles of things, we must first separate the ideas from the things, such as the ideas of Similarity, Unity, Number, Magnitude, Position, Motion: second, that we must assume an absolute Fair, Good, Just, and the like: third, that we must consider the ideas of relation, as Knowledge, Power: recollecting that the Things which we perceive have this or that appellation applied to them because they partake of this or that Idea; those things being just which participate in the idea of The Just, those being beautiful, which contain the idea of The Beautiful." And many of the arguments by which this doctrine was maintained are to be found in the Platonic dialogues. Thus the opinion that true knowledge consists in sensation, which had been asserted by Protagoras and others, is refuted in the Theætetus: and, we may add, so victoriously refuted, that the arguments there put forth8 have ever since exercised a strong influence upon the speculative world. It may be remarked that in the minds of Plato and of those who have since pursued the same paths of speculation, the interest of such discussions as those we are now referring to, was by no means limited to their bearing upon mere theory; but was closely connected with those great questions of morals which have always a practical import. Those who asserted that the only foundation of knowledge was sensation, asserted also that the only foundation of virtue was the desire of pleasure. And in Plato, the metaphysical part of the disquisitions concerning knowledge in general, though independent in its principles, always seems to be subordinate in its purpose to the questions concerning the knowledge of our duty.

Since Plato thus looked upon the Ideas which were involved in each department of knowledge as forming its only essential part, it was natural that he should look upon the study of Ideas as the true mode of pursuing knowledge. This he himself describes in the Philebus[3]. "The best way of arriving at truth is not very difficult to point out, but most hard to pursue. All the arts which have ever been discovered, were revealed in this manner. It is a gift of the gods to man, which, as I conceive, they sent down by some Prometheus, as by Prometheus they gave us the light of fire; and the ancients, more clear-

4

sighted than we, and less removed from the gods, handed down this traditionary doctrine: that whatever is said to be, comes of One and of Many, and comprehends in itself the Finite and the Infinite in coalition (being One Kind, and consisting of Infinite Individuals). And this being the state of things, we must, in each case, endeavour to seize the One Idea (the idea of the Kind) as the chief point; for we shall find that it is there. And when we have seized this one thing, we may then consider how it comprehends in itself two, or three, or any other number; and, again, examine each of these ramifications separately; till at last we9 perceive, not only that One is at the same time One and Many, but also how many. And when we have thus filled up the interval between the Infinite and the One, we may consider that we have done with each one. The gods then, as I have said, taught us by tradition thus to contemplate, and to learn, and to teach one another. But the philosophers of the present day seize upon the One, at hazard, too soon or too late, and then immediately snatch at the Infinite; but the intermediate steps escape them, in which resides the distinction between a truly logical and a mere disputatious discussion."

It would seem that what the author here describes as the most perfect form of exposition, is that which refers each object to its place in a classification containing a complete series of subordinations, and which gives a definition of each class. We have repeatedly remarked that, in sciences of classification, each new definition which gives a tenable and distinct separation of classes is an important advance in our knowledge; but that such definitions are rather the last than the first step in each advance. In the progress of real knowledge, these definitions are always the results of a laborious study of individual cases, and are never arrived at by a pure effort of thought, which is what Plato appears to have imagined as the true mode of philosophizing. And still less do the advances of other sciences consist in seizing at once upon the highest generality, and filling in afterwards all the intermediate steps between that and the special instances. On the contrary, as we have seen, the ascents from particular to general are all successive; and each step of this ascent requires time, and labour, and a patient examination of actual facts and objects.

It would, of course, be absurd to blame Plato for having inadequate views of the nature of progressive knowledge, at the time when knowledge could hardly be said to have begun its progress. But we already find in his speculations, as appears in the passages just quoted from his writings, several points brought into view which will require our continued attention10 as we proceed. In overlooking the necessity of a gradual and successive advance from the less general to the more general truths, Plato shared in a dimness of vision[4] which prevailed among philosophers to the time of Francis Bacon. In thinking too slightly of the study of actual nature, he manifested a bias from which the human intellect freed itself in the vigorous struggles which terminated the dark ages. In pointing out that all knowledge implies a unity of what we observe as manifold, which unity is given by the mind, Plato taught a lesson which has of late been too obscurely acknowledged, the recoil by which men repaired their long neglect of facts having carried them for a while so far as to think that facts were the whole of our knowledge. And in analysing this principle of Unity, by which we thus connect sensible things, into various Ideas, such as Number, Magnitude, Position, Motion, he made a highly important step, which it has been the business of philosophers in succeeding times to complete and to follow out.

5

But the efficacy of Plato's speculations in their bearing upon physical science, and upon theory in general, was much weakened by the confusion of practical with theoretical knowledge, which arose from the ethical propensities of the Socratic school. In the Platonic Dialogues, Art and Science are constantly spoken of indiscriminately. The skill possessed by the Painter, the Architect, the Shoemaker, is considered as a just example of human science, no less than the knowledge which the geometer or the astronomer possesses of the theoretical truths with which he is conversant. Not only so; but traditionary and mythological tales, mystical imaginations and fantastical etymologies, are mixed up, as no less choice ingredients, with the most acute logical analyses, and the most exact conduct of metaphysical controversies. There is no distinction made between the knowledge possessed by the theoretical psychologist and the11 physician, the philosophical teacher of morals and the legislator or the administrator of law. This, indeed, is the less to be wondered at, since even in our own time the same confusion is very commonly made by persons not otherwise ignorant or uncultured.

On the other hand, we may remark finally, that Plato's admiration of Ideas was not a barren imagination, even so far as regarded physical science. For, as we have seen[5], he had a very important share in the introduction of the theory of epicycles, having been the first to propose to astronomers in a distinct form, the problem of which that theory was the solution; namely, "to explain the celestial phenomena by the combination of equable circular motions." This demand of an ideal hypothesis which should exactly express the phenomena (as well as they could then be observed), and from which, by the interposition of suitable steps, all special cases might be deduced, falls in well with those views respecting the proper mode of seeking knowledge which we have quoted from the Philebus. And the Idea which could thus represent and replace all the particular Facts, being not only sought but found, we may readily suppose that the philosopher was, by this event, strongly confirmed in his persuasion that such an Idea was indeed what the inquirer ought to seek. In this conviction all his genuine followers up to modern times have participated; and thus, though they have avoided the error of those who hold that facts alone are valuable as the elements of our knowledge, they have frequently run into the opposite error of too much despising and neglecting facts, and of thinking that the business of the inquirer after truth was only a profound and constant contemplation of the conceptions of his own mind. But of this hereafter.

12

CHAPTER III.
Additional Remarks on Plato.

The leading points in Plato's writings which bear upon the philosophy of discovery are these:

1. The Doctrine of Ideas.
2. The Doctrine of the One and the Many.
3. The notion of the nature and aim of Science.
4. The survey of existing Sciences.

1. The Doctrine of Ideas is an attempt to solve a problem which in all ages forces itself upon the notice of thoughtful men; namely, How can certain and permanent knowledge be possible for man, since all his knowledge must be derived from transient and fluctuating sensations? And the answer given by this doctrine is, that certain and permanent knowledge is not derived from Sensations, but from Ideas. There are in the mind certain elements of knowledge which are not derived from sensation, and are only imperfectly exemplified in sensible objects; and when we reason concerning sensible things so as to obtain real knowledge, we do so by considering such things as partaking of the qualities of the Ideas concerning which there can be truth. The sciences of Geometry and Arithmetic show that there are truths which man can know; and the Doctrine of Ideas explains how this is possible.

So far the Doctrine of Ideas answers its primary purpose, and is a reply (by no means the least intelligible and satisfactory reply) to a question still agitated among philosophers: What is the ground of geometrical (and other necessary) truth?

But Plato seems, in many of his writings, to extend this doctrine much further; and to assume, not only Ideas of Space and its properties, from which geome13trical truths are derived; but of Relations, as the Relations of Like and Unlike, Greater and Less; and of mere material objects, as Tables and Chairs. Now to assume Ideas of such things as these solves no difficulty and is supported by no argument. In this respect the Ideal theory is of no value in Science.

It is curious that we have a very acute refutation of the Ideal theory in this sense, not only in Aristotle, the open opponent of Plato on this subject, but in the Platonic writings themselves: namely, in the Dialogue entitled Parmenides; which, on this and on other accounts, I consider to be the work not of Plato, but of an opponent of Plato[6].

2. I have spoken, in the preceding chapter, of Plato's doctrine that truth is to be obtained by discerning the One in the Many. This expression is used, it would seem, in a somewhat large and fluctuating way, to mean several things; as for instance, finding the one kind in many individuals (for instance, the one idea of dog in many dogs); or the one law in many phenomena (for instance, the eccentrics and epicycles in many planets). In any interpretation, it is too loose and indefinite a rule to be of much value in the formation of sciences, though it has been recently again propounded as important in modern times.

3. I have said, in the preceding chapter, that Plato, though he saw that scientific truths of great generality might be obtained and were to be arrived at by philosophers, overlooked the necessity of a gradual and successive advance from the less general to the more general; and I have described this as a 'dimness of vision.' I must now acknowledge that this is not a very appropriate phrase; for not only no acuteness of vision could have enabled Plato to see that gradual generalization in science of which, as yet, no example had appeared; but it was very fortunate for the progress of truth, at that time, that Plato had imagined to himself the object of science to be general14 and sublime truths which prove themselves to be true by the light of their own generality and symmetry. It is worth while to illustrate this notice of Plato by some references to his writings.

In the Sixth Book of the Republic, Plato treats of the then existing sciences as the instruments of a philosophical education. Among the most conspicuous of these is astronomy. He there ridicules the notion that astronomy is a sublime science because it makes men look upward. He asserts that the really sublime science is that which makes men look at the realities, which are suggested by the appearances seen in the heavens: namely, the spheres which revolve and carry the luminaries in their revolutions. Now it was no doubt the determined search for such "realities" as these which gave birth to the Greek Astronomy, that first and critical step in the progress of science. Plato, by his exhortations, if not by his suggestions, contributed effectually, as I conceive, to this step in science. In the same manner he requires a science of Harmonics which shall be free from the defects and inaccuracies which occur in actual instruments. This belief that the universe was full of mathematical relations, and that these were the true objects of scientific research, gave a vigour, largeness of mind, and confidence to the Greek speculators which no more cautious view of the problem of scientific discovery could have supplied. It was well that this advanced guard in the army of discoverers was filled with indomitable courage, boundless hopes, and creative minds.

But we must not forget that this disposition to what Bacon calls anticipation was full of danger as well as of hope. It led Plato into error, as it led Kepler afterwards, and many others in all ages of scientific activity. It led Plato into error, for instance, when it led him to assert (in the Timæus) that the four elements, Earth, Air, Fire and Water, have, for the forms of their particles respectively, the Cube, the Icosahedron, the Pyramid, and the Octahedron; and again, when it led him to despise the practical controversies of the musicians of his time; which con15troversies were, in fact, the proof of the truth of the mathematical theory of Harmonics. And in like manner it led Kepler into error when it led him to believe that he had found the reason of the number, size and motion of the planetary orbits in the application of the five regular solids to the frame of the universe[7].

How far the caution in forming hypotheses which Bacon's writings urge upon us is more severe than suits the present prospects of science, we may hereafter consider; but it is plainly very conceivable that a boldness in the invention and application of hypotheses which was propitious to science in its infancy, may be one of the greatest dangers of its more mature period: and further, that the happy effect of such a temper depended entirely upon the candour, skill and labour with which the hypotheses were compared with the observed phenomena.

4. Plato has given a survey of the sciences of his time as Francis Bacon has of his. Indeed Plato has given two such surveys: one, in the Republic, in reviewing, as I have said, the elements of a philosophical education; the other in the Timæus, as the portions of a theological view of the universe—such as has been called a Theodicæa, a justification of God. In the former passage of Plato, the sciences enumerated are Arithmetic, Plane Geometry, Solid Geometry, Astronomy and Harmonics[8]. In the Timæus we have a further notice of many other subjects, in a way which is intended, I conceive, to include such knowledge as Plato had then arrived at on the various parts of the universe. The subjects there referred to are, as I have elsewhere stated[9], these: light and heat, water, ice, gold, gems, rust and other natural objects:—odours, taste, hearing, lights, colour, and the powers of sense in general:—the parts and organs of the body, as the bones, the marrow, the brain, flesh, muscles, tendons, ligaments and nerves; the skin, the hair, the16

8

nails; the veins and arteries; respiration; generation; and in short, every obvious point of physiology. But the opinions thus delivered in the Timæus on the latter subject have little to do with the progress of real knowledge. The doctrines, on the other hand, which depend upon geometrical and arithmetical relations are portions or preludes of the sciences which the fulness of time brought forth.

5. I may, as further bearing upon the Platonic notion of science, notice Plato's view of the constitution of the human mind. According to him the Ideas which are the constituents of science form an Intelligible World, while the visible and tangible things which we perceive by our senses form the Visible World. In the visible world we have shadows and reflections of actual objects, and by these shadows and reflections we may judge of the objects, even when we cannot do so directly; as when men in a dark cavern judge of external objects by the shadows which they cast into the cavern. In like manner in the Intelligible World there are conceptions which are the usual objects of human thought, and about which we reason; but these are only shadows and reflections of the Ideas which are the real sources of truth. And the Reasoning Faculty, the Discursive Reason, the Logos, which thus deals with conceptions, is subordinate to the Intuitive Faculty, the Intuitive Reason, the Nous, which apprehends Ideas[10]. This recognition of a Faculty in man which contemplates the foundations—the Fundamental Ideas—of science, and by apprehending such Ideas, makes science possible, is consentaneous to the philosophy which I have all along presented, as the view taught us by a careful study of the history and nature of science. That new Fundamental Ideas are unfolded, and the Intuitive Faculty developed and enlarged by the progress of science and by an intimate acquaintance with its reasonings, Plato appears to have discerned in some measure, though dimly. And this is the less wonderful, inasmuch as this gradual and17 successive extension of the field of Intuitive Truth, in proportion as we become familiar with a larger amount of derived truth, is even now accepted by few, though proved by the reasonings of the greatest scientific discoverers in every age.

The leading defect in Plato's view of the nature of real science is his not seeing fully the extent to which experience and observation are the basis of all our knowledge of the universe. He considers the luminaries which appear in the heavens to be not the true objects of astronomy, but only some imperfect adumbration of them;—mere diagrams which may assist us in the study of a higher truth, as beautiful diagrams might illustrate the truths of geometry, but would not prove them. This notion of an astronomy which is an astronomy of Theories and not of Facts, is not tenable, for Theories are Facts. Theories and Facts are equally real; true Theories are Facts, and Facts are familiar Theories. But when Plato says that astronomy is a series of problems suggested by visible things, he uses expressions quite conformable to the true philosophy of science; and the like is true of all other sciences.

18

CHAPTER IV.
Aristotle.

The views of Aristotle with regard to the foundations of human knowledge are very different from those of his tutor Plato, and are even by himself put in opposition to them.

He dissents altogether from the Platonic doctrine that Ideas are the true materials of our knowledge; and after giving, respecting the origin of this doctrine, the account which we quoted in the last chapter, he goes on to reason against it. "Thus," he says[11], "they devised Ideas of all things which are spoken of as universals: much as if any one having to count a number of objects, should think that he could not do it while they were few, and should expect to count them by making them more numerous. For the kinds of things are almost more numerous than the special sensible objects, by seeking the causes of which they were led to their Ideas." He then goes on to urge several other reasons against the assumption of Ideas and the use of them in philosophical researches.

Aristotle himself establishes his doctrines by trains of reasoning. But reasoning must proceed from certain First Principles; and the question then arises, Whence are these First Principles obtained? To this he replies, that they are the result of Experience, and he even employs the same technical expression by which we at this day describe the process of collecting these principles from observed facts;—that they are obtained by Induction. I have already quoted passages in which this statement is made[12]. "The way of reasoning," he says[13], "is the same in philosophy,19 and in any art or science: we must collect the facts (τὰ ὑπάρχοντα), and the things to which the facts happen, and must have as large a supply of these as possible, and then we must examine them according to the terms of our syllogisms." ... "There are peculiar principles in each science; and in each case these principles must be obtained from experience. Thus astronomical observation supplies the principles of astronomical science. For the phenomena being rightly taken, the demonstrations of astronomy were discovered; and the same is the case with any other Art or Science. So that if the facts in each case be taken, it is our business to construct the demonstrations. For if in our natural history (κατὰ τὰν ἱστορί αν) we have omitted none of the facts and properties which belong to the subject, we shall learn what we can demonstrate and what we cannot." And again[14], "It is manifest that if any sensation be wanting, there must be some knowledge wanting, which we are thus prevented from having. For we acquire knowledge either by Induction (ἐπαγωγῆ) or by Demonstration: and Demonstration is from universals, but Induction from particulars. It is impossible to have universal theoretical propositions except by Induction: and we cannot make inductions without having sensation; for sensation has to do with particulars."

It is easy to show that Aristotle uses the term Induction, as we use it, to express the process of collecting a general proposition from particular cases in which it is exemplified. Thus in a passage which we have already quoted[15], he says, "Induction, and Syllogism from Induction, is when we attribute one extreme term to the middle by means of the other." The import of this technical phraseology will further appear by the example which he gives: "We find that several animals which are deficient in bile are long-lived, as man, the horse, the mule; hence we infer that all animals which are deficient in bile are long-lived."

20

.

We may observe, however, that both Aristotle's notion of induction, and many other parts of his philosophy, are obscure and imperfect, in consequence of his refusing to contemplate ideas as something distinct from sensation. It thus happens that he always assumes the ideas which enter into his proposition as given; and considers it as the philosopher's business to determine whether such propositions are true or not: whereas the most important feature in induction is, as we have said, the introduction of a new idea, and not its employment when once introduced. That the mind in this manner gives unity to that which is manifold,—that we are thus led to speculative principles which have an evidence higher than any others,—and that a peculiar sagacity in some men seizes upon the conceptions by which the facts may be bound into true propositions,—are doctrines which form no essential part of the philosophy of the Stagirite, although such views are sometimes recognized, more or less clearly, in his expressions. Thus he says[16], "There can be no knowledge when the sensation does not continue in the mind. For this purpose, it is necessary both to perceive, and to have some unity in the mind (αἰσθανομένοις ἐχειν ἔν τι[17] ἐν τῇ ψυχῇ); and many such perceptions having taken place, some difference is then perceived: and from the remembrance of these arises Reason. Thus from Sensation comes Memory, and from Memory of the same thing often repeated comes Experience: for many acts of Memory make up one Experience. And from Experience, or from any Universal Notion which takes a permanent place in the mind,—from the unity in the manifold, the same some one thing being found in many facts,—springs the first principle of Art and of Science; of Art, if it be employed about production; of Science, if about existence."

21

I will add to this, Aristotle's notice of Sagacity; since, although little or no further reference is made to this quality in his philosophy, the passage fixes our attention upon an important step in the formation of knowledge. "Sagacity" (ἀγχίνοια), he says[18], "is a hitting by guess (εὐστοχία τις) upon the middle term (the conception common to two cases) in an inappreciable time. As for example, if any one seeing that the bright side of the moon is always towards the sun, suddenly perceives why this is; namely, because the moon shines by the light of the sun:—or if he sees a person talking with a rich man, he guesses that he is borrowing money;—or conjectures that two persons are friends, because they are enemies of the same person."—To consider only the first of these examples;—the conception here introduced, that of a body shining by the light which another casts upon it, is not contained in the observed facts, but introduced by the mind. It is, in short, that conception which, in the act of induction, the mind superadds to the phenomena as they are presented by the senses: and to invent such appropriate conceptions, such "eustochies," is, indeed, the precise office of inductive sagacity.

At the end of this work (the Later Analytics) Aristotle ascribes our knowledge of principles to Intellect (νοῦς), or, as it appears necessary to translate the word, Intuition[19]. "Since, of our intellectual habits by which we aim at truth, some are always true, but some admit of being false, as Opinion and Reasoning, but Science and Intuition are always true; and since there is nothing which is more certain than Science except Intuition; and since Principles are better known to us than the Deductions from them; and since all Science is connected by reasoning, we cannot have Science respecting Principles. Considering this then, and that the beginning of Demonstration cannot be

11

Demonstration, nor the beginning of Science, Science; and since, as we have said, there is no other kind of truth, Intuition must be the beginning of Science."

22

What is here said, is, no doubt, in accordance with the doctrines which we have endeavoured to establish respecting the nature of Science, if by this Intuition we understand that contemplation of certain Fundamental Ideas, which is the basis of all rigorous knowledge. But notwithstanding this apparent approximation, Aristotle was far from having an habitual and practical possession of the principles which he thus touches upon. He did not, in reality, construct his philosophy by giving Unity to that which was manifold, or by seeking in Intuition principles which might be the basis of Demonstration; nor did he collect, in each subject, fundamental propositions by an induction of particulars. He rather endeavoured to divide than to unite; he employed himself, not in combining facts, but in analysing notions; and the criterion to which he referred his analysis was, not the facts of our experience, but our habits of language. Thus his opinions rested, not upon sound inductions, gathered in each case from the phenomena by means of appropriate Ideas; but upon the loose and vague generalizations which are implied in the common use of speech.

Yet Aristotle was so far consistent with his own doctrine of the derivation of knowledge from experience, that he made in almost every province of human knowledge, a vast collection of such special facts as the experience of his time supplied. These collections are almost unrivalled, even to the present day, especially in Natural History; in other departments, when to the facts we must add the right Inductive Idea, in order to obtain truth, we find little of value in the Aristotelic works. But in those parts which refer to Natural History, we find not only an immense and varied collection of facts and observations, but a sagacity and acuteness in classification which it is impossible not to admire. This indeed appears to have been the most eminent faculty in Aristotle's mind.

The influence of Aristotle in succeeding ages will come under our notice shortly.

23

CHAPTER V.
Additional Remarks on Aristotle.

1. ONE of the most conspicuous points in Aristotle's doctrines as bearing upon the philosophy of Science is his account of that mode of attaining truth which is called Induction; for we are accustomed to consider Induction as the process by which our Sciences have been formed; and we call them collectively the Inductive Sciences. Aristotle often speaks of Induction, as for instance, when he says that Socrates introduced the frequent use of it. But the cardinal passage on this subject is in his Analytics, in which he compares Syllogism and Induction as two modes of drawing conclusions[20]. He there says that all belief arises either from Syllogism or from Induction: and adds that Induction is, when by means of one extreme term we infer the other extreme to be true of the middle term. The example which he gives is this: knowing that particular animals are long-lived, as elephant, horse, mule; and finding that these animals agree in having no gall-

bladder; we infer, by Induction, that all animals which have no gall-bladder are long-lived. This may be done, he says, if the middle and the second extreme are convertible: as the following formal statement may show.

Elephant, horse, mule, &c. are long-lived.
Elephant, horse, mule, &c. are all gall-less.
If we might convert this proposition, and say

All gall-less animals are as elephant, horse, mule, &c.:

24

we might infer syllogistically that

All gall-less animals are long-lived.

And though we cannot infer this syllogistically, we infer it by Induction, when we have a sufficient amount of instances[21].

I have already elsewhere given this account of Induction, as a process employed in the formation of our knowledge[22]. What I have now to remark concerning Aristotle is, that it does not appear to have occurred to him, that in establishing such a proposition as that which he gives as his instance, the main difficulty is the discovery of a middle term which will allow us to frame such a proposition as we need. The zoologist who wanted to know what kind of animals are long-lived, might guess long before he guessed that the absence of the gall-bladder supplied the requisite middle term; (if the proposition were true; which it is not.) And in like manner in other cases, it is difficult to find a middle term, which enables us to collect a proposition by Induction. And herein consists the imperfection of his view of the subject; which considers the main point to be the proof of the proposition when the conceptions are given, whereas the main point really is, the discovery of conceptions which will make a true proposition possible.

2. Since the main characteristic of the steps which have occurred in the formation of the physical sciences, is not merely that they are propositions collected by Induction, but by the introduction of a new conception; it has been suggested that it is not a characteristic designation of these Sciences to call them Inductive Sciences. Almost every discovery involves in it the introduction of a new conception, as the element of a new proposition; and the novelty of the conception is more characteristic of the stages of discovery than the inductive application of it. Hence as25 bearing upon the Philosophy of Discovery, the statements of Aristotle concerning Induction, though acute and valuable, are not so valuable as they might seem. Even Francis Bacon, it has been asserted, erred in the same way (and of course with less excuse) in asserting Induction, of a certain kind, to be the great instrument for the promotion of knowledge, and in overlooking the necessity of the Invention which gives Induction its value.

3. The invention or discovery of a conception by which many facts of observation are conjoined so as to make them the materials of a proposition, is called in Plato, as we have seen, finding the One in the Many.

13

In the passage quoted from the Later Analytics, Aristotle uses the same expression, and speaks very justly respecting the formation of knowledge. Indeed the Titles of the chapters of this and many parts of Aristotle's works would lead us to expect just such a Philosophy of Discovery as is the object of our study at present. Thus we have, Anal. Post. B. II. chap. 13: "How we are to hunt (θηρεύειν) the predications of a Definition." Chap. 14: "Precepts for the invention of Problems and of a Middle Term:" and the like. But when we come to read these chapters, they contain little that is of value, and resolve themselves mostly into permutations of Aristotle's logical phraseology.

4. The part of the Aristotelian philosophy which has most permanently retained its place in modern Sciences is a part of which a use has been made quite different from that which was originally contemplated. The "Five words" which are explained in the Introduction to Aristotle's Categories: namely, the words Genus, Species, Difference, Property, Accident, were introduced mainly that they might be used in the propositions of which Syllogisms consist, and might thus be the elements of reasoning. But it has so happened that these words are rarely used in Sciences of Reasoning, but are abundantly and commonly used in26 the Sciences of Classification, as I have explained in speaking of the Classificatory Sciences[23].

5. Of Aristotle's actual contributions to the Physical Sciences I have spoken in the History of those Sciences[24]. I have[25] stated that he conceived the globular form of the earth so clearly and gave so forcibly the arguments for that doctrine, that we may look upon him as the most effective teacher of it. Also in the Appendix to that History, published in the third edition, I have given Aristotle's account of the Rainbow, as a further example of his industrious accumulation of facts, and of his liability to error in his facts.

6. We do not find Aristotle so much impressed as we might have expected by that great monument of Grecian ingenuity, the theory of epicycles and excentrics which his predecessor Plato urged so strongly upon the attention of his contemporaries. Aristotle proves, as I have said, the globular form of the earth by good and sufficient arguments. He also proves by arguments which seem to him quite conclusive[26], that the earth is in the center of the universe, and immoveable. As to the motions of the rest of the planets, he says little. The questions of their order, and their distances, and the like, belong, he says, to Astrology[27]. He remarks only that the revolution of the heaven itself, the outermost revolution, is simple and the quickest of all: that the revolutions of the others are slower, each moving in a direction opposite to the heaven in its own circle: and that it is reasonable that those which are nearest to the first revolution should take the longest time in describing their own circle, and those that are furthest off, the least time, and the intermediate ones in the order of their distances, "as also the mathematicians show."

In the Metaphysics[28] he enumerates the circular movements which had been introduced by the astro27nomers Eudoxus and Calippus for the explanation of the phenomena presented by the sun, moon and planets. These, he says, amount to fifty-five; and this, he says, must be the number of essences and principles which exist in the universe.

14

7. In the Sciences of Classification, and especially in the classification of animals, higher claims have been made for Aristotle, which I have discussed in the History[29]. I have there attempted to show that Aristotle's classification, inasmuch as it enumerates all the parts of animals, may be said to contain the materials of every subsequent classification: but that it cannot be said to anticipate any modern system, because the different grades of classification are not made subordinate to one another as a system of classification requires. I have the satisfaction of finding Mr. Owen agreeing with me in these views[30].

8. Francis Bacon's criticism on Aristotle which I have quoted in the Appendix to the History[31], is severe, and I think evidently the result of prejudice. He disparages Aristotle in comparison with the other philosophers of Greece. 'Their systems,' he says, 'had some savour of experience, and nature, and bodily things; while the Physics of Aristotle, in general, sound only of Logical Terms.

'Nor let anyone be moved by this: that in his books Of Animals, and in his Problems, and in others of his tracts, there is often a quoting of experiments. For he had made up his mind beforehand; and did not consult experience in order to make right propositions and axioms, but when he had settled his system to his will, he twisted experience round and made her bend to his system.'

I do not think that this can be said with any truth. I know no instances in which Aristotle has twisted experience round, and made her bend to his system. In28 his Problems, he is so far from giving dogmatical solutions of the questions proposed, that in most cases, he propounds two or three solutions as mere suggestions and conjectures. And both in his History of Animals, as I have said, and in others of his works, the want of system gives them an incoherent and tumultuary character, which even a false system would have advantageously removed; for, as I have said elsewhere, it is easier to translate a false system into a true one, than to introduce system into a mass of confusion.

9. It is curious that a fundamental error into which Aristotle fell in his view of the conditions which determine the formation of Science is very nearly the same as one of Francis Bacon's leading mistakes. Aristotle says, that Science consists in knowing the causes of things, as Bacon aims at acquiring a knowledge of the forms or essences of things and their qualities. But the history of all the sciences teaches us that sciences do not begin with such knowledge, and that in few cases only do they ever attain to it. Sciences begin by a knowledge of the laws of phenomena, and proceed by the discovery of the scientific ideas by which the phenomena are colligated, as I have shown in other works[32]. The discovery of causes is not beyond the human powers, as some have taught. Those who thus speak disregard the lessons taught by the history of Physical Astronomy, of Geology, of Physical Optics, Thermotics and other sciences. But the discovery of causes, and of the essential forms of qualities, is a triumph reserved for the later stages of each Science, when the knowledge of the laws of phenomena has already made great progress. It was not to be expected that Aristotle would discern this truth, when, as yet, there was no Science extant in which it had been exemplified. Yet in Astronomy, the theory of epicycles and excentrics had immense value, and even has still, as representing the laws of phenomena; while the attempt to find in29 it, as Aristotle wished to do, the ultimate causes of the motions of the universe, could only mislead. The

Aristotelian maxim, which sounds so plausible, and has been so generally accepted, that "to know truly is to know the causes of things," is a bad guide in scientific research. Instead of it we might substitute this: that "though we may aspire to know at last why things are, we must be content for a long time with knowing how they are."

10. Hence if we are asked whether Plato or Aristotle had the truer views of the nature and property of Science, we must give the preference to Plato; for though his notion of a real Intelligible World, of which the Visible world was a fleeting and changeable shadow, was extravagant, yet it led him to seek to determine the forms of the Intelligible Things, which are really the laws of visible phenomena; while Aristotle was led to pass lightly over such laws, because they did not at once reveal the causes which produced the phenomena.

11. Aristotle, throughout his works, takes numerous occasions to argue against Plato's doctrine of Ideas. Yet these Ideas, so far as they were the Intelligible Forms of Visible Things, were really fit objects of philosophical research; and the search after them had a powerful influence in promoting the progress of Science. And we may see in the effect of this search the answer to many of Aristotle's strongest arguments. For instance, Aristotle says that Plato, by way of explaining things, adds to them as many Ideas, and that this is just as if a man having to reckon a large number, were to begin by adding to it another large number. It is plain that to this we may reply, that the adopting the Ideas of Cycles, along with the motions of the Planets, does really explain the motions; and that the Cycles are not simply added to the phenomena, but include and supersede the phenomena: a finite number of Cycles include and represent an infinite number of separate phenomena.

To Aristotle's argument that Ideas cannot be the Causes or Principles of Things, we should reply, that30 though they cannot be this, they may nevertheless be, and must be, the Conditions and Principles of our Knowledge, which is what we want them to be.

I have given an account of the main features of Aristotle's philosophy, so far as it concerns the Physical Sciences, in the History of the Inductive Sciences, Book I.

31

CHAPTER VI.
The Later Greeks.

Thus while Plato was disposed to seek the essence of our knowledge in Ideas alone, Aristotle, slighting this source of truth, looked to Experience as the beginning of Science; and he attempted to obtain, by division and deduction, all that Experience did not immediately supply. And thus, with these two great names, began that struggle of opposite opinions which has ever since that time agitated the speculative world, as men have urged the claims of Ideas or of Experience to our respect, and as alternately each of these elements of knowledge has been elevated above its due place, while the other has been unduly depressed. We shall see the successive turns of this balanced struggle in the remaining portions of this review.

But we may observe that practically the influence of Plato predominated rather than that of Aristotle, in the remaining part of the history of ancient philosophy. It was, indeed, an habitual subject of dispute among men of letters, whether the sources of true knowledge are to be found in the Senses or in the Mind; the Epicureans taking one side of this alternative, and the Academics another, while the Stoics in a certain manner included both elements in their view. But none of these sects showed their persuasion that the materials of knowledge were to be found in the domain of Sense, by seeking them there. No one appears to have thought of following the example of Aristotle, and gathering together a store of observed facts. We may except, perhaps, assertions belonging to some provinces of Natural History, which were collected by various writers: but in these, the mixed32 character of the statements, the want of discrimination in the estimate of evidence, the credulity and love of the marvellous which the authors for the most part displayed, showed that instead of improving upon the example of Aristotle, they were wandering further and further from the path of real knowledge. And while they thus collected, with so little judgment, such statements as offered themselves, it hardly appears to have occurred to any one to enlarge the stores of observation by the aid of experiment; and to learn what the laws of nature were, by trying what were their results in particular cases. They used no instruments for obtaining an insight into the constitution of the universe, except logical distinctions and discussions; and proceeded as if the phenomena familiar to their predecessors must contain all that was needed as a basis for natural philosophy. By thus contenting themselves with the facts which the earlier philosophers had contemplated, they were led also to confine themselves to the ideas which those philosophers had put forth. For all the most remarkable alternatives of hypothesis, so far as they could be constructed with a slight and common knowledge of phenomena, had been promulgated by the acute and profound thinkers who gave the first impulse to philosophy: and it was not given to man to add much to the original inventions of their minds till he had undergone anew a long discipline of observation, and of thought employed upon observation. Thus the later authors of the Greek Schools became little better than commentators on the earlier; and the commonplaces with which the different schools carried on their debates,—the constantly recurring argument, with its known attendant answer,—the distinctions drawn finer and finer and leading to nothing,—render the speculations of those times a scholastic philosophy, in the same sense in which we employ the term when we speak of the labours of the middle ages. It will be understood that I now refer to that which is here my subject, the opinions concerning our knowledge of nature, and the methods in use for the purpose of obtaining such33 knowledge. Whether the moral speculations of the ancient world were of the same stationary kind, going their round in a limited circle, like their metaphysics and physics, must be considered on some other occasion.[33]

Mr. Grote, in his very interesting discussion of Socrates's teaching, notices also[34] the teaching of Hippocrates, which he conceives to have in one respect the same tendency as the philosophy of Socrates; namely, to turn away from the vague aggregate of doctrines and guesses which constituted the Physical Philosophy of that time, and to pursue instead a special and more practical course of inquiry: Hippocrates selecting Medicine and Socrates selecting Ethics. By this limitation of their subject, they avoided some of the errors of their predecessors. For, as Mr. Grote has also remarked, "the earlier speculators, Anaxagoras, Empedocles, Democritus, the Pythagoreans, all had still present to their minds the vast and undivided problems which have been transmitted down from

17

the old poets; bending their minds to the invention of some system which would explain them all at once, or assist the imagination in conceiving both how the Kosmos first began and how it continued to move on." There could be no better remedy for this ambitious error of the human mind than to have a definite subject of study, such as the diseases and the health of the human body. Accordingly, we see that the study of medicine did draw its cultivators away from this ancient but unprofitable field. Hippocrates[35] condemns those who, as Empedocles, set themselves to make out what man was from the beginning, how he began first to exist, and in what manner he was constructed. This is, he says, no part of medicine. In like manner he blames and refutes those who make some simple element, Hot, or Cold, or Moist, or Dry, the cause of34 diseases, and give medical precepts professing to be founded on this hypothesis.

These passages are marked by the prudence which practical study suggests to a calm and clear-sighted man. They can hardly be said to have opened the way to a Science of Medicine; for in the sense in which we here use the word Science, namely, a collection of general truths inferred from facts by successive discoverers, we have even yet no Science of Medicine. The question with regard to the number and nature of the Elements of which bodies are composed began to be agitated, as we have seen, at a very early period of Greek philosophy, and continued long to be regarded as a chief point of physiological doctrine. In Galen's work we have a treatise entitled, On the Elements according to Hippocrates; and the writer explains[36] that though Hippocrates has not written any work with the title On the Elements, yet that he has in his Treatise on the Nature of Man shown his opinion on that subject. That the doctrine of the Four Elements, Hot, Cold, Moist, Dry, subsisted long in the schools, we have evidence in Galen. He tells us[37] that when he was a student of nineteen years old a teacher urged this lore upon him, and regarded him as very contentious and perverse, because he offered objections to it. His account of the Dialogue between him and the teacher is curious. But in Hippocrates the doctrine of these four elements is replaced, in a great measure, by the doctrine of the Four Humours of which the human body is constituted; namely, Blood, Phlegm, Yellow Bile and Black Bile. Galen dwells with emphasis upon Hippocrates's proof that there must be more than one such element[38].

"What," he asks, "is the method of finding the Elements of bodies? There can, in my opinion, be no other than that which was introduced by Hippocrates; namely, we must inquire whether there be only one element, everywhere the same in kind, or whether35 there are more than one, various and unlike each other. And if the Element be not one only, but several, various and dissimilar, we must inquire in the second place, how many elements there are, and what, and of what kind they are, and how related in their association.

"Now that the First Element is not one only of which both our bodies and those of all other creatures were produced, Hippocrates shows from these considerations. And it is better first to put down his own expressions and then to expound them. 'I assert that if man consisted of one element only he could not fall sick; for there would be nothing which could derange his health, if he were all of one Element.'"

The doctrine of One Element did not prevail much after the time of Hippocrates: the doctrine of Four Elements continued, as I have said, long to hold possession of the

Schools, but does not appear as an important part of the doctrine of Hippocrates. The doctrine of the Four Humours (Blood, Phlegm, Yellow Bile and Black Bile) is more peculiarly his, and long retained its place as a principle of physiological Science.

But we are here not so much concerned with his discoveries in medicine as with his views respecting the method of acquiring sound knowledge, and in this respect, as has been said, he recommends by his practice a prudent limitation of the field of inquiry, a rejection of wide, ambitious, general assertions, and a practical study of his proper field.

In ascribing these merits to Hippocrates's medical speculations as to the ethical speculations of his contemporary Socrates, we assign considerable philosophical value to Hippocrates, no less than to Socrates. These merits were at that time the great virtues of physical as well as of ethical philosophy. But, as Mr. Grote well observes, the community of character which then subsisted between the physical and ethical speculations prevailing at that time, ceased to obtain in later times. Indeed, it ceased to exist just at that time, in consequence of the establishment of36 scientific astronomy by the exertions of Plato and his contemporaries. From that time the Common Sense (as we call it) of a man like Socrates, though it might be a good guide in ethics, was not a good guide in physics. I have shown elsewhere[39] how the Common Sense of Socrates was worthless in matters of astronomy. From that time one of the great intellectual lessons was, that in order to understand the external world, we must indeed observe carefully, but we must also guess boldly. Discovery here required an inventive mind like Plato's to deal with and arrange new and varied facts. But in ethics all the facts were old and familiar, and the generalizations of language by which they were grouped as Virtues and Vices, and the like, were common and well-known words. Here was no room for invention; and thus in the ethical speculations of Socrates or of any other moral teacher, we are not to look for any contributions to the Philosophy of Discovery.

physics *&* *discovery*

Nor do I find anything on this subject among later Greek writers, beyond the commendation of such intellectual virtues as Hippocrates and Galen, and other medical writers, schooled by the practice of their art, enjoined and praised. But before we quit the ancients I will point out some peculiarities which may be noticed in the Roman disciples of the Greek philosophy.

37

CHAPTER VII.
The Romans.

The Romans had no philosophy but that which they borrowed from the Greeks; and what they thus received, they hardly made entirely their own. The vast and profound question of which we have been speaking, the relation between Existence and our Knowledge of what exists, they never appear to have fathomed, even so far as to discern how wide and deep it is. In the development of the ideas by which nature is to be understood, they went no further than their Greek masters had gone, nor indeed was more to be looked for. And in the practical habit of accumulating observed facts as materials for knowledge, they were much less discriminating and more credulous than their Greek predecessors. The descent from Aristotle to Pliny, in the judiciousness of the authors and the value of their collections of facts, is immense.

Since the Romans were thus servile followers of their Greek teachers, and little acquainted with any example of new truths collected from the world around them, it was not to be expected that they could have any just conception of that long and magnificent ascent from one set of truths to others of higher order and wider compass, which the history of science began to exhibit when the human mind recovered its progressive habits. Yet some dim presentiment of the splendid career thus destined for the intellect of man appears from time to time to have arisen in their minds. Perhaps the circumstance which most powerfully contributed to suggest this vision, was the vast intellectual progress which they were themselves conscious of having made, through the introduction of the Greek38 philosophy; and to this may be added, perhaps, some other features of national character. Their temper was too stubborn to acquiesce in the absolute authority of the Greek philosophy, although their minds were not inventive enough to establish a rival by its side. And the wonderful progress of their political power had given them a hope in the progress of man which the Greeks never possessed. The Roman, as he believed the fortune of his State to be destined for eternity, believed also in the immortal destiny and endless advance of that Intellectual Republic of which he had been admitted a denizen.

It is easy to find examples of such feelings as I have endeavoured to describe. The enthusiasm with which Lucretius and Virgil speak of physical knowledge, manifestly arises in a great measure from the delight which they had felt in becoming acquainted with the Greek theories.

> Me vero primum dulces ante omnia Musæ
> Quarum sacra fero ingenti perculsus amore
> Accipiant, cœlique vias et sidera monstrent,
> Defectus Solis varios, Lunæque labores!...
> Felix qui potuit rerum cognoscere causas!
> Ye sacred Muses, with whose beauty fir'd,
> My soul is ravisht and my brain inspir'd:
> Whose Priest I am, whose holy fillets wear,
> Would you your Poet's first petition hear,
> Give me the ways of wand'ring stars to know,
> The depth of Heaven above and Earth below;
> Teach me the various labours of the Moon,
> And whence proceed th' eclipses of the Sun;
> Why flowing Tides prevail upon the main,
> And in what dark abyss they shrink again;
> What shakes the solid Earth; what cause delays
> The Summer Nights; and shortens Winter Days....
> Happy the man who, studying Nature's Laws,
> Through known effects can trace the secret cause!

Ovid[40] expresses a similar feeling.

> Felices animos quibus hæc cognoscere primis
> Inque domos superas scandere cura fuit!...

Admovere oculis distantia sidera nostris
39
Ætheraque ingenio supposuere suo.
Sic petitur cœlum: non ut ferat Ossam Olympus
Summaque Peliacus sidera tanget apex.
Thrice happy souls! to whom 'twas given to rise
To truths like these, and scale the spangled skies!
Far distant stars to clearest view they brought,
And girdled ether with their chain of thought.
So heaven is reached:—not as of old they tried
By mountains piled on mountains in their pride.

And from the whole tenour of these and similar passages, it is evident that the intellectual pleasure which arises from our first introduction to a beautiful physical theory had a main share in producing this enthusiasm at the contemplation of the victories of science; although undoubtedly the moral philosophy, which was never separated from the natural philosophy, and the triumph over superstitious fears, which a knowledge of nature was supposed to furnish, added warmth to the feeling of exultation.

We may trace a similar impression in the ardent expressions which Pliny[41] makes use of in speaking of the early astronomers, and which we have quoted in the History. "Great men! elevated above the common standard of human nature, by discovering the laws which celestial occurrences obey, and by freeing the wretched mind of man from the fears which eclipses inspired."

This exulting contemplation of what science had done, naturally led the mind to an anticipation of further achievements still to be performed. Expressions of this feeling occur in Seneca, and are of the most remarkable kind, as the following example will show[42]:

"Why do we wonder that comets, so rare a phenomenon, have not yet had their laws assigned?—that we should know so little of their beginning and their end, when their recurrence is at wide intervals? It is not yet fifteen hundred years since Greece,

Stellis numeros et nomina fecit,
40

'reckoned the stars, and gave them names.' There are still many nations which are acquainted with the heavens by sight only; which do not yet know why the moon disappears, why she is eclipsed. It is but lately that among us philosophy has reduced these matters to a certainty. The day shall come when the course of time and the labour of a maturer age shall bring to light what is yet concealed. One generation, even if it devoted itself to the skies, is not enough for researches so extensive. How then can it be so, when we divide this scanty allowance of years into no equal shares between our studies and our vices? These things then must be explained by a long succession of inquiries. We have but just begun to know how arise the morning and evening appearances, the stations, the progressions, and the retrogradations of the fixed stars which put themselves in our way;—which appearing perpetually in another and another place compel us to be curious. Some one will hereafter demonstrate in what region the comets wander; why they move so far asunder from the rest; of what size and nature they are. Let us be content with what we have discovered: let posterity contribute its share to truth." Again he adds[43] in the same strain: "Let us not wonder that what lies so deep is brought out so slowly. How many animals have become known for the first time in this age! And the members of future generations shall know many of which we are ignorant. Many things are reserved for ages to come, when our memory shall have passed away. The world would be a small thing indeed, if it did not contain matter of inquiry for all the world. Eleusis reserves something for the second visit of the worshipper. So too Nature does not at once disclose all HER mysteries. We think ourselves initiated; we are but in the vestibule. The arcana are not thrown open without distinction and without reserve. This age will see some things; that which comes after us, others."

41

While we admire the happy coincidence of these conjectures with the soundest views which the history of science teaches us, we must not forget that they are merely conjectures, suggested by very vague impressions, and associated with very scanty conceptions of the laws of nature. Seneca's Natural Questions, from which the above extract is taken, contains a series of dissertations on various subjects of Natural Philosophy; as Meteors, Rainbows, Lightnings, Springs, Rivers, Snow, Hail, Rain, Wind, Earthquakes and Comets. In the whole of these dissertations, the statements are loose, and the explanations of little or no value. Perhaps it may be worth our while to notice a case in which he refers to an observation of his own, although his conclusion from it be erroneous. He is arguing[44] against the opinion that Springs arise from the water which falls in rain. "In the first place," he says, "I, a very diligent digger in my vineyard, affirm that no rain is so heavy as to moisten the earth to the depth of more than ten feet. All the moisture is consumed in this outer crust, and descends not to the lower part." We have here something of the nature of an experiment; and indeed, as we may readily conceive, the instinct which impels man to seek truth by experiment can never be altogether extinguished. Seneca's experiment was deprived of its value by the indistinctness of his ideas, which led him to rest in the crude conception of the water being "consumed" in the superficial crust of the earth.

It is unnecessary to pursue further the reasonings of the Romans on such subjects, and we now proceed to the ages which succeeded the fall of their empire.

42

CHAPTER VIII.
Arabian Philosophers.

I have noticed certain additions to Physical Science made by the Arabians; namely, in Astronomy[45]. The discovery of the motion of the Sun's Apogee by Albategnius, and the discovery of the Moon's Variation by Aboul-Wefa; and in Optics[46] the assertion of Alhazen that the angle of refraction is not proportional to the angle of incidence, as Ptolemy had supposed: and certain steps in the philosophy of vision. We must also suppose, as the Arabic word alkali reminds us, that the Arabians contributed to lay the foundations of chemistry. The question which we have here to ask is, whether the

Arabians made any steps beyond their predecessors in the philosophy of discovery. And to this question, I conceive the answer must be this: that among them as among the Greeks, those who practically observed nature, and especially those who made discoveries in Science, must have had a practical acquaintance with some of the maxims which are exemplified in the formation of Science. To discover that the Apogee of the Sun was 17 degrees distant from the point where Ptolemy had placed it, Albategnius made careful observations, and referred them to the theory of the eccentric, so as to verify or correct that theory. And when, in the eleventh century, Arzachel found the Apogee to be less advanced than Albategnius had found it, he proceeded again to correct the theory by introducing a new movement of the equinoctial points, which was called the Trepidation.43 It appeared afterwards, however, that, in doing this, he had had too much confidence in the observations of his predecessors, and that no such movement as the Trepidation really existed. In like manner to correct Ptolemy's law of refraction, Alhazen had recourse to experiment: but he did not put his experiments in the form of a Table, as Ptolemy had done. If he had done this, he might possibly have discovered the law of sines, which Snell afterwards discovered.

But though the Arabian philosophers thus, in some cases, observed facts, and referred those facts to general mathematical laws, it does not appear that they were led to put in any new or striking general form such maxims as this: That the progress of Science consists in the exact observation of facts and in colligating them by ideas. Those of them who were dissatisfied with the existing philosophy as barren and useless (for instance Algazel[47]), were led to point at the faults and contradictions of that philosophy, but did not attempt, so far as I know, to substitute for it anything better. If they rejected Aristotle's Organon, they did not attempt to construct a new Organon for themselves.

Indeed they do not appear even to have had sufficient confidence in the real truth of the astronomical theories which they had adopted from the Greeks, always to correct and extend those where their observations showed that they required correction and extension. Sometimes they did this, but not generally enough. When Arzachel found by observation the Apogee of the Sun to be situated too far back, he ventured to correct Ptolemy's statement of its motion. But when Aboul-Wefa had really discovered the Variation of the Moon's motion, he did not express it by means of an epicycle. If he had done so, he would have made it unnecessary for Tycho Brahe at a later period to make the same discovery.

44

The moral of this incident is the same moral which we have perpetually to note as taught us at every step by the history of Science:—namely, the necessity of constant, careful and exact observation of Facts; and the advantage of devising a Theory, (even if it have to be afterwards rejected,) by which the Facts shall be bound together into a coherent whole.

45

CHAPTER IX.
The Schoolmen of the Middle Ages.

In the History of the Sciences I have devoted a Book to the state of Science in the middle ages, and have endeavoured to analyse the intellectual defects of that period. Among the characteristic features of the human mind during those times, I have noticed Indistinctness of Ideas, a Commentatorial Spirit, Mysticism, and Dogmatism. The account there given of this portion of the history of man belongs, in reality, rather to the History of Ideas than to the History of Progressive Science. For, as we have there remarked, theoretical Science was, during the period of which we speak, almost entirely stationary; and the investigation of the causes of such a state of things may be considered as a part of that review in which we are now engaged, of the vicissitudes of man's acquaintance with the methods of discovery. But when we offered to the world a history of science, to leave so large a chasm unexplained, would have made the series of events seem defective and broken; and the survey of the Middle Ages was therefore inserted. I would beg to refer to that portion of the former work the reader who wishes for information in addition to what is here given.

The Indistinctness of Ideas and the Commentatorial Disposition of those ages have already been here brought under our notice. Viewed with reference to the opposition between Experience and Ideas, on which point, as we have said, the succession of opinions in a great measure turns, it is clear that the commentatorial method belongs to the ideal side of the question: for the commentator seeks for such knowledge46 as he values, by analysing and illustrating what his author has said; and, content with this material of speculation, does not desire to add to it new stores of experience and observation. And with regard to the two other features in the character which we gave to those ages, we may observe that Dogmatism demands for philosophical theories the submission of mind, due to those revealed religious doctrines which are to guide our conduct and direct our hopes: while Mysticism elevates ideas into realities, and offers them to us as the objects of our religious regard. Thus the Mysticism of the middle ages and their Dogmatism alike arose from not discriminating the offices of theoretical and practical philosophy. Mysticism claimed for ideas the dignity and reality of principles of moral action and religious hope: Dogmatism imposed theoretical opinions respecting speculative points with the imperative tone of rules of conduct and faith.

If, however, the opposite claims of theory and practice interfered with the progress of science by the confusion they thus occasioned, they did so far more by drawing men away altogether from mere physical speculations. The Christian religion, with its precepts, its hopes, and its promises, became the leading subject of men's thoughts; and the great active truths thus revealed, and the duties thus enjoined, made all inquiries of mere curiosity appear frivolous and unworthy of man. The Fathers of the Church sometimes philosophized ill; but far more commonly they were too intent upon the great lessons which they had to teach, respecting man's situation in the eyes of his Heavenly Master, to philosophize at all respecting things remote from the business of life and of no importance in man's spiritual concerns.

Yet man has his intellectual as well as his spiritual wants. He has faculties which demand systems and reasons, as well as precepts and promises. The Christian doctor, who knew so much more than the heathen philosopher respecting the Creator and Governor of the universe, was not long content to know or to teach less, respecting the universe itself. While it was still main47tained that Theology was the only really important study, Theology was so extended and so fashioned as to include all other knowledge: and after no long time, the Fathers of the Church themselves became the authors of systems of universal knowledge.

But when this happened, the commentatorial spirit was still in its full vigour. The learned Christians could not, any more than the later Greeks or the Romans, devise, by the mere force of their own invention, new systems, full, comprehensive, and connected, like those of the heroic age of philosophy. The same mental tendencies which led men to look for speculative coherence and completeness in the view of the universe, led them also to admire and dwell upon the splendid and acute speculations of the Greeks. They were content to find, in those immortal works, the answers to the questions which their curiosity prompted; and to seek what further satisfaction they might require, in analysing and unfolding the doctrines promulgated by those great masters of knowledge. Thus the Christian doctors became, as to general philosophy, commentators upon the ancient Greek teachers.

Among these, they selected Aristotle as their peculiar object of admiration and study. The vast store, both of opinions and facts, which his works contain, his acute distinctions, his cogent reasons in some portions of his speculations, his symmetrical systems in almost all, naturally commended him to the minds of subtle and curious men. We may add that Plato, who taught men to contemplate Ideas separate from Things, was not so well fitted for general acceptance as Aristotle, who rejected this separation. For although the due apprehension of this opposition of Ideas and Sensations is a necessary step in the progress of true philosophy, it requires a clearer view and a more balanced mind than the common herd of students possess; and Aristotle, who evaded the necessary perplexities in which this antithesis involves us, appeared, to the temper of those times, the easier and the plainer guide of the two.

The Doctors of the middle ages having thus adopted48 Aristotle as their master in philosophy, we shall not be surprised to find them declaring, after him, that experience is the source of our knowledge of the visible world. But though, like the Greeks, they thus talked of experiment, like the Greeks, they showed little disposition to discover the laws of nature by observation of facts. This barren and formal recognition of experience or sensation as one source of knowledge, not being illustrated by a practical study of nature, and by real theoretical truths obtained by such a study, remained ever vague, wavering, and empty. Such a mere acknowledgment cannot, in any times, ancient or modern, be considered as indicating a just apprehension of the true basis and nature of science.

In imperfectly perceiving how, and how far, experience is the source of our knowledge of the external world, the teachers of the middle ages were in the dark; but so, on this subject, have been almost all the writers of all ages, with the exception of those who in recent times have had their minds enlightened by contemplating philosophically the modern progress of science. The opinions of the doctors of the middle ages on such subjects generally had those of Aristotle for their basis; but the subject was often still further analysed and systematized, with an acute and methodical skill hardly inferior to that of Aristotle himself.

The Stagirite, in the beginning of his Physics, had made the following remarks. "In all bodies of doctrine which involve principles, causes, or elements, Science and Knowledge arise from the knowledge of these; (for we then consider ourselves to know respecting any subject, when we know its first cause, its first principles, its ultimate elements.) It is evident, therefore, that in seeking a knowledge of nature, we must first know what are its principles. But the course of our knowledge is, from the things which are better known and more manifest to us, to the things which are more certain and evident in nature. For those things which are most evident in truth, are not most evident to us. [And consequently we must advance from things obscure in nature, but49 manifest to us, towards the things which are really in nature more clear and certain.] The things which are first obvious and apparent to us are complex; and from these we obtain, by analysis, principles and elements. We must proceed from universals to particulars. For the whole is better known to our senses than the parts, and for the same reason, the universal better known than the particular. And thus words signify things in a large and indiscriminate way, which is afterwards analysed by definition; as we see that the children at first call all men father, and all women mother, but afterwards learn to distinguish."

There are various assertions contained in this extract which came to be considered as standard maxims, and which occur constantly in the writers of the middle ages. Such are, for instance, the maxim, "Verè scire est per causas scire;" the remark, that compounds are known to us before their parts, and the illustration from the expressions used by children. Of the mode in which this subject was treated by the schoolmen, we may judge by looking at passages of Thomas Aquinas which treat of the subject of the human understanding. In the Summa Theologiæ, the eighty-fifth Question is On the manner and order of understanding, which subject he considers in eight Articles; and these must, even now, be looked upon as exhibiting many of the most important and interesting points of the subject. They are, First, Whether our understanding understands by abstracting ideas (species) from appearances; Second, Whether intelligible species abstracted from appearances are related to our understanding as that which we understand, or that by which we understand; Third, Whether our understanding does naturally understand universals first; Fourth, Whether our understanding can understand many things at once; Fifth, Whether our understanding understands by compounding and dividing; Sixth, Whether the understanding can err; Seventh, Whether one person can understand the same thing better than another; Eighth, Whether our understanding understands the indivisible sooner than the50 divisible. And in the discussion of the last point, for example, reference is made to the passage of Aristotle which we have already quoted. "It may seem," he says, "that we understand the indivisible before the divisible; for the Philosopher says that we understand and know by knowing principles and elements; but indivisibles are the principles and elements of divisible things. But to this we may reply, that in our receiving of science, principles and elements are not always first; for sometimes from the sensible effects we go on to the knowledge of intelligible principles and causes." We see that both the objection and the answer are drawn from Aristotle.

We find the same close imitation of Aristotle in Albertus Magnus, who, like Aquinas, flourished in the thirteenth century. Albertus, indeed, wrote treatises corresponding to almost all those of the Stagirite, and was called the Ape of Aristotle. In the beginning of his Physics, he says, "Knowledge does not always begin from that which is first according to the nature of things, but from that of which the knowledge is easiest.

For the human intellect, on account of its relation to the senses (propter reflexionem quam habet ad sensum), collects science from the senses; and thus it is easier for our knowledge to begin from that which we can apprehend by sense, imagination, and intellect, than from that which we apprehend by intellect alone." We see that he has somewhat systematized what he has borrowed.

This disposition to dwell upon and systematize the leading doctrines of metaphysics assumed a more definite and permanent shape in the opposition of the Realists and Nominalists. The opposition involved in this controversy is, in fact, that fundamental antithesis of Sense and Ideas about which philosophy has always been engaged; and of which we have marked the manifestation in Plato and Aristotle. The question, What is the object of our thoughts when we reason concerning the external world? must occur to all speculative minds: and the difficulties of the answer are manifest. We must reply, either that our own51 Ideas, or that Sensible Things, are the elements of our knowledge of nature. And then the scruples again occur,—how we have any general knowledge if our thoughts are fixed on particular objects; and, on the other hand,—how we can attain to any true knowledge of nature by contemplating ideas which are not identical with objects in nature. The two opposite opinions maintained on this subject were, on the one side,— that our general propositions refer to objects which are real, though divested of the peculiarities of individuals; and, on the other side,—that in such propositions, individuals are not represented by any reality, but bound together by a name. These two views were held by the Realists and Nominalists respectively: and thus the Realist manifested the adherence to Ideas, and the Nominalist the adherence to the impressions of Sense, which have always existed as opposite yet correlative tendencies in man.

The Realists were the prevailing sect in the Scholastic times: for example, both Thomas Aquinas and Duns Scotus, the Angelical and the Subtle Doctor, held this opinion, although opposed to each other in many of their leading doctrines on other subjects. And as the Nominalist, fixing his attention upon sensible objects, is obliged to consider what is the principle of generalization, in order that the possibility of any general proposition may be conceivable; so on the other hand, the Realist, beginning with the contemplation of universal ideas, is compelled to ask what is the principle of individuation, in order that he may comprehend the application of general propositions in each particular instance. This inquiry concerning the principle of individuation was accordingly a problem which occupied all the leading minds among the Schoolmen[48]. It will be apparent from what has been said, that it is only one of the many forms of the fundamental antithesis of the Ideas and the Senses, which we have constantly before us in this review.

52

The recognition of the derivation of our knowledge, in part at least, from Experience, though always loose and incomplete, appears often to be independent of the Peripatetic traditions. Thus Richard of St. Victor, a writer of contemplative theology in the twelfth century, says[49], that "there are three sources of knowledge, experience, reason, faith. Some things we prove by experiment, others we collect by reasoning, the certainty of others we hold by believing. And with regard to temporal matters, we obtain our knowledge by actual experience; the other guides belong to divine knowledge."

Richard also propounds a division of human knowledge which is clearly not derived directly from the ancients, and which shows that considerable attention must have been paid to such speculations. He begins by laying down clearly and broadly the distinction, which, as we have seen, is of primary importance, between practice and theory. Practice, he says, includes seven mechanical arts; those of the clothier, the armourer, the navigator, the hunter, the physician, and the player. Theory is threefold, divine, natural, doctrinal; and is thus divided into Theology, Physics, and Mathematics. Mathematics, he adds, treats of the invisible forms of visible things. We have seen that by many profound thinkers this word forms has been selected as best fitted to describe those relations of things which are the subject of mathematics. Again, Physics discovers causes from their effects and effects from their causes. It would not be easy at the present day to give a better account of the object of physical science. But Richard of St. Victor makes this account still more remarkably judicious, by the examples to which he alludes; which are earthquakes, the tides, the virtues of plants, the instincts of animals, the classification of minerals, plants and reptiles.

> Unde tremor terris, quâ vi maria alta tumescant,
> Herbarum vires, animos irasque ferarum,
> Omne genus fruticum, lapidum quoque, reptiliumque.
> 53

He further adds[50], "Physical science ascends from effects to causes, and descends again from causes to effects." This declaration Francis Bacon himself might have adopted. It is true, that Richard would probably have been little able to produce any clear and definite instances of knowledge, in which this ascent and descent were exemplified; but still the statement, even considered as a mere conjectural thought, contains a portion of that sagacity and comprehensive power which we admire so much in Bacon.

Richard of St. Victor, who lived in the twelfth century, thus exhibits more vigour and independence of speculative power than Thomas Aquinas, Albertus Magnus, and Duns Scotus, in the thirteenth. In the interval, about the end of the twelfth century, the writings of Aristotle had become generally known in the West; and had been elevated into the standard of philosophical doctrine, by the divines mentioned above, who felt a reverent sympathy with the systematizing and subtle spirit of the Stagirite as soon as it was made manifest to them. These doctors, following the example of their great forerunner, reduced every part of human knowledge to a systematic form; the systems which they thus framed were presented to men's minds as the only true philosophy, and dissent from them was no longer considered to be blameless. It was an offence against religion as well as reason to reject the truth, and the truth could be but one. In this manner arose that claim which the Doctors of the Church put forth to control men's opinions upon all subjects, and which we have spoken of in the History of Science as the Dogmatism of the Middle Ages. There is no difficulty in giving examples of this characteristic. We may take for instance a Statute of the University of Paris, occasioned by a Bull of Pope John XXI., in which it is enacted, "that no Master or Bachelor of any faculty, shall presume to read lectures upon any author in a private room, on account of the many perils which may arise therefrom; but54 shall read in public places, where all may resort, and may faithfully report what is there taught; excepting only books of Grammar and Logic, in which there can be no presumption." And certain errors of

Brescian are condemned in a Rescript[51] of the papal Legate Odo, with the following expressions: "Whereas, as we have been informed, certain Logical professors treating of Theology in their disputations, and Theologians treating of Logic, contrary to the command of the law are not afraid to mix and confound the lots of the Lord's heritage; we exhort and admonish your University, all and singular, that they be content with the landmarks of the Sciences and Faculties which our Fathers have fixed; and that having due fear of the curse pronounced in the law against him who removeth his neighbour's landmark, you hold such sober wisdom according to the Apostles, that ye may by no means incur the blame of innovation or presumption."

The account which, in the History of Science, I gave of Dogmatism as a characteristic of the middle ages, has been indignantly rejected by a very pleasing modern writer, who has, with great feeling and great diligence, brought into view the merits and beauties of those times, termed by him Ages of Faith. He urges[52] that religious authority was never claimed for physical science: and he quotes from Thomas Aquinas, a passage in which the author protests against the practice of confounding opinions of philosophy with doctrines of faith. We might quote in return the Rescript[53] of Stephen, bishop of Paris, in which he declares that there can be but one truth, and rejects the distinction of things being true according to philosophy and not according to the Catholic faith; and it might be added, that among the errors condemned in this document are some of Thomas Aquinas himself. We might further observe, that if no physical doctrines55 were condemned in the times of which we now speak, this was because, on such subjects, no new opinions were promulgated, and not because opinion was free. As soon as new opinions, even on physical subjects, attracted general notice, they were prohibited by authority, as we see in the case of Galileo[54].

But this disinclination to recognize philosophy as independent of religion, and this disposition to find in new theories, even in physical ones, something contrary to religion or scripture, are, it would seem, very natural tendencies of theologians; and it would be unjust to assert that these propensities were confined to the periods when the authority of papal Rome was highest; or that the spirit which has in a great degree controlled and removed such habits was introduced by the Reformation of religion in the sixteenth century. We must trace to other causes, the clear and general recognition of Philosophy, as distinct from Theology, and independent of her authority. In the earlier ages of the Church, indeed, this separation had been acknowledged. St. Augustin says, "A Christian should beware how he speaks on questions of natural philosophy, as if they were doctrines of Holy Scripture; for56 an infidel who should hear him deliver absurdities could not avoid laughing. Thus the Christian would be confused, and the infidel but little edified; for the infidel would conclude that our authors really entertained these extravagant opinions, and therefore they would despise them, to their own eternal ruin. Therefore the opinions of philosophers should never be proposed as dogmas of faith, or rejected as contrary to faith, when it is not certain that they are so." These words are quoted with approbation by Thomas Aquinas, and it is said[55], are cited in the same manner in every encyclopedical work of the middle ages. This warning of genuine wisdom was afterwards rejected, as we have seen; and it is only in modern times that its value has again been fully recognized. And this improvement we must ascribe, mainly, to the progress of physical science. For a great body of undeniable truths on physical subjects being accumulated, such as had no reference to nor connexion with the truths of religion, and yet such as possessed a strong interest for most men's minds, it was impossible longer to deny that there were wide provinces of knowledge which were not included in the dominions of Theology, and over which she had no authority. In the fifteenth and sixteenth centuries, the fundamental doctrines of mechanics, hydrostatics, optics, magnetics, chemistry, were established and promulgated; and along with them, a vast train of consequences, attractive to the mind by the ideal relations which they exhibited, and striking to the senses by the power which they gave man over nature. Here was a region in which philosophy felt herself entitled and impelled to assert her independence. From this region, there is a gradation of subjects in which philosophy advances more and more towards the peculiar domain of religion; and at some intermediate points there have been, and probably will always be, conflicts respecting the boundary57 line of the two fields of speculation. For the limit is vague and obscure, and appears to fluctuate and shift with the progress of time and knowledge.

Our business at present is not with the whole extent and limits of philosophy, but with the progress of physical science more particularly, and the methods by which it may be attained: and we are endeavouring to trace historically the views which have prevailed respecting such methods, at various periods of man's intellectual progress. Among the most conspicuous of the revolutions which opinions on this subject have undergone, is the transition from an implicit trust in the internal powers of man's mind to a professed dependence upon external observation; and from an unbounded reverence for the wisdom of the past, to a fervid expectation of change and improvement. The origin and progress of this disposition of mind;—the introduction of a state of things in which men not only obtained a body of indestructible truths from experience, and increased it from generation to generation, but professedly, and we may say, ostentatiously, declared such to be the source of their knowledge, and such their hopes of its destined career;—the rise, in short, of Experimental Philosophy, not only as a habit, but as a Philosophy of Experience, is what we must now endeavour to exhibit.

58

CHAPTER X.
The Innovators of the Middle Ages.

Raymond Lully.

1. General Remarks.—In the rise of Experimental Philosophy, understanding the term in the way just now stated, two features have already been alluded to: the disposition to cast off the prevalent reverence for the opinions and methods of preceding teachers with an eager expectation of some vast advantage to be derived from a change; and the belief that this improvement must be sought by drawing our knowledge from external observation rather than from mere intellectual efforts;—the Insurrection against Authority, and the Appeal to Experience. These two movements were closely connected; but they may easily be distinguished, and in fact, persons were very prominent in the former part of the task, who had no comprehension of the latter principle, from which alone the change derives its value. There were many Malcontents who had not the temper, talent or knowledge, which fitted them to be Reformers.

30

The authority which was questioned, in the struggle of which we speak, was that of the Scholastic System, the combination of Philosophy with Theology; of which Aristotle, presented in the form and manner which the Doctors of the Church had imposed upon him, is to be considered the representative. When there was demanded of men a submission of the mind, such as this system claimed, the natural love of freedom in man's bosom, and the speculative tendencies of his intellect, rose in rebellion, from time to time, against the ruling oppression. We find in all periods of the scholastic ages examples of this disposition of man to resist over59strained authority; the tendency being mostly, however, combined with a want of solid thought, and showing itself in extravagant pretensions and fantastical systems put forwards by the insurgents. We have pointed out one such opponent[56] of the established systems, even among the Arabian schoolmen, a more servile race than ever the Europeans were. We may here notice more especially an extraordinary character who appeared in the thirteenth century, and who may be considered as belonging to the Prelude of the Reform in Philosophy, although he had no share in the Reform itself.

2. Raymond Lully.—Raymond Lully is perhaps traditionally best known as an Alchemist, of which art he appears to have been a cultivator. But this was only one of the many impulses of a spirit ardently thirsty of knowledge and novelty. He had[57], in his youth, been a man of pleasure, but was driven by a sudden shock of feeling to resolve on a complete change of life. He plunged into solitude, endeavoured to still the remorse of his conscience by prayer and penance, and soon had his soul possessed by visions which he conceived were vouchsafed to him. In the feeling of religious enthusiasm thus excited, he resolved to devote his life to the diffusion of Christian truth among Heathens and Mahomedans. For this purpose, at the age of thirty he betook himself to the study of Grammar, and of the Arabic language. He breathed earnest supplications for an illumination from above; and these were answered by his receiving from heaven, as his admirers declare, his Ars Magna by which he was able without labour or effort to learn and apply all knowledge. The real state of the case is, that he put himself in opposition to the established systems, and propounded a New Art, from which he promised the most wonderful results; but that his Art really is merely a mode of combining ideal conceptions without any reference to real sources of knowledge, or any possibility60 of real advantage. In a Treatise addressed, in A.D. 1310, to King Philip of France, entitled Liber Lamentationis Duodecim Principiorum Philosophiæ contra Averroistas, Lully introduced Philosophy, accompanied by her twelve Principles, (Matter, Form, Generation, &c.) uttering loud complaints against the prevailing system of doctrine; and represents her as presenting to the king a petition that she may be upheld and restored by her favourite, the Author. His Tabula Generalis ad omnes Scientias applicabilis was begun the 15th September, 1292, in the Harbour of Tunis, and finished in 1293, at Naples. In order to frame an Art of thus tabulating all existing sciences, and indeed all possible knowledge, he divides into various classes the conceptions with which he has to deal. The first class contains nine Absolute Conceptions: Goodness, Greatness, Duration, Power, Wisdom, Will, Virtue, Truth, Majesty. The second class has nine Relative Conceptions: Difference, Identity, Contrariety, Beginning, Middle, End, Majority, Equality, Minority. The third class contains nine Questions: Whether? What? Whence? Why? How great? How circumstanced? When? Where? and How? The fourth class contains the nine Most General Subjects: God, Angel, Heaven, Man, Imaginativum, Sensitivum, Vegetativum, Elementativum, Instrumentativum. Then come nine Prædicaments, nine Moral Qualities,

and so on. These conceptions are arranged in the compartments of certain concentric moveable circles, and give various combinations by means of triangles and other figures, and thus propositions are constructed.

It must be clear at once, that real knowledge, which is the union of facts and ideas, can never result from this machinery for shifting about, joining and disjoining, empty conceptions. This, and all similar schemes, go upon the supposition that the logical combinations of notions do of themselves compose knowledge; and that really existing things may be arrived at by a successive system of derivation from our most general ideas. It is imagined that by distributing the nomenclature of abstract ideas according to the place which they can61 hold in our propositions, and by combining them according to certain conditions, we may obtain formulæ including all possible truths, and thus fabricate a science in which all sciences are contained. We thus obtain the means of talking and writing upon all subjects, without the trouble of thinking: the revolutions of the emblematical figures are substituted for the operations of the mind. Both exertion of thought, and knowledge of facts, become superfluous. And this reflection, adds an intelligent author[58], explains the enormous number of books which Lully is said to have written; for he might have written those even during his sleep, by the aid of a moving power which should keep his machine in motion. Having once devised this invention for manufacturing science, Lully varied it in a thousand ways, and followed it into a variety of developments. Besides Synoptical Tables, he employs Genealogical Trees, each of which he dignifies with the name of the Tree of Science. The only requisite for the application of his System was a certain agreement in the numbers of the classes into which different subjects were distributed; and as this symmetry does not really exist in the operations of our thoughts, some violence was done to the natural distinction and subordination of conceptions, in order to fit them for the use of the system.

Thus Lully, while he professed to teach an Art which was to shed new light upon every part of science, was in fact employed in a pedantic and trifling repetition of known truths or truisms; and while he complained of the errors of existing methods, he proposed in their place one which was far more empty, barren, and worthless, than the customary processes of human thought. Yet his method is spoken of[59] with 62some praise by Leibnitz, who indeed rather delighted in the region of ideas and words, than in the world of realities. But Francis Bacon speaks far otherwise and more justly on this subject[60]. "It is not to be omitted that some men, swollen with emptiness rather than knowledge, have laboured to produce a certain Method, not deserving the name of a legitimate Method, since it is rather a method of imposture: which yet is doubtless highly grateful to certain would-be philosophers. This method scatters about certain little drops of science in such a manner that a smatterer may make a perverse and ostentatious use of them with a certain show of learning. Such was the art of Lully, which consisted of nothing but a mass and heap of the words of each science; with the intention that he who can readily produce the words of any science shall be supposed to know the science itself. Such collections are like a rag shop, where you find a patch of everything, but nothing which is of any value."

63

CHAPTER XI.
The Innovators of the Middle Ages—continued.

Roger Bacon.

We now come to a philosopher of a very different character, who was impelled to declare his dissent from the reigning philosophy by the abundance of his knowledge, and by his clear apprehension of the mode in which real knowledge had been acquired and must be increased.

Roger Bacon was born in 1214, near Ilchester, in Somersetshire, of an old family. In his youth he was a student at Oxford, and made extraordinary progress in all branches of learning. He then went to the University of Paris, as was at that time the custom of learned Englishmen, and there received the degree of Doctor of Theology. At the persuasion of Robert Grostête, bishop of Lincoln, he entered the brotherhood of Franciscans in Oxford, and gave himself up to study with extraordinary fervour. He was termed by his brother monks Doctor Mirabilis. We know from his own works, as well as from the traditions concerning him, that he possessed an intimate acquaintance with all the science of his time which could be acquired from books; and that he had made many remarkable advances by means of his own experimental labours. He was acquainted with Arabic, as well as with the other languages common in his time. In the title of his works, we find the whole range of science and philosophy, Mathematics and Mechanics, Optics, Astronomy, Geography, Chronology, Chemistry, Magic, Music, Medicine, Grammar, Logic, Metaphysics, Ethics, and Theology; and judging from those which are published, these works are full of sound and exact64 knowledge. He is, with good reason, supposed to have discovered, or to have had some knowledge of, several of the most remarkable inventions which were made generally known soon afterwards; as gunpowder, lenses, burning specula, telescopes, clocks, the correction of the calendar, and the explanation of the rainbow.

Thus possessing, in the acquirements and habits of his own mind, abundant examples of the nature of knowledge and of the process of invention, Roger Bacon felt also a deep interest in the growth and progress of science, a spirit of inquiry respecting the causes which produced or prevented its advance, and a fervent hope and trust in its future destinies; and these feelings impelled him to speculate worthily and wisely respecting a Reform of the Method of Philosophizing. The manuscripts of his works have existed for nearly six hundred years in many of the libraries of Europe, and especially in those of England; and for a long period the very imperfect portions of them which were generally known, left the character and attainments of the author shrouded in a kind of mysterious obscurity. About a century ago, however, his Opus Majus was published[61] by Dr. S. Jebb, principally from a manuscript in the Library of Trinity College, Dublin; and this contained most or all of the separate works which were previously known to the public, along with others still more peculiar and characteristic. We are thus able to judge of Roger Bacon's knowledge and of his views, and they are in every way well worthy our attention.

65

The Opus Majus is addressed to Pope Clement the Fourth, whom Bacon had known when he was legate in England as Cardinal-bishop of Sabina, and who admired the talents of the monk, and pitied him for the persecutions to which he was exposed. On his elevation to the papal chair, this account of Bacon's labours and views was sent, at the earnest request of the pontiff. Besides the Opus Majus, he wrote two others, the Opus Minus and Opus Tertium; which were also sent to the pope, as the author says[62], "on account of the danger of roads, and the possible loss of the work." These works still exist unpublished, in the Cottonian and other libraries. The Opus Majus is a work equally wonderful with regard to its general scheme, and to the special treatises with which the outlines of the plan are filled up. The professed object of the work is to urge the necessity of a reform in the mode of philosophizing, to set forth the reasons why knowledge had not made a greater progress, to draw back attention to the sources of knowledge which had been unwisely neglected, to discover other sources which were yet almost untouched, and to animate men in the undertaking, by a prospect of the vast advantages which it offered. In the development of this plan, all the leading portions of science are expounded in the most complete shape which they had at that time assumed; and improvements of a very wide and striking kind are proposed in some of the principal of these departments. Even if the work had had no leading purpose, it would have been highly valuable as a treasure of the most solid knowledge and soundest speculations of the time; even if it had contained no such details, it would have been a work most remarkable for its general views and scope. It may be considered as, at the same time, the Encyclopedia and the Novum Organon of the thirteenth century.

Since this work is thus so important in the history of Inductive Philosophy I shall give, in a note, a view[63]66 of its divisions and contents. But I must now endeavour to point out more especially the way in which the various principles, which the reform of scientific method involved, are here brought into view.

One of the first points to be noticed for this purpose, is the resistance to authority; and at the stage of philosophical history with which we here have to do, this means resistance to the authority of Aristotle, as adopted and interpreted by the Doctors of the Schools. Bacon's work[64] is divided into Six Parts; and of these Parts, the First is, Of the four universal Causes of all Human Ignorance. The causes thus enumerated[65] are:—the force of unworthy authority;—traditionary habit;—the imperfection of the undisciplined senses;—and the disposition to conceal our ignorance and to make an ostentatious show of our knowledge. These influences involve every man, occupy every condition. They prevent our obtaining the most useful and large and fair doctrines of wisdom, the secret of all sciences and arts. He then proceeds to argue, from the testimony of philosophers themselves, that the authority of antiquity, and especially of Aristotle, is not infallible. "We find[66] their books full of doubts, obscurities, and perplexities. They scarce agree with each other in one empty question or67 one worthless sophism, or one operation of science, as one man agrees with another in the practical operations of medicine, surgery, and the like arts of Secular men. Indeed," he adds, "not only the philosophers, but the saints have fallen into errors which they have afterwards retracted," and this he instances in Augustin, Jerome, and others. He gives an admirable sketch[67] of the progress of philosophy from the Ionic School to Aristotle; of whom he speaks with great applause. "Yet," he adds[68], "those who came after him corrected him in some things, and added many things to his works, and shall go on adding to the end of the world." Aristotle, he adds, is now called peculiarly[69] the Philosopher, "yet there was a time when his philosophy was silent and unregarded, either on account of the rarity of copies of his works, or their difficulty, or from envy; till after the time of Mahomet,68 when Avicenna and Averroes, and others, recalled this philosophy into the full light of exposition. And although the Logic and some other works were translated by Boethius from the Greek, yet the philosophy of Aristotle first received a quick increase among the Latins at the time of Michael Scot; who, in the year of our Lord 1230, appeared, bringing with him portions of the books of Aristotle on Natural Philosophy and Mathematics. And yet a small part only of the works of this author is translated, and a still smaller part is in the hands of common students." He adds further[70] (in the Third Part of the Opus Majus, which is a Dissertation on language), that the translations which are current of these writings, are very bad and imperfect. With these views, he is moved to express himself somewhat impatiently[71] respecting these works: "If I had," he says, "power over the works of Aristotle, I would have them all burnt; for it is only a loss of time to study in them, and a cause of error, and a multiplication of ignorance beyond expression." "The common herd of students," he says, "with their heads, have no principle by which they can be excited to any worthy employment; and hence they mope and make asses of themselves over their bad translations, and lose their time, and trouble, and money."

The remedies which he recommends for these evils, are, in the first place, the study of that only perfect wisdom which is to be found in the sacred Scripture[72], in the next place, the study of mathematics and the use of experiment[73]. By the aid of these methods, 69Bacon anticipates the most splendid progress for human knowledge. He takes up the strain of hope and confidence which we have noticed as so peculiar in the Roman writers; and quotes some of the passages of Seneca which we adduced in illustration of this:—that the attempts in science were at first rude and imperfect, and were afterwards improved;—that the day will come, when what is still unknown shall be brought to light by the progress of time and the labours of a longer period;—that one age does not suffice for inquiries so wide and various;—that the people of future times shall know many things unknown to us;—and that the time shall arrive when posterity will wonder that we overlooked what was so obvious. Bacon himself adds anticipations more peculiarly in the spirit of his own time. "We have seen," he says, at the end of the work, "how Aristotle, by the ways which wisdom teaches, could give to Alexander the empire of the world. And this the Church ought to take into consideration against the infidels and rebels, that there may be a sparing of Christian blood, and especially on account of the troubles that shall come to pass in the days of Antichrist; which by the grace of God, it would be easy to obviate, if prelates and princes would encourage study, and join in searching out the secrets of nature and art."

It may not be improper to observe here that this belief in the appointed progress of knowledge, is not combined with any overweening belief in the unbounded and independent power of the human intellect. On the contrary, one of the lessons which Bacon draws from the state and prospects of knowledge, is the duty of faith and humility. "To him," he says[74], "who denies the truth of the faith because he is unable to understand it, I will propose in reply the course of nature, and as we have seen it in examples." And after giving some instances, he adds, "These, and the like, ought to move men and to excite them to the reception of divine truths. For if, in the vilest objects70 of creation, truths are found, before which the inward pride of man must bow, and believe though it cannot understand, how much more should man humble his mind before the glorious truths of God!" He had before said[75]: "Man is incapable of perfect wisdom in this life; it is hard for him to ascend towards perfection, easy to glide downwards to falsehoods and vanities: let him then not boast of his wisdom, or extol his knowledge. What he knows is little and worthless, in respect of that which he believes without knowing; and still less, in respect of that which he is ignorant of. He is mad who thinks highly of his wisdom; he most mad, who exhibits it as something to be wondered at." He adds, as another reason for humility, that he has proved by trial, he could teach in one year, to a poor boy, the marrow of all that the most diligent person could acquire in forty years' laborious and expensive study.

To proceed somewhat more in detail with regard to Roger Bacon's views of a Reform in Scientific Inquiry, we may observe that by making Mathematics and Experiment the two great points of his recommendation, he directed his improvement to the two essential parts of all knowledge, Ideas and Facts, and thus took the course which the most enlightened philosophy would have suggested. He did not urge the prosecution of experiment, to the comparative neglect of the existing mathematical sciences and conception; a fault which there is some ground for ascribing to his great namesake and successor Francis Bacon: still less did he content himself with a mere protest against the authority of the schools, and a vague demand for change, which was almost all that was done by those who put themselves forward as reformers in the intermediate time. Roger Bacon holds his way steadily between the two poles of human knowledge; which, as we have seen, it is far from easy to do. "There are two modes of knowing," says he[76]; "by argument, and by experi71ment. Argument concludes a question; but it does not make us feel certain, or acquiesce in the contemplation of truth, except the truth be also found to be so by experience." It is not easy to express more decidedly the clearly seen union of exact conceptions with certain facts, which, as we have explained, constitutes real knowledge.

One large division of the Opus Majus is "On the Usefulness of Mathematics," which is shown by a copious enumeration of existing branches of knowledge, as Chronology, Geography, the Calendar and (in a separate Part) Optics. There is a chapter[77], in which it is proved by reason, that all science requires mathematics. And the arguments which are used to establish this doctrine, show a most just appreciation of the office of mathematics in science. They are such as follows:—That other sciences use examples taken from mathematics as the most evident:—That mathematical knowledge is, as it were, innate in us, on which point he refers to the well-known dialogue of Plato, as quoted by Cicero:—That this science, being the easiest, offers the best introduction to the more difficult:—That in mathematics, things as known to us are identical with things as known to nature:—That we can here entirely avoid doubt and error, and obtain certainty and truth:—That mathematics is prior to other sciences in nature, because it takes cognizance of quantity, which is apprehended by intuition, (intuitu intellectus). "Moreover," he adds[78], "there have been found famous men, as Robert, bishop of Lincoln, and Brother Adam Marshman (de Marisco), and many others, who by the power of mathematics have been able to explain the causes of things; as may be seen in the writings of these men, for instance, concerning the Rainbow and Comets, and the generation of heat, and climates, and the celestial bodies."

72

But undoubtedly the most remarkable portion of the Opus Majus is the Sixth and last Part, which is entitled "De Scientia experimentali." It is indeed an extraordinary circumstance to find a writer of the thirteenth century, not only recognizing experiment as one source of knowledge, but urging its claims as something far more important than men had yet been aware of, exemplifying its value by striking and just examples, and speaking of its authority with a dignity of diction which sounds like a foremurmur of the Baconian sentences uttered nearly four hundred years later. Yet this is the character of what we here find[79]. "Experimental science, the sole mistress of speculative sciences, has three great Prerogatives among other parts of knowledge: First she tests by experiment the noblest conclusions of all other sciences: Next she discovers respecting the notions which other sciences deal with, magnificent truths to which these sciences of themselves can by no means attain: her Third dignity is, that she by her own power and without respect of other sciences, investigates the secret of nature."

The examples which Bacon gives of these "Prerogatives" are very curious, exhibiting, among some error and credulity, sound and clear views. His leading example of the First Prerogative, is the Rainbow, of which the cause, as given by Aristotle, is tested by reference to experiment with a skill which is, even to us now, truly admirable. The examples of the Second Prerogative are three:—first, the art of making an artificial sphere which shall move with the heavens by natural influences, which Bacon trusts may be done, though astronomy herself cannot do it—"et tunc," he says, "thesaurum unius regis valeret hoc instrumentum;"—secondly, the art of prolonging life, which experiment may teach, though medicine has no means of securing it except by regimen[80];—thirdly, the art of73 making gold finer than fine gold, which goes beyond the power of alchemy. The Third Prerogative of experimental science, arts independent of the received sciences, is exemplified in many curious examples, many of them whimsical traditions. Thus it is said that the character of a people may be altered by altering the air[81]. Alexander, it seems, applied to Aristotle to know whether he should exterminate certain nations which he had discovered, as being irreclaimably barbarous; to which the philosopher replied, "If you can alter their air, permit them to live, if not, put them to death." In this part, we find the suggestion that the fire-works made by children, of saltpetre, might lead to the invention of a formidable military weapon.

It could not be expected that Roger Bacon, at a time when experimental science hardly existed, could give any precepts for the discovery of truth by experiment. But nothing can be a better example of the method of such investigation, than his inquiry concerning the cause of the Rainbow. Neither Aristotle, nor Avicenna, nor Seneca, he says, have given us any clear knowledge of this matter, but experimental science can do so. Let the experimenter (experimentator) consider the cases in which he finds the same colours, as the hexagonal crystals from Ireland and India; by looking into these he will see colours like those of the rainbow. Many think that this arises from some special virtue of these stones and their hexagonal figure; let therefore the experimenter go on, and he will find the same in other transparent stones, in dark ones as well as in light-coloured. He will find the same effect also in other forms than the hexagon,74 if they be furrowed in the surface, as the Irish crystals are. Let him consider too, that he sees the same colours in the drops which are dashed from oars in the sunshine;—and in the spray thrown by a millwheel;—and in the dew-drops which lie on the grass in a meadow on a summer-morning;—and if a man takes water in his mouth and projects it on one side into a sunbeam;—and if in an oil-lamp hanging in the air, the rays fall in certain positions upon the surface of the oil;—and in many other ways, are colours produced. We have here a collection of instances, which are almost all examples of the same kind as the phenomenon under consideration; and by the help of a principle collected by induction from these facts, the colours of the rainbow were afterwards really explained.

With regard to the form and other circumstances of the bow he is still more precise. He bids us measure the height of the bow and of the sun, to show that the center of the bow is exactly opposite to the sun. He explains the circular form of the bow,—its being independent of the form of the cloud, its moving when we move, its flying when we follow,—by its consisting of the reflections from a vast number of minute drops. He does not, indeed, trace the course of the rays through the drop, or account for the precise magnitude which the bow assumes; but he approaches to the verge of this part of the explanation; and must be considered as having given a most happy example of experimental inquiry into nature, at a time when such examples were exceedingly scanty. In this respect, he was more fortunate than Francis Bacon, as we shall hereafter see.

We know but little of the biography of Roger Bacon, but we have every reason to believe that his influence upon his age was not great. He was suspected of magic, and is said to have been put into close confinement in consequence of this charge. In his work he speaks of Astrology as a science well worth cultivating. "But," says he, "Theologians and Decretists, not being learned in such matters and seeing that evil as well as good may be done, neglect and abhor such75 things, and reckon them among Magic Arts." We have already seen, that at the very time when Bacon was thus raising his voice against the habit of blindly following authority, and seeking for all science in Aristotle, Thomas Aquinas was employed in fashioning Aristotle's tenets into that fixed form in which they became the great impediment to the progress of knowledge. It would seem, indeed, that something of a struggle between the progressive and stationary powers of the human mind was going on at this time. Bacon himself says[82], "Never was there so great an appearance of wisdom, nor so much exercise of study in so many Faculties, in so many regions, as for this last forty years. Doctors are dispersed everywhere, in every castle, in every burgh, and especially by the students of two Orders, (he means the Franciscans and Dominicans, who were almost the only religious orders that distinguished themselves by an application to study[83],) which has not happened except for about forty years. And yet there was never so much ignorance, so much error." And in the part of his work which refers to Mathematics, he says of that study[84], that it is the door and the key of the sciences; and that the neglect of it for thirty or forty years has entirely ruined the studies of the Latins. According to these statements, some change, disastrous to the fortunes of science, must have taken place about 1230, soon after the foundation of the Dominican and Franciscan Orders[85]. Nor can we doubt that the adoption of the Aristotelian philosophy by these two Orders, in the form in which the Angelical Doctor had systematized it, was one of the events which most tended to defer, for three centuries, the reform which Roger Bacon urged as a matter of crying necessity in his own time.

76

CHAPTER XII.

The Revival of Platonism.

1. Causes of Delay in the Advance of Knowledge.—In the insight possessed by learned men into the method by which truth was to be discovered, the fourteenth and fifteenth centuries went backwards, rather than forwards, from the point which had been reached in the thirteenth. Roger Bacon had urged them to have recourse to experiment; but they returned with additional and exclusive zeal to the more favourite employment of reasoning upon their own conceptions. He had called upon them to look at the world without; but their eyes forthwith turned back upon the world within. In the constant oscillation of the human mind between Ideas and Facts, after having for a moment touched the latter, it seemed to swing back more impetuously to the former. Not only was the philosophy of Aristotle firmly established for a considerable period, but when men began to question its authority, they attempted to set up in its place a philosophy still more purely ideal, that of Plato. It was not till the actual progress of experimental knowledge for some centuries had given it a vast accumulation of force, that it was able to break its way fully into the circle of speculative science. The new Platonist schoolmen had to run their course, the practical discoverers had to prove their merit by their works, the Italian innovators had to utter their aspirations for a change, before the second Bacon could truly declare that the time for a fundamental reform was at length arrived.

It cannot but seem strange, to any one who attempts to trace the general outline of the intellectual progress of man, and who considers him as under the guidance77 of a Providential sway, that he should thus be permitted to wander so long in a wilderness of intellectual darkness; and even to turn back, by a perverse caprice as it might seem, when on the very border of the brighter and better land which was his destined inheritance. We do not attempt to solve this difficulty: but such a course of things naturally suggests the thought, that a progress in physical science is not the main object of man's career, in the eyes of the Power who directs the fortunes of our race. We can easily conceive that it may have been necessary to man's general welfare that he should continue to turn his eyes inwards upon his own heart and faculties, till Law and Duty, Religion and Government, Faith and Hope, had been fully incorporated with all the past acquisitions of human intellect; rather than that he should have rushed on into a train of discoveries tending to chain him to the objects and operations of the material world. The systematic Law[86] and philosophical Theology which acquired their ascendancy in men's minds at the time of which we speak, kept them engaged in a region of speculations which perhaps prepared the way for a profounder and wider civilization, for a more elevated and spiritual character, than might have been possible without such a preparation. The great Italian poet of the fourteenth century speaks with strong admiration of the founders of the system which prevailed in his time. Thomas, Albert, Gratian, Peter Lombard, occupy distinguished places in the Paradise. The first, who is the poet's instructor, says,—

Io fui degli agni della santa greggia
Che Domenico mena per cammino
U' ben s'impingua se non si vaneggia.
Questo che m'è a destra piu vicino
Frate e maestro fummi; ed esso Alberto
E di Cologna, ed io Tomas d'Aquino....
Quell' altro fiammeggiar esce del riso

De Grazian, che l'uno et l'altro foro
Ajutò si che piace in Paradiso.
I, then, was of the lambs that Dominic
Leads, for his saintly flock, along the way
Where well they thrive not swoln with vanity.
He nearest on my right-hand brother was
And master to me; Albert of Cologne
Is this; and of Aquinum Thomas, I....
That next resplendence issues from the smile
Of Gratian, who to either forum lent
Such help as favour wins in Paradise.

It appears probable that neither poetry, nor painting, nor the other arts which require for their perfection a lofty and spiritualized imagination, would have appeared in the noble and beautiful forms which they assumed in the fourteenth and fifteenth century, if men of genius had, at the beginning of that period, made it their main business to discover the laws of nature, and to reduce them to a rigorous scientific form. Yet who can doubt that the absence of these touching and impressive works would have left one of the best and purest parts of man's nature without its due nutriment and development? It may perhaps be a necessary condition in the progress of man, that the Arts which aim at beauty should reach their excellence before the Sciences which seek speculative truth; and if this be so, we inherit, from the middle ages, treasures which may well reconcile us to the delay which took place in their cultivation of experimental science.

However this may be, it is our business at present to trace the circumstances of this very lingering advance. We have already noticed the contest of the Nominalists and Realists, which was one form, though, with regard to scientific methods, an unprofitable one, of the antithesis of Ideas and Things. Though, therefore, this struggle continued, we need not dwell upon it. The Nominalists denied the real existence of Ideas, which doctrine was to a great extent implied in the prevailing systems; but the controversy in which they thus engaged, did not lead them to seek for knowledge in a new field and by new methods. The arguments79 which Occam the Nominalist opposes to those of Duns Scotus the Realist, are marked with the stamp of the same system, and consist only in permutations and combinations of the same elementary conceptions. It was not till the impulse of external circumstances was added to the discontent, which the more stirring intellects felt towards the barren dogmatism of their age, that the activity of the human mind was again called into full play, and a new career of progression entered upon, till then undreamt of, except by a few prophetic spirits.

2. Causes of Progress.—These circumstances were principally the revival of Greek and Roman literature, the invention of Printing, the Protestant Reformation, and a great number of curious discoveries and inventions in the arts, which were soon succeeded by important steps in speculative physical science. Connected with the first of these events, was the rise of a party of learned men who expressed their dissatisfaction with the Aristotelian philosophy, as it was then taught, and manifested a strong preference for the views of Plato. It is by no means suitable to our plan to give a detailed account of this new Platonic school; but we may notice a few of the writers who belong to it, so far at least as to indicate its influence upon the Methods of pursuing science.

In the fourteenth century[87], the frequent intercourse of the most cultivated persons of the Eastern and Western Empire, the increased study of the Greek language in Italy, the intellectual activity of the Italian States, the discovery of manuscripts of the classical authors, were circumstances which excited or nourished a new and zealous study of the works of Greek and Roman genius. The genuine writings of the ancients, when presented in their native life and beauty, instead of being seen only in those lifeless fragments and dull transformations which the scholastic system had exhibited, excited an intense enthusiasm. Europe, at that period, might be represented by Plato's beautiful80 allegory, of a man who, after being long kept in a dark cavern, in which his knowledge of the external world is gathered from the images which stream through the chinks of his prison, is at last led forth into the full blaze of day. It was inevitable that such a change should animate men's efforts and enlarge their faculties. Greek literature became more and more known, especially by the influence of learned men who came from Constantinople into Italy: these teachers, though they honoured Aristotle, reverenced Plato no less, and had never been accustomed to follow with servile submission of thought either these or any other leaders. The effect of such influences soon reveals itself in the works of that period. Dante has woven into his Divina Commedia some of the ideas of Platonism. Petrarch, who had formed his mind by the study of Cicero, and had thus been inspired with a profound admiration for the literature of Greece, learnt Greek from Barlaam, a monk who came as ambassador from the Emperor of the East to the Pope, in 1339. With this instructor, the poet read the works of Plato; struck by their beauty, he contributed, by his writings and his conversation, to awake in others an admiration and love for that philosopher, which soon became strongly and extensively prevalent among the learned in Italy.

3. Hermolaus Barbarus, &c.—Along with the feeling there prevailed also, among those who had learnt to relish the genuine beauties of the Greek and Latin writers, a strong disgust for the barbarisms in which the scholastic philosophy was clothed. Hermolaus Barbarus[88], who was born in 1454, at Venice, and had formed his taste by the study of classical literature, translated, among other learned works, Themistius's paraphrastic expositions of the Physics of Aristotle; with the view of trying whether the Aristotelian Natural Philosophy could not be presented in good Latin, which the scholastic teachers denied. In his Preface he expresses great indignation against those philosophers who have written and disputed on philosophical81 subjects in barbarous Latin, and in an uncultured style, so that all refined minds are repelled from these studies by weariness and disgust. They have, he says, by this barbarism, endeavoured to secure to themselves, in their own province, a supremacy without rivals or opponents. Hence they maintain that mathematics, philosophy, jurisprudence, cannot be expounded in correct Latin;—that between these sciences and the genuine Latin language there is a great gulf, as between things that cannot be brought together: and on this ground they blame those who combine the study of philology and eloquence with that of science. This opinion, adds Hermolaus, perverts and ruins our studies; and is highly prejudicial and unworthy in respect to the state. Hermolaus awoke in others, as for instance, in John Picus of Mirandula, the same dislike to the reigning school philosophy. As an opponent of the same kind, we may add Marius Nizolius of Bersallo, a scholar who carried his admiration of Cicero to an exaggerated extent, and who was led, by a controversy with the defenders of the scholastic philosophy, to publish (1553) a work On the True Principles and True

41

Method of Philosophizing. In the title of this work, he professes to give "the true principles of almost all arts and sciences, refuting and rejecting almost all the false principles of the Logicians and Metaphysicians." But although, in the work, he attacks the scholastic philosophy, he does little or nothing to justify the large pretensions of his title; and he excited, it is said, little notice. It is therefore curious that Leibnitz should have thought it worth his while to re-edit this work, which he did in 1670, adding remarks of his own.

4. Nicolaus Cusanus.—Without dwelling upon this opposition to the scholastic system on the ground of taste, I shall notice somewhat further those writers who put forwards Platonic views, as fitted to complete or to replace the doctrines of Aristotle. Among these, I may place Nicolaus Cusanus, (so called from Cus, a village on the Moselle, where he was born in 1401;) who was afterwards raised to the dignity of cardinal. We might, indeed, at first be tempted to include82 Cusanus among those persons who were led to reject the old philosophy by being themselves agents in the progressive movement of physical science. For he published, before Copernicus, and independently of him, the doctrine that the earth is in motion[89]. But it should be recollected that in order to see the possibility of this doctrine, and its claims to acceptance, no new reference to observation was requisite. The Heliocentric System was merely a new mode of representing to the mind facts, with which all astronomers had long been familiar. The system might very easily have been embraced and inculcated by Plato himself; as indeed it is said to have been actually taught by Pythagoras. The mere adoption of the Heliocentric view, therefore, without attempting to realize the system in detail, as Copernicus did, cannot entitle a writer of the fifteenth century to be looked upon as one of the authors of the discoveries of that period; and we must consider Cusanus as a speculative anti-Aristotelian, rather than as a practical reformer.

The title of Cusanus's book, De Doctâ Ignorantiâ, shows how far he was from agreeing with those who conceived that, in the works of Aristotle, they had a full and complete system of all human knowledge. At the outset of this book[90], he says, after pointing out some difficulties in the received philosophy, "If, therefore, the case be so, (as even the very profound Aristotle, in his First Philosophy, affirms,) that in things most manifest by nature, there is a difficulty, no less than for an owl to look at the sun; since the appetite of knowledge is not implanted in us in vain, we ought to desire to know that we are ignorant. If we can fully attain to this, we shall arrive at Instructed Ignorance." How far he was from placing the source of knowledge in experience, as opposed to ideas, we may see in the following passage[91] from another work of his, On Conjectures. "Conjectures must proceed from83 our mind, as the real world proceeds from the infinite Divine Reason. For since the human mind, the lofty likeness of God, participates, as it may, in the fruitfulness of the creative nature, it doth from itself, as the image of the Omnipotent Form, bring forth reasonable thoughts which have a similitude to real existences. Thus the Human Mind exists as a conjectural form of the world, as the Divine Mind is its real form." We have here the Platonic or ideal side of knowledge put prominently and exclusively forwards.

5. Marsilius Ficinus, &c.—A person who had much more influence on the diffusion of Platonism was Marsilius Ficinus, a physician of Florence. In that city there prevailed, at the time of which we speak, the greatest enthusiasm for Plato. George Gemistius Pletho,

when in attendance upon the Council of Florence, had imparted to many persons the doctrines of the Greek philosopher; and, among others, had infused a lively interest on this subject into the elder Cosmo, the head of the family of the Medici. Cosmo formed the plan of founding a Platonic academy. Ficinus[92], well instructed in the works of Plato, Plotinus, Proclus, and other Platonists, was selected to further this object, and was employed in translating the works of these authors into Latin. It is not to our present purpose to consider the doctrines of this school, except so far as they bear upon the nature and methods of knowledge; and therefore I must pass by, as I have in other instances done, the greater part of their speculations, which related to the nature of God, the immortality of the soul, the principles of Goodness and Beauty, and other points of the same order. The object of these and other Platonists of this school, however, was not to expel the authority of Aristotle by that of Plato. Many of them had come to the conviction that the highest ends of philosophy were to be reached only by bringing into accordance the doctrines of Plato and of Aristotle. Of this opinion was John Picus, Count of Mirandula and Concordia; and under84 this persuasion he employed the whole of his life in labouring upon a work, De Concordiâ Platonis et Aristotelis, which was not completed at the time of his death, in 1494; and has never been published. But about a century later, another writer of the same school, Francis Patricius[93], pointing out the discrepancies between the two Greek teachers, urged the propriety of deposing Aristotle from the supremacy he had so long enjoyed. "Now all these doctrines, and others not a few," he says[94], "since they are Platonic doctrines, philosophically most true, and consonant with the Catholic faith, whilst the Aristotelian tenets are contrary to the faith, and philosophically false, who will not, both as a Christian and a Philosopher, prefer Plato to Aristotle? And why should not hereafter, in all the colleges and monasteries of Europe, the reading and study of Plato be introduced? Why should not the philosophy of Aristotle be forthwith exiled from such places? Why must men continue to drink the mortal poison of impiety from that source?" with much more in the same strain.

The Platonic school, of which we have spoken, had, however, reached its highest point of prosperity before this time, and was already declining. About 1500, the Platonists appeared to triumph over the Peripatetics[95]; but the death of their great patron, Cardinal Bessarion, about this time, and we may add, the hollowness of their system in many points, and its want of fitness for the wants and expectations of the age, turned men's thoughts partly back to the established Aristotelian doctrines, and partly forwards to schemes of bolder and fresher promise.

6. Francis Patricius.—Patricius, of whom we have just spoken, was one of those who had arrived at the conviction that the formation of a new philosophy, and not merely the restoration of an old one, was needed. In 1593, appeared his Nova de Universis85 Philosophia; and the mode in which it begins[96] can hardly fail to remind us of the expressions which Francis Bacon soon afterwards used in the opening of a work of the same nature. "Francis Patricius, being about to found anew the true philosophy of the universe, dared to begin by announcing the following indisputable principles." Here, however, the resemblance between Patricius and true inductive philosophers ends. His principles are barren à priori axioms; and his system has one main element, Light, (Lux, or Lumen,) to which all operations of nature are referred. In general cultivation, and practical knowledge of nature, he was distinguished among his contemporaries. In various passages of his works he relates[97] observations which he had made in the course of his travels, in

Cyprus, Corfu, Spain, the mountains of the Modenese, and Dalmatia, which was his own country; his observations relate to light, the saltness of the sea, its flux and reflux, and other points of astronomy, meteorology, and natural history. He speaks of the sex of plants[98]; rejects judicial astrology; and notices the astronomical systems of Copernicus, Tycho, Fracastoro, and Torre. But the mode in which he speaks of experiments proves, what indeed is evident from the general scheme of his system, that he had no due appreciation of the place which observation must hold in real and natural philosophy.

7. Picus, Agrippa, &c.—It had been seen in the later philosophical history of Greece, how readily the ideas of the Platonic school lead on to a system of unfathomable and unbounded mysticism. John Picus, of Mirandula[99], added to the study of Plato and the86 Neoplatonists, a mass of allegorical interpretations of the Scriptures, and the dreams of the Cabbala, a Jewish system[100], which pretends to explain how all things are an emanation of the Deity. To this his nephew, Francis Picus, added a reference to inward illumination[101], by which knowledge is obtained, independently of the progress of reasoning. John Reuchlin, or Capnio, born 1455; John Baptist Helmont, born 1577; Francis Mercurius Helmont, born 1618, and others, succeeded John Picus in his admiration of the Cabbala: while others, as Jacob Bœhmen, rested upon internal revelations like Francis Picus. And thus we have a series of mystical writers, continued into modern times, who may be considered as the successors of the Platonic school; and who all exhibit views altogether erroneous with regard to the nature and origin of knowledge. Among the various dreams of this school are certain wide and loose analogies of terrestrial and spiritual things. Thus in the writings of Cornelius Agrippa (who was born 1487, at Cologne) we have such systems as the following[102]:—"Since there is a threefold world, elemental, celestial, and intellectual, and each lower one is governed by that above it, and receives the influence of its powers: so that the very Archetype and Supreme Author transfuses the virtues of his omnipotence into us through angels, heavens, stars, elements, animals, plants, stones,—into us, I say, for whose service he has framed and created all these things;—the Magi do not think it irrational that we should be able to ascend by the same degrees, the same worlds, to this Archetype of the world, the Author and First Cause of all, of whom all things are, and from whom they proceed; and should not only avail ourselves of those powers which exist in the nobler works of creation, but also should be able to attract other powers, and add them to these."

Agrippa's work, De Vanitate Scientiarum, may be87 said rather to have a skeptical and cynical, than a Platonic, character. It is a declamation[103], in a melancholy mood, against the condition of the sciences in his time. His indignation at the worldly success of men whom he considered inferior to himself, had, he says, metamorphosed him into a dog, as the poets relate of Hecuba of Troy, so that his impulse was to snarl and bark. His professed purpose, however, was to expose the dogmatism, the servility, the self-conceit, and the neglect of religious truth which prevailed in the reigning Schools of philosophy. His views of the nature of science, and the modes of improving its cultivation, are too imperfect and vague to allow us to rank him among the reformers of science.

8. Paracelsus, Fludd, &c.—The celebrated Paracelsus[104] put himself forwards as a reformer in philosophy, and obtained no small number of adherents. He was, in most respects, a shallow and impudent pretender; and had small knowledge of the literature or science of his time: but by the tone of his speaking and writing he manifestly belongs to

the mystical school of which we are now speaking. Perhaps by the boldness with which he proposed new systems, and by connecting these with the practical doctrines of medicine, he contributed something to the introduction of a new philosophy. We have seen in the History of Chemistry that he was the author of the system of Three Principles, (salt, sulphur, and mercury,) which replaced the ancient doctrine of Four Elements, and prepared the way for a true science of chemistry. But the salt, sulphur, and mercury of Paracelsus were not, he tells his disciples, the visible bodies which we call by those names, but certain invisible, astral, or sidereal elements. The astral salt is the basis of the solidity and incombustible parts in bodies; the astral sulphur is the source of combustion88 and vegetation; the astral mercury is the origin of fluidity and volatility. And again, these three elements are analogous to the three elements of man,—Body, Spirit, and Soul.

A writer of our own country, belonging to this mystical school, is Robert Fludd, or De Fluctibus, who was born in 1571, in Kent, and after pursuing his studies at Oxford, travelled for several years. Of all the Theosophists and Mystics, he is by much the most learned; and was engaged in various controversies with Mersenne, Gassendi, Kepler, and others. He thus brings us in contact with the next class of philosophers whom we have to consider, the practical reformers of philosophy;—those who furthered the cause of science by making, promulgating, or defending the great discoveries which now began to occupy men. He adopted the principle, which we have noticed elsewhere[105], of the analogy of the Macrocosm and Microcosm, the world of nature and the world of man. His system contains such a mixture and confusion of physical and metaphysical doctrines as might be expected from his ground-plan, and from his school. Indeed his object, the general object of mystical speculators, is to identify physical with spiritual truths. Yet the influence of the practical experimental philosophy which was now gaining ground in the world may be traced in him. Thus he refers to experiments on distillation to prove the existence and relation of the regions of water, air, and fire, and of the spirits which correspond to them; and is conceived, by some persons[106], to have anticipated Torricelli in the invention of the Barometer.

We need no further follow the speculations of this school. We see already abundant reason why the reform of the methods of pursuing science could not proceed from the Platonists. Instead of seeking knowledge by experiment, they immersed themselves deeper than even the Aristotelians had done in traditionary89 lore, or turned their eyes inwards in search of an internal illumination. Some attempts were made to remedy the defects of philosophy by a recourse to the doctrines of other sects of antiquity, when men began to feel more distinctly the need of a more connected and solid knowledge of nature than the established system gave them. Among these attempts were those of Berigard[107], Magernus, and especially Gassendi, to bring into repute the philosophy of the Ionian school, of Democritus and of Epicurus. But these endeavours were posterior in time to the new impulse given to knowledge by Copernicus, Kepler, and Galileo, and were influenced by views arising out of the success of these discoveries, and they must, therefore, be considered hereafter. In the mean time, some independent efforts (arising from speculative rather than practical reformers) were made to cast off the yoke of the Aristotelian dogmatism, and to apprehend the true form of that new philosophy which the most active and hopeful minds saw to be needed; and we must give some account of these attempts, before we can commit ourselves to the full stream of progressive philosophy.

45

CHAPTER XIII.
The Theoretical Reformers of Science.

We have already seen that Patricius, about the middle of the sixteenth century, announced his purpose of founding anew the whole fabric of philosophy; but that, in executing this plan, he ran into wide and baseless hypotheses, suggested by à priori conceptions rather than by external observation; and that he was further misled by fanciful analogies resembling those which the Platonic mystics loved to contemplate. The same time, and the period which followed it, produced several other essays which were of the same nature, with the exception of their being free from the peculiar tendencies of the Platonic school: and these insurrections against the authority of the established dogmas, although they did not directly substitute a better positive system in the place of that which they assailed, shook the authority of the Aristotelian system, and led to its overthrow; which took place as soon as these theoretical reformers were aided by practical reformers.

1. Bernardinus Telesius.—Italy, always, in modern times, fertile in the beginnings of new systems, was the soil on which these innovators arose. The earliest and most conspicuous of them is Bernardinus Telesius, who was born in 1508, at Cosenza, in the kingdom of Naples. His studies, carried on with great zeal and ability, first at Milan and then at Rome, made him well acquainted with the knowledge of his times; but his own reflections convinced him that the basis of science, as then received, was altogether erroneous; and led him to attempt a reform, with which view, in 1565, he published, at Rome, his91 work[108], "Bernardinus Telesius, of Cosenza, on the Nature of Things, according to principles of his own." In the preface of this work he gives a short account[109] of the train of reflection by which he was led to put himself in opposition to the Aristotelian philosophy. This kind of autobiography occurs not unfrequently in the writings of theoretical reformers; and shows how livelily they felt the novelty of their undertaking. After the storm and sack of Rome in 1527, Telesius retired to Padua, as a peaceful seat of the muses; and there studied philosophy and mathematics, with great zeal, under the direction of Jerome Amalthæus and Frederic Delphinus. In these studies he made great progress; and the knowledge which he thus acquired threw a new light upon his view of the Aristotelian philosophy. He undertook a closer examination of the Physical Doctrines of Aristotle; and as the result of this, he was astonished how it could have been possible that so many excellent men, so many nations, and even almost the whole human race, should, for so long a time, have allowed themselves to be carried away by a blind reverence for a teacher, who had committed errors so numerous and grave as he perceived to exist in "the philosopher." Along with this view of the insufficiency of the Aristotelian philosophy, arose, at an early period, the thought of erecting a better system in its place. With this purpose he left Padua, when he had received the degree of Doctor, and went to Rome, where he was encouraged in his design by the approval and friendly exhortations of distinguished men of letters, amongst whom were Ubaldino Bandinelli and Giovanni della Casa. From Rome he went to his native place, when the incidents and occupations of a married life for a while interrupted his philosophical project. But after his92 wife was dead, and his eldest son grown to manhood, he resumed with ardour the scheme of his youth; again studied the works of Aristotle and other philosophers, and

composed and published the first two books of his treatise. The opening to this work sufficiently exhibits the spirit in which it was conceived. Its object is stated in the title to be to show, that "the construction of the world, the magnitude and nature of the bodies contained in it, are not to be investigated by reasoning, which was done by the ancients, but are to be apprehended by the senses, and collected from the things themselves." And the Proem is in the same strain. "They who before us have inquired concerning the construction of this world and of the things which it contains, seem indeed to have prosecuted their examination with protracted vigils and great labour, but never to have looked at it." And thus, he observes, they found nothing but error. This he ascribes to their presumption. "For, as it were, attempting to rival God in wisdom, and venturing to seek for the principles and causes of the world by the light of their own reason, and thinking they had found what they had only invented, they made an arbitrary world of their own." "We then," he adds, "not relying on ourselves, and of a duller intellect than they, propose to ourselves to turn our regards to the world itself and its parts."

The execution of the work, however, by no means corresponds to the announcement. The doctrines of Aristotle are indeed attacked; and the objections to these, and to other received opinions, form a large part of the work. But these objections are supported by à priori reasoning, and not by experiments. And thus, rejecting the Aristotelian physics, he proposes a system at least equally baseless; although, no doubt, grateful to the author from its sweeping and apparently simple character. He assumes three principles, Heat, Cold, and Matter: Heat is the principle of motion, Cold of immobility, and Matter is the corporeal substratum, in which these incorporeal and active principles produce their effects. It is easy to imagine that, by combining93 and separating these abstractions in various ways, a sort of account of many natural phenomena may be given; but it is impossible to ascribe any real value to such a system. The merit of Telesius must be considered to consist in his rejection of the Aristotelian errors, in his perception of the necessity of a reform in the method of philosophizing, and in his persuasion that this reform must be founded on experiments rather than on reasoning. When he said[110], "We propose to ourselves to turn our eyes to the world itself, and its parts, their passions, actions, operations, and species," his view of the course to be followed was right; but his purpose remained but ill fulfilled, by the arbitrary edifice of abstract conceptions which his system exhibits.

Francis Bacon, who, about half a century later, treated the subject of a reform of philosophy in a far more penetrating and masterly manner, has given us his judgment of Telesius. In his view, he takes Telesius as the restorer of the Atomic philosophy, which Democritus and Parmenides taught among the ancients; and according to his custom, he presents an image of this philosophy in an adaptation of a portion of ancient mythology[111]. The Celestial Cupid, who with Cœlus, was the parent of the Gods and of the Universe, is exhibited as a representation of matter and its properties, according to the Democritean philosophy. "Concerning Telesius," says Bacon, "we think well, and acknowledge him as a lover of truth, a useful contributor to science, an amender of some tenets, the first of recent men. But we have to do with him as the restorer of the philosophy of Parmenides, to whom much reverence is due." With regard to this philosophy, he pronounces a judgment which very truly expresses the cause of its rashness and emptiness. "It is," he says, "such a system[112] as naturally94 proceeds from the intellect, abandoned to its own impulse, and not rising from experience to theory continuously and successively." Accordingly, he says that, "Telesius, although learned in the Peripatetic philosophy (if that were anything), which indeed, he has turned against the teachers of it, is hindered by his affirmations, and is more successful in destroying than in building."

The work of Telesius excited no small notice, and was placed in the Index Expurgatorius. It made many disciples, a consequence probably due to its spirit of system-making, no less than to its promise of reform, or its acuteness of argument; for till trial and reflection have taught man modesty and moderation, he can never be content to receive knowledge in the small successive instalments in which nature gives it forth to him. It is the makers of large systems, arranged with an appearance of completeness and symmetry, who, principally, give rise to Schools of philosophy.

2. (Thomas Campanella).—Accordingly, Telesius may be looked upon as the founder of a School. His most distinguished successor was Thomas Campanella, who was born in 1568, at Stilo, in Calabria. He showed great talents at an early age, prosecuting his studies at Cosenza, the birth-place of the great opponent of Aristotle and reformer of philosophy. He, too, has given us an account[113] of the course of thought by which he was led to become an innovator. "Being afraid that not genuine truth, but falsehood in the place of truth, was the tenant of the Peripatetic School, I examined all the Greek, Latin, and Arabic commentators of Aristotle, and hesitated more and more, as I sought to learn whether what they have said were also to be read in the world itself, which I had been taught by learned men was the living book of God. And as my doctors could not satisfy my scruples, I resolved to read all the books of Plato, Pliny, Galen, the Stoics,95 and the Democriteans, and especially those of Telesius; and to compare them with that first and original writing, the world; that thus from the primary autograph, I might learn if the copies contained anything false." Campanella probably refers here to an expression of Plato, who says, "the world is God's epistle to mankind." And this image, of the natural world as an original manuscript, while human systems of philosophy are but copies, and may be false ones, became a favourite thought of the reformers, and appears repeatedly in their writings from this time. "When I held my public disputation at Cosenza," Campanella proceeds, "and still more, when I conversed privately with the brethren of the monastery, I found little satisfaction in their answers; but Telesius delighted me, on account of his freedom in philosophizing, and because he rested upon the nature of things, and not upon the assertions of men."

With these views and feelings, it is not wonderful that Campanella, at the early age of twenty-two (1590,) published a work remarkable for the bold promise of its title: "Thomas Campanella's Philosophy demonstrated to the senses, against those who have philosophized in an arbitrary and dogmatical manner, not taking nature for their guide; in which the errors of Aristotle and his followers are refuted from their own assertions and the laws of nature: and all the imaginations feigned in the place of nature by the Peripatetics are altogether rejected; with a true defence of Bernardin Telesius of Cosenza, the greatest of philosophers; confirmed by the opinions of the ancients, here elucidated and defended, especially those of the Platonists."

This work was written in answer to a book published against Telesius by a Neapolitan professor named Marta; and it was the boast of the young author that he had only employed eleven months in the composition of his defence, while his adversary had been engaged eleven years in preparing his attack. Campanella found a favourable reception in the house of the Marchese Lavelli, and there employed himself in the composition of an additional work, entitled On the96 Sense of Things and Magic, and in other literary labours. These, however, are full of the indications of an enthusiastic temper, inclined to mystical devotion, and of opinions bearing the cast of pantheism. For instance, the title of the book last quoted sets forth as demonstrated in the course of the work, that "the world is the living and intelligent statue of God; and that all its parts, and particles of parts, are endowed some with a clearer, some with a more obscure sense, such as suffices for the preservation of each and of the whole." Besides these opinions, which could not fail to make him obnoxious to the religious authorities, Campanella[114] engaged in schemes of political revolution, which involved him in danger and calamity. He took part in a conspiracy, of which the object was to cast off the tyranny of Spain, and to make Calabria a republic. This design was discovered; and Campanella, along with others, was thrown into prison and subjected to torture. He was kept in confinement twenty-seven years; and at last obtained his liberation by the interposition of Pope Urban VIII. He was, however, still in danger from the Neapolitan Inquisition; and escaped in disguise to Paris, where he received a pension from the king, and lived in intercourse with the most eminent men of letters. He died there in 1639.

Campanella was a contemporary of Francis Bacon, whom we must consider as belonging to an epoch to which the Calabrian school of innovators was only a prelude. I shall not therefore further follow the connexion of writers of this order. Tobias Adami, a Saxon writer, an admirer of Campanella's works, employed himself, about 1620, in adapting them to the German public, and in recommending them strongly to German philosophers. Descartes, and even Bacon, may be considered as successors of Campanella; for they too were theoretical reformers; but they enjoyed the advantage of the light which had, in the mean time, been thrown upon the philosophy of science, by the great practical advances of Kepler, Galileo, and others. To these97 practical reformers we must soon turn our attention: but we may first notice one or two additional circumstances belonging to our present subject.

Campanella remarks that both the Peripatetics and the Platonists conducted the learner to knowledge by a long and circuitous path, which he wished to shorten by setting out from the sense. Without speaking of the methods which he proposed, we may notice one maxim[115] of considerable value which he propounds, and to which we have already been led. "We begin to reason from sensible objects, and definition is the end and epilogue of science. It is not the beginning of our knowing, but only of our teaching."

3. (Andrew Cæsalpinus.)—The same maxim had already been announced by Cæsalpinus, a contemporary of Telesius; (he was born at Arezzo in 1520, and died at Rome in 1603). Cæsalpinus is a great name in science, though professedly an Aristotelian. It has been seen in the History of Science[116], that he formed the first great epoch of the science of botany by his systematic arrangement of plants, and that in this task he had no successor for nearly a century. He also approached near to the great discovery of the circulation of the blood[117]. He takes a view of science which includes the remark that we have just quoted from Campanella: "We reach perfect knowledge by three steps: Induction, Division, Definition. By Induction, we collect likeness and agreement from

49

observation; by Division, we collect unlikeness and disagreement; by Definition, we learn the proper substance of each object. Induction makes universals from particulars, and offers to the mind all intelligible matter; Division discovers the difference of universals, and leads to species; Definition resolves species into their principles and elements[118]." Without asserting this to be rigorously correct, it is incomparably more true and philosophical than the opposite view,98 which represents definition as the beginning of our knowledge; and the establishment of such a doctrine is a material step in inductive philosophy[119].

4. (Giordano Bruno.)—Among the Italian innovators of this time we must notice the unfortunate Giordano Bruno, who was born at Nola about 1550 and burnt at Rome in 1600. He is, however, a reformer of a different school from Campanella; for he derives his philosophy from Ideas and not from Observation. He represents himself as the author of a new doctrine, which he terms the Nolan Philosophy. He was a zealous promulgator and defender of the Copernican system of the universe, as we have noticed in the History of Science[120]. Campanella also wrote in defence of that system.

It is worthy of remark that a thought which is often quoted from Francis Bacon, occurs in Bruno's Cena di Cenere, published in 1584; I mean, the notion that the later times are more aged than the earlier. In the course of the dialogue, the Pedant, who is one of the interlocutors, says, "In antiquity is wisdom;" to which the Philosophical Character replies, "If you knew what you were talking about, you would see that your principle leads to the opposite result of that which you wish to infer;—I mean, that we are older, and have lived longer, than our predecessors." He then proceeds to apply this, by tracing the course of astronomy through the earlier astronomers up to Copernicus.

5.(Peter Ramus.)—I will notice one other reformer of this period, who attacked the Aristotelian system on another side, on which it was considered to be most impregnable. This was Peter Ramus,(born in Picardy in 1515,) who ventured to denounce the Logic of Aristotle as unphilosophical and useless. After showing an extraordinary aptitude for the acquirement of knowledge in his youth, when he proceeded to the degree of Master of Arts, he astonished his examiners by99 choosing for the subject of the requisite disputation the thesis[121], "that what Aristotle has said is all wrong." This position, so startling in 1535, he defended for the whole day, without being defeated. This was, however, only a formal academical exercise, which did not necessarily imply any permanent conviction of the opinion thus expressed. But his mind was really labouring to detect and remedy the errors which he thus proclaimed. From him, as from the other reformers of this time, we have an account of this mental struggle[122]. He says, in a work on this subject, "I will candidly and simply explain how I was delivered from the darkness of Aristotle. When, according to the laws of our university, I had spent three years and a half in the Aristotelian philosophy, and was now invested with the philosophical laurel as a Master of Arts, I took an account of the time which I had consumed in this study, and considered on what subjects I should employ this logical art of Aristotle, which I had learnt with so much labour and noise, I found it made me not more versed in history or antiquities, more eloquent in discourse, more ready in verse, more wise in any subject. Alas for me! how was I overpowered, how deeply did I groan, how did I deplore my lot and my nature, how did I deem myself to be by some unhappy and dismal fate and frame of mind abhorrent from the Muses, when I found that I was one who, after all my pains, could reap no benefit from that wisdom of which I heard so much, as being contained in the Logic of Aristotle." He then relates that he was led to the study of the Dialogues of Plato, and was delighted with the kind of analysis of the subjects discussed which Socrates is there represented as executing. "Well," he adds, "I began thus to reflect within myself— (I should have thought it impious to say it to another)—What, I100 pray you, prevents me from socratizing; and from asking, without regard to Aristotle's authority, whether Aristotle's Logic be true and correct? It may be that that philosopher leads us wrong; and if so, no wonder that I cannot find in his books the treasure which is not there. What if his dogmas be mere figments? Do I not tease and torment myself in vain, trying to get a harvest from a barren soil?" He convinced himself that the Aristotelian logic was worthless: and constructed a new system of Logic, founded mainly on the Platonic process of exhausting a subject by analytical classification of its parts. Both works, his Animadversions on Aristotle, and his Logic, appeared in 1543. The learned world was startled and shocked to find a young man, on his first entrance into life, condemning as faulty, fallacious, and useless, that part of Aristotle's works which had always hitherto been held as a masterpiece of philosophical acuteness, and as the Organon of scientific reasoning. And in truth, it must be granted that Ramus does not appear to have understood the real nature and object of Aristotle's Logic; while his own system could not supply the place of the old one, and was not of much real value. This dissent from the established doctrines was, however, not only condemned but punished. The printing and selling of his books was forbidden through France; and Ramus was stigmatized by a sentence[123] which declared him rash, arrogant, impudent, and ignorant, and prohibited from teaching logic and philosophy. He was, however, afterwards restored to the office of professor: and though much attacked, persisted in his plan of reforming, not only Logic but Physics and Metaphysics. He made his position still more dangerous by adopting the reformed religion; and during the unhappy civil wars of France, he was deprived of his professorship, driven from Paris, and had his library plundered. He endeavoured, but in vain, to engage a German professor, Schegk, to undertake the101 reform of the Aristotelian Physics; a portion of knowledge in which he felt himself not to be strong. Unhappily for himself, he afterwards returned to Paris, where he perished in the massacre of St. Bartholomew in 1572.

Ramus's main objection to the Aristotelian Logic is, that it is not the image of the natural process of thought; an objection which shows little philosophical insight; for the course by which we obtain knowledge may well differ from the order in which our knowledge, when obtained, is exhibited. We have already seen that Ramus's contemporaries, Cæsalpinus and Campanella, had a wiser view; placing definition as the last step in knowing, but the first in teaching. But the effect which Ramus produced was by no means slight. He aided powerfully in turning the minds of men to question the authority of Aristotle on all points; and had many followers, especially among the Protestants. Among the rest, Milton, our great poet, published "Artis Logicæ plenior Institutio ad Petri Rami methodum concinnata;" but this work, appearing in 1672, belongs to a succeeding period.

6.(The Reformers in general).—It is impossible not to be struck with the series of misfortunes which assailed the reformers of philosophy of the period we have had to review. Roger Bacon was repeatedly condemned and imprisoned; and, not to speak of others who suffered under the imputation of magical arts, Telesius is said[124] to have been driven from Naples to his native city by calumny and envy; Cæsalpinus was accused of atheism[125]; Campanella was imprisoned for twenty-seven years and tortured; Giordano Bruno was burnt at Rome as a heretic; Ramus was persecuted during his life, and finally murdered by his personal enemy Jacques Charpentier, in a massacre of which the plea was religion. It is true, that for the most part these misfortunes were not principally due to the attempts102 at philosophical reform, but were connected rather with politics or religion. But we cannot doubt that the spirit which led men to assail the received philosophy, might readily incline them to reject some tenets of the established religion; since the boundary line of these subjects is difficult to draw. And as we have seen, there was in most of the persons of whom we have spoken, not only a well-founded persuasion of the defects of existing systems, but an eager spirit of change, and a sanguine anticipation of some wide and lofty philosophy, which was soon to elevate the minds and conditions of men. The most unfortunate were, for the most part, the least temperate and judicious reformers. Patricius, who, as we have seen, declared himself against the Aristotelian philosophy, lived and died at Rome in peace and honour[126].

7.(Melancthon.)—It is not easy to point out with precision the connexion between the efforts at a Reform in Philosophy, and the great Reformation of Religion in the sixteenth century. The disposition to assert (practically at least) a freedom of thinking, and to reject the corruptions which tradition had introduced and authority maintained, naturally extended its influence from one subject to another; and especially in subjects so nearly connected as theology and philosophy. The Protestants, however, did not reject the Aristotelian system; they only reformed it, by going back to the original works of the author, and by reducing it to a conformity with Scripture. In this reform, Melancthon was the chief author, and wrote works on Logic, Physics, Morals, and Metaphysics, which were used among Protestants. On the subject of the origin of our knowledge, his views contained a very philosophical improvement of the Aristotelian doctrines. He recognized the importance of Ideas, as well as of Experience. "We could not," he says[127], "proceed to reason at all, except there were by nature103 innate in man certain fixed points, that is, principles of science;—as Number, the recognition of Order and Proportion, logical, geometrical, physical and moral Principles. Physical principles are such as these,—everything which exists proceeds from a cause,—a body cannot be in two places at once,—time is a continued series of things or of motions,—and the like." It is not difficult to see that such Principles partake of the nature of the Fundamental Ideas which we have attempted to arrange and enumerate in a previous part of this work.

Before we proceed to the next chapter, which treats of the Practical Reformers of Scientific Method, let us for an instant look at the strong persuasion implied in the titles of the works of this period, that the time of a philosophical revolution was at hand. Telesius published De Rerum Natura juxta propria principia; Francis Helmont, Philosophia vulgaris refutata; Patricius, Nova de Universis Philosophia; Campanella, Philosophia sensibus demonstrata, adversus errores Aristotelis; Bruno professed himself the author of a Nolan Philosophy; and Ramus of a New Logic. The age announced itself pregnant; and the eyes of all who took an interest in the intellectual fortunes of the race, were looking eagerly for the expected offspring.

104

CHAPTER XIV.

The Practical Reformers of Science.

1. Character of the Practical Reformers.—We now come to a class of speculators who had perhaps a greater share in bringing about the change from stationary to progressive knowledge, than those writers who so loudly announced the revolution. The mode in which the philosophers of whom we now speak produced their impressions on men's minds, was very different from the procedure of the theoretical reformers. What these talked of, they did; what these promised, they performed. While the theorists concerning knowledge proclaimed that great advances were to be made, the practical discoverers went steadily forwards. While one class spoke of a complete Reform of scientific Methods, the other, boasting little, and often thinking little of Method, proved the novelty of their instrument by obtaining new results. While the metaphysicians were exhorting men to consult experience and the senses, the physicists were examining nature by such means with unparalleled success. And while the former, even when they did for a moment refer to facts, soon rushed back into their own region of ideas, and tried at once to seize the widest generalizations, the latter, fastening their attention upon the phenomena, and trying to reduce them to laws, were carried forwards by steps measured and gradual, such as no conjectural view of scientific method had suggested; but leading to truths as profound and comprehensive as any which conjecture had dared to anticipate. The theoretical reformers were bold, self-confident, hasty, contemptuous of antiquity, ambitious of ruling all future speculations, as they whom they105 sought to depose had ruled the past. The practical reformers were cautious, modest, slow, despising no knowledge, whether borrowed from tradition or observation, confident in the ultimate triumph of science, but impressed with the conviction that each single person could contribute a little only to its progress. Yet though thus working rather than speculating,—dealing with particulars more than with generals,—employed mainly in adding to knowledge, and not in defining what knowledge is, or how additions are to be made to it,—these men, thoughtful, curious, and of comprehensive minds, were constantly led to important views on the nature and methods of science. And these views, thus suggested by reflections on their own mental activity, were gradually incorporated with the more abstract doctrines of the metaphysicians, and had a most important influence in establishing an improved philosophy of science. The indications of such views we must now endeavour to collect from the writings of the discoverers of the times preceding the seventeenth century.

Some of the earliest of these indications are to be found in those who dealt with Art rather than with Science. I have already endeavoured to show that the advance of the arts which give us a command over the powers of nature, is generally prior to the formation of exact and speculative knowledge concerning those powers. But Art, which is thus the predecessor of Science, is, among nations of acute and active intellects, usually its parent. There operates, in such a case, a speculative spirit, leading men to seek for the reasons of that which they find themselves able to do. How slowly, and with what repeated deviations men follow this leading, when under the influence of a partial and dogmatical philosophy, the late birth and slow growth of sound physical theory shows. But at the period of which we now speak, we find men, at length, proceeding in obedience to the impulse which thus drives them from practice to theory;—from an acquaintance with phenomena to a free and intelligent inquiry concerning their causes.

2. Leonardo da Vinci.—I have already noted, in the History of Science, that the Indistinctness of Ideas, which was long one main impediment to the progress of science in the middle ages, was first remedied among architects and engineers. These men, so far at least as mechanical ideas were concerned, were compelled by their employments to judge rightly of the relations and properties of the materials with which they had to deal; and would have been chastised by the failure of their works, if they had violated the laws of mechanical truth. It was not wonderful, therefore, that these laws became known to them first. We have seen, in the History, that Leonardo da Vinci, the celebrated painter, who was also an engineer, is the first writer in whom we find the true view of the laws of equilibrium of the lever in the most general case. This artist, a man of a lively and discursive mind, is led to make some remarks[128] on the formation of our knowledge, which may show the opinions on that subject that already offered themselves at the beginning of the sixteenth century[129]. He expresses himself as follows:—"Theory is the general, Experiments are the soldiers. The interpreter of the artifices of nature is Experience: she is never deceived. Our judgment sometimes is deceived, because it expects effects which Experience refuses to allow." And again, "We must consult Experience, and vary the circumstances till we have drawn from them general rules; for it is she who furnishes true rules. But of what use, you ask, are these rules; I reply, that they direct us in the researches of nature and the operations of art. They prevent our imposing upon ourselves and others by promising ourselves results which we cannot obtain.

"In the study of the sciences which depend on mathematics, those who do not consult nature but authors, are not the children of nature, they are only her grand107children. She is the true teacher of men of genius. But see the absurdity of men! They turn up their noses at a man who prefers to learn from nature herself rather than from authors who are only her clerks."

In another place, in reference to a particular case, he says, "Nature begins from the Reason and ends in Experience; but for all that, we must take the opposite course; begin from the Experiment and try to discover the Reason."

Leonardo was born forty-six years before Telesius; yet we have here an estimate of the value of experience far more just and substantial than the Calabrian school ever reached. The expressions contained in the above extracts, are well worthy our notice;—that experience is never deceived;—that we must vary our experiments, and draw from them general rules;—that nature is the original source of knowledge, and books only a derivative substitute;—with a lively image of the sons and grandsons of nature. Some of these assertions have been deemed, and not without reason, very similar to those made by Bacon a century later. Yet it is probable that the import of such expressions, in Leonardo's mind, was less clear and definite than that which they acquired by the progress of sound philosophy. When he says that theory is the general and experiments the soldiers, he probably meant that theory directs men what experiments to make; and had not in his mind the notion of a theoretical Idea ordering and brigading the Facts. When he says that Experience is the interpreter of Nature, we may recollect, that in a more correct use of this image, Experience and Nature are the writing, and the Intellect of man the interpreter. We may add, that the clear apprehension of the importance of Experience led, in this as in other cases, to an unjust depreciation of the value of what science owed to books. Leonardo would have made little progress, if he had attempted to master a complex science, astronomy for instance, by means of observation alone, without the aid of books.

But in spite of such criticism, Leonardo's maxims show extraordinary sagacity and insight; and they108 appear to us the more remarkable, when we see how rare such views are for a century after his time.

3. Copernicus.—For we by no means find, even in those practical discoverers to whom, in reality, the revolution in science, and consequently in the philosophy of science, was due, this prompt and vigorous recognition of the supreme authority of observation as a ground of belief; this bold estimate of the probable worthlessness of traditional knowledge; and this plain assertion of the reality of theory founded upon experience. Among such discoverers, Copernicus must ever hold a most distinguished place. The heliocentric theory of the universe, established by him with vast labour and deep knowledge, was, for the succeeding century, the field of discipline and exertion of all the most active speculative minds. Men, during that time, proved their freedom of thought, their hopeful spirit, and their comprehensive view, by adopting, inculcating, and following out the philosophy which this theory suggested. But in the first promulgation of the theory, in the works of Copernicus himself, we find a far more cautious and reserved temper. He does not, indeed, give up the reality of his theory, but he expresses himself so as to avoid shocking those who might (as some afterwards did) think it safe to speak of it as an hypothesis rather than a truth. In his preface addressed to the Pope[130], after speaking of the difficulties in the old and received doctrines, by which he was led to his own theory, he says, "Hence I began to think of the mobility of the earth; and although the opinion seemed absurd, yet because I knew that to others before me this liberty had been conceded, of imagining any kinds of circles in order to explain the phenomena of the stars, I thought it would also be readily granted me, that I might try whether, by supposing the earth to be in motion, I might not arrive at a better explanation than theirs, of the revolutions of the celestial orbs." Nor does he anywhere assert that the seeming109 absurdity had become a certain truth, or betray any feeling of triumph over the mistaken belief of his predecessors. And, as I have elsewhere shown, his disciples[131] indignantly and justly defended him from the charge of disrespect towards Ptolemy and other ancient astronomers. Yet Copernicus is far from compromising the value or evidence of the great truths which he introduced to general acceptance; and from sinking in his exposition of his discoveries below the temper which had led to them. His quotation from Ptolemy, that "He who is to follow philosophy must be a freeman in mind," is a grand and noble maxim, which it well became him to utter.

4. Fabricius.—In another of the great discoverers of this period, though employed on a very different subject, we discern much of the same temper. Fabricius of Acquapendente[132], the tutor and forerunner of our Harvey, and one of that illustrious series of Paduan professors who were the fathers of anatomy[133], exhibits something of the same respect for antiquity, in the midst of his original speculations. Thus in a dissertation[134] On the Action of the Joints, he quotes Aristotle's Mechanical Problems to prove that in all animal motion there must be some quiescent fulcrum; and finds merit

even in Aristotle's ignorance. "Aristotle," he says[135], "did not know that motion was produced by the muscle; and after staggering about from one supposition to another, at last is compelled by the facts themselves to recur to an innate spirit, which, he conceives, is contrasted, and which pulls and pushes. And here we cannot help admiring the genius of Aristotle, who, though ignorant of the muscle, invents something which produces nearly the same effect as the muscle, namely, contraction and pulling." He then, with great acuteness, points out the distinction between Aristotle's opinions, thus favourably interpreted, and those of Galen. In all this, we see110 something of the wish to find all truths in the writings of the ancients, but nothing which materially interferes with freedom of inquiry. The anatomists have in all ages and countries been practically employed in seeking knowledge from observation. Facts have ever been to them a subject of careful and profitable study; while the ideas which enter into the wider truths of the science, are, as we have seen, even still involved in obscurity, doubt, and contest.

5. Maurolycus.—Francis Maurolycus of Messana, whose mathematical works were published in 1575, was one of the great improvers of the science of optics in his time. In his Preface to his Treatise on the Spheres, he speaks of previous writers on the same subject; and observes that as they have not superseded one another, they have not rendered it unfit for any one to treat the subject afresh. "Yet," he says, "it is impossible to amend the errors of all who have preceded us. This would be a task too hard for Atlas, although he supports the heavens. Even Copernicus is tolerated, who makes the sun to be fixed, and the earth to move round it in a circle, and who is more worthy of a whip or a scourge than of a refutation." The mathematicians and astronomers of that time were not the persons most sensible of the progress of physical knowledge; for the basis of their science, and a great part of its substance, were contained in the writings of the ancients; and till the time of Kepler, Ptolemy's work was, very justly, looked upon as including all that was essential in the science.

6. Benedetti.—But the writers on Mechanics were naturally led to present themselves as innovators and experimenters; for all that the ancients had taught concerning the doctrine of motion was erroneous; while those who sought their knowledge from experiment, were constantly led to new truths. John Baptist Benedetti, a Venetian nobleman, in 1599, published his Speculationum Liber, containing, among other matter, a treatise on Mechanics, in which several of the Aristotelian errors were refuted. In the Preface to this Treatise, he says, "Many authors have written111 much, and with great ability, on Mechanics; but since nature is constantly bringing to light something either new, or before unnoticed, I too wished to put forth a few things hitherto unattempted, or not sufficiently explained." In the doctrine of motion he distinctly and at some length condemns and argues against all the Aristotelian doctrines concerning motion, weight, and many other fundamental principles of physics. Benedetti is also an adherent of the Copernican doctrine. He states[136] the enormous velocity which the heavenly bodies must have, if the earth be the centre of their motions; and adds, "which difficulty does not occur according to the beautiful theory of the Samian Aristarchus, expounded in a divine manner by Nicolas Copernicus; against which the reasons alleged by Aristotle are of no weight." Benedetti throughout shows no want of the courage or ability which were needed in order to rise in opposition against the dogmas of the Peripatetics. He does not, however, refer to experiment in a very direct manner; indeed most of the facts on which the elementary truths of mechanics rest, were known and

admitted by the Aristotelians; and therefore could not be adduced as novelties. On the contrary, he begins with à priori maxims, which experience would not have confirmed. "Since," he says[137], "we have undertaken the task of proving that Aristotle is wrong in his opinions concerning motion, there are certain absolute truths, the objects of the intellect known of themselves, which we must lay down in the first place." And then, as an example of these truths, he states this: "Any two bodies of equal size and figure, but of different materials, will have their natural velocities in the same proportion as their weights;" where by their natural velocities, he means the velocities with which they naturally fall downwards.

7. Gilbert.—The greatest of these practical reformers of science is our countryman, William Gilbert; if,112 indeed, in virtue of the clear views of the prospects which were then opening to science, and of the methods by which her future progress was to be secured, while he exemplified those views by physical discoveries, he does not rather deserve the still higher praise of being at the same time a theoretical and a practical reformer. Gilbert's physical researches and speculations were employed principally upon subjects on which the ancients had known little or nothing; and on which therefore it could not be doubtful whether tradition or observation was the source of knowledge. Such was magnetism; for the ancients were barely acquainted with the attractive property of the magnet. Its polarity, including repulsion as well as attraction, its direction towards the north, its limited variation from this direction, its declination from the horizontal position, were all modern discoveries. Gilbert's work[138] on the magnet and on the magnetism of the earth, appeared in 1600; and in this, he repeatedly maintains the superiority of experimental knowledge over the physical philosophy of the ancients. His preface opens thus: "Since in making discoveries and searching out the hidden causes of things, stronger reasons are obtained from trustworthy experiments and demonstrable arguments, than from probable conjectures and the dogmas of those who philosophize in the usual manner," he has, he says, "endeavoured to proceed from common magnetical experiments to the inward constitution of the earth." As I have stated in the History of Magnetism[139], Gilbert's work contains all the fundamental facts of that science, so fully stated, that we have, at this day, little to add to them. He is not, however, by the advance which he thus made, led to depreciate the ancients, but only to claim for himself the same liberty of philosophizing which113 they had enjoyed[140]. "To those ancient and first parents of philosophy, Aristotle, Theophrastus, Ptolemy, Hippocrates, Galen, be all due honour; from them it was that the stream of wisdom has been derived down to posterity. But our age has discovered and brought to light many things which they, if they were yet alive, would gladly embrace. Wherefore we also shall not hesitate to expound, by probable hypotheses, those things which by long experience we have ascertained."

In this work the author not only adopts the Copernican doctrine of the earth's motion, but speaks[141] of the contrary supposition as utterly absurd, founding his argument mainly on the vast velocities which such a supposition requires us to ascribe to the celestial bodies. Dr. Gilbert was physician to Queen Elizabeth and to James the First, and died in 1603. Some time after his death the executors of his brother published another work of his, De Mundo nostro Sublunari Philosophia Nova, in which similar views are still more comprehensively presented. In this he says, "The two lords of philosophy, Aristotle and Galen, are held in worship like gods, and rule the schools;—the former by some destiny obtained a sway and influence among philosophers, like that of

57

his pupil Alexander among the kings of the earth;—Galen, with like success, holds his triumph among the physicians of Europe." This comparison of Aristotle to Alexander was also taken hold of by Bacon. Nor is Gilbert an unworthy precursor of Bacon in the view he gives of the History of Science, which occupies the first three chapters of his Philosophy. He traces this history from "the simplicity and ignorance of the ancients," through "the fabrication of the fable of the four elements," to Aristotle and Galen. He mentions with due disapproval the host of commentators which succeeded, the alchemists, the "shipwreck of science in the deluge of the Goths," and the revival of letters and genius in the time of "our grandfathers." "This114 later age," he says, "has exploded the Barbarians, and restored the Greeks and Latins to their pristine grace and honour. It remains, that if they have written aught in error, this should be remedied by better and more productive processes (frugiferis institutis), not to be contemned for their novelty; (for nothing which is true is really new, but is perfect from eternity, though to weak man it may be unknown;) and that thus Philosophy may bear her fruit." The reader of Bacon will not fail to recognize, in these references to "fruit-bearing" knowledge, a similarity of expression with the Novum Organon.

Bacon does not appear to me to have done justice to his contemporary. He nowhere recognizes in the labours of Gilbert a community of purpose and spirit with his own. On the other hand, he casts upon him a reflection which he by no means deserves. In the Advancement of Learning[142], he says, "Another error is, that men have used to infect their meditations, opinions, and doctrines, with some conceits which they have most admired, or some sciences to which they have most applied; and given all things else a tincture according to them, utterly untrue and improper.... So have the alchemists made a philosophy out of a few experiments of the furnace; and Gilbertus, our countryman, hath made a philosophy out of the observations of a loadstone," (in the Latin, philosophiam etiam e magnete elicuit). And in the same manner he mentions him in the Novum Organon[143], as affording an example of an empirical kind of philosophy, which appears to those daily conversant with the experiments, probable, but to other persons incredible and empty. But instead of blaming Gilbert for disturbing and narrowing science by a too constant reference to magnetical rules, we might rather censure Bacon, for not seeing how important in all natural philosophy are those laws of attraction and repulsion of which magnetical phenomena are the most obvious115 illustration. We may find ground for such a judgment in another passage in which Bacon speaks of Gilbert. In the Second Book[144] of the Novum Organon, having classified motions, he gives, as one kind, what he calls, in his figurative language, motion for gain, or motion of need, by which a body shuns heterogeneous, and seeks cognate bodies. And he adds, "The Electrical operation, concerning which Gilbert and others since him have made up such a wonderful story, is nothing less than the appetite of a body, which, excited by friction, does not well tolerate the air, and prefers another tangible body if it be found near." Bacon's notion of an appetite in the body is certainly much less philosophical than Gilbert's, who speaks of light bodies as drawn towards amber by certain material radii[145]; and we might perhaps venture to say that Bacon here manifests a want of clear mechanical ideas. Bacon, too, showed his inferior aptitude for physical research in rejecting the Copernican doctrine which Gilbert adopted. In the Advancement of Learning[146], suggesting a history of the opinions of philosophers, he says that he would have inserted in it even recent theories, as those of Paracelsus; of Telesius, who restored the philosophy of Parmenides; or Patricius, who resublimed the fumes of Platonism; or Gilbert, who brought back the dogmas of

Philolaus. But Bacon quotes[147] with pleasure Gilbert's ridicule of the Peripatetics' definition of heat. They had said, that heat is that which separates heterogeneous and unites homogeneous matter; which, said Gilbert, is as if any one were to define man as that which sows wheat and plants vines.

Galileo, another of Gilbert's distinguished contemporaries, had a higher opinion of him. He says[148], "I extremely admire and envy this author. I think him worthy of the greatest praise for the many new and true observations which he has made, to the disgrace116 of so many vain and fabling authors; who write, not from their own knowledge only, but repeat everything they hear from the foolish and vulgar, without attempting to satisfy themselves of the same by experience; perhaps that they may not diminish the size of their books."

8. Galileo.—Galileo was content with the active and successful practice of experimental inquiry; and did not demand that such researches should be made expressly subservient to that wider and more ambitious philosophy, on which the author of the Novum Organon employed his powers. But still it now becomes our business to trace those portions of Galileo's views which have reference to the theory, as well as the practice, of scientific investigation. On this subject, Galileo did not think more profoundly, perhaps, than several of his contemporaries; but in the liveliness of expression and illustration with which he recommended his opinions on such topics, he was unrivalled. Writing in the language of the people, in the attractive form of dialogue, with clearness, grace, and wit, he did far more than any of his predecessors had done to render the new methods, results, and prospects of science familiar to a wide circle of readers, first in Italy, and soon, all over Europe. The principal points inculcated by him were already becoming familiar to men of active and inquiring minds; such as,—that knowledge was to be sought from observation, and not from books;—that it was absurd to adhere to, and debate about, the physical tenets of Aristotle and the rest of the ancients. On persons who followed this latter course, Galileo fixed the epithet of Paper Philosophers[149]; because, as he wrote in a letter to Kepler, this sort of men fancied that philosophy was to be studied like the Æneid or Odyssey, and that the true reading of nature was to be detected by the collation of texts. Nothing so much shook the authority of the received system of Physics as the experimental discoveries, directly contradicting117 it, which Galileo made. By experiment, as I have elsewhere stated[150], he disproved the Aristotelian doctrine that bodies fall quickly or slowly in proportion to their weight. And when he had invented the telescope, a number of new discoveries of the most striking kind (the inequalities of the moon's surface, the spots in the sun, the moon-like phases of Venus, the satellites of Jupiter, the ring of Saturn,) showed, by the evidence of the eyes, how inadequate were the conceptions, and how erroneous the doctrines of the ancients, respecting the constitution of the universe. How severe the blow was to the disciples of the ancient schools, we may judge by the extraordinary forms of defence in which they tried to intrench themselves. They would not look through Galileo's glasses; they maintained that what was seen was an illusion of witchcraft; and they tried, as Galileo says[151], with logical arguments, as if with magical incantations, to charm the new planets out of the sky. No one could be better fitted than Galileo for such a warfare. His great knowledge, clear intellect, gaiety, and light irony, (with the advantage of being in the right,) enabled him to play with his adversaries as he pleased. Thus when an Aristotelian[152] rejected the discovery of the irregularities in the moon's surface,

because, according to the ancient doctrine, her form was a perfect sphere, and held that the apparent cavities were filled with an invisible crystal substance, Galileo replied, that he had no objection to assent to this, but that then he should require his adversary in return to believe that there were on the same surface invisible crystal mountains ten times as high as those visible ones which he had actually observed and measured.

We find in Galileo many thoughts which have since become established maxims of modern philosophy. "Philosophy," he says[153], "is written in that great book, I mean the Universe, which is constantly open before our eyes; but it cannot be understood,118 unless we first know the language and learn the characters in which it is written." With this thought he combines some other lively images. One of his interlocutors says concerning another, "Sarsi perhaps thinks that philosophy is a book made up of the fancies of men, like the Iliad or Orlando Furioso, in which the matter of least importance is, that what is written be true." And again, with regard to the system of authority, he says, "I think I discover in him a firm belief that, in philosophizing, it is necessary to lean upon the opinion of some celebrated author; as if our mind must necessarily remain unfruitful and barren till it be married to another man's reason."—"No," he says, "the case is not so.—When we have the decrees of Nature, authority goes for nothing; reason is absolute[154]."

In the course of Galileo's controversies, questions of the logic of science came under discussion. Vincenzio di Grazia objected to a proof from induction which Galileo adduced, because all the particulars were not enumerated; to which the latter justly replies[155], that if induction were required to pass through all the cases, it would be either useless or impossible;—impossible when the cases are innumerable; useless when they have each already been verified, since then the general proposition adds nothing to our knowledge.

One of the most novel of the characters which Science assumes in Galileo's hands is, that she becomes cautious. She not only proceeds leaning upon Experience, but she is content to proceed a little way at a time. She already begins to perceive that she must rise to the heights of knowledge by many small and separate steps. The philosopher is desirous to know much, but resigned to be ignorant for a time of that which cannot yet be known. Thus when Galileo discovered the true law of the motion of a falling body[156], that the velocity increases proportionally to the time from the beginning of the fall, he did not insist upon119 immediately assigning the cause of this law. "The cause of the acceleration of the motions of falling bodies is not," he says, "a necessary part of the investigation." Yet the conception of this acceleration, as the result of the continued action of the force of gravity upon the falling body, could hardly fail to suggest itself to one who had formed the idea of force. In like manner, the truth that the velocities, acquired by bodies falling down planes of equal heights, are all equal, was known to Galileo and his disciples, long before he accounted for it[157], by the principle, apparently so obvious, that the momentum generated is as the moving force which generates it. He was not tempted to rush at once, from an experimental truth to a universal system. Science had learnt that she must move step by step; and the gravity of her pace already indicated her approaching maturity and her consciousness of the long path which lay before her.

But besides the genuine philosophical prudence which thus withheld Galileo from leaping hastily from one inference to another, he had perhaps a preponderating inclination towards facts; and did not feel, so much as some other persons of his time, the need of reducing them to ideas. He could bear to contemplate laws of motion without being urged by an uncontrollable desire to refer them to conceptions of force.

9. Kepler.—In this respect his friend Kepler differed from him; for Kepler was restless and unsatisfied till he had reduced facts to laws, and laws to causes; and never acquiesced in ignorance, though he tested with the most rigorous scrutiny that which presented itself in the shape of knowledge to fill the void. It may be seen in the History of Astronomy[158] with what perseverance, energy, and fertility of invention, Kepler pursued his labours, (enlivened and relieved by the most curious freaks of fancy,) with a view of discovering the rules which regulate the motions of the planet120 Mars. He represents this employment under the image of a warfare; and describes[159] his object to be "to triumph over Mars, and to prepare for him, as for one altogether vanquished, tabular prisons and equated eccentric fetters;" and when, "the enemy, left at home a despised captive, had burst all the chains of the equations, and broken forth of the prisons of the tables;"—when "it was buzzed here and there that the victory is vain, and that the war is raging anew as violently as before;"—that is, when the rules which he had proposed did not coincide with the facts;—he by no means desisted from his attempts, but "suddenly sent into the field a reserve of new physical reasonings on the rout and dispersion of the veterans," that is, tried new suppositions suggested by such views as he then entertained of the celestial motions. His efforts to obtain the formal laws of the planetary motions resulted in some of the most important discoveries ever made in astronomy; and if his physical reasonings were for the time fruitless, this arose only from the want of that discipline in mechanical ideas which the minds of mathematicians had still to undergo; for the great discoveries of Newton in the next generation showed that, in reality, the next step of the advance was in this direction. Among all Kepler's fantastical expressions, the fundamental thoughts were sound and true; namely, that it was his business, as a physical investigator, to discover a mathematical rule which governed and included all the special facts; and that the rules of the motions of the planets must conform to some conception of causation.

The same characteristics,—the conviction of rule and cause, perseverance in seeking these, inventiveness in devising hypotheses, love of truth in trying and rejecting them, and a lively Fancy playing with the Reason without interrupting her,—appear also in his work on Optics; in which he tried to discover the exact law of optical refraction[160]. In this undertaking121 he did not succeed entirely; nor does he profess to have done so. He ends his numerous attempts by saying, "Now, reader, you and I have been detained sufficiently long while I have been attempting to collect into one fagot the measures of different refractions."

In this and in other expressions, we see how clearly he apprehended that colligation of facts which is the main business of the practical discoverer. And by his peculiar endowments and habits, Kepler exhibits an essential portion of this process, which hardly appears at all in Galileo. In order to bind together facts, theory is requisite as well as observation,—the cord as well as the fagots. And the true theory is often, if not always, obtained by trying several and selecting the right. Now of this portion of the discoverer's exertions, Kepler is a most conspicuous example. His fertility in devising suppositions, his undaunted industry in calculating the results of them, his entire honesty and candour in resigning them if these results disagreed with the facts, are a very instructive spectacle; and are fortunately exhibited to us in the most lively manner in his own garrulous narratives. Galileo urged men by precept as well as example to begin their philosophy from observation; Kepler taught them by his practice that they must proceed from observation by means of hypotheses. The one insisted upon facts; the other dealt no less copiously with ideas. In the practical, as in the speculative portion of our history, this antithesis shows itself; although in the practical part we cannot have the two elements separated, as in the speculative we sometimes have.

In the History of Science[161], I have devoted several pages to the intellectual character of Kepler, inasmuch as his habit of devising so great a multitude of hypotheses, so fancifully expressed, had led some writers to look upon him as an inquirer who transgressed the most fixed rules of philosophical inquiry. This opinion has arisen, I conceive, among those who have122 forgotten the necessity of Ideas as well as Facts for all theory; or who have overlooked the impossibility of selecting and explicating our ideas without a good deal of spontaneous play of the mind. It must, however, always be recollected that Kepler's genius and fancy derived all their scientific value from his genuine and unmingled love of truth. These qualities appeared, not only in the judgment he passed upon hypotheses, but also in matters which more immediately concerned his reputation. Thus when Galileo's discovery of the telescope disproved several opinions which Kepler had published and strenuously maintained, he did not hesitate a moment to retract his assertions and range himself by the side of Galileo, whom he vigorously supported in his warfare against those who were incapable of thus cheerfully acknowledging the triumph of new facts over their old theories.

10. Tycho.—There remains one eminent astronomer, the friend and fellow-labourer of Kepler, whom we must not separate from him as one of the practical reformers of science. I speak of Tycho Brahe, who is, I think, not justly appreciated by the literary world in general, in consequence of his having made a retrograde step in that portion of astronomical theory which is most familiar to the popular mind. Though he adopted the Copernican view of the motion of the planets about the sun, he refused to acknowledge the annual and diurnal motion of the earth. But notwithstanding this mistake, into which he was led by his interpretation of Scripture rather than of nature, Tycho must ever be one of the greatest names in astronomy. In the philosophy of science also, the influence of what he did is far from inconsiderable; and especially its value in bringing into notice these two points:—that not only are observations the beginning of science, but that the progress of science may often depend upon the observer's pursuing his task regularly and carefully for a long time, and with well devised instruments; and again, that observed facts offer a succession of laws which we discover as our observations become better, and as our theories are better adapted to the123 observations. With regard to the former point, Tycho's observatory was far superior to all that had preceded it[162], not only in the optical, but in the mechanical arrangements; a matter of almost equal consequence. And hence it was that his observations inspired in Kepler that confidence which led him to all his labours and all his discoveries. "Since," he says[163], "the divine goodness has given us in Tycho Brahe an exact observer, from whose observations this error of eight minutes in the calculations of the Ptolemaic hypothesis is detected, let us acknowledge and make use

of this gift of God: and since this error cannot be neglected, these eight minutes alone have prepared the way for an entire reform of Astronomy, and are to be the main subject of this work."

With regard to Tycho's discoveries respecting the moon, it is to be recollected that besides the first inequality of the moon's motion, (the equation of the centre, arising from the elliptical form of her orbit,) Ptolemy had discovered a second inequality, the evection, which, as we have observed in the History of this subject[164], might have naturally suggested the suspicion that there were still other inequalities. In the middle ages, however, such suggestions, implying a constant progress in science, were little attended to; and, we have seen, that when an Arabian astronomer[165] had really discovered another inequality of the moon, it was soon forgotten, because it had no place in the established systems. Tycho not only rediscovered the lunar inequality, (the variation,) thus once before won and lost, but also two other inequalities; namely[166], the change of inclination of the moon's orbit as the line of nodes moves round, and an inequality in the motion of the line of nodes. Thus, as I have elsewhere said, it appeared that the discovery of a rule is a step to the discovery of deviations from that rule, which require to be expressed in other rules. It124 became manifest to astronomers, and through them to all philosophers, that in the application of theory to observation, we find, not only the stated phenomena, for which the theory does account, but also residual phenomena, which are unaccounted for, and remain over and above the calculation. And it was seen further, that these residual phenomena might be, altogether or in part, exhausted by new theories.

These were valuable lessons; and the more valuable inasmuch as men were now trying to lay down maxims and methods for the conduct of science. A revolution was not only at hand, but had really taken place, in the great body of real cultivators of science. The occasion now required that this revolution should be formally recognized;—that the new intellectual power should be clothed with the forms of government;—that the new philosophical republic should be acknowledged as a sister state by the ancient dynasties of Aristotle and Plato. There was needed some great Theoretical Reformer, to speak in the name of the Experimental Philosophy; to lay before the world a declaration of its rights and a scheme of its laws. And thus our eyes are turned to Francis Bacon, and others who like him attempted this great office. We quit those august and venerable names of discoverers, whose appearance was the prelude and announcement of the new state of things then opening; and in doing so, we may apply to them the language which Bacon applies to himself[167]:—

Χαίρετε Κήρυκες Διὸ ς ἄγγελοι ἠδὲ καὶ ἀνδρῶν.

Hail, Heralds, Messengers of Gods and Men!
125

CHAPTER XV.
Francis Bacon.

(I.) 1. General Remarks.—It is a matter of some difficulty to speak of the character and merits of this illustrious man, as regards his place in that philosophical history with which we are here engaged. If we were to content ourselves with estimating him

63

according to the office which, as we have just seen, he claims for himself[168], as merely the harbinger and announcer of a sounder method of scientific inquiry than that which was recognized before him, the task would be comparatively easy. For we might select from his writings those passages in which he has delivered opinions and pointed out processes, then novel and strange, but since confirmed by the experience of actual discoverers, and by the judgments of the wisest of succeeding philosophers; and we might pass by, without disrespect, but without notice, maxims and proposals which have not been found available for use;—views so indistinct and vague, that we are even yet unable to pronounce upon their justice;—and boundless anticipations, dictated by the sanguine hopes of a noble and comprehensive intellect. But if we thus reduce the philosophy of Bacon to that portion which the subsequent progress of science has rigorously verified, we shall have to pass over many of those declarations which have excited most notice in his writings, and shall lose sight of many of those striking thoughts which his admirers most love to dwell upon. For he is usually spoken126 of, at least in this country, as a teacher who not only commenced, but in a great measure completed, the Philosophy of Induction. He is considered, not only as having asserted some general principles, but laid down the special rules of scientific investigation; as not only one of the Founders, but the supreme Legislator of the modern Republic of Science; not only the Hercules who slew the monsters that obstructed the earlier traveller, but the Solon who established a constitution fitted for all future time.

2. Nor is it our purpose to deny that of such praise he deserves a share which, considering the period at which he lived, is truly astonishing. But it is necessary for us in this place to discriminate and select that portion of his system which, bearing upon physical science, has since been confirmed by the actual history of science. Many of Bacon's most impressive and captivating passages contemplate the extension of the new methods of discovering truth to intellectual, to moral, to political, as well as to physical science. And how far, and how, the advantages of the inductive method may be secured for those important branches of speculation, it will at some future time be a highly interesting task to examine. But our plan requires us at present to omit the consideration of these; for our purpose is to learn what the genuine course of the formation of science is, by tracing it in those portions of human knowledge, which, by the confession of all, are most exact, most certain, most complete. Hence we must here deny ourselves the dignity and interest which float about all speculations in which the great moral and political concerns of men are involved. It cannot be doubted that the commanding position which Bacon occupies in men's estimation arises from his proclaiming a reform in philosophy of so comprehensive a nature;—a reform which was to infuse a new spirit into every part of knowledge. Physical Science has tranquilly and noiselessly adopted many of his suggestions; which were, indeed, her own natural impulses, not borrowed from him; and she is too deeply and satisfactorily absorbed in contemplating her re127sults, to talk much about the methods of obtaining them which she has thus instinctively pursued. But the philosophy which deals with mind, with manners, with morals, with polity, is conscious still of much obscurity and perplexity; and would gladly borrow aid from a system in which aid is so confidently promised. The aphorisms and phrases of the Novum Organon are far more frequently quoted by metaphysical, ethical, and even theological writers, than they are by the authors of works on physics.

3. Again, even as regards physics, Bacon's fame rests upon something besides the novelty of the maxims which he promulgated. That a revolution in the method of scientific research was going on, all the greatest physical investigators of the sixteenth century were fully aware, as we have shown in the last chapter. But their writings conveyed this conviction to the public at large somewhat slowly. Men of letters, men of the world, men of rank, did not become familiar with the abstruse works in which these views were published; and above all, they did not, by such occasional glimpses as they took of the state of physical science, become aware of the magnitude and consequences of this change. But Bacon's lofty eloquence, wide learning, comprehensive views, bold pictures of the coming state of things, were fitted to make men turn a far more general and earnest gaze upon the passing change. When a man of his acquirements, of his talents, of his rank and position, of his gravity and caution, poured forth the strongest and loftiest expressions and images which his mind could supply, in order to depict the "Great Instauration" which he announced;—in order to contrast the weakness, the blindness, the ignorance, the wretchedness, under which men had laboured while they followed the long beaten track, with the light, the power, the privileges, which they were to find in the paths to which he pointed;—it was impossible that readers of all classes should not have their attention arrested, their minds stirred, their hopes warmed; and should not listen with wonder and with pleasure to the strains of 128 prophetic eloquence in which so great a subject was presented. And when it was found that the prophecy was verified; when it appeared that an immense change in the methods of scientific research really had occurred;—that vast additions to man's knowledge and power had been acquired, in modes like those which had been spoken of;—that further advances might be constantly looked for;—and that a progress, seemingly boundless, was going on in the direction in which the seer had thus pointed;—it was natural that men should hail him as the leader of the revolution; that they should identify him with the event which he was the first to announce; that they should look upon him as the author of that which he had, as they perceived, so soon and so thoroughly comprehended.

4. For we must remark, that although (as we have seen) he was not the only, nor the earliest writer, who declared that the time was come for such a change, he not only proclaimed it more emphatically, but understood it, in its general character, much more exactly, than any of his contemporaries. Among the maxims, suggestions and anticipations which he threw out, there were many of which the wisdom and the novelty were alike striking to his immediate successors;—there are many which even now, from time to time, we find fresh reason to admire, for their acuteness and justice. Bacon stands far above the herd of loose and visionary speculators who, before and about his time, spoke of the establishment of new philosophies. If we must select some one philosopher as the Hero of the revolution in scientific method, beyond all doubt Francis Bacon must occupy the place of honour.

We shall, however, no longer dwell upon these general considerations, but shall proceed to notice some of the more peculiar and characteristic features of Bacon's philosophy; and especially those views, which, occurring for the first time in his writings, have been fully illustrated and confirmed by the subsequent progress of science, and have become a portion of the permanent philosophy of our times.

(II.) 5. A New Era announced.—The first great129 feature which strikes us in Bacon's philosophical views is that which we have already noticed;—his confident and emphatic announcement of a New Era in the progress of science, compared with which the advances of former times were poor and trifling. This was with Bacon no loose and shallow opinion, taken up on light grounds and involving only vague, general notions. He had satisfied himself of the justice of such a view by a laborious course of research and reflection. In 1605, at the age of forty-four, he published his Treatise of the Advancement of Learning, in which he takes a comprehensive and spirited survey of the condition of all branches of knowledge which had been cultivated up to that time. This work was composed with a view to that reform of the existing philosophy which Bacon always had before his eyes; and in the Latin edition of his works, forms the First Part of the Instauratio Magna. In the Second Part of the Instauratio, the Novum Organon, published in 1620, he more explicitly and confidently states his expectations on this subject. He points out how slightly and feebly the examination of nature had been pursued up to his time, and with what scanty fruit. He notes the indications of this in the very limited knowledge of the Greeks who had till then been the teachers of Europe, in the complaints of authors concerning the subtilty and obscurity of the secrets of nature, in the dissensions of sects, in the absence of useful inventions resulting from theory, in the fixed form which the sciences had retained for two thousand years. Nor, he adds[169], is this wonderful; for how little of his thought and labour has man bestowed upon science! Out of twenty-five centuries scarce six have been favourable to the progress of knowledge. And even in those favoured times, natural philosophy received the smallest share of man's attention; while the portion so given was marred by controversy and dogmatism; and even those who have bestowed a little thought upon130 this philosophy, have never made it their main study, but have used it as a passage or drawbridge to serve other objects. And thus, he says, the great Mother of the Sciences is thrust down with indignity to the offices of a handmaid; is made to minister to the labours of medicine or mathematics, or to give the first preparatory tinge to the immature minds of youth. For these and similar considerations of the errors of past time, he draws hope for the future, employing the same argument which Demosthenes uses to the Athenians: "That which is worst in the events of the past, is the best as a ground of trust in the future. For if you had done all that became you, and still had been in this condition, your case might be desperate; but since your failure is the result of your own mistakes, there is good hope that, correcting the error of your course, you may reach a prosperity yet unknown to you."

(III.) 6. A change of existing Method.—All Bacon's hope of improvement indeed was placed in an entire change of the Method by which science was pursued; and the boldness, and at the same time (the then existing state of science being considered), the definiteness of his views of the change that was requisite, are truly remarkable.

That all knowledge must begin with observation, is one great principle of Bacon's philosophy; but I hardly think it necessary to notice the inculcation of this maxim as one of his main services to the cause of sound knowledge, since it had, as we have seen, been fully insisted upon by others before him, and was growing rapidly into general acceptance without his aid. But if he was not the first to tell men that they must collect their knowledge from observation, he had no rival in his peculiar office of teaching them how science must thus be gathered from experience.

66

It appears to me that by far the most extraordinary parts of Bacon's works are those in which, with extreme earnestness and clearness, he insists upon a graduated and successive induction, as opposed to a hasty transit from special facts to the highest generalizations. The131 nineteenth Axiom of the First Book of the Novum Organon contains a view of the nature of true science most exact and profound, and, so far as I am aware, at the time perfectly new. "There are two ways, and can only be two, of seeking and finding truth. The one, from sense and particulars, takes a flight to the most general axioms, and from those principles and their truth, settled once for all, invents and judges of intermediate axioms. The other method collects axioms from sense and particulars, ascending continuously and by degrees, so that in the end it arrives at the most general axioms; this latter way is the true one, but hitherto untried."

It is to be remarked, that in this passage Bacon employs the term axioms to express any propositions collected from facts by induction, and thus fitted to become the starting-point of deductive reasonings. How far propositions so obtained may approach to the character of axioms in the more rigorous sense of the term, we have already in some measure examined; but that question does not here immediately concern us. The truly remarkable circumstance is to find this recommendation of a continuous advance from observation, by limited steps, through successive gradations of generality, given at a time when speculative men in general had only just begun to perceive that they must begin their course from experience in some way or other. How exactly this description represents the general structure of the soundest and most comprehensive physical theories, all persons who have studied the progress of science up to modern times can bear testimony; but perhaps this structure of science cannot in any other way be made so apparent as by those Tables of successive generalizations in which we have exhibited the history and constitution of some of the principal physical sciences, in the Chapter of a preceding work which treats of the Logic of Induction. And the view which Bacon thus took of the true progress of science was not only new, but, so far as I am aware, has never been adequately illustrated up to the present day.

132

7. It is true, as I observed in the last chapter, that Galileo had been led to see the necessity, not only of proceeding from experience in the pursuit of knowledge, but of proceeding cautiously and gradually; and he had exemplified this rule more than once, when, having made one step in discovery, he held back his foot, for a time, from the next step, however tempting. But Galileo had not reached this wide and commanding view of the successive subordination of many steps, all leading up at last to some wide and simple general truth. In catching sight of this principle, and in ascribing to it its due importance, Bacon's sagacity, so far as I am aware, wrought unassisted and unrivalled.

8. Nor is there any wavering or vagueness in Bacon's assertion of this important truth. He repeats it over and over again; illustrates it by a great number of the most lively metaphors and emphatic expressions. Thus he speaks of the successive floors (tabulata) of induction; and speaks of each science as a pyramid[170] which has observation and experience for its basis. No images can better exhibit the relation of general and particular truths, as our own Inductive Tables may serve to show.

(IV.) 9. Comparison of the New and Old Method. Again; not less remarkable is his contrasting this true Method of Science (while it was almost, as he says, yet untried) with the ancient and vicious Method, which began, indeed, with facts of observation, but rushed at once and with no gradations, to the most general principles. For this was the course which had been actually followed by all those speculative reformers who had talked so loudly of the necessity of beginning our philosophy from experience. All these men, if they attempted to frame physical doctrines at all, had caught up a few facts of observation, and had133 erected a universal theory upon the suggestions which these offered. This process of illicit generalization, or, as Bacon terms it, Anticipation of Nature (anticipatio naturæ), in opposition to the Interpretation of Nature, he depicts with singular acuteness, in its character and causes. "These two ways," he says[171] "both begin from sense and particulars; but their discrepancy is immense. The one merely skims over experience and particulars in a cursory transit; the other deals with them in a due and orderly manner. The one, at its very outset, frames certain general abstract principles, but useless; the other gradually rises to those principles which have a real existence in nature."

"The former path," he adds[172], "that of illicit and hasty generalization, is one which the intellect follows when abandoned to its own impulse; and this it does from the requisitions of logic. For the mind has a yearning which makes it dart forth to generalities, that it may have something to rest in; and after a little dallying with experience, becomes weary of it; and all these evils are augmented by logic, which requires these generalities to make a show with in its disputations."

"In a sober, patient, grave intellect," he further adds, "the mind, by its own impulse, (and more especially if it be not impelled by the sway of established opinions) attempts in some measure that other and true way, of gradual generalization; but this it does with small profit; for the intellect, except it be regulated and aided, is a faculty of unequal operation, and altogether unapt to master the obscurity of things."

The profound and searching wisdom of these remarks appears more and more, as we apply them to the various attempts which men have made to obtain knowledge; when they begin with the contemplation of a few facts, and pursue their speculations, as upon most subjects they have hitherto generally done; for almost all such attempts have led immediately to some process134 of illicit generalization, which introduces an interminable course of controversy. In the physical sciences, however, we have the further inestimable advantage of seeing the other side of the contrast exemplified: for many of them, as our inductive Tables show us, have gone on according to the most rigorous conditions of gradual and successive generalization; and in consequence of this circumstance in their constitution, possess, in each part of their structure, a solid truth, which is always ready to stand the severest tests of reasoning and experiment.

We see how justly and clearly Bacon judged concerning the mode in which facts are to be employed in the construction of science. This, indeed, has ever been deemed his great merit: insomuch that many persons appear to apprehend the main substance of his doctrine to reside in the maxim that facts of observation, and such facts alone, are the essential elements of all true science.

(V.) 10. Ideas are necessary.—Yet we have endeavoured to establish the doctrine that facts are but one of two ingredients of knowledge both equally necessary;—that Ideas are no less indispensable than facts themselves; and that except these be duly unfolded and applied, facts are collected in vain. Has Bacon then neglected this great portion of his subject? Has he been led by some partiality of view, or some peculiarity of circumstances, to leave this curious and essential element of science in its pristine obscurity? Was he unaware of its interest and importance?

We may reply that Bacon's philosophy, in its effect upon his readers in general, does not give due weight or due attention to the ideal element of our knowledge. He is considered as peculiarly and eminently the asserter of the value of experiment and observation. He is always understood to belong to the experiential, as opposed to the ideal school. He is held up in contrast to Plato and others who love to dwell upon that part of knowledge which has its origin in the intellect of man.

11. Nor can it be denied that Bacon has, in the135 finished part of his Novum Organon, put prominently forwards the necessary dependence of all our knowledge upon Experience, and said little of its dependence, equally necessary, upon the Conceptions which the intellect itself supplies. It will appear, however, on a close examination, that he was by no means insensible or careless of this internal element of all connected speculation. He held the balance, with no partial or feeble hand, between phenomena and ideas. He urged the Colligation of Facts, but he was not the less aware of the value of the Explication of Conceptions.

12. This appears plainly from some remarkable Aphorisms in the Novum Organon. Thus, in noticing the causes of the little progress then made by science[173], he states this:—"In the current Notions, all is unsound, whether they be logical or physical. Substance, quality, action, passion, even being, are not good Conceptions; still less are heavy, light, dense, rare, moist, dry, generation, corruption, attraction, repulsion, element, matter, form, and others of that kind; all are fantastical and ill-defined." And in his attempt to exemplify his own system, he hesitates[174] in accepting or rejecting the notions of elementary, celestial, rare, as belonging to fire, since, as he says, they are vague and ill-defined notions (notiones vagæ nec bene terminatæ). In that part of his work which appears to be completed, there is not, so far as I have noticed, any attempt to fix and define any notions thus complained of as loose and obscure. But yet such an undertaking appears to have formed part of his plan; and in the Abecedarium Naturæ[175], which consists of the heads of various portions of his great scheme, marked by letters of the alphabet, we find the titles of a series of dissertations "On the Conditions of Being," which must have had for their object the elucidation of divers Notions essential to science, and which would have136 been contributions to the Explication of Conceptions, such as we have attempted in a former part of this work. Thus some of the subjects of these dissertations are;—Of Much and Little;—Of Durable and Transitory;—Of Natural and Monstrous;—Of Natural and Artificial. When the philosopher of induction came to discuss these, considered as conditions of existence, he could not do otherwise than develope, limit, methodize, and define the Ideas involved in these Notions, so as to make them consistent with themselves, and a fit basis of demonstrative reasoning. His task would have been of the same nature as ours has been, in that part of this work which treats of the Fundamental Ideas of the various classes of sciences.

13. Thus Bacon, in his speculative philosophy, took firmly hold of both the handles of science; and if he had completed his scheme, would probably have given due attention to Ideas, no less than to Facts, as an element of our knowledge; while in his view of the general method of ascending from facts to principles, he displayed a sagacity truly wonderful. But we cannot be surprised, that in attempting to exemplify the method which he recommended, he should have failed. For the method could be exemplified only by some important discovery in physical science; and great discoveries, even with the most perfect methods, do not come at command. Moreover, although the general structure of his scheme was correct, the precise import of some of its details could hardly be understood, till the actual progress of science had made men somewhat familiar with the kind of steps which it included.

(VI.) 14. Bacon's Example.—Accordingly, Bacon's Inquisition into the Nature of Heat, which is given in the Second Book of the Novum Organon as an example of the mode of interrogating Nature, cannot be looked upon otherwise than as a complete failure. This will be evident if we consider that, although the exact nature of heat is still an obscure and controverted matter, the science of Heat now consists of many important truths; and that to none of these137 truths is there any approximation in Bacon's essay. From his process he arrives at this, as the "forma or true definition" of heat;—"that it is an expansive, restrained motion, modified in certain ways, and exerted in the smaller particles of the body." But the steps by which the science of Heat really advanced were (as may be seen in the history[176] of the subject) these;—The discovery of a measure of heat or temperature (the thermometer); the establishment of the laws of conduction and radiation; of the laws of specific heat, latent heat, and the like. Such steps have led to Ampère's hypothesis[177], that heat consists in the vibrations of an imponderable fluid; and to Laplace's hypothesis, that temperature consists in the internal radiation of such a fluid. These hypotheses cannot yet be said to be even probable; but at least they are so modified as to include some of the preceding laws which are firmly established; whereas Bacon's hypothetical motion includes no laws of phenomena, explains no process, and is indeed itself an example of illicit generalization.

15. One main ground of Bacon's ill fortune in this undertaking appears to be, that he was not aware of an important maxim of inductive science, that we must first obtain the measure and ascertain the laws of phenomena, before we endeavour to discover their causes. The whole history of thermotics up to the present time has been occupied with the former step, and the task is not yet completed: it is no wonder, therefore, that Bacon failed entirely, when he so prematurely attempted the second. His sagacity had taught him that the progress of science must be gradual; but it had not led him to judge adequately how gradual it must be, nor of what different kinds of inquiries, taken in due order, it must needs consist, in order to obtain success.

Another mistake, which could not fail to render it unlikely that Bacon should really exemplify his138 precepts by any actual advance in science, was, that he did not justly appreciate the sagacity, the inventive genius, which all discovery requires. He conceived that he could supersede the necessity of such peculiar endowments. "Our method of discovery in science," he says[178], "is of such a nature, that there is not much left to acuteness and strength of genius, but all degrees of genius and intellect are brought nearly to the same level." And he illustrates this by comparing his method to a pair of compasses, by means of which a person with no manual skill may draw a perfect circle. In the same spirit he speaks of proceeding by due rejections; and appears to imagine that when we have obtained a collection of facts, if we go on successively rejecting what is false, we shall at last find that we have, left in our hands, that scientific truth which we seek. I need not observe how far this view is removed from the real state of the case. The necessity of a conception which must be furnished by the mind in order to bind together the facts, could hardly have escaped the eye of Bacon, if he had cultivated more carefully the ideal side of his own philosophy. And any attempts which he could have made to construct such conceptions by mere rule and method, must have ended in convincing him that nothing but a peculiar inventive talent could supply that which was thus not contained in the facts, and yet was needed for the discovery.

(VII.) 16. His Failure.—Since Bacon, with all his acuteness, had not divined circumstances so important in the formation of science, it is not wonderful that his attempt to reduce this process to a Technical Form is of little value. In the first place, he says[179], we must prepare a natural and experimental history, good and sufficient; in the next place, the instances thus collected are to be arranged in Tables in some orderly way; and then we must apply a legitimate and true induction. And in his example[180], he first collects a139 great number of cases in which heat appears under various circumstances, which he calls "a Muster of Instances before the intellect," (comparentia instantiarum ad intellectum,) or a Table of the Presence of the thing sought. He then adds a Table of its Absence in proximate cases, containing instances where heat does not appear; then a Table of Degrees, in which it appears with greater or less intensity. He then adds[181], that we must try to exclude several obvious suppositions, which he does by reference to some of the instances he has collected; and this step he calls the Exclusive, or the Rejection of Natures. He then observes, (and justly,) that whereas truth emerges more easily from error than from confusion, we may, after this preparation, give play to the intellect, (fiat permissio intellectus,) and make an attempt at induction, liable afterwards to be corrected; and by this step, which he terms his First Vindemiation, or Inchoate Induction, he is led to the proposition concerning heat, which we have stated above.

17. In all the details of his example he is unfortunate. By proposing to himself to examine at once into the nature of heat, instead of the laws of special classes of phenomena, he makes, as we have said, a fundamental mistake; which is the less surprising since he had before him so few examples of the right course in the previous history of science. But further, his collection of instances is very loosely brought together; for he includes in his list the hot taste of aromatic plants, the caustic effects of acids, and many other facts which cannot be ascribed to heat without a studious laxity in the use of the word. And when he comes to that point where he permits his intellect its range, the conception of motion upon which it at once fastens, appears to be selected with little choice or skill, the suggestion being taken from flame[182], boiling liquids, a blown fire, and some other cases. If from such examples we could imagine heat to be motion, we140 ought at least to have some gradation to cases of heat where no motion is visible, as in a red-hot iron. It would seem that, after a large collection of instances had been looked at, the intellect, even in its first attempts, ought not to have dwelt upon such an hypothesis as this.

71

18. After these steps, Bacon speaks of several classes of instances which, singling them out of the general and indiscriminate collection of facts, he terms Instances with Prerogative: and these he points out as peculiar aids and guides to the intellect in its task. These Instances with Prerogative have generally been much dwelt upon by those who have commented on the Novum Organon. Yet, in reality, such a classification, as has been observed by one of the ablest writers of the present day[183], is of little service in the task of induction. For the instances are, for the most part, classed, not according to the ideas which they involve, or to any obvious circumstance in the facts of which they consist, but according to the extent or manner of their influence upon the inquiry in which they are employed. Thus we have Solitary Instances, Migrating Instances, Ostensive Instances, Clandestine Instances, so termed according to the degree in which they exhibit, or seem to exhibit, the property whose nature we would examine. We have Guide-Post Instances, (Instantiæ Crucis,) Instances of the Parted Road, of the Doorway, of the Lamp, according to the guidance they supply to our advance. Such a classification is much of the same nature as if, having to teach the art of building, we were to describe tools with reference to the amount and place of the work which they must do, instead of pointing out their construction and use:—as if we were to inform the pupil that we must have tools for lifting a stone up, tools for moving it sideways, tools for laying it square, tools for cementing it firmly. Such an enumeration of ends would convey little instruction as to the means.141 Moreover, many of Bacon's classes of instances are vitiated by the assumption that the "form," that is, the general law and cause of the property which is the subject of investigation, is to be looked for directly in the instances; which, as we have seen in his inquiry concerning heat, is a fundamental error.

19. Yet his phraseology in some cases, as in the instantia crucis, serves well to mark the place which certain experiments hold in our reasonings: and many of the special examples which he gives are full of acuteness and sagacity. Thus he suggests swinging a pendulum in a mine, in order to determine whether the attraction of the earth arises from the attraction of its parts; and observing the tide at the same moment in different parts of the world, in order to ascertain whether the motion of the water is expansive or progressive; with other ingenious proposals. These marks of genius may serve to counterbalance the unfavourable judgment of Bacon's aptitude for physical science which we are sometimes tempted to form, in consequence of his false views on other points; as his rejection of the Copernican system, and his undervaluing Gilbert's magnetical speculations. Most of these errors arose from a too ambitious habit of intellect, which would not be contented with any except very wide and general truths; and from an indistinctness of mechanical, and perhaps, in general, of mathematical ideas:—defects which Bacon's own philosophy was directed to remedy, and which, in the progress of time, it has remedied in others.

(VIII.) 20. His Idols.—Having thus freely given our judgment concerning the most exact and definite portion of Bacon's precepts, it cannot be necessary for us to discuss at any length the value of those more vague and general Warnings against prejudice and partiality, against intellectual indolence and presumption, with which his works abound. His advice and exhortations of this kind are always expressed with energy and point, often clothed in the happiest forms of imagery; and hence it has come to pass, that such passages are perhaps more familiar to the general reader142 than any other part of his writings. Nor are Bacon's counsels without their importance, when we have to do with those subjects in which prejudice and partiality exercise their peculiar sway. Questions of politics and morals, of manners, taste, or history, cannot be subjected to a scheme of rigorous induction; and though on such matters we venture to assert general principles, these are commonly obtained with some degree of insecurity, and depend upon special habits of thought, not upon mere logical connexion. Here, therefore, the intellect may be perverted, by mixing, with the pure reason, our gregarious affections, or our individual propensities; the false suggestions involved in language, or the imposing delusions of received theories. In these dim and complex labyrinths of human thought, the Idol of the Tribe, or of the Den, of the Forum, or of the Theatre, may occupy men's minds with delusive shapes, and may obscure or pervert their vision of truth. But in that Natural Philosophy with which we are here concerned, there is little opportunity for such influences. As far as a physical theory is completed through all the steps of a just induction, there is a clear daylight diffused over it which leaves no lurking-place for prejudice. Each part can be examined separately and repeatedly; and the theory is not to be deemed perfect till it will bear the scrutiny of all sound minds alike. Although, therefore, Bacon, by warning men against the idols of fallacious images above spoken of, may have guarded them from dangerous error, his precepts have little to do with Natural Philosophy: and we cannot agree with him when he says[184], that the doctrine concerning these idols bears the same relation to the interpretation of nature as the doctrine concerning sophistical paralogisms bears to common logic.

(IX.) 21. His Aim, Utility.—There is one very prominent feature in Bacon's speculations which we must not omit to notice; it is a leading and constant143 object with him to apply his knowledge to Use. The insight which he obtains into nature, he would employ in commanding nature for the service of man. He wishes to have not only principles but works. The phrase which best describes the aim of his philosophy is his own[185], "Ascendendo ad axiomata, descendendo ad opera." This disposition appears in the first aphorism of the Novum Organon, and runs through the work. "Man, the minister and interpreter of nature, does and understands, so far as he has, in fact or in thought, observed the course of nature; and he cannot know or do more than this." It is not necessary for us to dwell much upon this turn of mind; for the whole of our present inquiry goes upon the supposition that an acquaintance with the laws of nature is worth our having for its own sake. It may be universally true, that Knowledge is Power; but we have to do with it not as Power, but as Knowledge. It is the formation of Science, not of Art, with which we are here concerned. It may give a peculiar interest to the history of science, to show how it constantly tends to provide better and better for the wants and comforts of the body; but that is not the interest which engages us in our present inquiry into the nature and course of philosophy. The consideration of the means which promote man's material well-being often appears to be invested with a kind of dignity, by the discovery of general laws which it involves; and the satisfaction which rises in our minds at the contemplation of such cases, men sometimes ascribe, with a false ingenuity, to the love of mere bodily enjoyment. But it is never difficult to see that this baser and coarser element is not the real source of our admiration. Those who hold that it is the main business of science to construct instruments for the uses of life, appear sometimes to be willing to accept the consequence which follows from such a doctrine, that the first shoemaker was a philosopher worthy of the highest144 admiration[186]. But those who maintain such paradoxes, often, by a happy inconsistency, make it their own aim, not to

73

devise some improved covering for the feet, but to delight the mind with acute speculations, exhibited in all the graces of wit and fancy.

It has been said[187] that the key of the Baconian doctrine consists in two words, Utility and Progress. With regard to the latter point, we have already seen that the hope and prospect of a boundless progress in human knowledge had sprung up in men's minds, even in the early times of imperial Rome; and were most emphatically expressed by that very Seneca who disdained to reckon the worth of knowledge by its value in food and clothing. And when we say that Utility was the great business of Bacon's philosophy, we forget one-half of his characteristic phrase: "Ascendendo ad aximomata," no less than "descendendo ad opera," was, he repeatedly declared, the scheme of his path. He constantly spoke, we are told by his secretary[188], of two kinds of experiments, experimenta fructifera, and experimenta lucifera.

Again; when we are told by modern writers that Bacon merely recommended such induction as all men instinctively practise, we ought to recollect his own earnest and incessant declarations to the contrary. The induction hitherto practised is, he says, of no use for obtaining solid science. There are two ways[189], "hæc via in usu est," "altera vera, sed intentata." Men have constantly been employed in anticipation; in illicit induction. The intellect left to itself rushes on in this road[190]; the conclusions so obtained are persuasive[191]; far more persuasive than inductions made with due caution[192]. But still this method must be rejected if we would obtain true knowledge. We shall then at length have ground of good hope for science when we145 proceed in another manner[193]. We must rise, not by a leap, but by small steps, by successive advances, by a gradation of ascents, trying our facts, and clearing our notions at every interval. The scheme of true philosophy, according to Bacon, is not obvious and simple, but long and technical, requiring constant care and self-denial to follow it. And we have seen that, in this opinion, his judgment is confirmed by the past history and present condition of science.

Again; it is by no means a just view of Bacon's character to place him in contrast to Plato. Plato's philosophy was the philosophy of Ideas; but it was not left for Bacon to set up the philosophy of Facts in opposition to that of Ideas. That had been done fully by the speculative reformers of the sixteenth century. Bacon had the merit of showing that Facts and Ideas must be combined; and not only so, but of divining many of the special rules and forms of this combination, when as yet there were no examples of them, with a sagacity hitherto quite unparalleled.

(X.) 22. His Perseverance.—With Bacon's unhappy political life we have here nothing to do. But we cannot but notice with pleasure how faithfully, how perseveringly, how energetically he discharged his great philosophical office of a Reformer of Methods. He had conceived the purpose of making this his object at an early period. When meditating the continuation of his Novum Organon, and speaking of his reasons for trusting that his work will reach some completeness of effect, he says[194], "I am by two arguments thus persuaded. First, I think thus from the zeal and constancy of my mind, which has not waxed old in this design, nor, after so many years, grown cold and indifferent; I remember that about forty years ago I composed a juvenile work about these things, which with great contrivance and a pompous title I called temporis partum maximum, or the most considerable146 birth of time; Next, that on account of its usefulness, it may hope the Divine blessing." In stating the grounds of hope for future progress in the sciences, he says[195]: "Some hope may, we conceive, be ministered to men by our own example: and this we say, not for the sake of boasting, but because it is useful to be said. If any despond, let them look at me, a man among all others of my age most occupied with civil affairs, nor of very sound health, (which brings a great loss of time;) also in this attempt the first explorer, following the footsteps of no man, nor communicating on these subjects with any mortal; yet, having steadily entered upon the true road and made my mind submit to things themselves, one who has, in this undertaking, made, (as we think,) some progress." He then proceeds to speak of what may be done by the combined and more prosperous labours of others, in that strain of noble hope and confidence, which rises again and again, like a chorus, at intervals in every part of his writings. In the Advancement of Learning he had said, "I could not be true and constant to the argument I handle, if I were not willing to go beyond others, but yet not more willing than to have others go beyond me again." In the Preface to the Instauratio Magna, he had placed among his postulates those expressions which have more than once warmed the breast of a philosophical reformer[196]. "Concerning ourselves we speak not; but as touching the matter which we have in hand, this we ask;—that men be of good hope, neither feign and imagine to themselves this our Reform as something of infinite dimension and beyond the grasp of mortal man, when in truth it is the end and true limit of infinite error; and is by no means unmindful of the condition of mortality and humanity, not confiding that such a thing can be carried to its perfect close in the space of a single age, but assigning it as a task to a succession of generations." In a later portion of the Instauratio he147 says: "We bear the strongest love to the human republic our common country; and we by no means abandon the hope that there will arise and come forth some man among posterity, who will be able to receive and digest all that is best in what we deliver; and whose care it will be to cultivate and perfect such things. Therefore, by the blessing of the Deity, to tend to this object, to open up the fountains, to discover the useful, to gather guidance for the way, shall be our task; and from this we shall never, while we remain in life, desist."

(XI.) 23. His Piety.—We may add, that the spirit of piety as well as of hope which is seen in this passage, appears to have been habitual to Bacon at all periods of his life. We find in his works several drafts of portions of his great scheme, and several of them begin with a prayer. One of these entitled, in the edition of his works, "The Student's Prayer," appears to me to belong probably to his early youth. Another, entitled "The Writer's Prayer," is inserted at the end of the Preface of the Instauratio, as it was finally published. I will conclude my notice of this wonderful man by inserting here these two prayers.

"To God the Father, God the Word, God the Spirit, we pour forth most humble and hearty supplications; that he, remembering the calamities of mankind, and the pilgrimage of this our life, in which we wear out days few and evil, would please to open to us new refreshments out of the fountains of his goodness for the alleviating of our miseries. This also we humbly and earnestly beg, that human things may not prejudice such as are divine; neither that, from the unlocking of the gates of sense, and the kindling of a greater natural light, anything of incredulity, or intellectual night, may arise in our minds towards divine mysteries. But rather, that by our mind thoroughly cleansed and purged from fancy and vanities, and yet subject and perfectly given up to the Divine oracles, there may be given unto faith the things that are faith's."

"Thou, O Father, who gavest the visible light as the first-born of thy creatures, and didst pour into148 man the intellectual light as the top and consummation of thy workmanship, be pleased to protect and govern this work, which coming from thy goodness, returneth to thy glory. Thou, after thou hadst reviewed the works which thy hands had made, beheldest that everything was very good, and thou didst rest with complacency in them. But man, reflecting on the works which he had made, saw that all was vanity and vexation of spirit, and could by no means acquiesce in them. Wherefore, if we labour in thy works with the sweat of our brows, thou wilt make us partakers of thy vision and thy Sabbath. We humbly beg that this mind may be steadfastly in us; and that thou, by our hands, and also by the hands of others on whom thou shalt bestow the same spirit, wilt please to convey a largess of new alms to thy family of mankind. These things we commend to thy everlasting love, by our Jesus, thy Christ, God with us. Amen."

149

CHAPTER XVI.
Additional Remarks on Francis Bacon.

Francis Bacon and his works have recently been discussed and examined by various writers in France and Germany as well as England[197]. Not to mention smaller essays, M. Bouillet has published a valuable edition of his philosophical works; Count Joseph de Maistre wrote a severe critique of his philosophy, which has been published since the death of the author; M. Charles Remusat has written a lucid and discriminating Essay on the subject; and in England we have had a new edition of the works published, with a careful and thoughtful examination of the philosophy which they contain, written by one of the editors: a person especially fitted for such an examination by an acute intellect, great acquaintance with philosophical literature, and a wide knowledge of modern science. Robert Leslie Ellis, the editor of whom I speak, died during the publication of the edition, and before he had done full justice to his powers; but he had already written various dissertations on Bacon's philosophy, which accompany the different Treatises in the new edition.

Mr. Ellis has given a more precise view than any of his predecessors had done of the nature of Bacon's150 induction and of his philosophy of discovery. Bacon's object was to discover the 'natures' or essences of things, in order that he might reproduce these natures or essences at will; he conceived that these natures were limited in number, and manifested in various combinations in the bodies which exist in the universe; so that by accumulating observations of them in a multitude of cases, we may learn by induction in what they do and in what they do not consist; the Induction which is to be used for this purpose consists in a great measure of excluding the cases which do not exhibit the 'nature' in question; and by such exclusion, duly repeated, we have at last left in our hands the elements of which the proposed nature consists. And the knowledge which is thus obtained may be applied to reproduce the things so analysed. As exhibiting this view clearly we may take a passage in the Sylva Sylvarum: "Gold has these natures: greatness of weight, closeness of parts, fixation, pliantness or softness, immunity from rust, colour or tincture of yellow. Therefore the sure way, though most about, to make gold, is to know the causes of the several natures before rehearsed, and the axioms concerning the same.

For if a man can make a metal, that hath all these properties, let men dispute whether it be gold or no." He means that however they dispute, it is gold for all practical purposes.

For such an Induction as this, Bacon claims the merit both of being certain, and of being nearly independent of the ingenuity of the inquirer. It is a method which enables all men to make exact discoveries, as a pair of compasses enables all men to draw an exact circle.

Now it is necessary for us, who are exploring the progress of the true philosophy of discovery, to say plainly that this part of Bacon's speculation is erroneous and valueless. No scientific discovery ever has been made in this way. Men have not obtained truths concerning the natural world by seeking for the natures of things, and by extracting them from phenomena by rejecting the cases in which they were not.151 On the contrary, they have begun by ascertaining the laws of the phenomena; and have then gone on, not by a mechanical method which levels all intellect, but by special efforts of the brightest intellects to catch hold of the ideas by which these laws of phenomena might be interpreted and expressed in more general terms. These two steps, the finding the laws of phenomena, and finding the conceptions by which those laws can be expressed, are really the course of discovery, as the history of science exhibits it to us.

Bacon, therefore, according to the view now presented, was wrong both as to his object and as to his method. He was wrong in taking for his object the essences of things,—the causes of abstract properties: for these man cannot, or can very rarely discover; and all Bacon's ingenuity in enumerating and classifying these essences and abstract properties has led, and could lead, to no result. The vast results of modern science have been obtained, not by seeking and finding the essences of things, but by exploring the laws of phenomena and the causes of those laws.

And Bacon's method, as well as his object, is vitiated by a pervading error:—the error of supposing that to be done by method which must be done by mind;—that to be done by rule which must be done by a flight beyond rule;—that to be mainly negative which is eminently positive;—that to depend on other men which must depend on the discoverer himself;—that to be mere prose which must have a dash of poetry;—that to be a work of mere labour which must be also a work of genius.

Mr. Ellis has seen very clearly and explained very candidly that this method thus recommended by Bacon has not led to discovery. "It is," he says, "neither to the technical part of his method nor to the details of his view of the nature and progress of science, that his great fame is justly owing. His merits are of another kind. They belong to the spirit rather than to the positive precepts of his philosophy."

As the reader of the last chapter will see, this amounts to much the same as the account which I152 had given of the positive results of Bacon's method, and the real value of that portion of his philosophy which he himself valued most. But still there remain, as I have also noted, portions of Bacon's speculations which have a great and enduring value, namely, his doctrine that Science is the Interpretation of Nature, his distinction of this Interpretation of Nature from the vicious and premature Anticipation of Nature which had generally prevailed till then; and the recommendation of a graduated and successive induction by which alone the highest and most general truths were to be reached. These are points which he urges with great clearness and with great earnestness; and these are important points in the true philosophy of discovery.

I may add that Mr. Ellis agrees with me in noting the invention of the conception by which the laws of phenomena are interpreted as something additional to Induction, both in the common and in the Baconian sense of the word. He says (General Preface, Art. 9), "In all cases this process [scientific discovery] involves an element to which nothing corresponds in the Tables of Comparence and Exclusion; namely the application to the facts of a principle of arrangement, an idea, existing in the mind of the discoverer antecedently to the act of induction." It may be said that this principle or idea is aimed at in the Baconian analysis. "And this is in one sense true: but it must be added, that this analysis, if it be thought right to call it so, is of the essence of the discovery which results from it. To take for granted that it has been already effected is simply a petitio principii. In most cases the mere act of induction follows as a matter of course as soon as the appropriate idea has been introduced." And as an example he takes Kepler's invention of the ellipse, as the idea by which Mars's motions could be reduced to law; making the same use of this example which we have repeatedly made of it.

Mr. Ellis may at first sight appear to express himself more favourably than I have done, with regard to153 the value of Bacon's Inquisitio in Naturam Calidi in the Second Book of the Novum Organon. He says of one part of it[198]: "Bacon here anticipates not merely the essential character of the most recent theory of heat, but also the kind of evidence by which it has been established.... The merit of having perceived the true significance of the production of heat by friction belongs of right to Bacon."

But notwithstanding this, Mr. Ellis's general judgment on this specimen of Bacon's application of his own method does not differ essentially from mine. He examines the Inquisitio at some length, and finally says: "If it were affirmed that Bacon, after having had a glimpse of the truth suggested by some obvious phenomena, had then recourse, as he himself expresses it, to certain 'differentiæ inanes' in order to save the phenomena, I think it would be hard to dispute the truth of the censure."

Another of the Editors of this edition (Mr. Spedding) fixes his attention upon another of the features of the method of discovery proposed by Bacon, and is disposed to think that the proposed method has never yet had justice done it, because it has not been tried in the way and on the scale that Bacon proposes[199]. Bacon recommended that a great collection of facts should be at once made and accumulated, regarding every branch of human knowledge; and conceived that, when this had been done by common observers, philosophers might extract scientific truths from this mass of facts by the application of a right method. This separation of the offices of the observer and discoverer, Mr. Spedding thinks is shown to be possible by such practical examples as meteorological observations, made by ordinary observers, and reduced to tables and laws by a central calculator; by hydrographical observations made by ships provided with proper instructions, and reduced to general laws by the154 man of science in his study; by magnetical observations made by many persons in every part of the world, and reduced into subservience to theory by mathematicians at home.

And to this our reply will be, in the terms which the history of all the Sciences has taught us, that such methods of procedure as this do not belong to the Epoch of Discovery, but to the Period of verification and application of the discovery which follows. When a theory has been established in its general form, our knowledge of the distribution of its phenomena in time and space can be much promoted by ordinary observers scattered over the earth, and succeeding each other in time, provided they are furnished with instruments and methods of observation, duly constructed on the principles of science; but such observers cannot in any degree supersede the discoverer who is first to establish the theory, and to introduce into the facts a new principle of order. When the laws of nature have been caught sight of, much may be done, even by ordinary observers, in verifying and exactly determining them; but when a real discovery is to be made, this separation of the observer and the theorist is not possible. In those cases, the questioning temper, the busy suggestive mind, is needed at every step, to direct the operating hand or the open gaze. No possible accumulation of facts about mixture and heat, collected in the way of blind trial, could have led to the doctrines of chemistry, or crystallography, or the atomic theory, or voltaic and chemical and magnetic polarity, or physiology, or any other science. Indeed not only is an existing theory requisite to supply the observer with instruments and methods, but without theory he cannot even describe his observations. He says that he mixes an acid and an alkali; but what is an acid? What is an alkali? How does he know them? He classifies crystals according to their forms: but till he has learnt what is distinctive in the form of a crystal, he cannot distinguish a cube from a square prism, even if he had a goniometer and could use it. And the like impossibility hangs over all the other subjects. To155 report facts for scientific purposes without some aid from theory, is not only useless, but impossible.

When Mr. Spedding says, "I could wish that men of science would apply themselves earnestly to the solution of this practical problem: What measures are to be taken in order that the greatest variety of judicious observations of nature all over the world may be carried on in concert upon a common plan and brought to a common centre:"—he is urging upon men of science to do what they have always done, so far as they have had any power, and in proportion as the state of science rendered such a procedure possible and profitable to science. In Astronomy, it has been done from the times of the Greeks and even of the Chaldeans, having been begun as soon as the heavens were reduced to law at all. In meteorology, it has been done extensively, though to little purpose, because the weather has not yet been reduced to rule. Men of science have shown how barometers, thermometers, hygrometers, and the like, may be constructed; and these may be now read by any one as easily as a clock; but of ten thousand meteorological registers thus kept by ordinary observers, what good has come to science? Again: The laws of the tides have been in a great measure determined by observations in all parts of the globe, because theory pointed out what was to be observed. In like manner the facts of terrestrial magnetism were ascertained with tolerable completeness by extended observations, then, and then only, when a most recondite and profound branch of mathematics had pointed out what was to be observed, and most ingenious instruments had been devised by men of science for observing. And even with these, it requires an education to use the instruments. But in many cases no education in the use of instruments devised by others can supersede the necessity of a theoretical and suggestive spirit in the inquirer himself. He must devise his own instruments and his own methods, if he is to make any discovery. What chemist, or inquirer about polarities, or about optical

79

laws yet undiscovered, can make any progress by using another156 man's experiments and observations? He must invent at every step of his observation; and the observer and theorist can no more be dissevered, than the body and soul of the inquirer.

That persons of moderate philosophical powers may, when duly educated, make observations which may be used by greater discoverers than themselves, is true. We have examples of such a subordination of scientific offices in astronomy, in geology, and in many other departments. But still, as I have said, a very considerable degree of scientific education is needed even for the subordinate labourers in science; and the more considerable in proportion as science advances further and further; since every advance implies a knowledge of what has already been done, and requires a new precision or generality in the new points of inquiry.

157

CHAPTER XVII.
From Bacon to Newton.

1. Harvey.—We have already seen that Bacon was by no means the first mover or principal author of the revolution in the method of philosophizing which took place in his time; but only the writer who proclaimed in the most impressive and comprehensive manner, the scheme, the profit, the dignity, and the prospects of the new philosophy. Those, therefore, who after him, took up the same views are not to be considered as his successors, but as his fellow-labourers; and the line of historical succession of opinions must be pursued without special reference to any one leading character, as the principal figure of the epoch. I resume this line, by noticing a contemporary and fellow-countryman of Bacon, Harvey, the discoverer of the circulation of the blood. This discovery was not published and generally accepted till near the end of Bacon's life; but the anatomist's reflections on the method of pursuing science, though strongly marked with the character of the revolution that was taking place, belong to a very different school from the Chancellor's. Harvey was a pupil of Fabricius of Acquapendente, whom we noticed among the practical reformers of the sixteenth century. He entertained, like his master, a strong reverence for the great names which had ruled in philosophy up to that time, Aristotle and Galen; and was disposed rather to recommend his own method by exhibiting it as the true interpretation of ancient wisdom, than to boast of its novelty. It is true, that he assigns, as his reason for158 publishing some of his researches[200], "that by revealing the method I use in searching into things, I might propose to studious men, a new and (if I mistake not) a surer path to the attainment of knowledge[201];" but he soon proceeds to fortify himself with the authority of Aristotle. In doing this, however, he has the very great merit of giving a living and practical character to truths which exist in the Aristotelian works, but which had hitherto been barren and empty professions. We have seen that Aristotle had asserted the importance of experience as one root of knowledge; and in this had been followed by the schoolmen of the middle ages: but this assertion came with very different force and effect from a man, the whole of whose life had been spent in obtaining, by means of experience, knowledge which no man had possessed before. In Harvey's general reflections, the necessity of both the elements of knowledge, sensations and ideas, experience and reason, is fully brought into view, and rightly connected with the metaphysics of Aristotle. He puts the antithesis of these two elements

with159 great clearness. "Universals are chiefly known to us, for science is begot by reasoning from universals to particulars; yet that very comprehension of universals in the understanding springs from the perception of singulars in our sense." Again, he quotes Aristotle's apparently opposite assertions:—that made in his Physics[202], "that we must advance from things which are first known to us, though confusedly, to things more distinctly intelligible in themselves; from the whole to the part; from the universal to the particular;" and that made in the Analytics[203]; that "Singulars are more known to us and do first exist according to sense: for nothing is in the understanding which was not before in the sense." Both, he says, are true, though at first they seem to clash: for "though in knowledge we begin with sense, sensation itself is a universal thing." This he further illustrates; and quotes Seneca, who says, that "Art itself is nothing but the reason of the work, implanted in the Artist's mind:" and adds, "the same way by which we gain an Art, by the very same way we attain any kind of science or knowledge whatever; for as Art is a habit whose object is something to be done, so Science is a habit whose object is something to be known; and as the former proceedeth from the imitation of examples, so this latter, from the knowledge of things natural. The source of both is from sense and experience; since [but?] it is impossible that Art should be rightly purchased by the one or Science by the other without a direction from ideas." Without here dwelling on the relation of Art and Science, (very justly stated by Harvey, except that ideas exist in a very different form in the mind of the Artist and the Scientist) it will be seen that this doctrine, of science springing from experience with a direction from ideas, is exactly that which we have repeatedly urged, as the true view of the subject. From this view, Harvey proceeds to infer the importance of a reference to sense in his own160 subject, not only for first discovering, but for receiving knowledge: "Without experience, not other men's but our own, no man is a proper disciple of any part of natural knowledge; without experimental skill in anatomy, he will no better apprehend what I shall deliver concerning generation, than a man born blind can judge of the nature and difference of colours, or one born deaf, of sounds." "If we do otherwise, we may get a humid and floating opinion, but never a solid and infallible knowledge: as is happenable to those who see foreign countries only in maps, and the bowels of men falsely described in anatomical tables. And hence it comes about, that in this rank age, we have many sophisters and bookwrights, but few wise men and philosophers." He had before declared "how unsafe and degenerate a thing it is, to be tutored by other men's commentaries, without making trial of the things themselves; especially since Nature's book is so open and legible." We are here reminded of Galileo's condemnation of the "paper philosophers." The train of thought thus expressed by the practical discoverers, spread rapidly with the spread of the new knowledge that had suggested it, and soon became general and unquestioned.

2. Descartes.—Such opinions are now among the most familiar and popular of those which are current among writers and speakers; but we should err much if we were to imagine that after they were once propounded they were never resisted or contradicted. Indeed, even in our own time, not only are such maxims very often practically neglected or forgotten, but the opposite opinions, and views of science quite inconsistent with those we have been explaining, are often promulgated and widely accepted. The philosophy of pure ideas has its commonplaces, as well as the philosophy of experience. And at the time of which we speak, the former philosophy, no less than the latter, had its great asserter and expounder; a man in his own time more admired than Bacon, regarded with more deference by a large body of disciples all over Europe, and more powerful in stirring up

men's161 minds to a new activity of inquiry. I speak of Descartes, whose labours, considered as a philosophical system, were an endeavour to revive the method of obtaining knowledge by reasoning from our own ideas only, and to erect it in opposition to the method of observation and experiment. The Cartesian philosophy contained an attempt at a counter-revolution. Thus in this author's Principia Philosophiæ[204], he says that "he will give a short account of the principal phenomena of the world, not that he may use them as reasons to prove anything; for," adds he, "we desire to deduce effects from causes, not causes from effects; but only in order that out of the innumerable effects which we learn to be capable of resulting from the same causes, we may determine our mind to consider some rather than others." He had before said, "The principles which we have obtained [by pure à priori reasoning] are so vast and so fruitful, that many more consequences follow from them than we see contained in this visible world, and even many more than our mind can ever take a full survey of." And he professes to apply this method in detail. Thus in attempting to state the three fundamental laws of motion, he employs only à priori reasonings, and is in fact led into error in the third law which he thus obtains[205]. And in his Dioptrics[206] he pretends to deduce the laws of reflection and refraction of light from certain comparisons (which are, in truth, arbitrary,) in which the radiation of light is represented by the motion of a ball impinging upon the reflecting or refracting body. It might be represented as a curious instance of the caprice of fortune, which appears in scientific as in other history, that Kepler, professing to derive all his knowledge from experience, and exerting himself with the greatest energy and perseverance, failed in detecting the law of refraction; while Descartes, who professed to be able to despise experiment, obtained the true law of sines. But as we have stated162 in the History[207], Descartes appears to have learnt this law from Snell's papers. And whether this be so or not, it is certain that notwithstanding the profession of independence which his philosophy made, it was in reality constantly guided and instructed by experience. Thus in explaining the Rainbow (in which his portion of the discovery merits great praise) he speaks[208] of taking a globe of glass, allowing the sun to shine on one side of it, and noting the colours produced by rays after two refractions and one reflection. And in many other instances, indeed in all that relates to physics, the reasonings and explanations of Descartes and his followers were, consciously or unconsciously, directed by the known facts, which they had observed themselves or learnt from others.

But since Descartes thus, speculatively at least, set himself in opposition to the great reform of scientific method which was going on in his time, how, it may be asked, did he acquire so strong an influence over the most active minds of his time? How is it that he became the founder of a large and distinguished school of philosophers? How is it that he not only was mainly instrumental in deposing Aristotle from his intellectual throne, but for a time appeared to have established himself with almost equal powers, and to have rendered the Cartesian school as firm a body as the Peripatetic had been?

The causes to be assigned for this remarkable result are, I conceive, the following. In the first place, the physicists of the Cartesian school did, as I have just stated, found their philosophy upon experiment, and did not practically, or indeed, most of them, theoretically, assent to their master's boast of showing what the phenomena must be, instead of looking to see what they are. And as Descartes had really incorporated in his philosophy all the chief physical discoveries of his own and preceding times, and had delivered, in a more general and systematic shape than163 any one before him, the principles which he thus established, the physical philosophy of his school was in reality far the best then current; and was an immense improvement upon the Aristotelian doctrines, which had not yet been displaced as a system. Another circumstance which gained him much favour, was the bold and ostentatious manner in which he professed to begin his philosophy by liberating himself from all preconceived prejudice. The first sentence of his philosophy contains this celebrated declaration: "Since," he says, "we begin life as infants, and have contracted various judgments concerning sensible things before we possess the entire use of our reason, we are turned aside from the knowledge of truth by many prejudices: from which it does not appear that we can be any otherwise delivered, than if once in our life we make it our business to doubt of everything in which we discern the smallest suspicion of uncertainty." In the face of this sweeping rejection or unhesitating scrutiny of all preconceived opinions, the power of the ancient authorities and masters in philosophy must obviously shrink away; and thus Descartes came to be considered as the great hero of the overthrow of the Aristotelian dogmatism. But in addition to these causes, and perhaps more powerful than all in procuring the assent of men to his doctrines, came the deductive and systematic character of his philosophy. For although all knowledge of the external world is in reality only to be obtained from observation, by inductive steps,—minute, perhaps, and slow, and many, as Galileo and Bacon had already taught;—the human mind conforms to these conditions reluctantly and unsteadily, and is ever ready to rush to general principles, and then to employ itself in deducing conclusions from these by synthetical reasonings; a task grateful, from the distinctness and certainty of the result, and the accompanying feeling of our own sufficiency. Hence men readily overlooked the precarious character of Descartes' fundamental assumptions, in their admiration of the skill with which a varied and complex Universe was evolved out of them. And the complete and164 systematic character of this philosophy attracted men no less than its logical connexion. I may quote here what a philosopher[209] of our own time has said of another writer: "He owed his influence to various causes; at the head of which may be placed that genius for system which, though it cramps the growth of knowledge, perhaps finally atones for that mischief by the zeal and activity which it rouses among followers and opponents, who discover truth by accident when in pursuit of weapons for their warfare. A system which attempts a task so hard as that of subjecting vast provinces of human knowledge to one or two principles, if it presents some striking instances of conformity to superficial appearances, is sure to delight the framer; and for a time to subdue and captivate the student too entirely for sober reflection and rigorous examination. In the first instance consistency passes for truth. When principles in some instances have proved sufficient to give an unexpected explanation of facts, the delighted reader is content to accept as true all other deductions from the principles. Specious premises being assumed to be true, nothing more can be required than logical inference. Mathematical forms pass current as the equivalent of mathematical certainty. The unwary admirer is satisfied with the completeness and symmetry of the plan of his house, unmindful of the need of examining the firmness of the foundation and the soundness of the materials. The system-maker, like the conqueror, long dazzles and overawes the world; but when their sway is past, the vulgar herd, unable to measure their astonishing faculties, take revenge by trampling on fallen greatness." Bacon showed his wisdom in his reflections on this subject, when he said that "Method, carrying a show of total and perfect knowledge, hath a tendency to generate acquiescence."

The main value of Descartes' physical doctrines consisted in their being arrived at in a way incon165sistent with his own professed method, namely, by a reference to observation. But though he did in reality begin from facts, his system was nevertheless a glaring example of that error which Bacon had called Anticipation; that illicit generalization which leaps at once from special facts to principles of the widest and remotest kind; such, for instance, as the Cartesian doctrine, that the world is an absolute plenum, every part being full of matter of some kind, and that all natural effects depend on the laws of motion. Against this fault, to which the human mind is so prone, Bacon had lifted his warning voice in vain, so far as the Cartesians were concerned; as indeed, to this day, one theorist after another pursues his course, and turns a deaf ear to the Verulamian injunctions; perhaps even complacently boasts that he founds his theory upon observation; and forgets that there are, as the aphorism of the Novum Organon declares, two ways by which this may be done;—the one hitherto in use and suggested by our common tendencies, but barren and worthless; the other almost untried, to be pursued only with effort and self-denial, but alone capable of producing true knowledge.

3. Gassendi.—Thus the lessons which Bacon taught were far from being generally accepted and applied at first. The amount of the influence of these two men, Bacon and Descartes, upon their age, has often been a subject of discussion. The fortunes of the Cartesian school have been in some measure traced in the History of Science. But I may mention the notice taken of these two philosophers by Gassendi, a contemporary and countryman of Descartes. Gassendi, as I have elsewhere stated[210], was associated with Descartes in public opinion, as an opponent of the Aristotelian dogmatism; but was not in fact a follower or profound admirer of that writer. In a Treatise on Logic, Gassendi gives an account of the Logic of various sects and authors; treating, in order, of the166 Logic of Zeno (the Eleatic), of Euclid (the Megarean), of Plato, of Aristotle, of the Stoics, of Epicurus, of Lullius, of Ramus; and to these he adds the Logic of Verulam, and the Logic of Cartesius. "We must not," he says, "on account of the celebrity it has obtained, pass over the Organon or Logic of Francis Bacon Lord Verulam, High Chancellor of England, whose noble purpose in our time it has been, to make an Instauration of the Sciences." He then gives a brief account of the Novum Organon, noticing the principal features in its rules, and especially the distinction between the vulgar induction which leaps at once from particular experiments to the more general axioms, and the chastised and gradual induction, which the author of the Organon recommends. In his account of the Cartesian Logic, he justly observes, that "He too imitated Verulam in this, that being about to build up a new philosophy from the foundation, he wished in the first place to lay aside all prejudice: and having then found some solid principle, to make that the groundwork of his whole structure. But he proceeds by a very different path from that which Verulam follows; for while Verulam seeks aid from things, to perfect the cogitation of the intellect, Cartesius conceives, that when we have laid aside all knowledge of things, there is, in our thoughts alone, such a resource, that the intellect may by its own power arrive at a perfect knowledge of all, even the most abstruse things."

The writings of Descartes have been most admired, and his method most commended, by those authors who have employed themselves upon metaphysical rather than physical subjects of inquiry. Perhaps we might say that, in reference to such subjects, this method is not so vicious as at first, when contrasted with the Baconian induction, it seems to be: for it might be urged that the thoughts from which Descartes begins his reasonings are, in reality, experiments of the kind which the subject requires us to consider: each such thought is a fact in the intellectual world; and of such facts, the metaphysician seeks to discover the laws. I shall not here examine the validity of this167 plea; but shall turn to the consideration of the actual progress of physical science, and its effect on men's minds.

4. *Actual progress in Science.*—The practical discoverers were indeed very active and very successful during the seventeenth century, which opened with Bacon's survey and exhortations. The laws of nature, of which men had begun to obtain a glimpse in the preceding century, were investigated with zeal and sagacity, and the consequence was that the foundations of most of the modern physical sciences were laid. That mode of research by experiment and observation, which had, a little time ago, been a strange, and to many, an unwelcome innovation, was now become the habitual course of philosophers. The revolution from the philosophy of tradition to the philosophy of experience was completed. The great discoveries of Kepler belonged to the preceding century. They are not, I believe, noticed, either by Bacon or by Descartes; but they gave a strong impulse to astronomical and mechanical speculators, by showing the necessity of a sound science of motion. Such a science Galileo had already begun to construct. At the time of which I speak, his disciples[211] were still labouring at this task, and at other problems which rapidly suggested themselves. They had already convinced themselves that air had weight; in 1643 Torricelli proved this practically by the invention of the Barometer; in 1647 Pascal proved it still further by sending the Barometer to the top of a mountain. Pascal and Boyle brought into clear view the fundamental laws of fluid equilibrium; Boyle and Mariotte determined the law of the compression of air as regulated by its elasticity. Otto Guericke invented the air-pump, and by his "Madgeburg Experiments" on a vacuum, illustrated still further the effects of the air. Guericke pursued what Gilbert had begun, the observation of electrical pheno168mena; and these two physicists made an important step, by detecting repulsion as well as attraction in these phenomena. Gilbert had already laid the foundations of the science of Magnetism. The law of refraction, at which Kepler had laboured in vain, was, as we have seen, discovered by Snell (about 1621), and published by Descartes. Mersenne had discovered some of the more important parts of the theory of Harmonics. In sciences of a different kind, the same movement was visible. Chemical doctrines tended to assume a proper degree of generality, when Sylvius in 1679 taught the opposition of acid and alkali, and Stahl, soon after, the phlogistic theory of combustion. Steno had remarked the most important law of crystallography in 1669, that the angles of the same kind of crystals are always equal. In the sciences of classification, about 1680, Ray and Morison in England resumed the attempt to form a systematic botany, which had been interrupted for a hundred years, from the time of the memorable essay of Cæsalpinus. The grand discovery of the circulation of the blood by Harvey about 1619, was followed in 1651 by Pecquet's discovery of the course of the chyle. There could now no longer be any question whether science was progressive, or whether observation could lead to new truths.

Among these cultivators of science, such sentiments as have been already quoted became very familiar;—that knowledge is to be sought from nature herself by observation and experiment;—that in such matters tradition is of no force when opposed to experience, and that mere reasonings without facts cannot lead to solid knowledge. But I

85

do not know that we find in these writers any more special rules of induction and scientific research which have since been confirmed and universally adopted. Perhaps too, as was natural in so great a revolution, the writers of this time, especially the second-rate ones, were somewhat too prone to disparage the labours and talents of Aristotle and the ancients in general, and to overlook the ideal element of our knowledge, in their zealous study of169 phenomena. They urged, sometimes in an exaggerated manner, the superiority of modern times in all that regards science, and the supreme and sole importance of facts in scientific investigations. There prevailed among them also a lofty and dignified tone of speaking of the condition and prospects of science, such as we are accustomed to admire in the Verulamian writings; for this, in a less degree, is epidemic among those who a little after his time speak of the new philosophy.

5. Otto Guericke, &c.—I need not illustrate these characteristics at any great length. I may as an example notice Otto Guericke's Preface to his Experimenta Magdeburgica (1670). He quotes a passage from Kircher's Treatise on the Magnetic Art, in which the author says, "Hence it appears how all philosophy, except it be supported by experiments, is empty, fallacious, and useless; what monstrosities philosophers, in other respects of the highest and subtlest genius, may produce in philosophy by neglecting experiment. Thus Experience alone is the Dissolver of Doubts, the Reconciler of Difficulties, the sole Mistress of Truth, who holds a torch before us in obscurity, unties our knots, teaches us the true causes of things." Guericke himself reiterates the same remark, adding that "philosophers, insisting upon their own thoughts and arguments merely, cannot come to any sound conclusion respecting the natural constitution of the world." Nor were the Cartesians slow in taking up the same train of reflection. Thus Gilbert Clark who, in 1660, published[212] a defence of Descartes' doctrine of a plenum in the universe, speaks in a tone which reminds us of Bacon, and indeed was very probably caught from him: "Natural philosophy formerly consisted entirely of loose and most doubtful controversies, carried on in high-sounding words, fit rather to delude than to instruct men. But at last (by the favour of the Deity)170 there shone forth some more divine intellects, who taking as their counsellors reason and experience together, exhibited a new method of philosophizing. Hence has been conceived a strong hope that philosophers may embrace, not a shadow or empty image of Truth, but Truth herself: and that Physiology (Physics) scattering these controversies to the winds, will contract an alliance with Mathematics. Yet this is hardly the work of one age; still less of one man. Yet let not the mind despond, or doubt not that, one party of investigators after another following the same method of philosophizing, at last, under good auguries, the mysteries of nature being daily unlocked as far as human feebleness will allow, Truth may at last appear in full, and these nuptial torches may be lighted."

As another instance of the same kind, I may quote the preface to the First volume of the Transactions of the Academy of Sciences at Paris: "It is only since the present century," says the writer, "that we can reckon the revival of Mathematics and Physics. M. Descartes and other great men have laboured at this work with so much success, that in this department of literature, the whole face of things has been changed. Men have quitted a sterile system of physics, which for several generations had been always at the same point; the reign of words and terms is passed; men will have things; they establish principles which they understand, they follow those principles; and thus they make progress. Authority has ceased to have more weight than Reason: that which was received without contradiction because it had been long received, is now examined, and often rejected: and philosophers have made it their business to consult, respecting natural things, Nature herself rather than the Ancients." These had now become the commonplaces of those who spoke concerning the course and method of the Sciences.

6. Hooke.—In England, as might be expected, the influence of Francis Bacon was more directly visible. We find many writers, about this time, repeating the truths which Bacon had proclaimed, and in almost171 every case showing the same imperfections in their views which we have noticed in him. We may take as an example of this Hooke's Essay, entitled "A General Scheme or Idea of the present state of Natural Philosophy, and how its defects may be remedied by a Methodical proceeding in the making Experiments and collecting Observations; whereby to compile a Natural History as a solid basis for the superstructure of true Philosophy." This Essay may be looked upon as an attempt to adapt the Novum Organon to the age which succeeded its publication. We have in this imitation, as in the original, an enumeration of various mistakes and impediments which had in preceding times prevented the progress of knowledge; exhortations to experiment and observation as the only solid basis of Science; very ingenious suggestions of trains of inquiry, and modes of pursuing them; and a promise of obtaining scientific truths when facts have been duly accumulated. This last part of his scheme the author calls a Philosophical Algebra; and he appears to have imagined that it might answer the purpose of finding unknown causes from known facts, by means of certain regular processes, in the same manner as Common Algebra finds unknown from known quantities. But this part of the plan appears to have remained unexecuted. The suggestion of such a method was a result of the Baconian notion that invention in a discoverer might be dispensed with. We find Hooke adopting the phrases in which this notion is implied: thus he speaks of the understanding as "being very prone to run into the affirmative way of judging, and wanting patience to follow and prosecute the negative way of inquiry, by rejection of disagreeing natures." And he follows Bacon also in the error of attempting at once to obtain from the facts the discovery of a "nature," instead of investigating first the measures and the laws of phenomena. I return to more general notices of the course of men's thoughts on this subject.

7. Royal Society.—Those who associated themselves together for the prosecution of science quoted Bacon as their leader, and exulted in the progress172 made by the philosophy which proceeded upon his principles. Thus in Oldenburg's Dedication of the Transactions of the Royal Society of London for 1670, to Robert Boyle, he says; "I am informed by such as well remember the best and worst days of the famous Lord Bacon, that though he wrote his Advancement of Learning and his Instauratio Magna in the time of his greatest power, yet his greatest reputation rebounded first from the most intelligent foreigners in many parts of Christendom:" and after speaking of his practical talents and his public employments, he adds, "much more justly still may we wonder how, without any great skill in Chemistry, without much pretence to the Mathematics or Mechanics, without optic aids or other engines of late invention, he should so much transcend the philosophers then living, in judicious and clear instructions, in so many useful observations and discoveries, I think I may say beyond the records of many ages." And in the end of the Preface to the same volume, he speaks with great exultation of the advance of science all over Europe, referring undoubtedly to facts then familiar. "And now let envy snarl, it cannot stop the wheels of active philosophy, in no part of the known

world;—not in France, either in Paris or in Caen;—not in Italy, either in Rome, Naples, Milan, Florence, Venice, Bononia or Padua;—in none of the Universities either on this or on that side of the seas, Madrid and Lisbon, all the best spirits in Spain and Portugal, and the spacious and remote dominions to them belonging;—the Imperial Court and the Princes of Germany; the Northern Kings and their best luminaries; and even the frozen Muscovite and Russian have all taken the operative ferment: and it works high and prevails every way, to the encouragement of all sincere lovers of knowledge and virtue."

Again, in the Preface for 1672, he pursues the same thought into detail: "We must grant that in the last age, when operative philosophy began to recover ground, and to tread on the heels of triumphant Philology; emergent adventures and great successes173 were encountered by dangerous oppositions and strong obstructions. Galilæus and others in Italy suffered extremities for their celestial discoveries; and here in England Sir Walter Raleigh, when he was in his greatest lustrous, was notoriously slandered to have erected a school of atheism, because he gave countenance to chemistry, to practical arts, and to curious mechanical operations, and designed to form the best of them into a college. And Queen Elizabeth's Gilbert was a long time esteemed extravagant for his magnetisms; and Harvey for his diligent researches in pursuance of the circulation of the blood. But when our renowned Lord Bacon had demonstrated the methods for a perfect restoration of all parts of real knowledge; and the generous and philosophical Peireskius had, soon after, agitated in all parts to redeem the most instructive antiquities, and to excite experimental essays and fresh discoveries; the success became on a sudden stupendous; and effective philosophy began to sparkle, and even to flow into beams of shining light all over the world."

The formation of the Royal Society of London and of the Academy of Sciences of Paris, from which proceeded the declamations just quoted, were among many indications, belonging to this period, of the importance which states as well as individuals had by this time begun to attach to the cultivation of science. The English Society was established almost immediately when the restoration of the monarchy appeared to give a promise of tranquillity to the nation (in 1660), and the French Academy very soon afterwards (in 1666). These measures were very soon followed by the establishment of the Observatories of Paris and Greenwich (in 1667 and 1675); which may be considered to be a kind of public recognition of the astronomy of observation, as an object on which it was the advantage and the duty of nations to bestow their wealth.

8. Bacon's New Atalantis.—When philosophers had their attention turned to the boundless prospect of increase to the knowledge and powers and pleasures of174 man which the cultivation of experimental philosophy seemed to promise, it was natural that they should think of devising institutions and associations by which such benefits might be secured. Bacon had drawn a picture of a society organized with a view to such purpose, in his fiction of the "New Atalantis." The imaginary teacher who explains this institution to the inquiring traveller, describes it by the name of Solomon's House; and says[213], "The end of our foundation is the knowledge of causes and secret motions of things; and the enlarging the bounds of the human empire to effecting of things possible." And, as parts of this House, he describes caves and wells, chambers and towers, baths and gardens, parks and pools, dispensatories and furnaces, and many other contrivances, provided for the purpose of making experiments of many kinds. He describes also the

various employments of the Fellows of this College, who take a share in its researches. There are merchants of light, who bring books and inventions from foreign countries; depredators, who gather the experiments which exist in books; mystery-men, who collect the experiments of the mechanical arts; pioneers or miners, who invent new experiments; and compilers, "who draw the experiments of the former into titles and tables, to give the better light for the drawing of observations and axioms out of them." There are also dowry-men or benefactors, that cast about how to draw out of the experiments of their fellows things of use and practice for man's life; lamps, that direct new experiments of a more penetrating light than the former; inoculators, that execute the experiments so directed. Finally, there are the interpreters of nature, that raise the former discoveries by experiments into greater observations (that is, more general truths), axioms and aphorisms. Upon this scheme we may remark, that fictitious as it undisguisedly is, it still serves to exhibit very clearly some of the main features of the author's[175] philosophy:—namely, his steady view of the necessity of ascending from facts to the most general truths by several stages;—an exaggerated opinion of the aid that could be derived in such a task from technical separation of the phenomena and a distribution of them into tables;—a belief, probably incorrect, that the offices of experimenter and interpreter may be entirely separated, and pursued by different persons with a certainty of obtaining success!—and a strong determination to make knowledge constantly subservient to the uses of life.

9. Cowley.—Another project of the same kind, less ambitious but apparently more directed to practice, was published a little later (1657) by another eminent man of letters in this country. I speak of Cowley's "Proposition for the Advancement of Experimental Philosophy." He suggests that a College should be established at a short distance from London, endowed with a revenue of four thousand pounds, and consisting of twenty professors with other members. The objects of the labours of these professors he describes to be, first, to examine all knowledge of nature delivered to us from former ages and to pronounce it sound or worthless; second, to recover the lost inventions of the ancients; third, to improve all arts that we now have; lastly, to discover others that we yet have not. In this proposal we cannot help marking the visible declension from Bacon's more philosophical view. For we have here only a very vague indication of improving old arts and discovering new, instead of the two clear Verulamian antitheses, Experiments and Axioms deduced from them, on the one hand, and on the other an ascent to general Laws, and a derivation, from these, of Arts for daily use. Moreover the prominent place which Cowley has assigned to the verifying the knowledge of former ages and recovering "the lost inventions and drowned lands of the ancients," implies a disposition to think too highly of traditionary knowledge; a weakness which Bacon's scheme shows him to have fully overcome. And thus it has been up to the present day, that with all Bacon's mistakes, in[176] the philosophy of scientific method few have come up to him, and perhaps none have gone beyond him.

Cowley exerted himself to do justice to the new philosophy in verse as well as prose, and his Poem to the Royal Society expresses in a very noble manner those views of the history and prospects of philosophy which prevailed among the men by whom the Royal Society was founded. The fertility and ingenuity of comparison which characterize Cowley's poetry are well known; and these qualities are in this instance largely employed for the embellishment of his subject. Many of the comparisons which he exhibits are apt and striking. Philosophy is a ward whose estate (human knowledge) is, in his nonage, kept from him by his guardians and tutors; (a case which the ancient rhetoricians were fond of taking as a subject of declamation;) and these wrong-doers retain him in unjust tutelage and constraint for their own purposes; until

> Bacon at last, a mighty man, arose,
> (Whom a wise King, and Nature, chose
> Lord Chancellor of both their laws,)
> And boldly undertook the injured pupil's cause.

Again, Bacon is one who breaks a scarecrow Priapus which stands in the garden of knowledge. Again, Bacon is one who, instead of a picture of painted grapes, gives us real grapes from which we press "the thirsty soul's refreshing wine." Again, Bacon is like Moses, who led the Hebrews forth from the barren wilderness, and ascended Pisgah;—

> Did on the very border stand
> Of the blest promised land,
> And from the mountain's top of his exalted wit
> Saw it himself and showed us it.

The poet however adds, that Bacon discovered, but did not conquer this new world; and that the men whom he addresses must subdue these regions. These "champions" are then ingeniously compared to Gideon's band:

> Their old and empty pitchers first they brake,
> And with their hands then lifted up the light.
> 177

There were still at this time some who sneered at or condemned the new philosophy; but the tide of popular opinion was soon strongly in its favour. I have elsewhere[214] noticed a pasquinade of the poet Boileau in 1682, directed against the Aristotelians. At this time, and indeed for long afterwards, the philosophers of France were Cartesians. The English men of science, although partially and for a time they accepted some of Descartes' opinions, for the most part carried on the reform independently, and in pursuance of their own views. And they very soon found a much greater leader than Descartes to place at their head, and to take as their authority, so far as they acknowledged authority, in their speculations. I speak of Newton, whose influence upon the philosophy of science I must now consider.

10. Barrow.—I will, however, first mention one other writer who may, in more than one way, be regarded as the predecessor of Newton. I speak of Isaac Barrow, whom Newton succeeded as Professor of Mathematics in the University of Cambridge, and who in his mathematical speculations approached very near to Newton's method of Fluxions. He afterwards (in 1673) became Master of Trinity College, which office he held till his death in 1677. But the passages which I shall quote belong to an earlier period, (when Barrow was about 22 years old,) and may be regarded as expressions of the opinions which were then current among active-minded and studious young men. They manifest a complete familiarity with the writings both of Bacon and of Descartes, and a very just appreciation of both. The discourse of which I speak is an academical exercise delivered in 1652, on the thesis Cartesiana hypothesis haud satisfacit præcipuis naturæ phænomenis. By the "Cartesian hypothesis," he does not mean the hypothesis that the planets are

moved by vortices of etherial matter: I believe that this Cartesian tenet never had any disciples in England; it178 certainly never took any hold of Cambridge. By the Cartesian hypothesis, Barrow means the doctrine that all the phenomena of nature can be accounted for by matter and motion; and allowing that the motions of the planets are to be so accounted for, (which is Newtonian as well as Cartesian doctrine,) he denies that the Cartesian hypothesis accounts for "the generations, properties, and specific operations of animals, plants, minerals, stones, and other natural bodies," in doing which he shows a sound philosophical judgment. But among the parts of this discourse most bearing on our present purpose are those where he mentions Bacon. "Against Cartesius," he says, "I pit the chymists and others, but especially as the foremost champion of this battle, our Verulam, a man of great name and of great judgment, who condemned this philosophy before it was born." "He," adds Barrow, "several times in his Organon, warned men against all hypotheses of this kind, and noticed beforehand that there was not much to be expected from those principles which are brought into being by violent efforts of argumentation from the brains of particular men: for that, as upon the phenomena of the stars, various constructions of the heavens may be devised, so also upon the phenomena of the Universe, still more dogmas may be founded and constructed; and yet all such are mere inventions: and as many philosophies of this kind as are or shall be extant, so many fictitious and theatrical worlds are made." The reference is doubtless to Aphorism LXII. of the First Book of the Novum Organon, in which Bacon is speaking of his "Idols of the Theatre." After making the remark which Barrow has adopted, Bacon adds, "Such theatrical fables have also this in common with those of dramatic poets, that the dramatic story is more regular and elegant than true histories are, and is made so as to be agreeable." Barrow, having this in his mind, goes on to say: "And though Cartesius has dressed up the stage of his theatre more prettily than any other person, and made his drama more like history, still he is not exempt from the like censure." And he then refers to Cartesius's own declaration, that179 he did not learn his system from things themselves, but tried to impose his own laws upon things; thus inverting the order of true philosophy.

Other parts of Bacon's work to which Barrow refers are those where he speaks of the Form, or Formal Cause of a body, and says that in comparison with that, the Efficient Cause and the Material Cause are things unimportant and superficial, and contribute little to true and active science[215]. And again, his classification of the various kinds of motions[216],—the motus libertatis, motus nexus, motus continuitatis, motus ad lucrum, fugæ, unionis, congregationis; and the explanation of electrical attraction (about which Gilbert and others had written) as motus ad lucrum.

These passages show that Barrow had read the Novum Organon in a careful and intelligent manner, and presumed his Cambridge hearers to be acquainted with the work. Nor is his judgment of Descartes less wise and philosophical. He rejects, as we have seen, his system as a true scheme of the universe, and condemns altogether his à priori mode of philosophizing; but this does not prevent his accepting Descartes' real discoveries, and admiring the boldness and vigour of his attempts to reform philosophy. There is, in Barrow's works, academic verse, as well as prose, on the subject of the Cartesian hypothesis. In this, Descartes himself is highly praised, though his doctrines are very partially accepted. The writer says: "Pardon us, great Cartesius, if the Muse resists you. Pardon! We follow you, Inquiring Spirit that you are, while we reject your system. As you

91

have taught us free thought, and broken down the rule of tyranny, we undauntedly speculate, even in opposition to you."

Descartes is even yet spoken of, especially by French writers, as the person who first asserted and established the freedom of inquiry which is the boast of modern philosophy; but this is said with reference to metaphysics, not to physics. In physical philosophy,180 though he caught hold of some of the discoveries which were then coming into view, the method in which he reasoned or professed to reason was altogether vicious; and was, as I have already said, an attempt to undo what the reformers, both theoretical and practical, had been doing:—to discredit the philosophy of experience, and to restore the reign of à priori systems.

It was, however, now, too late to make any such attempt; and nothing came of it to interrupt the progress of a better philosophy of discovery.

181

CHAPTER XVIII.
Newton.

1. BOLD and extensive as had been the anticipations of those whose minds were excited by the promise of the new philosophy, the discoveries of Newton respecting the mechanics of the universe, brought into view truths more general and profound than those earlier philosophers had hoped or imagined. With these vast accessions to human knowledge, men's thoughts were again set in action; and philosophers made earnest and various attempts to draw, from these extraordinary advances in science, the true moral with regard to the conduct and limits of the human understanding. They not only endeavoured to verify and illustrate, by these new portions of science, what had recently been taught concerning the methods of obtaining sound knowledge; but they were also led to speculate concerning many new and more interesting questions relating to this subject. They saw, for the first time, or at least far more clearly than before, the distinction between the inquiry into the laws, and into the causes of phenomena. They were tempted to ask, how far the discovery of causes could be carried; and whether it would soon reach, or clearly point to, the ultimate cause. They were driven to consider whether the properties which they discovered were essential properties of all matter, necessarily and primarily involved in its essence, though revealed to us at a late period by their derivative effects. These questions even now agitate the thoughts of speculative men. Some of them have already, in this work, been discussed, or arranged in the places which our view of the philosophy of these subjects assigns to them. But we182 must here notice them as they occurred to Newton himself and his immediate followers.

2. The general Baconian notion of the method of philosophizing,—that it consists in ascending from phenomena, through various stages of generalization, to truths of the highest order,—received, in Newton's discovery of the universal mutual gravitation of every particle of matter, that pointed actual exemplification, for want of which it had hitherto been almost overlooked, or at least very vaguely understood. That great truth, and the steps by which it was established, afford, even now, by far the best example of the successive ascent, from one scientific truth to another,—of the repeated transition from

less to more general propositions,—which we can yet produce; as may be seen in the Table which exhibits the relation of these steps in Book II. of the Novum Organon Renovatum. Newton himself did not fail to recognize this feature in the truths which he exhibited. Thus he says[217], "By the way of Analysis we proceed from compounds to ingredients, as from motions to the forces producing them; and in general, from effects to their causes, and from particular causes to more general ones, till the argument ends in the most general." And in like manner in another Query[218]: "The main business of natural philosophy is to argue from phenomena without feigning hypotheses, and to deduce causes from effects, till we come to the First Cause, which is certainly not mechanical."

3. Newton appears to have had a horror of the term hypothesis, which probably arose from his acquaintance with the rash and illicit general assumptions of Descartes. Thus in the passage just quoted, after declaring that gravity must have some other cause than matter, he says, "Later philosophers banish the consideration of such a cause out of Natural Philosophy, feigning hypotheses for explaining all things mechanically, and referring other causes to metaphysics." In the celebrated Scholium at the end of183 the Principia he says, "Whatever is not deduced from the phenomena, is to be termed hypothesis; and hypotheses, whether metaphysical or physical, or occult causes, or mechanical, have no place in experimental philosophy. In this philosophy, propositions are deduced from phenomena, and rendered general by induction." And in another place, he arrests the course of his own suggestions, saying, "Verum hypotheses non fingo." I have already attempted to show that this is, in reality, a superstitious and self-destructive spirit of speculation. Some hypotheses are necessary, in order to connect the facts which are observed; some new principle of unity must be applied to the phenomena, before induction can be attempted. What is requisite is, that the hypothesis should be close to the facts, and not connected with them by the intermediation of other arbitrary and untried facts; and that the philosopher should be ready to resign it as soon as the facts refuse to confirm it. We have seen in the History[219], that it was by such a use of hypotheses, that both Newton himself, and Kepler, on whose discoveries those of Newton were based, made their discoveries. The suppositions of a force tending to the sun and varying inversely as the square of the distance; of a mutual force between all the bodies of the solar system; of the force of each body arising from the attraction of all its parts; not to mention others, also propounded by Newton,—were all hypotheses before they were verified as theories. It is related that when Newton was asked how it was that he saw into the laws of nature so much further than other men, he replied, that if it were so, it resulted from his keeping his thoughts steadily occupied upon the subject which was to be thus penetrated. But what is this occupation of the thoughts, if it be not the process of keeping the phenomena clearly in view, and trying, one after another, all the plausible hypotheses which seem likely to connect them, till at last the true law is discovered? Hypotheses so used are a necessary element of discovery.

184

4. With regard to the details of the process of discovery, Newton has given us some of his views, which are well worthy of notice, on account of their coming from him; and which are real additions to the philosophy of this subject. He speaks repeatedly of the analysis and synthesis of observed facts; and thus marks certain steps in scientific research, very important, and not, I think, clearly pointed out by his predecessors. Thus

he says[220], "As in Mathematics, so in Natural Philosophy, the investigation of difficult things by the method of analysis ought ever to precede the method of composition. This analysis consists in making experiments and observations, and in drawing general conclusions from them by induction, and admitting of no objections against the conclusions, but such as are taken from experiments or other certain truths. And although the arguing from experiments and observations by induction be no demonstration of general conclusions; yet it is the best way of arguing which the nature of things admits of, and may be looked upon as so much the stronger, by how much the induction is more general." And he then observes, as we have quoted above, that by this way of analysis we proceed from compounds to ingredients, from motions to forces, from effects to causes, and from less to more general causes. The analysis here spoken of includes the steps which in our Novum Organon we call the decomposition of facts, the exact observation and measurement of the phenomena, and the colligation of facts; the necessary intermediate step, the selection and explication of the appropriate conception, being passed over by Newton, in the fear of seeming to encourage the fabrication of hypotheses. The synthesis of which Newton here speaks consists of those steps of deductive reasoning, proceeding from the conception once assumed, which are requisite for the comparison of its consequences with the observed facts. This, his statement of the process of research, is, as far as it goes, perfectly exact.

185

5. In speaking of Newton's precepts on the subject, we are naturally led to the celebrated "Rules of Philosophizing," inserted in the second edition of the Principia. These rules have generally been quoted and commented on with an almost unquestioning reverence. Such Rules, coming from such an authority, cannot fail to be highly interesting to us; but at the same time, we cannot here evade the necessity of scrutinizing their truth and value, according to the principles which our survey of this subject has brought into view. The Rules stand at the beginning of that part of the Principia (the Third Book) in which he infers the mutual gravitation of the sun, moon, planets, and all parts of each. They are as follows:

"Rule I. We are not to admit other causes of natural things than such as both are true, and suffice for explaining their phenomena.

"Rule II. Natural effects of the same kind are to be referred to the same causes, as far as can be done.

"Rule III. The qualities of bodies which cannot be increased or diminished in intensity, and which belong to all bodies in which we can institute experiments, are to be held for qualities of all bodies whatever.

"Rule IV. In experimental philosophy, propositions collected from phenomena by induction, are to be held as true either accurately or approximately, notwithstanding contrary hypotheses; till other phenomena occur by which they may be rendered either more accurate or liable to exception."

In considering these Rules, we cannot help remarking, in the first place, that they are constructed with an intentional adaptation to the case with which Newton has to deal,—the induction of Universal Gravitation; and are intended to protect the reasonings before which they stand. Thus the first Rule is designed to strengthen the inference of gravitation from the celestial phenomena, by describing it as a vera causa, a true cause; the second Rule countenances the doctrine that the planetary motions are governed by mechanical186 forces, as terrestrial motions are; the third rule appears intended to justify the assertion of gravitation, as a universal quality of bodies; and the fourth contains, along with a general declaration of the authority of induction, the author's usual protest against hypotheses, levelled at the Cartesian hypotheses especially.

6. Of the First Rule.—We, however, must consider these Rules in their general application, in which point of view they have often been referred to, and have had very great authority allowed them. One of the points which has been most discussed, is that maxim which requires that the causes of phenomena which we assign should be true causes, veræ causæ. Of course this does not mean that they should be the true or right cause; for although it is the philosopher's aim to discover such causes, he would be little aided in his search of truth, by being told that it is truth which he is to seek. The rule has generally been understood to prescribe that in attempting to account for any class of phenomena, we must assume such causes only, as from other considerations, we know to exist. Thus gravity, which was employed in explaining the motions of the moon and planets, was already known to exist and operate at the earth's surface.

Now the Rule thus interpreted is, I conceive, an injurious limitation of the field of induction. For it forbids us to look for a cause, except among the causes with which we are already familiar. But if we follow this rule, how shall we ever become acquainted with any new cause? Or how do we know that the phenomena which we contemplate do really arise from some cause which we already truly know? If they do not, must we still insist upon making them depend upon some of our known causes; or must we abandon the study of them altogether? Must we, for example, resolve to refer the action of radiant heat to the air, rather than to any peculiar fluid or ether, because the former is known to exist, the latter is merely assumed for the purpose of explanation? But why should we do this? Why should we not endeavour to learn the cause from the effects, even if it be not already known187 to us? We can infer causes, which are new when we first become acquainted with them. Chemical Forces, Optical Forces, Vital Forces, are known to us only by chemical and optical and vital phenomena; must we, therefore, reject their existence or abandon their study? They do not conform to the double condition, that they shall be sufficient and also real: they are true, only so far as they explain the facts, but are they, therefore, unintelligible or useless? Are they not highly important and instructive subjects of speculation? And if the gravitation which rules the motions of the planets had not existed at the earth's surface;—if it had been there masked and concealed by the superior effect of magnetism, or some other extraneous force,—might not Newton still have inferred, from Kepler's laws, the tendency of the planets to the sun; and from their perturbations, their tendency to each other? His discoveries would still have been immense, if the cause which he assigned had not been a vera causa in the sense now contemplated.

7. But what do we mean by calling gravity a "true cause"? How do we learn its reality? Of course, by its effects, with which we are familiar;—by the weight and fall of bodies about us. These strike even the most careless observer. No one can fail to see that all bodies which we come in contact with are heavy;—that gravity acts in our neighbourhood here upon earth. Hence, it may be said, this cause is at any rate a true cause, whether it explains the celestial phenomena or not.

But if this be what is meant by a vera causa, it appears strange to require that in all cases we should find such a one to account for all classes of phenomena. Is it reasonable or prudent to demand that we shall reduce every set of phenomena, however minute, or abstruse, or complicated, to causes so obviously existing as to strike the most incurious, and to be familiar among men? How can we expect to find such veræ causæ for the delicate and recondite phenomena which an exact and skilful observer detects in chemical, or optical, or electrical experiments? The facts188 themselves are too fine for vulgar apprehension; their relations, their symmetries, their measures require a previous discipline to understand them. How then can their causes be found among those agencies with which the common unscientific herd of mankind are familiar? What likelihood is there that causes held for real by such persons, shall explain facts which such persons cannot see or cannot understand?

Again: if we give authority to such a rule, and require that the causes by which science explains the facts which she notes and measures and analyses, shall be causes which men, without any special study, have already come to believe in, from the effects which they casually see around them, what is this, except to make our first rude and unscientific persuasions the criterion and test of our most laborious and thoughtful inferences? What is it, but to give to ignorance and thoughtlessness the right of pronouncing upon the convictions of intense study and long-disciplined thought? "Electrical atmospheres" surrounding electrized bodies, were at one time held to be a "true cause" of the effects which such bodies produce. These atmospheres, it was said, are obvious to the senses; we feel them like a spider's web on the hands and face. Æpinus had to answer such persons, by proving that there are no atmospheres, no effluvia, but only repulsion. He thus, for a true cause in the vulgar sense of the term, substituted an hypothesis; yet who doubts that what he did was an advance in the science of electricity?

8. Perhaps some persons may be disposed to say, that Newton's Rule does not enjoin us to take those causes only which we clearly know, or suppose we know, to be really existing and operating, but only causes of such kinds as we have already satisfied ourselves do exist in nature. It may be urged that we are entitled to infer that the planets are governed in their motions by an attractive force, because we find, in the bodies immediately subject to observation and experiment, that such motions are produced by attractive forces, for example, by that of the earth. It may189 be said that we might on similar grounds infer forces which unite particles of chemical compounds, or deflect particles of light, because we see adhesion and deflection produced by forces.

But it is easy to show that the Rule, thus laxly understood, loses all significance. It prohibits no hypothesis; for all hypotheses suppose causes such as, in some case or other, we have seen in action. No one would think of explaining phenomena by referring them to forces and agencies altogether different from any which are known; for on this supposition, how could he pretend to reason about the effects of the assumed causes, or undertake to prove that they would explain the facts? Some close similarity with some known kind of cause is requisite, in order that the hypothesis may have the appearance of an explanation. No forces, or virtues, or sympathies, or fluids, or ethers, would be excluded by this interpretation of veræ causæ. Least of all, would such an interpretation reject the Cartesian hypothesis of vortices; which undoubtedly, as I conceive, Newton intended to condemn by his Rule. For that such a case as a whirling fluid, carrying bodies round a centre in orbits, does occur, is too obvious to require proof. Every eddying stream, or blast that twirls the dust in the road, exhibits examples of such action, and would justify the assumption of the vortices which carry the planets in their courses; as indeed, without doubt, such facts suggested the Cartesian explanation of the solar system. The vortices, in this mode of considering the subject, are at the least as real a cause of motion as gravity itself.

9. Thus the Rule which enjoins "true causes," is nugatory, if we take veræ causæ in the extended sense of any causes of a real kind, and unphilosophical, if we understand the term of those very causes which we familiarly suppose to exist. But it may be said that we are to designate as "true causes," not those which are collected in a loose, confused and precarious manner, by undisciplined minds, from obvious phenomena, but those which are justly and rigorously inferred.190 Such a cause, it may be added, gravity is; for the facts of the downward pressures and downward motions of bodies at the earth's surface lead us, by the plainest and strictest induction, to the assertion of such a force. Now to this interpretation of the Rule there is no objection; but then, it must be observed, that on this view, terrestrial gravity is inferred by the same process as celestial gravitation; and the cause is no more entitled to be called "true," because it is obtained from the former, than because it is obtained from the latter class of facts. We thus obtain an intelligible and tenable explanation of a vera causa; but then, by this explanation, its verity ceases to be distinguishable from its other condition, that it "suffices for the explanation of the phenomena." The assumption of universal gravitation accounts for the fall of a stone; it also accounts for the revolutions of the Moon or of Saturn; but since both these explanations are of the same kind, we cannot with justice make the one a criterion or condition of the admissibility of the other.

10. But still, the Rule, so understood, is so far from being unmeaning or frivolous, that it expresses one of the most important tests which can be given of a sound physical theory. It is true, the explanation of one set of facts may be of the same nature as the explanation of the other class: but then, that the cause explains both classes, gives it a very different claim upon our attention and assent from that which it would have if it explained one class only. The very circumstance that the two explanations coincide, is a most weighty presumption in their favour. It is the testimony of two witnesses in behalf of the hypothesis; and in proportion as these two witnesses are separate and independent, the conviction produced by their agreement is more and more complete. When the explanation of two kinds of phenomena, distinct, and not apparently connected, leads us to the same cause, such a coincidence does give a reality to the cause, which it has not while it merely accounts for those appearances which suggested the supposition.191 This coincidence of propositions inferred from separate classes of facts, is exactly what we noticed in the Novum Organon Renovatum (b. ii. c. 5, sect. 3), as one of the most decisive characteristics of a true theory, under the name of Consilience of Inductions.

That Newton's First Rule of Philosophizing, so understood, authorizes the inferences which he himself made, is really the ground on which they are so firmly believed by philosophers. Thus when the doctrine of a gravity varying inversely as the square of the distance from the body, accounted at the same time for the relations of times and distances in the planetary orbits and for the amount of the moon's deflection from the tangent of her orbit, such a doctrine became most convincing: or again, when the doctrine of the universal gravitation of all parts of matter, which explained so admirably the inequalities of the moon's motions, also gave a satisfactory account of a phenomenon utterly different, the precession of the equinoxes. And of the same kind is the evidence in favour of the undulatory theory of light, when the assumption of the length of an undulation, to which we are led by the colours of thin plates, is found to be identical with that length which explains the phenomena of diffraction; or when the hypothesis of transverse vibrations, suggested by the facts of polarization, explains also the laws of double refraction. When such a convergence of two trains of induction points to the same spot, we can no longer suspect that we are wrong. Such an accumulation of proof really persuades us that we have to do with a vera causa. And if this kind of proof be multiplied;—if we again find other facts of a sort uncontemplated in framing our hypothesis, but yet clearly accounted for when we have adopted the supposition;—we are still further confirmed in our belief; and by such accumulation of proof we may be so far satisfied, as to believe without conceiving it possible to doubt. In this case, when the validity of the opinion adopted by us has been repeatedly confirmed by its sufficiency in unforeseen cases, so that all doubt is removed and forgotten, the192 theoretical cause takes its place among the realities of the world, and becomes a true cause.

11. Newton's Rule then, to avoid mistakes, might be thus expressed: That "we may, provisorily, assume such hypothetical cause as will account for any given class of natural phenomena; but that when two different classes of facts lead us to the same hypothesis, we may hold it to be a true cause." And this Rule will rarely or never mislead us. There are no instances, in which a doctrine recommended in this manner has afterwards been discovered to be false. There have been hypotheses which have explained many phenomena, and kept their ground long, and have afterwards been rejected. But these have been hypotheses which explained only one class of phenomena; and their fall took place when another kind of facts was examined and brought into conflict with the former. Thus the system of eccentrics and epicycles accounted for all the observed motions of the planets, and was the means of expressing and transmitting all astronomical knowledge for two thousand years. But then, how was it overthrown? By considering the distances as well as motions of the heavenly bodies. Here was a second class of facts; and when the system was adjusted so as to agree with the one class, it was at variance with the other. These cycles and epicycles could not be true, because they could not be made a just representation of the facts. But if the measures of distance as well as of position had conspired in pointing out the cycles and epicycles, as the paths of the planets, the paths so determined could not have been otherwise than their real paths; and the epicyclical theory would have been, at least geometrically, true.

12. Of the Second Rule.—Newton's Second Rule directs that "natural events of the same kind are to be referred to the same causes, so far as can be done." Such a precept at first appears to help us but little; for all systems, however little solid, profess to conform

to such a rule. When any theorist undertakes to explain a class of facts, he assigns causes which, according193 to him, will by their natural action, as seen in other cases, produce the effects in question. The events which he accounts for by his hypothetical cause, are, he holds, of the same kind as those which such a cause is known to produce. Kepler, in ascribing the planetary motions to magnetism, Descartes, in explaining them by means of vortices, held that they were referring celestial motions to the causes which give rise to terrestrial motions of the same kind. The question is, Are the effects of the same kind? This once settled, there will be no question about the propriety of assigning them to the same cause. But the difficulty is, to determine when events are of the same kind. Are the motions of the planets of the same kind with the motion of a body moving freely in a curvilinear path, or do they not rather resemble the motion of a floating body swept round by a whirling current? The Newtonian and the Cartesian answered this question differently. How then can we apply this Rule with any advantage?

13. To this we reply, that there is no way of escaping this uncertainty and ambiguity, but by obtaining a clear possession of the ideas which our hypothesis involves, and by reasoning rigorously from them. Newton asserts that the planets move in free paths, acted on by certain forces. The most exact calculation gives the closest agreement of the results of this hypothesis with the facts. Descartes asserts that the planets are carried round by a fluid. The more rigorously the conceptions of force and the laws of motion are applied to this hypothesis, the more signal is its failure in reconciling the facts to one another. Without such calculation, we can come to no decision between the two hypotheses. If the Newtonian hold that the motions of the planets are evidently of the same kind as those of a body describing a curve in free space, and therefore, like that, to be explained by a force acting upon the body; the Cartesian denies that the planets do move in free space. They are, he maintains, immersed in a plenum. It is only when it appears that comets pass through this plenum in all194 directions with no impediment, and that no possible form and motion of its whirlpools can explain the forces and motions which are observed in the solar system, that he is compelled to allow the Newtonian's classification of events of the same kind.

Thus it does not appear that this Rule of Newton can be interpreted in any distinct and positive manner, otherwise than as enjoining that, in the task of induction, we employ clear ideas, rigorous reasoning, and close and fair comparison of the results of the hypothesis with the facts. These are, no doubt, important and fundamental conditions of a just induction; but in this injunction we find no peculiar or technical criterion by which we may satisfy ourselves that we are right, or detect our errors. Still, of such general prudential rules, none can be more wise than one which thus, in the task of connecting facts by means of ideas, recommends that the ideas be clear, the facts, correct, and the chain of reasoning which connects them, without a flaw.

14. Of the Third Rule.—The Third Rule, that "qualities which are observed without exception be held to be universal," as I have already said, seems to be intended to authorize the assertion of gravitation as a universal attribute of matter. We formerly stated, in treating of Mechanical Ideas[221], that this application of such a Rule appears to be a mode of reasoning far from conclusive. The assertion of the universality of any property of bodies must be grounded upon the reason of the case, and not upon any arbitrary maxim. Is it intended by this Rule to prohibit any further examination how far

gravity is an original property of matter, and how far it may be resolved into the result of other agencies? We know perfectly well that this was not Newton's intention; since the cause of gravity was a point which he proposed to himself as a subject of inquiry. It would certainly be very unphilosophical to pretend, by this Rule of Philosophizing, to prejudge the question of such hypotheses as that of Mosotti,195 That gravity is the excess of the electrical attraction over electrical repulsion, and yet to adopt this hypothesis, would be to suppose electrical forces more truly universal than gravity; for according to the hypothesis, gravity, being the inequality of the attraction and repulsion, is only an accidental and partial relation of these forces. Nor would it be allowable to urge this Rule as a reason of assuming that double stars are attracted to each other by a force varying according to the inverse square of the distance; without examining, as Herschel and others have done, the orbits which they really describe. But if the Rule is not available in such cases, what is its real value and authority? and in what cases are they exemplified?

15. In a former work[222], it was shown that the fundamental laws of motion, and the properties of matter which these involve, are, after a full consideration of the subject, unavoidably assumed as universally true. It was further shown, that although our knowledge of these laws and properties be gathered from experience, we are strongly impelled, (some philosophers think, authorized,) to look upon these as not only universally, but necessarily true. It was also stated, that the law of gravitation, though its universality may be deemed probable, does not apparently involve the same necessity as the fundamental laws of motion. But it was pointed out that these are some of the most abstruse and difficult questions of the whole of philosophy; involving the profound, perhaps insoluble, problem of the identity or diversity of Ideas and Things. It cannot, therefore, be deemed philosophical to cut these Gordian knots by peremptory maxims, which encourage us to decide without rendering a reason. Moreover, it appears clear that the reason which is rendered for this Rule by the Newtonians is quite untenable; namely, that we know extension, hardness, and inertia, to be universal qualities of bodies by experience alone, and that we have the same196 evidence of experience for the universality of gravitation. We have already observed that we cannot, with any propriety, say that we find by experience all bodies are extended. This could not be a just assertion, unless we conceive the possibility of our finding the contrary. But who can conceive our finding by experience some bodies which are not extended? It appears, then, that the reason given for the Third Rule of Newton involves a mistake respecting the nature and authority of experience. And the Rule itself cannot be applied without attempting to decide, by the casual limits of observation, questions which necessarily depend upon the relations of ideas.

16. Of the Fourth Rule.—Newton's Fourth Rule is, that "Propositions collected from phenomena by induction, shall be held to be true, notwithstanding contrary hypotheses; but shall be liable to be rendered more accurate, or to have their exceptions pointed out, by additional study of phenomena." This Rule contains little more than a general assertion of the authority of induction, accompanied by Newton's usual protest against hypotheses.

The really valuable part of the Fourth Rule is that which implies that a constant verification, and, if necessary, rectification, of truths discovered by induction, should go on in the scientific world. Even when the law is, or appears to be, most certainly exact and universal, it should be constantly exhibited to us afresh in the form of experience and observation. This is necessary, in order to discover exceptions and modifications if such exist: and if the law be rigorously true, the contemplation of it, as exemplified in the world of phenomena, will best give us that clear apprehension of its bearings which may lead us to see the ground of its truth.

The concluding clause of this Fourth Rule appears, at first, to imply that all inductive propositions are to be considered as merely provisional and limited, and never secure from exception. But to judge thus would be to underrate the stability and generality of scientific truths; for what man of science can suppose that we197 shall hereafter discover exceptions to the universal gravitation of all parts of the solar system? And it is plain that the author did not intend the restriction to be applied so rigorously; for in the Third Rule, as we have just seen, he authorizes us to infer universal properties of matter from observation, and carries the liberty of inductive inference to its full extent. The Third Rule appears to encourage us to assert a law to be universal, even in cases in which it has not been tried; the Fourth Rule seems to warn us that the law may be inaccurate, even in cases in which it has been tried. Nor is either of these suggestions erroneous; but both the universality and the rigorous accuracy of our laws are proved by reference to Ideas rather than to Experience; a truth, which, perhaps, the philosophers of Newton's time were somewhat disposed to overlook.

17. The disposition to ascribe all our knowledge to Experience, appears in Newton and the Newtonians by other indications; for instance, it is seen in their extreme dislike to the ancient expressions by which the principles and causes of phenomena were described, as the occult causes of the Schoolmen, and the forms of the Aristotelians, which had been adopted by Bacon. Newton says[223], that the particles of matter not only possess inertia, but also active principles, as gravity, fermentation, cohesion; he adds, "These principles I consider not as Occult Qualities, supposed to result from the Specific Forms of things, but as General Laws of Nature, by which the things themselves are formed: their truth appearing to us by phenomena, though their causes be not yet discovered. For these are manifest qualities, and their causes only are occult. And the Aristotelians gave the name of occult qualities, not to manifest qualities, but to such qualities only as they supposed to lie hid in bodies, and to the unknown causes of manifest effects: such as would be the causes of gravity, and of magnetick and electrick attractions,198 and of fermentations, if we should suppose that these forces or actions arose from qualities unknown to us, and incapable of being discovered and made manifest. Such occult qualities put a stop to the improvement of Natural Philosophy, and therefore of late years have been rejected. To tell us that every species of things is endowed with an occult specific quality by which it acts and produces manifest effects, is to tell us nothing: but to derive two or three general principles of motion from phenomena, and afterwards to tell us how the properties and actions of all corporeal things follow from these manifest principles, would be a great step in philosophy, though the causes of those principles were not yet discovered: and therefore I scruple not to propose the principles of motion above maintained, they being of very general extent, and leave their causes to be found out."

18. All that is here said is highly philosophical and valuable; but we may observe that the investigation of specific forms in the sense in which some writers had used the phrase, was by no means a frivolous or unmeaning object of inquiry. Bacon and others had used

form as equivalent to law[224]. If we could ascertain that arrangement of the particles of a crystal from which its external crystalline form and other properties arise, this arrangement would be the internal form of the crystal. If the undulatory theory be true, the form of light is transverse vibrations: if the emission theory be maintained, the form of light is particles moving in straight lines, and deflected by various forces. Both the terms, form and law, imply an ideal connexion of sensible phenomena; form supposes mat199ter which is moulded to the form; law supposes objects which are governed by the law. The former term refers more precisely to existences, the latter to occurrences. The latter term is now the more familiar, and is, perhaps, the better metaphor: but the former also contains the essential antithesis which belongs to the subject, and might be used in expressing the same conclusions.

But occult causes, employed in the way in which Newton describes, had certainly been very prejudicial to the progress of knowledge, by stopping inquiry with a mere word. The absurdity of such pretended explanations had not escaped ridicule. The pretended physician in the comedy gives an example of an occult cause or virtue.

Mihi demandatur
A doctissimo Doctore
Quare Opium facit dormire:
Et ego respondeo,
Quia est in eo
Virtus dormitiva,
Cujus natura est sensus assoupire.
19. But the most valuable part of the view presented to us in the quotation just given from Newton is the distinct separation, already noticed as peculiarly brought into prominence by him, of the determination of the laws of phenomena, and the investigation of their causes. The maxim, that the former inquiry must precede the latter, and that if the general laws of facts be discovered, the result is highly valuable, although the causes remain unknown, is extremely important; and had not, I think, ever been so strongly and clearly stated, till Newton both repeatedly promulgated the precept, and added to it the weight of the most striking examples.

We have seen that Newton, along with views the most just and important concerning the nature and methods of science, had something of the tendency, prevalent in his time, to suspect or reject, at least speculatively, all elements of knowledge except observation. This tendency was, however, in him so200 corrected and restrained by his own wonderful sagacity and mathematical habits, that it scarcely led to any opinion which we might not safely adopt. But we must now consider the cases in which this tendency operated in a more unbalanced manner, and led to the assertion of doctrines which, if consistently followed, would destroy the very foundations of all general and certain knowledge.

201

CHAPTER XIX.
Locke and his French Followers.

1. IN the constant opposition and struggle of the schools of philosophy, which consider our Senses and our Ideas respectively, as the principal sources of our knowledge, we have seen that at the period of which we now treat, the tendency was to exalt the external and disparage the internal element. The disposition to ascribe our knowledge to observation alone, had already, in Bacon's time, led him to dwell to a disproportionate degree upon that half of his subject; and had tinged Newton's expressions, though it had not biassed his practice. But this partiality soon assumed a more prominent shape, becoming extreme in Locke, and extravagant in those who professed to follow him.

Indeed Locke appears to owe his popularity and influence as a popular writer mainly to his being one of the first to express, in a plain and unhesitating manner, opinions which had for some time been ripening in the minds of a large portion of the cultivated public. Hobbes had already promulgated the main doctrines which Locke afterwards urged, on the subject of the origin and nature of our knowledge: but in him these doctrines were combined with offensive opinions on points of morals, government, and religion, so that their access to general favour was impeded: and it was to Locke that they were indebted for the extensive influence which they soon after obtained. Locke owed this authority mainly to the intellectual circumstances of the time. Although a writer of great merit, he by no means possesses such metaphysical acuteness or such philosophical largeness of view,202 or such a charm of writing, as must necessarily give him the high place he has held in the literature of Europe. But he came at a period when the reign of Ideas was tottering to its fall. All the most active and ambitious spirits had gone over to the new opinions, and were prepared to follow the fortunes of the Philosophy of Experiment, then in the most prosperous and brilliant condition, and full of still brighter promise. There were, indeed, a few learned and thoughtful men who still remained faithful to the empire of Ideas; partly, it may be, from a too fond attachment to ancient systems; but partly, also, because they knew that there were subjects of vast importance, in which experience did not form the whole foundation of our knowledge. They knew, too, that many of the plausible tenets of the new philosophy were revivals of fallacies which had been discussed and refuted in ancient times. But the advocates of mere experience came on with a vast store of weighty truth among their artillery, and with the energy which the advance usually bestows. The ideal system of philosophy could, for the present, make no effectual resistance; Locke, by putting himself at the head of the assault, became the hero of his day: and his name has been used as the watchword of those who adhere to the philosophy of the senses up to our own times.

2. Locke himself did not assert the exclusive authority of the senses in the extreme unmitigated manner in which some who call themselves his disciples have done. But this is the common lot of the leaders of revolutions, for they are usually bound by some ties of affection and habit to the previous state of things, and would not destroy all traces of that condition: while their followers attend, not to their inconsistent wishes, but to the meaning of the revolution itself; and carry out, to their genuine and complete results, the principles which won the victory, and which have been brought out more sharp from the conflict. Thus Locke himself does not assert that all our ideas are derived from Sensation, but from Sensation and Reflection. But it was easily seen that,203 in this assertion, two very heterogeneous elements were conjoined: that while to pronounce Sensation the origin of ideas, is a clear decided tenet, the acceptance or rejection of which determines the general character of our philosophy; to make the same declaration concerning

Reflection, is in the highest degree vague and ambiguous; since reflection may either be resolved into a mere modification of sensation, as was done by one school, or may mean all that the opposite school opposes to sensation, under the name of Ideas. Hence the clear and strong impression which fastened upon men's minds, and which does in fact represent all the systematic and consistent part of Locke's philosophy, was, that in it all our ideas are represented as derived from Sensation.

3. We need not spend much time in pointing out the inconsistencies into which Locke fell; as all must fall into inconsistencies who recognize no source of knowledge except the senses. Thus he maintains that our Idea of Space is derived from the senses of sight and touch; our Idea of Solidity from the touch alone. Our Notion of Substance is an unknown support of unknown qualities, and is illustrated by the Indian fable of the tortoise which supports the elephant, which supports the world. Our Notion of Power or Cause is in like manner got from the senses. And yet, though these ideas are thus mere fragments of our experience, Locke does not hesitate to ascribe to them necessity and universality when they occur in propositions. Thus he maintains the necessary truth of geometrical properties: he asserts that the resistance arising from solidity is absolutely insurmountable[225]; he conceives that nothing short of Omnipotence can annihilate a particle of matter[226]; and he has no misgivings in arguing upon the axiom that Every thing must have a cause. He does not perceive that, upon his own account of the origin of our knowledge, we can have no right to make any of these assertions. If204 our knowledge of the truths which concern the external world were wholly derived from experience, all that we could venture to say would be,—that geometrical properties of figures are true as far as we have tried them;—that we have seen no example of a solid body being reduced to occupy less space by pressure, or of a material substance annihilated by natural means;—and that wherever we have examined, we have found that every change has had a cause. Experience can never entitle us to declare that what she has not seen is impossible; still less, that things which she can not see are certain. Locke himself intended to throw no doubt upon the certainty of either human or divine knowledge; but his principles, when men discarded the temper in which he applied them, and the checks to their misapplication which he conceived that he had provided, easily led to a very comprehensive skepticism. His doctrines tended to dislodge from their true bases the most indisputable parts of knowledge; as, for example, pure and mixed mathematics. It may well be supposed, therefore, that they shook the foundations of many other parts of knowledge in the minds of common thinkers.

It was not long before these consequences of the overthrow of ideas showed themselves in the speculative world. I have already in a previous work[227] mentioned Hume's skeptical inferences from Locke's maxim, that we have no ideas except those which we acquire by experience; and the doctrines set up in opposition to this by the metaphysicians of Germany. I might trace the progress of the sensational opinions in Britain till the reaction took place here also: but they were so much more clearly and decidedly followed out in France, that I shall pursue their history in that country.

4. The French Followers of Locke, Condillac, &c.—Most of the French writers who adopted Locke's leading doctrines, rejected the "Reflection," which formed205 an anomalous part of his philosophy, and declared that Sensation alone was the source of ideas. Among these writers, Condillac was the most distinguished. He expressed the

leading tenet of their school in a clear and pointed manner by saying that "All ideas are transformed sensations." We have already considered this phrase[228], and need not here dwell upon it.

Opinions such as these tend to annihilate, as we have seen, one of the two co-ordinate elements of our knowledge. Yet they were far from being so prejudicial to the progress of science, or even of the philosophy of science, as might have been anticipated. One reason of this was, that they were practically corrected, especially among the cultivators of Natural Philosophy, by the study of mathematics; for that study did really supply all that was requisite on the ideal side of science, so far as the ideas of space, time, and number, were concerned, and partly also with regard to the idea of cause and some others. And the methods of discovery, though the philosophy of them made no material advance, were practically employed with so much activity, and in so many various subjects, that a certain kind of prudence and skill in this employment was very widely diffused.

5. Importance of Language.—In one respect this school of metaphysicians rendered a very valuable service to the philosophy of science. They brought into prominent notice the great importance of words and terms in the formation and progress of knowledge, and pointed out that the office of language is not only to convey and preserve our thoughts, but to perform the analysis in which reasoning consists. They were led to this train of speculation, in a great measure, by taking pure mathematical science as their standard example of substantial knowledge. Condillac, rejecting, as we have said, almost all those ideas on which universal and demonstrable truths must be based, was still not at all disposed to question the reality of206 human knowledge; but was, on the contrary, a zealous admirer of the evidence and connexion which appear in those sciences which have the ideas of space and number for their foundation, especially the latter. He looked for the grounds of the certainty and reality of the knowledge which these sciences contain; and found them, as he conceived, in the nature of the language which they employ. The Signs which are used in arithmetic and algebra enable us to keep steadily in view the identity of the same quantity under all the forms which, by composition and decomposition, it may be made to assume; and these Signs also not only express the operations which are performed, but suggest the extension of the operations according to analogy. Algebra, according to him, is only a very perfect language; and language answers its purpose of leading us to truth, by possessing the characteristics of algebra. Words are the symbols of certain groups of impressions or facts; they are so selected and applied as to exhibit the analogies which prevail among these facts; and these analogies are the truths of which our knowledge consists. "Every language is an analytical method; every analytical method is a language[229];" these were the truths "alike new and simple," as he held, which he conceived that he had demonstrated. "The art of speaking, the art of writing, the art of reasoning, the art of thinking, are only, at bottom, one and the same art[230]." Each of these operations consists in a succession of analytical operations; and words are the marks by which we are able to fix our minds upon the steps of this analysis.

6. The analysis of our impressions and notions does in reality lead to truth, not only in virtue of the identity of the whole with its parts, as Condillac held, but also in virtue of certain Ideas which govern the synthesis of our sensations, and which contain the elements of universal truths, as we have all along endeavoured to show. But although

Condillac overlooked or rejected this doctrine, the importance of words, as207 marking the successive steps of this synthesis and analysis, is not less than he represented it to be. Every truth, once established by induction from facts, when it is become familiar under a brief and precise form of expression, becomes itself a fact; and is capable of being employed, along with other facts of a like kind, as the materials of fresh inductions. In this successive process, the term, like the cord of a fagot, both binds together the facts which it includes, and makes it possible to manage the assemblage as a single thing. On occasion of most discoveries in science, the selection of a technical term is an essential part of the proceeding. In the History of Science, we have had numerous opportunities of remarking this; and the List of technical terms given as an Index to that work, refers us, by almost every word, to one such occasion. And these terms, which thus have had so large a share in the formation of science, and which constitute its language, do also offer the means of analyzing its truths, each into its constituent truths; and these into facts more special, till the original foundations of our most general propositions are clearly exhibited. The relations of general and particular truths are most evidently represented by the Inductive Tables given in Book II. of the Novum Organon Renovatum. But each step in each of these Tables has its proper form of expression, familiar among the cultivators of science; and the analysis which our Tables display, is commonly performed in men's minds, when it becomes necessary, by fixing the attention successively upon a series of words, not upon the lines of a Table. Language offers to the mind such a scale or ladder as the Table offers to the eye; and since such Tables present to us, as we have said, the Logic of Induction, that is, the formal conditions of the soundness of our reasoning from facts, we may with propriety say that a just analysis of the meaning of words is an essential portion of Inductive Logic.

In saying this, we must not forget that a decomposition of general truths into ideas, as well as into facts, belongs to our philosophy; but the point we208 have here to remark, is the essential importance of words to the latter of these processes. And this point had not ever had its due weight assigned to it till the time of Condillac and other followers of Locke, who pursued their speculations in the spirit I have just described. The doctrine of the importance of terms is the most considerable addition to the philosophy of science which has been made since the time of Bacon[231].

7. The French Encyclopedists.—The French Encyclopédie, published in 1751, of which Diderot and Dalembert were the editors, may be considered as representing the leading characters of European philosophy during the greater part of the eighteenth century. The writers in this work belong for the most part to the school of Locke and Condillac; and we may make a few remarks upon them, in order to bring into view one or two points in addition to what we have already said of that school. The Discours Préliminaire, written by Dalembert, is celebrated as containing a view of the origin of our knowledge, and the connexion and classification of the sciences.

A tendency of the speculations of the Encyclopedists, as of the School of Locke in general, is to reject all ideal principles of connexion among facts, as something which experience, the only source of true knowledge, does not give. Hence all certain knowledge consists only in the recognition of the same thing under different aspects, or different forms of expression. Axioms are not the result of an original relation of ideas, but of the use, or it may be the abuse[232], of words. In like manner, the propositions of Geometry are a series of modifications,—of distortions, so to speak,—of one original truth; much as if the proposition were stated in the successive forms of expression presented by a language which was constantly growing more and209 more artificial. Several of the sciences which rest upon physical principles, that is, (says the writer,) truths of experience or simple hypotheses, have only an experimental or hypothetical certainty. Impenetrability added to the idea of extent is a mystery in addition: the nature of motion is a riddle for philosophers: the metaphysical principle of the laws of percussion is equally concealed from them. The more profoundly they study the idea of matter and of the properties which represent it, the more obscure this idea becomes; the more completely does it escape them.

8. This is a very common style of reflection, even down to our own times. I have endeavoured to show that concerning the Fundamental Ideas of space, of force and resistance, of substance, external quality, and the like, we know enough to make these Ideas the grounds of certain and universal truths;—enough to supply us with axioms from which we can demonstratively reason. If men wish for any other knowledge of the nature of matter than that which ideas, and facts conformable to ideas, give them, undoubtedly their desire will be frustrated, and they will be left in a mysterious vacancy; for it does not appear how such knowledge as they ask for could be knowledge at all. But in reality, this complaint of our ignorance of the real nature of things proceeds from the rejection of ideas, and the assumption of the senses alone as the ground of knowledge. "Observation and calculation are the only sources of truth:" this is the motto of the school of which we now speak. And its import amounts to this:—that they reject all ideas except the idea of number, and recognize the modifications which parts undergo by addition and subtraction as the only modes in which true propositions are generated. The laws of nature are assemblages of facts: the truths of science are assertions of the identity of things which are the same. "By the avowal of almost all philosophers," says a writer of this school[233], "the most sublime210 truths, when once simplified and reduced to their lowest terms, are converted into facts, and thenceforth present to the mind only this proposition; the white is white, the black is black."

These statements are true in what they positively assert, but they involve error in the denial which by implication they convey. It is true that observation and demonstration are the only sources of scientific truth; but then, demonstration may be founded on other grounds besides the elementary properties of number. It is true that the theory of gravitation is but the assertion of a general fact; but this is so, not because a sound theory does not involve ideas, but because our apprehension of a fact does.

9. Another characteristic indication of the temper of the Encyclopedists and of the age to which they belong, is the importance by them assigned to those practical Arts which minister to man's comfort and convenience. Not only, in the body of the Encyclopedia, are the Mechanical Arts placed side by side with the Sciences, and treated at great length; but in the Preliminary Discourse, the preference assigned to the liberal over the mechanical Arts is treated as a prejudice[234], and the value of science is spoken of as measured by its utility. "The discovery of the Mariner's Compass is not less advantageous to the human race than the explanation of its properties would be to physics.—Why should we not esteem those to whom we owe the fusee and the escapement of watches as much as the inventors of Algebra?" And in the classification of

sciences which accompanies the Discourse, the labours of artisans of all kinds have a place.

This classification of the various branches of science contained in the Dissertation is often spoken of. It has for its basis the classification proposed by Bacon, in which the parts of human knowledge are arranged according to the faculties of the mind in which they originate; and these faculties are taken, both by Bacon and by Dalembert, as Memory, Reason, and Imagi211nation. The insufficiency of Bacon's arrangement as a scientific classification is so glaring, that the adoption of it, with only superficial modifications, at the period of the Encyclopedia, is a remarkable proof of the want of original thought and real philosophy at the time of which we speak.

10. We need not trace further the opinion which derives all our knowledge from the senses in its application to the philosophy of Science. Its declared aim is to reduce all knowledge to the knowledge of Facts; and it rejects all inquiries which involve the Idea of Cause, and similar Ideas, describing them as "metaphysical," or in some other damnatory way. It professes, indeed, to discard all Ideas; but, as we have long ago seen, some Ideas or other are inevitably included even in the simplest Facts. Accordingly the speculations of this school are compelled to retain the relations of Position, Succession, Number and Resemblance, which are rigorously ideal relations. The philosophy of Sensation, in order to be consistent, ought to reject these Ideas along with the rest, and to deny altogether the possibility of general knowledge.

When the opinions of the Sensational School had gone to an extreme length, a Reaction naturally began to take place in men's minds. Such have been the alternations of opinion, from the earliest ages of human speculation. Man may perhaps have existed in an original condition in which he was only aware of the impressions of Sense; but his first attempts to analyse his perceptions brought under his notice Ideas as a separate element, essential to the existence of knowledge. Ideas were thenceforth almost the sole subject of the study of philosophers; of Plato and his disciples, professedly; of Aristotle, and still more of the followers and commentators of Aristotle, practically. And this continued till the time of Galileo, when the authority of the Senses again began to be asserted; for it was shown by the great discoveries which were then made, that the Senses had at least some share in the promotion of knowledge. As discoveries more numerous and more striking were supplied by Obser212vation, the world gradually passed over to the opinion that the share which had been ascribed to Ideas in the formation of real knowledge was altogether a delusion, and that Sensation alone was true. But when this was asserted as a general doctrine, both its manifest falsity and its alarming consequences roused men's minds, and made them recoil from the extreme point to which they were approaching. Philosophy again oscillated back towards Ideas; and over a great part of Europe, in the clearest and most comprehensive minds, this regression from the dogmas of the Sensational School is at present the prevailing movement. We shall conclude our review by noticing a few indications of this state of things.

213

CHAPTER XX.
The Reaction against the Sensational School.

1. WHEN Locke's Essay appeared, it was easily seen that its tendency was to urge, in a much more rigorous sense than had previously been usual, the ancient maxim of Aristotle, adopted by the schoolmen of the middle ages, that "nothing exists in the intellect but what has entered by the senses." Leibnitz expressed in a pointed manner the limitation with which this doctrine had always been understood. "Nihil est in intellectu quod non prius fuerit in sensu;—nempe," he added, "nisi intellectus ipse." To this it has been objected[235], that we cannot say that the intellect is in the intellect. But this remark is obviously frivolous; for the faculties of the understanding (which are what the argument against the Sensational School requires us to reserve) may be said to be in the understanding, with as much justice as we may assert there are in it the impressions derived from sense. And when we take account of these faculties, and of the Ideas to which, by their operation, we necessarily subordinate our apprehension of phenomena, we are led to a refutation of the philosophy which makes phenomena, unconnected by Ideas, the source of all knowledge. The succeeding opponents of the Lockian school insisted upon and developed in various ways this remark of Leibnitz, or some equivalent view.

2. It was by inquiries into the foundations of Morals that English philosophers were led to question the truth of Locke's theory. Dr. Price, in his Review214 of the Principal Questions in Morals, first published in 1757, maintained that we cannot with propriety assert all our ideas to be derived from sensation and reflection. He pointed out, very steadily, the other source. "The power, I assert, that understands, or the faculty within us that discerns truth, and that compares all the objects of thought and judges of them, is a spring of new ideas[236]." And he exhibits the antithesis in various forms. "Were not sense and knowledge entirely different, we should rest satisfied with sensible impressions, such as light, colours and sounds, and inquire no further about them, at least when the impressions are strong and vigorous: whereas, on the contrary, we necessarily desire some further acquaintance with them, and can never be satisfied till we have subjected them to the survey of reason. Sense presents particular forms to the mind, but cannot rise to any general ideas. It is the intellect that examines and compares the presented forms, that rises above individuals to universal and abstract ideas; and thus looks downward upon objects, takes in at one view an infinity of particulars, and is capable of discovering general truths. Sense sees only the outside of things, reason acquaints itself with their natures. Sensation is only a mode of feeling in the mind; but knowledge implies an active and vital energy in the mind[237]."

3. The necessity of refuting Hume's inferences from the mere sensation system led other writers to limit, in various ways, their assent to Locke. Especially was this the case with a number of intelligent metaphysicians in Scotland, as Reid, Beattie, Dugald Stewart, and Thomas Brown. Thus Reid asserts[238], "that the account which Mr. Locke himself gives of the Idea of Power cannot be reconciled to his favourite doctrine, that all our simple ideas have their origin from sensation or reflection." Reid remarks, that our memory and our reasoning power come in for a share in the215 origin of this idea: and in speaking of reasoning, he obviously assumes the axiom that every event must have a cause. By succeeding writers of this school, the assumption of the fundamental principles, to which our nature in such cases irresistibly directs us, is more clearly pointed out. Thus Stewart defends the form of expression used by Price[239]: "A variety of intuitive

judgments might be mentioned, involving simple ideas, which it is impossible to trace to any origin but to the power which enables us to form these judgments. Thus it is surely an intuitive truth that the sensations of which I am conscious, and all those I remember, belong to one and the same being, which I call myself. Here is an intuitive judgment involving the simple idea of Identity. In like manner, the changes which I perceive in the universe impress me with a conviction that some cause must have operated to produce them. Here is an intuitive judgment involving the simple Idea of Causation. When we consider the adjacent angles made by a straight line standing upon another, and perceive that their sum is equal to two right angles, the judgment we form involves a simple idea of Equality. To say, therefore, that the Reason or the Understanding is a source of new ideas, is not so exceptionable a mode of speaking as has been sometimes supposed. According to Locke, Sense furnishes our ideas, and Reason perceives their agreements and disagreements. But the truth is, that these agreements and disagreements are in many instances, simple ideas, of which no analysis can be given; and of which the origin must therefore be referred to Reason, according to Locke's own doctrine." This view, according to which the Reason or Understanding is the source of certain simple ideas, such as Identity, Causation, Equality, which ideas are necessarily involved in the intuitive judgments which we form, when we recognize fundamental truths of science, approaches very near in effect to the doctrine which in several works I have presented, of Fundamental Ideas belonging to216 each science, and manifesting themselves in the axioms of the science. It may be observed, however, that by attempting to enumerate these ideas and axioms, so as to lay the foundations of the whole body of physical science, and by endeavouring, as far as possible, to simplify and connect each group of such Ideas, I have at least given a more systematic form to this doctrine. I have, moreover, traced it into many consequences to which it necessarily leads, but which do not appear to have been contemplated by the metaphysicians of the Scotch school. But I gladly acknowledge my obligations to the writers of that school; and I trust that in the near agreement of my views on such points with theirs, there is ground for believing the system of philosophy which I have presented, to be that to which the minds of thoughtful men, who have meditated on such subjects, are generally tending.

4. As a further instance that such a tendency is at work, I may make a quotation from an eminent English philosophical writer of another school. "If you will be at the pains," says Archbishop Whately[240], "carefully to analyze the simplest description you hear of any transaction or state of things, you will find that the process which almost invariably takes place is, in logical language, this: that each individual has in his mind certain major premises or principles relative to the subject in question;—that observation of what actually presents itself to the senses, supplies minor premises; and that the statement given (and which is reported as a thing experienced) consists, in fact, of the conclusions drawn from the combinations of these premises." The major premises here spoken of are the Fundamental Ideas, and the Axioms and Propositions to which they lead; and whatever is regarded as a fact of observation is necessarily a conclusion in which these propositions are assumed; for these contain, as we have said, the conditions of our experience.217 Our experience conforms to these axioms and their consequences, whether or not the connexion be stated in a logical manner, by means of premises and a conclusion.

5. The same persuasion is also suggested by the course which the study of metaphysics has taken of late years in France. In that country, as we have seen, the Sensational System, which was considered as the necessary consequence of the revolution begun by Locke, obtained a more complete ascendancy than it did in England; and in that country too, the reaction, among metaphysical and moral writers, when its time came, was more decided and rapid than it was among Locke's own countrymen. It would appear that M. Laromiguière was one of the first to give expression to this feeling, of the necessity of a modification of the sensational philosophy. He began by professing himself the disciple of Condillac, even while he was almost unconsciously subverting the fundamental principles of that writer. And thus, as M. Cousin justly observes[241], his opinions had the more powerful effect from being presented, not as thwarting and contradicting, but as sharing and following out the spirit of his age. M. Laromiguière's work, entitled Essai sur les Facultés de l'Ame, consists of lectures given to the Faculty of Letters of the Academy of Paris, in the years 1811, 1812 and 1813. In the views which these lectures present, there is much which the author has in common with Condillac. But he is led by his investigation to assert[242], that it is not true that sensation is the sole fundamental element of our thoughts and our understanding. Attention also is requisite: and here we have an element of quite another kind. For sensation is passive; attention is active. Attention does not spring out of sensation; the passive principle is not the reason of the active principle. Activity and passivity are two facts entirely different. Nor can this activity be defined or derived; being, as the author218 says, a fundamental idea. The distinction is manifest by its own nature; and we may find evidence of it in the very forms of language. To look is more than to see; to hearken is more than to hear. The French language marks this distinction with respect to other senses also. "On voit, et l'on regarde; on entend, et l'on écoute; on sent, et l'on flaire; on goûte, et l'on savoure." And thus the mere sensation, or capacity of feeling, is only the occasion on which the attention is exercised; while the attention is the foundation of all the operations of the understanding.

The reader of my works will have seen how much I have insisted upon the activity of the mind, as the necessary basis of all knowledge. In all observation and experience, the mind is active, and by its activity apprehends all sensations in subordination to its own ideas; and thus it becomes capable of collecting knowledge from phenomena, since ideas involve general relations and connexions, which sensations of themselves cannot involve. And thus we see that, in this respect also, our philosophy stands at that point to which the speculations of the most reflecting men have of late constantly been verging.

6. M. Cousin himself, from whom we have quoted the above account of Laromiguière, shares in this tendency, and has argued very energetically and successfully against the doctrines of the Sensational School. He has made it his office once more to bring into notice among his countrymen, the doctrine of ideas as the sources of knowledge; and has revived the study of Plato, who may still be considered as one of the great leaders of the ideal school. But the larger portion of M. Cousin's works refers to questions out of the reach of our present review, and it would be unsuitable to dwell longer upon them in this place.

7. We turn to speculations more closely connected with our present subject. M. Ampère, a French man of science, well entitled by his extensive knowledge, and large and profound views, to deal with the philo219sophy of the sciences, published in 1834, his

Essai sur la Philosophie des Sciences, ou Exposition analytique d'une Classification Naturelle de toutes les Connaissances Humaines. In this remarkable work we see strong evidence of the progress of the reaction against the system which derives our knowledge from sensation only. The author starts from a maxim, that in classing the sciences, we must not only regard the nature of the objects about which each science is concerned, but also the point of view under which it considers them: that is, the ideas which each science involves. M. Ampère also gives briefly his views of the intellectual constitution of man; a subject on which he had long and sedulously employed his thoughts; and these views are far from belonging to the Sensational School. Human thought, he says, is composed of phenomena and of conceptions. Phenomena are external, or sensitive; and internal, or active. Conceptions are of four kinds; primitive, as space and motion, duration and cause; objective, as our idea of matter and substance; onomatic, or those which we associate with the general terms which language presents to us; and explicative, by which we ascend to causes after a comparative study of phenomena. He teaches further, that in deriving ideas from sensation, the mind is not passive; but exerts an action which, when voluntary, is called attention, but when it is, as it often is, involuntary, may be termed reaction.

I shall not dwell upon the examination of these opinions[243]; but I may remark, that both in the recognition of conceptions as an original and essential element of the mind, and in giving a prominent place to the active function of the mind, in the origin of our knowledge, this view approaches to that which I have presented in preceding works; although undoubtedly with considerable differences.

8. The classification of the sciences which M.220 Ampère proposes, is founded upon a consideration of the sciences themselves; and is, the author conceives, in accordance with the conditions of natural classifications, as exhibited in Botany and other sciences. It is of a more symmetrical kind, and exhibits more steps of subordination, than that to which I have been led; it includes also practical Art as well as theoretical Science; and it is extended to moral and political as well as physical Sciences. It will not be necessary for me here to examine it in detail: but I may remark, that it is throughout a dichotomous division, each higher member being subdivided into two lower ones, and so on. In this way, M. Ampère obtains sciences of the First Order, each of which is divided into two sciences of the Second, and four of the Third Order. Thus Mechanics is divided into Cinematics, Statics, Dynamics, and Molecular Mechanics; Physics is divided into Experimental Physics, Chemistry, Stereometry, and Atomology; Geology is divided into Physical Geography, Mineralogy, Geonomy, and Theory of the Earth. Without here criticizing these divisions or their principle, I may observe that Cinematics, the doctrine of motion without reference to the force which produces it, is a portion of knowledge which our investigation has led us also to see the necessity of erecting into a separate science; and which we have termed Pure Mechanism. Of the divisions of Geology, Physical Geography, especially as explained by M. Ampère, is certainly a part of the subject, both important and tolerably distinct from the rest. Geonomy contains what we have termed in the History, Descriptive Geology;—the exhibition of the facts separate from the inquiry into their causes; while our Physical Geology agrees with M. Ampère's Theory of the Earth. Mineralogy appears to be placed by him in a different place from that which it occupies in our scheme: but in fact, he uses the term for a different science; he applies it to the classification not of simple minerals, but of rocks, which is a science auxiliary to geology, and which has sometimes been called Petralogy. What we have termed

Mineralogy, M. Ampère unites with221 Chemistry. "It belongs," he says[244], "to Chemistry, and not to Mineralogy, to inquire how many atoms of silicium and of oxygen compose silica; to tell us that its primitive form is a rhombohedron of certain angles, that it is called quartz, &c.; leaving, on one hand, to Molecular Geometry the task of explaining the different secondary forms which may result from the primitive form; and on the other hand, leaving to Mineralogy the office of describing the different varieties of quartz, and the rocks in which they occur, according as the quartz is crystallized, transparent, coloured, amorphous, solid, or in sand." But we may remark, that by adopting this arrangement, we separate from Mineralogy almost all the knowledge, and absolutely all the general knowledge, which books professing to treat of that science have usually contained. The consideration of Mineralogical Classifications, which, as may be seen in the History of Science, is so curious and instructive, is forced into the domain of Chemistry, although many of the persons who figure in it were not at all properly chemists. And we lose, in this way, the advantage of that peculiar office which, in our arrangement, Mineralogy fills; of forming a rigorous transition from the sciences of classification to those which consider the mathematical properties of bodies; and connecting the external characters and the internal constitution of bodies by means of a system of important general truths. I conceive, therefore, that our disposition of this science, and our mode of applying the name, are far more convenient than those of M. Ampère.

9. We have seen the reaction against the pure sensational doctrines operating very powerfully in England and in France. But it was in Germany that these doctrines were most decidedly rejected; and systems in extreme opposition to these put forth with confidence, and received with applause. Of the authors who gave this impulse to opinions in that country, Kant222 was the first, and by far the most important. I have in the History of Ideas (b. iii. c. 3), endeavoured to explain how he was aroused, by the skepticism of Hume, to examine wherein the fallacy lay which appeared to invalidate all reasonings from effect to cause; and how this inquiry terminated in a conviction that the foundations of our reasonings on this and similar points were to be sought in the mind, and not in the phenomena;—in the subject, and not in the object. The revolution in the customary mode of contemplating human knowledge which Kant's opinions involved, was most complete. He himself, with no small justice, compares[245] it with the change produced by Copernicus's theory of the solar system. "Hitherto," he says, "men have assumed that all our knowledge must be regulated by the objects of it; yet all attempts to make out anything concerning objects à priori by means of our conceptions," (as for instance their geometrical properties) "must, on this foundation, be unavailing. Let us then try whether we cannot make out something more in the problems of metaphysics, by assuming that objects must be regulated by our knowledge, since this agrees better with that supposition, which we are prompted to make, that we can know something of them à priori. This thought is like that of Copernicus, who, when he found that nothing was to be made of the phenomena of the heavens so long as everything was supposed to turn about the spectator, tried whether the matter might not be better explained if he made the spectator turn, and left the stars at rest. We may make the same essay in metaphysics, as to what concerns our intuitive knowledge respecting objects. If our apprehension of objects must be regulated by the properties of the objects, I cannot comprehend how we can possibly know anything about them à priori. But if the object, as apprehended by us, be regulated by the constitution of our faculties of apprehension, I can readily

113

conceive223 this possibility." From this he infers that our experience must be regulated by our conceptions.

10. This view of the nature of knowledge soon superseded entirely the doctrines of the Sensational School among the metaphysicians of Germany. These philosophers did not gradually modify and reject the dogmas of Locke and Condillac, as was done in England and France[246]; nor did they endeavour to ascertain the extent of the empire of Ideas by a careful survey of its several provinces, as we have been doing in this series of works. The German metaphysicians saw at once that Ideas and Things, the Subjective and the Objective elements of our knowledge, were, by Kant's system, brought into opposition and correlation, as equally real and equally indispensable. Seeing this, they rushed at once to the highest and most difficult problem of philosophy,—to determine what this correlation is;—to discover how Ideas and Things are at the same time opposite and identical;—how the world, while it is distinct from and independent of us, is yet, as an object of our knowledge, governed by the conditions of our thoughts. The attempts to solve this problem, taken in the widest sense, including the forms which it assumes in Morals, Politics, the Arts, and Religion, as well as in the Material Sciences, have, since that time, occupied the most profound speculators of Germany; and have given rise to a number of systems, which, rapidly succeeding each other, have, each in its day, been looked upon as a complete solution of the problem. To trace the characters of these various systems, does not belong to the business of the present chapter: my task is ended when I have shown, as I have now done, how the progress of thought in the philosophical world, followed from the earliest up to the present time, has224 led to that recognition of the co-existence and joint necessity of the two opposite elements of our knowledge; and when I have pointed out processes adapted to the extension of our knowledge, which a true view of its nature has suggested or may suggest.

The latter portion of this task occupies the Third Book of the Novum Organon Renovatum. With regard to the recent succession of German systems of philosophy, I shall add something in a subsequent chapter: and I shall also venture to trace further than I have yet done, the bearing of the philosophy of science upon the theological view of the universe and the moral and religious condition of man.

225

CHAPTER XXI.
Further Advance of the Sensational School.
M. Auguste Comte.

I shall now take the liberty of noticing the views published by a contemporary writer; not that it forms part of my design to offer any criticism upon the writings of all those who have treated of those subjects on which we are now employed; but because we can more distinctly in this manner point out the contrasts and ultimate tendencies of the several systems of opinion which have come under our survey: and since from among these systems we have endeavoured to extract and secure the portion of truth which remains in each, and to reject the rest, we are led to point out the errors on which our attention is thus fixed, in recent as well as older writers.

M. Auguste Comte published in 1830 the first, and in 1835 the second volume of his Cours de Philosophie Positive; of which the aim is not much different from that of the present work, since as he states (p. viii.) such a title as the Philosophy of the Sciences would describe a part of his object, and would be inappropriate only by excluding that portion (not yet published) which refers to speculations concerning social relations.

1. M. Comte on Three States of Science.—By employing the term Philosophie Positive, he wishes to distinguish the philosophy involved in the present state of our sciences from the previous forms of human knowledge. For according to him, each branch of knowledge passes, in the course of man's history, through three different states; it is first theological, then metaphysical, then positive. By the latter term226 he implies a state which includes nothing but general representations of facts;—phenomena arranged according to relations of succession and resemblance. This "positive philosophy" rejects all inquiry after causes, which inquiry he holds to be void of sense[247] and inaccessible. All such conceptions belong to the "metaphysical" state of science which deals with abstract forces, real entities, and the like. Still more completely does he reject, as altogether antiquated and absurd, the "theological" view of phenomena. Indeed he conceives[248] that any one's own consciousness of what passes within himself is sufficient to convince him of the truth of the law of the three phases through which knowledge must pass. "Does not each of us," he says, "in contemplating his own history, recollect that he has been successively a theologian in his infancy, a metaphysician in his youth, and a physicist in his ripe age? This may easily be verified for all men who are up to the level of their time."

It is plain from such statements, and from the whole course of his work, that M. Comte holds, in their most rigorous form, the doctrines to which the speculations of Locke and his successors led; and which tended, as we have seen, to the exclusion of all ideas except those of number and resemblance. As M. Comte refuses to admit into his philosophy the fundamental idea of Cause, he of course excludes most of the other ideas, which are, as we endeavoured to show, the foundations of science; such as the ideas of Media by which secondary qualities are made known to us; the ideas of Chemical Attraction, of Polar Forces, and the like. He would reduce all science to the mere expression of laws of phenomena, expressed in formulæ of space, time, and number; and would condemn as unmeaning, and as belonging to an obsolete state of science, all endeavours to determine the causes of phenomena, or even to refer them to any of the other ideas just mentioned.

227

2. M. Comte rejects the Search of Causes.—In a previous work[249] I have shown, I trust decisively, that it is the genuine office of science to inquire into the causes as well as the laws of phenomena;—that such an inquiry cannot be avoided; and that it has been the source of almost all the science we possess. I need not here repeat the arguments there urged; but I may make a remark or two upon M. Comte's hypothesis, that all science is first "metaphysical" and then "positive;" since it is in virtue of this hypothesis that he rejects the investigation of causes, as worthy only of the infancy of science. All discussions concerning ideas, M. Comte would condemn as "metaphysical," and would consider as mere preludes to positive philosophy. Now I venture to assert, on the

contrary, that discussions concerning ideas, and real discoveries, have in every science gone hand in hand. There is no science in which the pretended order of things can be pointed out. There is no science in which the discoveries of the laws of phenomena, when once begun, have been carried on independently of discussions concerning ideas. There is no science in which the expression of the laws of phenomena can at this time dispense with ideas which have acquired their place in science in virtue of metaphysical considerations. There is no science in which the most active disquisitions concerning ideas did not come after, not before, the first discovery of laws of phenomena. In Astronomy, the discovery of the phenomenal laws of the epicyclical motions of the heavens led to assumptions of the metaphysical principle of equable circular motions: Kepler's discoveries would never have been made but for his metaphysical notions. These discoveries of the laws of phenomena did not lead immediately to Newton's theory, because a century of metaphysical discussions was requisite as a preparation. Newton then discovered, not merely a law of phenomena, but a cause; and therefore he was the228 greatest of discoverers. The same is the case in Optics; the ancients possessed some share of our knowledge of facts; but meddled little with the metaphysical reasonings of the subject. In modern times when men began to inquire into the nature of light, they soon extended their knowledge of its laws. When this series of discoveries had come to a pause, a new series of brilliant discoveries of laws of phenomena went on, inseparably connected with a new series of views of the nature and cause of light. In like manner, the most modern discoveries in chemistry involve indispensably the idea of polar forces. The metaphysics (in M. Comte's sense) of each subject advances in a parallel line with the knowledge of physical laws. The Explication of Conceptions must go on, as we have already shown, at the same rate as the Colligation of Facts.

M. Comte will say[250] that Newton's discovery of gravitation only consists in exhibiting the astronomical phenomena of the universe as one single fact under different points of view. But this fact involves the idea of force, that is, of cause. And that this idea is not a mere modification of the ideas of time and space, we have shown: if it were so, how could it lead to the axiom that attraction is mutual, an indispensable part of the Newtonian theory? M. Comte says[251] that we do not know what attraction is, since we can only define it by identical phrases: but this is just as true of space, or time, or motion; and is in fact exactly the characteristic of a fundamental idea. We do not obtain such ideas from definitions, but we possess them not the less truly because we cannot define them.

That M. Comte's hypothesis is historically false, is obvious by such examples as I have mentioned. Metaphysical discussions have been essential steps in the progress of each science. If we arbitrarily reject all these portions of scientific history as useless trifling,229 belonging to the first rude attempts at knowledge, we shall not only distort the progress of things, but pervert the plainest facts. Of this we have an example in M. Comte's account of Kepler's mechanical speculations. We have seen, in the History of Physical Astronomy, that Kepler's second law, (that the planets describe areas about the sun proportional to the times,) was proved by him, by means of calculations founded on the observations of Tycho; but that the mechanical reason of it was not assigned till a later period, when it appeared as the first proposition of Newton's Principia. It is plain from the writings of Kepler, that it was impossible for him to show how this law resulted from the forces which were in action; since the forces which he considered were not those tending to the centre, which really determine the property in question, but forces exerted by the sun in the direction of the planet's motion, without which forces Kepler conceived that the motion could not go on. In short, the state of mechanical science in Kepler's time was such that no demonstration of the law could be given. The terms in which such a demonstration must be expressed had not at that time acquired a precise significance; and it was in virtue of many subsequent metaphysical discussions (as M. Comte would term them) that these terms became capable of expressing sound mechanical reasoning. Kepler did indeed pretend to assign what he called a "physical proof" of his law, depending upon this, that the sun's force is less at greater distances; a condition which does not at all influence the result. Thus Kepler's reason for his law proves nothing but the confusion of thought in which he was involved on such subjects. Yet M. Comte assigns to Kepler the credit of having proved this law by sound mechanical reasoning, as well as established it as a matter of fact[252]. "This discovery by Kepler,"230 he adds, "is the more remarkable, inasmuch as it occurred before the science of dynamics had really been created by Galileo." We may remark that inasmuch as M. Comte perceived this incongruity in the facts as he stated them, it is the more remarkable that he did not examine them more carefully.

3. Causes in Physics.—The condemnation of the inquiry into causes which is conveyed in M. Comte's notion of the three stages of Science, he again expresses more in detail, in stating[253] what he calls his Fundamental theory of hypotheses. This "theory" is, that we may employ hypotheses in our natural philosophy, but these hypotheses must always be such as admit of a positive verification. We must have no suppositions concerning the agents by which effects are produced. All such suppositions have an anti-scientific character, and can only impede the real progress of physics. There can be no use in the ethers and imaginary fluids to which some persons refer the phenomena of heat, light, electricity and magnetism. And in agreement with this doctrine, M. Comte in his account[254] of the231 Science of Optics, condemns, as utterly unphilosophical and absurd, both the theory of emission and that of undulation.

To this we reply, that theory of one kind or other is indispensable to the expression of the phenomena; and that when the laws are expressed, and apparently explained, by means of a theory, to forbid us to inquire whether it be really true or false, is a pedantic and capricious limitation of our knowledge, to which the intellect of man neither can nor should submit. If any one holds the adoption of one or other of these theories to be indifferent, let him express the laws of phenomena of diffraction in terms of the theory of emission[255]. If any one rejects the doctrine of undulation, let him point out some other way of connecting double refraction with polarization. And surely no man of science will contend that the beautiful branch of science which refers to that connexion is not a portion of our positive knowledge.

M. Comte's contempt for the speculations of the undulationists seems to have prevented his acquainting himself with their reasonings, and even with the laws of phenomena on which they have reasoned, although these form by far the most striking and beautiful addition which Science has received in modern times. He adduces, as an insuperable objection to the undulatory theory, a difficulty which is fully removed by calculation in every work on the subject:—the existence of shadow[256]. He barely mentions the subject of diffraction, and Young's law of interferences;—speaks of Fresnel as having applied this principle to the phenomena of coloured rings, "on which the

117

ingenious labours of Newton left much to desire;" as if Fresnel's labours on this subject had been the supplement of those of Newton: and after regretting that "this principle of interferences has not yet been distinctly232 disentangled from chemical conceptions on the nature of light," concludes his chapter. He does not even mention the phenomena of dipolarization, of circular and elliptical polarization, or of the optical properties of crystals; discoveries of laws of phenomena quite as remarkable as any which can be mentioned.

M. Comte's favourite example of physical research is Thermotics, and especially Fourier's researches with regard to heat. It is shown[257] in the History of Thermotics, that the general phenomena of radiation required the assumption of a fluid to express them; as appears in the theory of exchanges[258]. And the explanation of the principal laws of radiation, which Fourier gives, depends upon the conception of material molecular radiation. The flux of caloric, of which Fourier speaks, cannot be conceived otherwise than as implying a material flow. M. Comte apologizes[259] for this expression, as too figurative, and says that it merely indicates a fact. But what is the flow of a current of fluid except a fact? And is it not evident that without such expressions, and the ideas corresponding to them, Fourier could neither have conveyed nor conceived his theory?

In concluding this discussion it must be recollected, that though it is a most narrow and untenable rule to say that we will admit no agency of ethers and fluids into philosophy; yet the reality of such agents is only to be held in the way, and to the extent, which the laws of phenomena indicate. It is not only allowable, but inevitable to assume, as the vehicle of heat and light, a medium possessing some of the properties of more familiar kinds of matter. But the idea of such a medium, which we possess, and on which we cannot but reason, can be fully developed only by an assiduous study of the cases in which it is applicable. It may be, that as science advances, all our knowledge may converge to one general and single aspect of the233 universe. We abandon and reject this hope, if we refuse to admit those ideas which must be our stepping-stones in advancing to such a point: and we no less frustrate such an expectation, if we allow ourselves to imagine that from our present position we can stride at once to the summit.

4. Causes in other Sciences.—But if it is, in the sciences just mentioned, impracticable to reduce our knowledge to laws of phenomena alone, without referring to causes, media, and other agencies; how much more plainly is it impossible to confine our thoughts to phenomena, and to laws of succession and resemblance, in other sciences, as chemistry, physiology, and geology? Who shall forbid us, or why should we be forbidden, to inquire whether chemical and galvanic forces are identical; whether irritability is a peculiar vital power; whether geological causes have been uniform or paroxysmal? To exclude such inquiries, would be to secure ourselves from the poison of error by abstaining from the banquet of truth:—it would be to attempt to feed our minds with the meagre diet of space and number, because we may find too delightful a relish in such matters as cause and end, symmetry and affinity, organization and development.

Thus M. Comte's arrangement of the progress of science as successively metaphysical and positive, is contrary to history in fact, and contrary to sound philosophy in principle. Nor is there any better foundation for his statement that theological views are to be found only in the rude infantine condition of human knowledge, and vanish as science advances. Even in material sciences this is not the case. We have shown in the

118

chapter on Final Causes, that physiologists have been directed in their remarks by the conviction of a purpose in every part of the structure of animals; and that this idea, which had its rise after the first observations, has gone on constantly gaining strength and clearness, so that it is now the basis of a large portion of the science. We have seen, too, in the Book on the palætiological sciences, that the researches of that class do by no means lead us to reject an origin of the series234 of events, nor to suppose this origin to be included in the series of natural laws. Science has not at all shown any reason for denying either the creation or the purpose of the universe.

This is true of those aspects of the universe which have become the subjects of rigorous science: but how small a portion of the whole do they form! Especially how minute a proportion does our knowledge bear to our ignorance, if we admit into science, as M. Comte advises, only the laws of phenomena! Even in the best explored fields of science, how few such laws do we know! Meteorology, climate, terrestrial magnetism, the colours and other properties of bodies, the conditions of musical and articulate sound, and a thousand other facts of physics, are not defined by any known laws. In physiology we may readily convince ourselves how little we know of laws, since we can hardly study one species without discovering some unguessed property, or apply the microscope without seeing some new structure in the best known organs. And when we go on to social and moral and political matters, we may well doubt whether any one single rigorous rule of phenomena has ever been stated, although on such subjects man's ideas have been busily and eagerly working ever since his origin. What a wanton and baseless assumption it would be, then, to reject those suggestions of a Governor of the universe which we derive from man's moral and spiritual nature, and from the institutions of society, because we fancy we see in the small field of our existing "positive knowledge" a tendency to exclude "theological views!" Because we can explain the motion of the stars by a general Law which seems to imply no hyperphysical agency, and can trace a few more limited laws in other properties of matter, we are exhorted to reject convictions irresistibly suggested to us by our bodies and our souls, by history and antiquities, by conscience and human law.

5. M. Comte's practical philosophy.—It is not merely as a speculative doctrine that M. Comte urges the necessity of our thus following the guidance of235 "positive philosophy." The fevered and revolutionary condition of human society at present arises, according to him[260], from the simultaneous employment of three kinds of philosophy radically incompatible;—theological, metaphysical, and positive philosophy. The remedy for the evil is to reject the two former, and to refer everything to that positive philosophy, of which the destined triumph cannot be doubtful. In like manner, our European education[261], still essentially theological, metaphysical, and literary, must be replaced by a positive education, suited to the spirit of our epoch.

With these practical consequences of M. Comte's philosophy we are not here concerned: but the notice of them may serve to show how entirely the rejection of the theological view pervades his system; and how closely this rejection is connected with the principles which lead him also to reject the fundamental ideas of the sciences as we have presented them.

119

6. M. Comte on Hypotheses.—In the detail of M. Comte's work, I do not find any peculiar or novel remarks on the induction by which the sciences are formed; except we may notice, as such, his permission of hypotheses to the inquirer, already referred to. "There can only be," he says[262], "two general modes fitted to reveal to us, in a direct and entirely rational manner, the true law of any phenomenon;—either the immediate analysis of this phenomenon, or its exact and evident relation to some more extended law, previously established;—in a word, induction, or deduction. But both these ways would certainly be insufficient, even with regard to the simplest phenomenon, in the eyes of any one who fully comprehends the essential difficulties of the intimate study of nature, if we did not often begin by anticipating the result, and making a provisory supposition, at first essentially conjectural, even with respect to some of the notions which constitute the final object of inquiry. Hence236 the introduction, which is strictly indispensable, of hypotheses in natural philosophy." We have already seen that the "permissio intellectus" had been noticed as a requisite step in discovery, as long before as the time of Bacon.

7. M. Comte's Classification of Sciences.—I do not think it necessary to examine in detail M. Comte's views of the philosophy of the different sciences; but it may illustrate the object of the present work, to make a remark upon his attempt to establish a distinction between physical and chemical science. This distinction he makes to consist in three points[263];—that Physics considers general and Chemistry special properties;—that Physics considers masses and Chemistry molecules;—that in Physics the mode of arrangement of the molecules remains constant, while in Chemistry this arrangement is necessarily altered. M. Comte however allows that these lines of distinction are vague and insecure; for, among many others, magnetism, a special property, belongs to physics, and breaks down his first criterion; and molecular attractions are a constant subject of speculation in physics, so that the second distinction cannot be insisted on. To which we may add that the greater portion of chemistry does not attend at all to the arrangement of the molecules, so that the third character is quite erroneous. The real distinction of these branches of science is, as we have seen, the fundamental ideas which they employ. Physics deals with relations of space, time, and number, media, and scales of qualities, according to intensity and other differences; while chemistry has for its subject elements and attractions as shown in composition; and polarity, though in different senses, belongs to both. The failure of this attempt of M. Comte at distinguishing these provinces of science by their objects, may be looked upon as an illustration of the impossibility of establishing a philosophy of the sciences on any other ground than the ideas which they involve.

237

We have thus traced to its extreme point, so far as the nature of science is concerned, one of those two antagonistic opinions, of which the struggle began in the outset of philosophy, and has continued during the whole of her progress;—namely, the opinions which respectively make our sensations and our ideas the origin of our knowledge. The former, if it be consistent with itself, must consider all knowledge of causes as impossible, since no sensation can give us the idea of cause. And when this opinion is applied to science, it reduces it to the mere investigation of laws of phenomena, according to relations of space, time, and number. I purposely abstain, as far as possible, from the consideration of the other consequences, not strictly belonging to the physical sciences, which were drawn from the doctrine that all our ideas are only transformed sensations. The materialism, the atheism, the sensualist morality, the anarchical polity, which some of the disciples of the Sensational School erected upon the fundamental dogmas of their sect, do not belong to our present subject, and are matters too weighty to be treated of as mere accessories.

The above Remarks were written before I had seen the third volume of M. Comte's work, or the subsequent volumes. But I do not find, in anything which those volumes contain, any ground for altering what I have written. Indeed they are occupied altogether with subjects which do not come within the field of my present speculations.

238

CHAPTER XXII.
Mr. Mill's Logic[264].

The History of the Inductive Sciences was published in 1837, and the Philosophy of the Inductive Sciences in 1840. In 1843 Mr. Mill published his System of Logic, in which he states that without the aid derived from the facts and ideas in my volumes, the corresponding portion of his own would most probably not have been written, and quotes parts of what I have said with commendation. He also, however, dissents from me on several important and fundamental points, and argues against what I have said thereon. I conceive that it may tend to bring into a clearer light the doctrines which I have tried to establish, and the truth of them, if I discuss some of the differences between us, which I shall proceed to do[265].

Mr. Mill's work has had, for a work of its abstruse character, a circulation so extensive, and admirers so numerous and so fervent, that it needs no commendation of mine. But if my main concern at present had not been with the points in which Mr. Mill differs from me, I should have had great pleasure in pointing out passages, of which there are many, in which Mr. Mill appears to me to have been very happy in promoting or in expressing philosophical truth.

There is one portion of his work indeed which tends to give it an interest of a wider kind than be239longs to that merely scientific truth to which I purposely and resolutely confined my speculations in the works to which I have referred. Mr. Mill has introduced into his work a direct and extensive consideration of the modes of dealing with moral and political as well as physical questions; and I have no doubt that this part of his book has, for many of his readers, a more lively interest than any other. Such a comprehensive scheme seems to give to doctrines respecting science a value and a purpose which they cannot have, so long as they are restricted to mere material sciences. I still retain the opinion, however, upon which I formerly acted, that the philosophy of science is to be extracted from the portions of science which are universally allowed to be most certainly established, and that those are the physical sciences. I am very far from saying, or thinking, that there is no such thing as Moral and Political Science, or that no method can be suggested for its promotion; but I think that by attempting at present to include the Moral Sciences in the same formulæ with the Physical, we open far more controversies than we close; and that in the moral as in the physical sciences, the first step towards

121

showing how truth is to be discovered, is to study some portion of it which is assented to so as to be beyond controversy.

I. What is Induction?—1. Confining myself, then, to the material sciences, I shall proceed to offer my remarks on Induction with especial reference to Mr. Mill's work. And in order that we may, as I have said, proceed as intelligibly as possible, let us begin by considering what we mean by Induction, as a mode of obtaining truth; and let us note whether there is any difference between Mr. Mill and me on this subject.

"For the purposes of the present inquiry," Mr. Mill says (i. 347[266]), "Induction may be defined the opera240tion of discovering and forming general propositions:" meaning, as appears by the context, the discovery of them from particular facts. He elsewhere (i. 370) terms it "generalization from experience:" and again he speaks of it with greater precision as the inference of a more general proposition from less general ones.

2. Now to these definitions and descriptions I assent as far as they go; though, as I shall have to remark, they appear to me to leave unnoticed a feature which is very important, and which occurs in all cases of Induction, so far as we are concerned with it. Science, then, consists of general propositions, inferred from particular facts, or from less general propositions, by Induction; and it is our object to discern the nature and laws of Induction in this sense. That the propositions are general, or are more general than the facts from which they are inferred, is an indispensable part of the notion of Induction, and is essential to any discussion of the process, as the mode of arriving at Science, that is, at a body of general truths.

3. I am obliged therefore to dissent from Mr. Mill when he includes, in his notion of Induction, the process by which we arrive at individual facts from other facts of the same order of particularity.

Such inference is, at any rate, not Induction alone; if it be Induction at all, it is Induction applied to an example.

For instance, it is a general law, obtained by Induction from particular facts, that a body falling vertically downwards from rest, describes spaces proportional to the squares of the times. But that a particular body will fall through 16 feet in one second and 64 feet in two seconds, is not an induction simply, it is a result obtained by applying the inductive law to a particular case.

But further, such a process is often not induction at all. That a ball striking another ball directly will communicate to it as much momentum as the striking ball itself loses, is a law established by induction: but if, from habit or practical skill, I make one billiard-ball strike another, so as to produce the velocity which241 I wish, without knowing or thinking of the general law, the term Induction cannot then be rightly applied. If I know the law and act upon it, I have in my mind both the general induction and its particular application. But if I act by the ordinary billiard-player's skill, without thinking of momentum or law, there is no Induction in the case.

4. This distinction becomes of importance, in reference to Mr. Mill's doctrine, because he has extended his use of the term Induction, not only to the cases in which the general induction is consciously applied to a particular instance; but to the cases in which the particular instance is dealt with by means of experience, in that rude sense in which experience can be asserted of brutes; and in which, of course, we can in no way imagine that the law is possessed or understood, as a general proposition. He has thus, as I conceive, overlooked the broad and essential difference between speculative knowledge and practical action; and has introduced cases which are quite foreign to the idea of science, alongside with cases from which we may hope to obtain some views of the nature of science and the processes by which it must be formed.

5. Thus (ii. 232) he says, "This inference of one particular fact from another is a case of induction. It is of this sort of induction that brutes are capable." And to the same purpose he had previously said (i. 251), "He [the burnt child who shuns the fire] is not generalizing: he is inferring a particular from particulars. In the same way also, brutes reason ... not only the burnt child, but the burnt dog, dreads the fire."

6. This confusion, (for such it seems to me,) of knowledge with practical tendencies, is expressed more in detail in other places. Thus he says (i. 118), "I cannot dig the ground unless I have an idea of the ground and of a spade, and of all the other things I am operating upon."

7. This appears to me to be a use of words which can only tend to confuse our idea of knowledge by obliterating all that is distinctive in human knowledge.242 It seems to me quite false to say that I cannot dig the ground, unless I have an idea of the ground and of my spade. Are we to say that we cannot walk the ground, unless we have an idea of the ground, and of our feet, and of our shoes, and of the muscles of our legs? Are we to say that a mole cannot dig the ground, unless he has an idea of the ground and of the snout and paws with which he digs it? Are we to say that a pholas cannot perforate a rock, unless he have an idea of the rock, and of the acid with which he corrodes it?

8. This appears to me, as I have said, to be a line of speculation which can lead to nothing but confusion. The knowledge concerning which I wish to inquire is human knowledge. And in order that I may have any chance of success in the inquiry, I find it necessary to single out that kind of knowledge which is especially and distinctively human. Hence, I pass by, in this part of my investigation, all the knowledge, if it is to be so called, which man has in no other way than brutes have it;—all that merely shows itself in action. For though action may be modified by habit, and habit by experience, in animals as well as in men, such experience, so long as it retains that merely practical form, is no part of the materials of science. Knowledge in a general form, is alone knowledge for that purpose; and to that, therefore, I must confine my attention; at least till I have made some progress in ascertaining its nature and laws, and am thus prepared to compare such knowledge,—human knowledge properly so called,—with mere animal tendencies to action; or even with practical skill which does not include, as for the most part practical skill does not include, speculative knowledge.

9. And thus, I accept Mr. Mill's definition of Induction only in its first and largest form; and reject, as useless and mischievous for our purposes, his extension of the term

to the practical influence which experience of one fact exercises upon a creature dealing with similar facts. Such influence cannot be resolved into ideas and induction, without, as I conceive, making all our subsequent investigation vague and hete243rogeneous, indefinite and inconclusive. If we must speak of animals as learning from experience, we may at least abstain from applying to them terms which imply that they learn, in the same way in which men learn astronomy from the stars, and chemistry from the effects of mixture and heat. And the same may be said of the language which is to be used concerning what men learn, when their learning merely shows itself in action, and does not exist as a general thought. Induction must not be applied to such cases. Induction must be confined to cases where we have in our minds general propositions, in order that the sciences, which are our most instructive examples of the process we have to consider, may be, in any definite and proper sense, Inductive Sciences.

10. Perhaps some persons may be inclined to say that this difference of opinion, as to the extent of meaning which is to be given to the term Induction, is a question merely of words; a matter of definition only. This is a mode in which men in our time often seem inclined to dispose of philosophical questions; thus evading the task of forming an opinion upon such questions, while they retain the air of looking at the subject from a more comprehensive point of view. But as I have elsewhere said, such questions of definition are never questions of definition merely. A proposition is always implied along with the definition; and the truth of the proposition depends upon the settlement of the definition. This is the case in the present instance. We are speaking of Induction, and we mean that kind of Induction by which the sciences now existing among men have been constructed. On this account it is, that we cannot include, in the meaning of the term, mere practical tendencies or practical habits; for science is not constructed of these. No accumulation of these would make up any of the acknowledged sciences. The elements of such sciences are something of a kind different from practical habits. The elements of such sciences are principles which we know; truths which can be contemplated as being true. Practical habits, practical skill, instincts and244 the like, appear in action, and in action only. Such endowments or acquirements show themselves when the occasion for action arrives, and then, show themselves in the act; without being put, or being capable of being put, in the form of truths contemplated by the intellect. But the elements and materials of Science are necessary truths contemplated by the intellect. It is by consisting of such elements and such materials, that Science is Science. Hence a use of the term Induction which requires us to obliterate this distinction, must make it impossible for us to arrive at any consistent and intelligible view of the nature of Science, and of the mental process by which Sciences come into being. We must, for the purpose which Mr. Mill and I have in common, retain his larger and more philosophical definition of Induction,—that it is the inference of a more general proposition from less general ones.

11. Perhaps, again, some persons may say, that practical skill and practical experience lead to science, and may therefore be included in the term Induction, which describes the formation of science. But to this we reply, that these things lead to science as occasions only, and do not form part of science; and that science begins then only when we look at the facts in a general point of view. This distinction is essential to the philosophy of science. The rope-dancer may, by his performances, suggest, to himself or to others, properties of the center of gravity; but this is so, because man has a tendency to speculate and to think of general truths, as well as a tendency to dance on a rope on

special occasions, and to acquire skill in such dancing by practice. The rope-dancer does not dance by Induction, any more than the dancing dog does. To apply the terms Science and Induction to such cases, carries us into the regions of metaphor; as when we call birds of passage "wise meteorologists," or the bee "a natural chemist, who turns the flower-dust into honey." This is very well in poetry: but for our purposes we must avoid recognizing these cases as really belonging to the sciences of meteorology and chemis245try,—as really cases of Induction. Induction for us is general propositions, contemplated as such, derived from particulars.

Science may result from experience and observation by Induction; but Induction is not therefore the same thing as experience and observation. Induction is experience or observation consciously looked at in a general form. This consciousness and generality are necessary parts of that knowledge which is science. And accordingly, on the other hand, science cannot result from mere Instinct, as distinguished from Reason; because Instinct by its nature is not conscious and general, but operates blindly and unconsciously in particular cases, the actor not seeing or thinking of the rule which he obeys.

12. A little further on I shall endeavour to show that not only a general thought, but a general word or phrase is a requisite element in Induction. This doctrine, of course, still more decidedly excludes the case of animals, and of mere practical knowledge in man. A burnt child dreads the fire; but reason must be unfolded, before the child learns to understand the words "fire will hurt you." The burnt dog never thus learns to understand words. And this difference points to an entirely different state of thought in the two cases: or rather, to a difference between a state of rational thought on the one hand, and of mere practical instinct on the other.

13. Besides this difference of speculative thought and practical instinct which thus are, as appears to me, confounded in Mr. Mill's philosophy, in such a way as tends to destroy all coherent views of human knowledge, there is another set of cases to which Mr. Mill applies the term Induction, and to which it appears to me to be altogether inapplicable. He employs it to describe the mode in which superstitious men, in ignorant ages, were led to the opinion that striking natural events presaged or accompanied calamities. Thus he says (i. 389), "The opinion so long prevalent that a comet or any other unusual appearance in the heavenly regions was the precursor of calamities to246 mankind, or at least to those who witnessed it; the belief in the oracles of Delphi and Dodona; the reliance on astrology, or on the weather-prophecies in almanacs; were doubtless inductions supposed to be grounded on experience;" and he speaks of these insufficient inductions being extinguished by the stronger inductions subsequently obtained by scientific inquiry. And in like manner, he says in another place (i. 367), "Let us now compare different predictions: the first, that eclipses will occur whenever one planet or satellite is so situated as to cast its shadow upon another: the second, that they will occur whenever some great calamity is impending over mankind."

14. Now I cannot see how anything but confusion can arise from applying the term Induction to superstitious fancies like those here mentioned. They are not imperfect truths, but entire falsehoods. Of that, Mr. Mill and I are agreed: how then can they exemplify the progress towards truth? They were not collected from the facts by seeking a law of their occurrence; but were suggested by an imagination of the anger of superior

powers shown by such deviations from the ordinary course of nature. If we are to speak of inductions to any purpose, they must be such inductions as represent the facts, in some degree at least. It is not meant, I presume, that these opinions are in any degree true: to what purpose then are they adduced? If I were to hold that my dreams predict or conform to the motions of the stars or of the clouds, would this be an induction? It would be so, as much one as those here so denominated: yet what but confusion could arise from classing it among scientific truths? Mr. Mill himself has explained (ii. 389) the way in which such delusions as the prophecies of almanac-makers, and the like, obtain credence; namely, by the greater effect which the positive instances produce on ordinary minds in comparison with the negative, when the rule has once taken possession of their thoughts. And this being, as he says, the recognized explanation of such cases, why should we not leave them to their due place, and not confound and perplex the whole of247 our investigation by elevating them to the rank of "inductions"? The very condemnation of such opinions is that they are not at all inductive. When we have made any progress in our investigation of the nature of science, to attempt to drive us back to the wearisome discussion of such elementary points as these, is to make progress hopeless.

II. Induction or Description?—15. In the cases hitherto noticed, Mr. Mill extends the term Induction, as I think, too widely, and applies it to cases to which it is not rightly applicable. I have now to notice a case of an opposite kind, in which he does not apply it where I do, and condemns me for using it in such a case. I had spoken of Kepler's discovery of the Law, that the planets move round the sun in ellipses, as an example of Induction. The separate facts of any planet (Mars, for instance,) being in certain places at certain times, are all included in the general proposition which Kepler discovered, that Mars describes an ellipse of a certain form and position. This appears to me a very simple but a very distinct example of the operation of discovering general propositions; general, that is, with reference to particular facts; which operation Mr. Mill, as well as myself, says is Induction. But Mr. Mill denies this operation in this case to be Induction at all (i. 357). I should not have been prepared for this denial by the previous parts of Mr. Mill's book, for he had said just before (i. 350), "such facts as the magnitudes of the bodies of the solar system, their distances from each other, the figure of the earth and its rotation ... are proved indirectly, by the aid of inductions founded on other facts which we can more easily reach." If the figure of the earth and its rotation are proved by Induction, it seems very strange, and is to me quite incomprehensible, how the figure of the earth's orbit and its revolution (and of course, of the figure of Mars's orbit and his revolution in like manner,) are not also proved by Induction. No, says Mr. Mill, Kepler, in putting together a number of places of the planet into one figure, only performed an act of description. "This descriptive operation," he248 adds (i. 359), "Mr. Whewell, by an aptly chosen expression, has termed Colligation of Facts." He goes on to commend my observations concerning this process, but says that, according to the old and received meaning of the term, it is not Induction at all.

16. Now I have already shown that Mr. Mill himself, a few pages earlier, had applied the term Induction to cases undistinguishable from this in any essential circumstance. And even in this case, he allows that Kepler did really perform an act of Induction (i. 358), "namely, in concluding that, because the observed places of Mars were correctly represented by points in an imaginary ellipse, therefore Mars would continue to revolve in

that same ellipse; and even in concluding that the position of the planet during the time which had intervened between the two observations must have coincided with the intermediate points of the curve." Of course, in Kepler's Induction, of which I speak, I include all this; all this is included in speaking of the orbit of Mars: a continuous line, a periodical motion, are implied in the term orbit. I am unable to see what would remain of Kepler's discovery, if we take from it these conditions. It would not only not be an induction, but it would not be a description, for it would not recognize that Mars moved in an orbit. Are particular positions to be conceived as points in a curve, without thinking of the intermediate positions as belonging to the same curve? If so, there is no law at all, and the facts are not bound together by any intelligible tie.

In another place (ii. 209) Mr. Mill returns to his distinction of Description and Induction; but without throwing any additional light upon it, so far as I can see.

17. The only meaning which I can discover in this attempted distinction of Description and Induction is, that when particular facts are bound together by their relation in space, Mr. Mill calls the discovery of the connexion Description, but when they are connected by other general relations, as time, cause and the like, Mr. Mill terms the discovery of the connexion Induc249tion. And this way of making a distinction, would fall in with the doctrine of other parts of Mr. Mill's book, in which he ascribes very peculiar attributes to space and its relations, in comparison with other Ideas, (as I should call them). But I cannot see any ground for this distinction, of connexion according to space and other connexions of facts.

To stand upon such a distinction, appears to me to be the way to miss the general laws of the formation of science. For example: The ancients discovered that the planets revolved in recurring periods, and thus connected the observations of their motions according to the Idea of Time. Kepler discovered that they revolved in ellipses, and thus connected the observations according to the Idea of Space. Newton discovered that they revolved in virtue of the Sun's attraction, and thus connected the motions according to the Idea of Force. The first and third of these discoveries are recognized on all hands as processes of Induction. Why is the second to be called by a different name? or what but confusion and perplexity can arise from refusing to class it with the other two? It is, you say, Description. But such Description is a kind of Induction, and must be spoken of as Induction, if we are to speak of Induction as the process by which Science is formed: for the three steps are all, the second in the same sense as the first and third, in co-ordination with them, steps in the formation of astronomical science.

18. But, says Mr. Mill (i. 363), "it is a fact surely that the planet does describe an ellipse, and a fact which we could see if we had adequate visual organs and a suitable position." To this I should reply: "Let it be so; and it is a fact, surely, that the planet does move periodically: it is a fact, surely, that the planet is attracted by the sun. Still, therefore, the asserted distinction fails to find a ground." Perhaps Mr. Mill would remind us that the elliptical form of the orbit is a fact which we could see if we had adequate visual organs and a suitable position: but that force is a thing which we cannot see. But this distinction also250 will not bear handling. Can we not see a tree blown down by a storm, or a rock blown up by gunpowder? Do we not here see force:—see it, that is, by its effects, the only way in which we need to see it in the case of a planet, for the purposes of our argument?

Are not such operations of force, Facts which may be the objects of sense? and is not the operation of the sun's Force a Fact of the same kind, just as much as the elliptical form of orbit which results from the action? If the latter be "surely a Fact," the former is a Fact no less surely.

19. In truth, as I have repeatedly had occasion to remark, all attempts to frame an argument by the exclusive or emphatic appropriation of the term Fact to particular cases, are necessarily illusory and inconclusive. There is no definite and stable distinction between Facts and Theories; Facts and Laws; Facts and Inductions. Inductions, Laws, Theories, which are true, are Facts. Facts involve Inductions. It is a fact that the moon is attracted by the earth, just as much as it is a Fact that an apple falls from a tree. That the former fact is collected by a more distinct and conscious Induction, does not make it the less a Fact. That the orbit of Mars is a Fact—a true Description of the path—does not make it the less a case of Induction.

20. There is another argument which Mr. Mill employs in order to show that there is a difference between mere colligation which is description, and induction in the more proper sense of the term. He notices with commendation a remark which I had made (i. 364), that at different stages of the progress of science the facts had been successfully connected by means of very different conceptions, while yet the later conceptions have not contradicted, but included, so far as they were true, the earlier: thus the ancient Greek representation of the motions of the planets by means of epicycles and eccentrics, was to a certain degree of accuracy true, and is not negatived, though superseded, by the modern representation of the planets as describing ellipses round the sun. And he then reasons that251 this, which is thus true of Descriptions, cannot be true of Inductions. He says (i. 367), "Different descriptions therefore may be all true: but surely not different explanations." He then notices the various explanations of the motions of the planets— the ancient doctrine that they are moved by an inherent virtue; the Cartesian doctrine that they are moved by impulse and by vortices; the Newtonian doctrine that they are governed by a central force; and he adds, "Can it be said of these, as was said of the different descriptions, that they are all true as far as they go? Is it not true that one only can be true in any degree, and that the other two must be altogether false?"

21. And to this questioning, the history of science compels me to reply very distinctly and positively, in the way which Mr. Mill appears to think extravagant and absurd. I am obliged to say, Undoubtedly, all these explanations may be true and consistent with each other, and would be so if each had been followed out so as to show in what manner it could be made consistent with the facts. And this was, in reality, in a great measure done[267]. The doctrine that the heavenly bodies were moved by vortices was successively modified, so that it came to coincide in its results with the doctrine of an inverse-quadratic centripetal force, as I have remarked in the History[268]. When this point was reached, the vortex was merely a machinery, well or ill devised, for producing such a centripetal force, and therefore did not contradict the doctrine of a centripetal force. Newton himself does not appear to have been averse to explaining gravity by impulse. So little is it true that if the one theory be true the other must be false. The attempt to explain gravity by the impulse of streams of particles flowing through the universe in all directions, which I have mentioned in the Philosophy[269] so far from being incon252sistent with the Newtonian theory, that it is founded entirely upon it. And

even with regard to the doctrine, that the heavenly bodies move by an inherent virtue; if this doctrine had been maintained in any such way that it was brought to agree with the facts, the inherent virtue must have had its laws determined; and then, it would have been found that the virtue had a reference to the central body; and so, the "inherent virtue" must have coincided in its effect with the Newtonian force; and then, the two explanations would agree, except so far as the word "inherent" was concerned. And if such a part of an earlier theory as this word inherent indicates, is found to be untenable, it is of course rejected in the transition to later and more exact theories, in Inductions of this kind, as well as in what Mr. Mill calls Descriptions. There is therefore still no validity discoverable in the distinction which Mr. Mill attempts to draw between "descriptions" like Kepler's law of elliptical orbits, and other examples of induction.

22. When Mr. Mill goes on to compare what he calls different predictions—the first, the true explanation of eclipses by the shadows which the planets and satellites cast upon one another, and the other, the belief that they will occur whenever some great calamity is impending over mankind, I must reply, as I have stated already, (Art. 17), that to class such superstitions as the last with cases of Induction, appears to me to confound all use of words, and to prevent, as far as it goes, all profitable exercise of thought. What possible advantage can result from comparing (as if they were alike) the relation of two descriptions of a phenomenon, each to a certain extent true, and therefore both consistent, with the relation of a scientific truth to a false and baseless superstition?

23. But I may make another remark on this example, so strangely introduced. If, under the influence of fear and superstition, men may make such mistakes with regard to laws of nature, as to imagine that eclipses portend calamities, are they quite secure from mistakes in description? Do not the very per253sons who tell us how eclipses predict disasters, also describe to us fiery swords seen in the air, and armies fighting in the sky? So that even in this extreme case, at the very limit of the rational exercise of human powers, there is nothing to distinguish Description from Induction.

I shall now leave the reader to judge whether this feature in the history of science,— that several views which appear at first quite different are yet all true,—which Mr. Mill calls a curious and interesting remark of mine, and which he allows to be "strikingly true" of the Inductions which he calls Descriptions, (i. 364) is, as he says, "unequivocally false" of other Inductions. And I shall confide in having general assent with me, when I continue to speak of Kepler's Induction of the elliptical orbits.

I now proceed to another remark.

III. In Discovery a new Conception is introduced.—

24. There is a difference between Mr. Mill and me in our view of the essential elements of this Induction of Kepler, which affects all other cases of Induction, and which is, I think, the most extensive and important of the differences between us. I must therefore venture to dwell upon it a little in detail.

I conceive that Kepler, in discovering the law of Mars's motion, and in asserting that the planet moved in an ellipse, did this;—he bound together particular observations of separate places of Mars by the notion, or, as I have called it, the conception, of an ellipse, which was supplied by his own mind. Other persons, and he too, before he made this discovery, had present to their minds the facts of such separate successive positions of the planet; but could not bind them together rightly, because they did not apply to them this conception of an ellipse. To supply this conception, required a special preparation, and a special activity in the mind of the discoverer. He, and others before him, tried other ways of connecting the special facts, none of which fully succeeded. To discover such a connexion, the mind must be conversant with certain relations of space, and with certain kinds of figures.254 To discover the right figure was a matter requiring research, invention, resource. To hit upon the right conception is a difficult step; and when this step is once made, the facts assume a different aspect from what they had before: that done, they are seen in a new point of view; and the catching this point of view, is a special mental operation, requiring special endowments and habits of thought. Before this, the facts are seen as detached, separate, lawless; afterwards, they are seen as connected, simple, regular; as parts of one general fact, and thereby possessing innumerable new relations before unseen. Kepler, then, I say, bound together the facts by superinducing upon them the conception of an ellipse; and this was an essential element in his Induction.

25. And there is the same essential element in all Inductive discoveries. In all cases, facts, before detached and lawless, are bound together by a new thought. They are reduced to law, by being seen in a new point of view. To catch this new point of view, is an act of the mind, springing from its previous preparation and habits. The facts, in other discoveries, are brought together according to other relations, or, as I have called them, Ideas;—the Ideas of Time, of Force, of Number, of Resemblance, of Elementary Composition, of Polarity, and the like. But in all cases, the mind performs the operation by an apprehension of some such relations; by singling out the one true relation; by combining the apprehension of the true relation with the facts; by applying to them the Conception of such a relation.

26. In previous writings, I have not only stated this view generally, but I have followed it into detail, exemplifying it in the greater part of the History of the principal Inductive Sciences in succession. I have pointed out what are the Conceptions which have been introduced in every prominent discovery in those sciences; and have noted to which of the above Ideas, or of the like Ideas, each belongs. The performance of this task is the office of the greater part of my Philosophy of the Inductive Sciences. For that work255 is, in reality, no less historical than the History which preceded it. The History of the Inductive Sciences is the history of the discoveries, mainly so far as concerns the Facts which were brought together to form sciences. The Philosophy is, in the first ten Books, the history of the Ideas and Conceptions, by means of which the facts were connected, so as to give rise to scientific truths. It would be easy for me to give a long list of the Ideas and Conceptions thus brought into view, but I may refer any reader who wishes to see such a list, to the Tables of Contents of the History, and of the first ten Books of the Philosophy.

27. That these Ideas and Conceptions are really distinct elements of the scientific truths thus obtained, I conceive to be proved beyond doubt, not only by considering that the discoveries never were made, nor could be made, till the right Conception was

130

obtained, and by seeing how difficult it often was to obtain this element; but also, by seeing that the Idea and the Conception itself, as distinct from the Facts, was, in almost every science, the subject of long and obstinate controversies;—controversies which turned upon the possible relations of Ideas, much more than upon the actual relations of Facts. The first ten Books of the Philosophy to which I have referred, contain the history of a great number of these controversies. These controversies make up a large portion of the history of each science; a portion quite as important as the study of the facts; and a portion, at every stage of the science, quite as essential to the progress of truth. Men, in seeking and obtaining scientific knowledge, have always shown that they found the formation of right conceptions in their own minds to be an essential part of the process.

28. Moreover, the presence of a Conception of the mind as a special element of the inductive process, and as the tie by which the particular facts are bound together, is further indicated, by there being some special new term or phrase introduced in every induction; or at least some term or phrase thenceforth steadily applied to the facts, which had not been256 applied to them before; as when Kepler asserted that Mars moved round the sun in an elliptical orbit, or when Newton asserted that the planets gravitate towards the sun; these new terms, elliptical orbit, and gravitate, mark the new conceptions on which the inductions depend. I have in the Philosophy[270] further illustrated this application of "technical terms," that is, fixed and settled terms, in every inductive discovery; and have spoken of their use in enabling men to proceed from each such discovery to other discoveries more general. But I notice these terms here, for the purpose of showing the existence of a conception in the discoverer's mind, corresponding to the term thus introduced; which conception, the term is intended to convey to the minds of those to whom the discovery is communicated.

29. But this element of discovery,—right conceptions supplied by the mind in order to bind the facts together,—Mr. Mill denies to be an element at all. He says, of Kepler's discovery of the elliptical orbit (i. 363), "It superadded nothing to the particular facts which it served to bind together;" yet he adds, "except indeed the knowledge that a resemblance existed between the planetary orbit and other ellipses;" that is, except the knowledge that it was an ellipse;—precisely the circumstance in which the discovery consisted. Kepler, he says, "asserted as a fact that the planet moved in an ellipse. But this fact, which Kepler did not add to, but found in the motion of the planet ... was the very fact, the separate parts of which had been separately observed; it was the sum of the different observations."

30. That the fact of the elliptical motion was not merely the sum of the different observations, is plain from this, that other persons, and Kepler himself before his discovery, did not find it by adding together the observations. The fact of the elliptical orbit was not the sum of the observations merely; it was the257 sum of the observations, seen under a new point of view, which point of view Kepler's mind supplied. Kepler found it in the facts, because it was there, no doubt, for one reason; but also, for another, because he had, in his mind, those relations of thought which enabled him to find it. We may illustrate this by a familiar analogy. We too find the law in Kepler's book; but if we did not understand Latin, we should not find it there. We must learn Latin in order to find the law in the book. In like manner, a discoverer must know the language of science, as well as look at the book of nature, in order to find scientific truth. All the discussions

131

and controversies respecting Ideas and Conceptions of which I have spoken, may be looked upon as discussions and controversies respecting the grammar of the language in which nature speaks to the scientific mind. Man is the Interpreter of Nature; not the Spectator merely, but the Interpreter. The study of the language, as well as the mere sight of the characters, is requisite in order that we may read the inscriptions which are written on the face of the world. And this study of the language of nature, that is, of the necessary coherencies and derivations of the relations of phenomena, is to be pursued by examining Ideas, as well as mere phenomena;—by tracing the formation of Conceptions, as well as the accumulation of Facts. And this is what I have tried to do in the books already referred to.

31. Mr. Mill has not noticed, in any considerable degree, what I have said of the formation of the Conceptions which enter into the various sciences; but he has, in general terms, denied that the Conception is anything different from the facts themselves. "If," he says (i. 301), "the facts are rightly classed under the conceptions, it is because there is in the facts themselves, something of which the conception is a copy." But it is a copy which cannot be made by a person without peculiar endowments; just as a person cannot copy an ill-written inscription, so as to make it convey sense, unless he understand the language. "Conceptions," Mr. Mill says (ii. 217), "do not258 develope themselves from within, but are impressed from without." But what comes from without is not enough: they must have both origins, or they cannot make knowledge. "The conception," he says again (ii. 221), "is not furnished by the mind till it has been furnished to the mind." But it is furnished to the mind by its own activity, operating according to its own laws. No doubt, the conception may be formed, and in cases of discovery, must be formed, by the suggestion and excitement which the facts themselves produce; and must be so moulded as to agree with the facts. But this does not make it superfluous to examine, out of what materials such conceptions are formed, and how they are capable of being moulded so as to express laws of nature; especially, when we see how large a share this part of discovery—the examination how our ideas can be modified so as to agree with nature,—holds, in the history of science.

32. I have already (Art. 28) given, as evidence that the conception enters as an element in every induction, the constant introduction in such cases, of a new fixed term or phrase. Mr. Mill (ii. 282) notices this introduction of a new phrase in such cases as important, though he does not appear willing to allow that it is necessary. Yet the necessity of the conception at least, appears to result from the considerations which he puts forward. "What darkness," he says, "would have been spread over geometrical demonstration, if wherever the word circle is used, the definition of a circle was inserted instead of it." "If we want to make a particular combination of ideas permanent in the mind, there is nothing which clenches it like a name specially devoted to express it." In my view, the new conception is the nail which connects the previous notions, and the name, as Mr. Mill says, clenches the junction.

33. I have above (Art. 30) referred to the difficulty of getting hold of the right conception, as a proof that induction is not a mere juxtaposition of facts. Mr. Mill does not dispute that it is often difficult to hit upon the right conception. He says (i. 360),259 "that a conception of the mind is introduced, is indeed most certain, and Mr. Whewell has rightly stated elsewhere, that to hit upon the right conception is often a far more difficult,

and more meritorious achievement, than to prove its applicability when obtained. But," he adds, "a conception implies and corresponds to something conceived; and although the conception itself is not in the facts, but in our mind, it must be a conception of something which really is in the facts." But to this I reply, that its being really in the facts, does not help us at all towards knowledge, if we cannot see it there. As the poet says,

It is the mind that sees: the outward eyes
Present the object, but the mind descries.
And this is true of the sight which produces knowledge, as well as of the sight which produces pleasure and pain, which is referred to in the Tale.

34. Mr. Mill puts his view, as opposed to mine, in various ways, but, as will easily be understood, the answers which I have to offer are in all cases nearly to the same effect. Thus, he says (ii. 216), "the tardy development of several of the physical sciences, for example, of Optics, Electricity, Magnetism, and the higher generalizations of Chemistry, Mr. Whewell ascribes to the fact that mankind had not yet possessed themselves of the idea of Polarity, that is, of opposite properties in opposite directions. But what was there to suggest such an idea, until by a separate examination of several of these different branches of knowledge it was shown that the facts of each of them did present, in some instances at least, the curious phenomena of opposite properties in opposite directions?" But on this I observe, that these facts did not, nor do yet, present this conception to ordinary minds. The opposition of properties, and even the opposition of directions, which are thus apprehended by profound cultivators of science, are of an abstruse and recondite kind; and to conceive any one kind of polarity in its proper generality, is a process which few persons hitherto appear to have mastered; still less, have men in general come to conceive of them all260 as modifications of a general notion of Polarity. The description which I have given of Polarity in general, "opposite properties in opposite directions," is of itself a very imperfect account of the manner in which corresponding antitheses are involved in the portions of science into which Polar relations enter. In excuse of its imperfection, I may say, that I believe it is the first attempt to define Polarity in general; but yet, the conception of Polarity has certainly been strongly and effectively present in the minds of many of the sagacious men who have discovered and unravelled polar phenomena. They attempted to convey this conception, each in his own subject, sometimes by various and peculiar expressions, sometimes by imaginary mechanism by which the antithetical results were produced; their mode of expressing themselves being often defective or imperfect, often containing what was superfluous; and their meaning was commonly very imperfectly apprehended by most of their hearers and readers. But still, the conception was there, gradually working itself into clearness and distinctness, and in the mean time, directing their experiments, and forming an essential element of their discoveries. So far would it be from a sufficient statement of the case to say, that they conceived polarity because they saw it;—that they saw it as soon as it came into view;—and that they described it as they saw it.

35. The way in which such conceptions acquire clearness and distinctness is often by means of Discussions of Definitions. To define well a thought which already enters into trains of discovery, is often a difficult matter. The business of such definition is a part of the business of discovery. These, and other remarks connected with these, which I had made in the Philosophy, Mr. Mill has quoted and adopted (ii. 242). They appear to me to

point very distinctly to the doctrine to which he refuses his assent,—that there is a special process in the mind, in addition to the mere observation of facts, which is necessary at every step in the progress of knowledge. The Conception must be formed before it can be defined. The Definition261 gives the last stamp of distinctness to the Conception; and enables us to express, in a compact and lucid form, the new scientific propositions into which the new Conception enters.

36. Since Mr. Mill assents to so much of what has been said in the Philosophy, with regard to the process of scientific discovery, how, it may be asked, would he express these doctrines so as to exclude that which he thinks erroneous? If he objects to our saying that when we obtain a new inductive truth, we connect phenomena by applying to them a new Conception which fits them, in what terms would he describe the process? If he will not agree to say, that in order to discover the law of the facts, we must find an appropriate Conception, what language would he use instead of this? This is a natural question; and the answer cannot fail to throw light on the relation in which his views and mine stand to each other.

Mr. Mill would say, I believe, that when we obtain a new inductive law of facts, we find something in which the facts resemble each other; and that the business of making such discoveries is the business of discovering such resemblances. Thus, he says (of me,) (ii. 211), "his Colligation of Facts by means of appropriate Conceptions, is but the ordinary process of finding by a comparison of phenomena, in what consists their agreement or resemblance." And the Methods of experimental Inquiry which he gives (i. 450, &c.), proceed upon the supposition that the business of discovery may be thus more properly described.

37. There is no doubt that when we discover a law of nature by induction, we find some point in which all the particular facts agree. All the orbits of the planets agree in being ellipses, as Kepler discovered; all falling bodies agree in being acted on by a uniform force, as Galileo discovered; all refracted rays agree in having the sines of incidence and refraction in a constant ratio, as Snell discovered; all the bodies in the universe agree in attracting each other, as Newton discovered; all chemical compounds agree in being constituted of elements in definite proportions, as262 Dalton discovered. But it appears to me a most scanty, vague, and incomplete account of these steps in science, to say that the authors of them discovered something in which the facts in each case agreed. The point in which the cases agree, is of the most diverse kind in the different cases—in some, a relation of space, in others, the action of a force, in others, the mode of composition of a substance;—and the point of agreement, visible to the discoverer alone, does not come even into his sight, till after the facts have been connected by thoughts of his own, and regarded in points of view in which he, by his mental acts, places them. It would seem to me not much more inappropriate to say, that an officer, who disciplines his men till they move together at the word of command, does so by finding something in which they agree. If the power of consentaneous motion did not exist in the individuals, he could not create it: but that power being there, he finds it and uses it. Of course I am aware that the parallel of the two cases is not exact; but in the one case, as in the other, that in which the particular things are found to agree, is something formed in the mind of him who brings the agreement into view.

IV. Mr. Mill's Four Methods of Inquiry.—38. Mr. Mill has not only thus described the business of scientific discovery; he has also given rules for it, founded on this description. It may be expected that we should bestow some attention upon the methods of inquiry which he thus proposes. I presume that they are regarded by his admirers as among the most valuable parts of his book; as certainly they cannot fail to be, if they describe methods of scientific inquiry in such a manner as to be of use to the inquirer.

Mr. Mill enjoins four methods of experimental inquiry, which he calls the Method of Agreement, the Method of Difference, the Method of Residues, and the Method of Concomitant Variations[271]. They are all263 described by formulæ of this kind:—Let there be, in the observed facts, combinations of antecedents, ABC, BC, ADE, &c. and combinations of corresponding consequents, abc, bc, ade, &c.; and let the object of inquiry be, the consequence of some cause A, or the cause of some consequence a. The Method of Agreement teaches us, that when we find by experiment such facts as abc the consequent of ABC, and ade the consequent of ADE, then a is the consequent of A. The Method of Difference teaches us that when we find such facts as abc the consequent of ABC, and bc the consequent of BC, then a is the consequent of A. The Method of Residues teaches us, that if abc be the consequent of ABC, and if we have already ascertained that the effect of A is a, and the effect of B is b, then we may infer that the effect of C is c. The Method of Concomitant Variations teaches us, that if a phenomenon a varies according as another phenomenon A varies, there is some connexion of causation direct or indirect, between A and a.

39. Upon these methods, the obvious thing to remark is, that they take for granted the very thing which is most difficult to discover, the reduction of the phenomena to formulæ such as are here presented to us. When we have any set of complex facts offered to us; for instance, those which were offered in the cases of discovery which I have mentioned,—the facts of the planetary paths, of falling bodies, of refracted rays, of cosmical motions, of chemical analysis; and when, in any of these cases, we would discover the law of nature which governs them, or, if any one chooses so to term it, the feature in which all the cases agree, where are we to look for our A, B, C and a, b, c? Nature does not present to us the cases in this form; and how are we to reduce them to this form? You say, when we find the combination of ABC with abc and ABD with abd, then we may draw our inference. Granted: but when and where are we to find such combinations? Even now that the discoveries are made, who will point out to us what are the A, B, C and a, b, c elements of the cases which have just been enumerated?264 Who will tell us which of the methods of inquiry those historically real and successful inquiries exemplify? Who will carry these formulæ through the history of the sciences, as they have really grown up; and show us that these four methods have been operative in their formation; or that any light is thrown upon the steps of their progress by reference to these formulæ?

40. Mr. Mill's four methods have a great resemblance to Bacon's "Prerogatives of Instances;" for example, the Method of Agreement to the Instantiæ Ostensivæ; the Method of Differences to the Instantiæ Absentiæ in Proximo, and the Instantiæ Crucis; the Method of Concomitant Variations to the Instantiæ Migrantes. And with regard to the value of such methods, I believe all study of science will convince us more and more of the wisdom of the remarks which Sir John Herschel has made upon them[272].

"It has always appeared to us, we must confess, that the help which the classification of instances under their different titles of prerogative, affords to inductions, however just such classification may be in itself, is yet more apparent than real. The force of the instance must be felt in the mind before it can be referred to its place in the system; and before it can be either referred or appreciated it must be known; and when it is appreciated, we are ready enough to weave our web of induction, without greatly troubling ourselves whence it derives the weight we acknowledge it to have in our decisions.... No doubt such instances as these are highly instructive; but the difficulty in physics is to find such, not to perceive their force when found."

V. His Examples.—41. If Mr. Mill's four methods had been applied by him in his book to a large body of conspicuous and undoubted examples of discovery, well selected and well analysed, extending along the whole history of science, we should have been better265 able to estimate the value of these methods. Mr. Mill has certainly offered a number of examples of his methods; but I hope I may say, without offence, that they appear to me to be wanting in the conditions which I have mentioned. As I have to justify myself for rejecting Mr. Mill's criticism of doctrines which I have put forward, and examples which I have adduced, I may, I trust, be allowed to offer some critical remarks in return, bearing upon the examples which he has given, in order to illustrate his doctrines and precepts.

42. The first remark which I have to make is, that a large proportion of his examples (i. 480, &c.) is taken from one favourite author; who, however great his merit may be, is too recent a writer to have had his discoveries confirmed by the corresponding investigations and searching criticisms of other labourers in the same field, and placed in their proper and permanent relation to established truths; these alleged discoveries being, at the same time, principally such as deal with the most complex and slippery portions of science, the laws of vital action. Thus Mr. Mill has adduced, as examples of discoveries, Prof. Liebig's doctrine—that death is produced by certain metallic poisons through their forming indecomposable compounds; that the effect of respiration upon the blood consists in the conversion of peroxide of iron into protoxide—that the antiseptic power of salt arises from its attraction for moisture—that chemical action is contagious; and others. Now supposing that we have no doubt of the truth of these discoveries, we must still observe that they cannot wisely be cited, in order to exemplify the nature of the progress of knowledge, till they have been verified by other chemists, and worked into their places in the general scheme of chemistry; especially, since it is tolerably certain that in the process of verification, they will be modified and more precisely defined. Nor can I think it judicious to take so large a proportion of our examples from a region of science in which, of all parts of our material knowledge, the conceptions both of266 ordinary persons, and even of men of science themselves, are most loose and obscure, and the genuine principles most contested; which is the case in physiology. It would be easy, I think, to point out the vague and indeterminate character of many of the expressions in which the above examples are propounded, as well as their doubtful position in the scale of chemical generalization; but I have said enough to show why I cannot give much weight to these, as cardinal examples of the method of discovery; and therefore I shall not examine in detail how far they support Mr. Mill's methods of inquiry.

43. Mr. Liebig supplies the first and the majority of Mr. Mill's examples in chapter IX. of his Book on Induction. The second is an example for which Mr. Mill states himself to be indebted to Mr. Alexander Bain; the law established being this, that (i. 487) electricity cannot exist in one body without the simultaneous excitement of the opposite electricity in some neighbouring body, which Mr. Mill also confirms by reference to Mr. Faraday's experiments on voltaic wires.

I confess I am quite at a loss to understand what there is in the doctrine here ascribed to Mr. Bain which was not known to the electricians who, from the time of Franklin, explained the phenomena of the Leyden vial. I may observe also that the mention of an "electrified atmosphere" implies a hypothesis long obsolete. The essential point in all those explanations was, that each electricity produced by induction the opposite electricity in neighbouring bodies, as I have tried to make apparent in the History[273]. Faraday has, more recently, illustrated this universal co-existence of opposite electricities with his usual felicity.

But the conjunction of this fact with voltaic phenomena, implies a non-recognition of some of the simplest doctrines of the subject. "Since," it is said (i. 488), "common or machine electricity, and voltaic electricity267 may be considered for the present purpose to be identical, Faraday wished to know, &c." I think Mr. Faraday would be much astonished to learn that he considered electricity in equilibrium, and electricity in the form of a voltaic current, to be, for any purpose, identical. Nor do I conceive that he would assent to the expression in the next page, that "from the nature of a voltaic charge, the two opposite currents necessary to the existence of each other are both accommodated in one wire." Mr. Faraday has, as it appears to me, studiously avoided assenting to this hypothesis.

44. The next example is the one already so copiously dwelt upon by Sir John Herschel, Dr. Wells's researches on the production of Dew. I have already said[274] that "this investigation, although it has sometimes been praised as an original discovery, was in fact only resolving the phenomenon into principles already discovered namely, the doctrine of a constituent temperature of vapour, the different conducting power of different bodies, and the like. And this agrees in substance with what Mr. Mill says (i. 497); that the discovery, when made, was corroborated by deduction from the known laws of aqueous vapour, of conduction, and the like. Dr. Wells's researches on Dew tended much in this country to draw attention to the general principles of Atmology; and we may see, in this and in other examples which Mr. Mill adduces, that the explanation of special phenomena by means of general principles, already established, has, for common minds, a greater charm, and is more complacently dwelt on, than the discovery of the general principles themselves.

45. The next example, (i. 502) is given in order to illustrate the Method of Residues, and is the discovery by M. Arago that a disk of copper affects the vibrations of the magnetic needle. But this apparently detached fact affords little instruction compared with the singularly sagacious researches by which Mr. Faraday268 discovered the cause of this effect to reside in the voltaic currents which the motion of the magnetic needle developed in the copper. I have spoken of this discovery in the History[275]. Mr. Mill however is

quoting Sir John Herschel in thus illustrating the Method of Residues. He rightly gives the Perturbations of the Planets and Satellites as better examples of the method[276].

46. In the next chapter (c. x.) Mr. Mill speaks of Plurality of causes and of the Intermixture of effects, and gives examples of such cases. He here teaches (i. 517) that chemical synthesis and analysis, (as when oxygen and hydrogen compose water, and when water is resolved into oxygen and hydrogen,) is properly transformation, but that because we find that the weight of the compound is equal to the sum of the weights of the elements, we take up the notion of chemical composition. I have endeavoured to show[277] that the maxim, that the sum of the weights of the elements is equal to the weight of the compound, was, historically, not proved from experiment, but assumed in the reasonings upon experiments.

47. I have now made my remarks upon nearly all the examples which Mr. Mill gives of scientific inquiry, so far as they consist of knowledge which has really been obtained. I may mention, as points which appear to me to interfere with the value of Mr. Mill's references to examples, expressions which I cannot reconcile with just conceptions of scientific truth; as when he says (i. 523), "some other force which impinges on the first force;" and very frequently indeed, of the "tangential force," as co-ordinate with the centripetal force.

When he speaks (ii. 20, Note) of "the doctrine now universally received that the earth is a great natural magnet with two poles," he does not recognize the recent theory of Gauss, so remarkably coincident with269 a vast body of facts[278]. Indeed in his statement, he rejects no less the earlier views proposed by Halley, theorized by Euler, and confirmed by Hansteen, which show that we are compelled to assume at least four poles of terrestrial magnetism; which I had given an account of in the first edition of the History.

There are several other cases which he puts, in which, the knowledge spoken of not having been yet acquired, he tells us how he would set about acquiring it; for instance, if the question were (i. 526) whether mercury be a cure for a given disease; or whether the brain be a voltaic pile (ii. 21); or whether the moon be inhabited (ii. 100); or whether all crows are black (ii. 124); I confess that I have no expectation of any advantage to philosophy from discussions of this kind.

48. I will add also, that I do not think any light can be thrown upon scientific methods, at present, by grouping along with such physical inquiries as I have been speaking of, speculations concerning the human mind, its qualities and operations. Thus he speaks (i. 508) of human characters, as exemplifying the effect of plurality of causes; of (i. 518) the phenomena of our mental nature, which are analogous to chemical rather than to dynamical phenomena; of (i. 518) the reason why susceptible persons are imaginative; to which I may add, the passage where he says (i. 444), "let us take as an example of a phenomenon which we have no means of fabricating artificially, a human mind." These, and other like examples, occur in the part of his work in which he is speaking of scientific inquiry in general, not in the Book on the Logic of the Moral Sciences; and are, I think, examples more likely to lead us astray than to help our progress, in discovering the laws of Scientific Inquiry, in the ordinary sense of the term.

VI. Mr. Mill against Hypothesis.—49. I will now pass from Mr. Mill's methods, illustrated by such examples as those which I have been considering, to270 the views respecting the conditions of Scientific Induction to which I have been led, by such a survey as I could make, of the whole history of the principal Inductive Sciences; and especially, to those views to which Mr. Mill offers his objections[279].

Mr. Mill thinks that I have been too favourable to the employment of hypotheses, as means of discovering scientific truth; and that I have countenanced a laxness of method, in allowing hypotheses to be established, merely in virtue of the accordance of their results with the phenomena. I believe I should be as cautious as Mr. Mill, in accepting mere hypothetical explanations of phenomena, in any case in which we had the phenomena, and their relations, placed before both of us in an equally clear light. I have not accepted the Undulatory theory of Heat, though recommended by so many coincidences and analogies[280]. But I see some grave reasons for not giving any great weight to Mr. Mill's admonitions;—reasons drawn271 from the language which he uses on the subject, and which appears to me inconsistent with the conditions of the cases to which he applies it. Thus, when he says (ii. 22) that the condition of a hypothesis accounting for all the known phenomena is "often fulfilled equally well by two conflicting hypotheses," I can only say that I know of no such case in the history of Science, where the phenomena are at all numerous and complicated; and that if such a case were to occur, one of the hypotheses might always be resolved into the other. When he says, that "this evidence (the agreement of the results of the hypothesis with the phenomena) cannot be of the smallest value, because we cannot have in the case of such an hypothesis the assurance that if the hypothesis be false it must lead to results at variance with the true facts," we must reply, with due submission, that we have, in the case spoken of, the most complete evidence of this; for any change in the hypothesis would make it incapable of accounting for the facts. When he says that "if we give ourselves the license of inventing the causes as well as their laws, a person of fertile imagination might devise a hundred modes of accounting for any given fact;" I reply, that the question is about accounting for a large and complex series of facts, of which the laws have been ascertained: and as a test of Mr. Mill's assertion, I would propose as a challenge to any person of fertile imagination to devise any one other hypothesis to account for the perturbations of the moon, or the coloured fringes of shadows, besides the hypothesis by which they have actually been explained with such curious completeness. This challenge has been repeatedly offered, but never in any degree accepted; and I entertain no apprehension that Mr. Mill's supposition will ever be verified by such a performance.

50. I see additional reason for mistrusting the precision of Mr. Mill's views of that accordance of phenomena with the results of a hypothesis, in several others of the expressions which he uses (ii. 23). He speaks of a hypothesis being a "plausible explanation272 of all or most of the phenomena;" but the case which we have to consider is where it gives an exact representation of all the phenomena in which its results can be traced. He speaks of its being certain that the laws of the phenomena are "in some measure analogous" to those given by the hypothesis; the case to be dealt with being, that they are in every way identical. He speaks of this analogy being certain, from the fact that the hypothesis can be "for a moment tenable;" as if any one had recommended a hypothesis which is tenable only while a small part of the facts are considered, when it is

inconsistent with others which a fuller examination of the case discloses. I have nothing to say, and have said nothing, in favour of hypotheses which are not tenable. He says there are many such "harmonies running through the laws of phenomena in other respects radically distinct;" and he gives as an instance, the laws of light and heat. I have never alleged such harmonies as grounds of theory, unless they should amount to identities; and if they should do this, I have no doubt that the most sober thinkers will suppose the causes to be of the same kind in the two harmonizing instances. If chlorine, iodine and brome, or sulphur and phosphorus, have, as Mr. Mill says, analogous properties, I should call these substances analogous: but I can see no temptation to frame an hypothesis that they are identical (which he seems to fear), so long as Chemistry proves them distinct. But any hypothesis of an analogy in the constitution of these elements (suppose, for instance, a resemblance in their atomic form or composition) would seem to me to have a fair claim to trial; and to be capable of being elevated from one degree of probability to another by the number, variety, and exactitude of the explanations of phenomena which it should furnish.

VII. Against prediction of Facts.—51. These expressions of Mr. Mill have reference to a way in which hypotheses may be corroborated, in estimating the value of which, it appears that he and I differ. "It seems to be thought," he says (ii. 23), "that an hypo273thesis of the sort in question is entitled to a more favourable reception, if, besides accounting for the facts previously known, it has led to the anticipation and prediction of others which experience afterwards verified." And he adds, "Such predictions and their fulfilment are indeed well calculated to strike the ignorant vulgar;" but it is strange, he says, that any considerable stress should be laid upon such a coincidence by scientific thinkers. However strange it may seem to him, there is no doubt that the most scientific thinkers, far more than the ignorant vulgar, have allowed the coincidence of results predicted by theory with fact afterwards observed, to produce the strongest effects upon their conviction; and that all the best-established theories have obtained their permanent place in general acceptance in virtue of such coincidences, more than of any other evidence. It was not the ignorant vulgar alone, who were struck by the return of Halley's comet, as an evidence of the Newtonian theory. Nor was it the ignorant vulgar, who were struck with those facts which did so much strike men of science, as curiously felicitous proofs of the undulatory theory of light,—the production of darkness by two luminous rays interfering in a special manner; the refraction of a single ray of light into a conical pencil; and other complex yet precise results, predicted by the theory and verified by experiment. It must, one would think, strike all persons in proportion to their thoughtfulness, that when Nature thus does our bidding, she acknowledges that we have learnt her true language. If we can predict new facts which we have not seen, as well as explain those which we have seen, it must be because our explanation is not a mere formula of observed facts, but a truth of a deeper kind. Mr. Mill says, "If the laws of the propagation of light agree with those of the vibrations of an elastic fluid in so many respects as is necessary to make the hypothesis a plausible explanation of all or most of the phenomena known at the time, it is nothing strange that they should accord with each other in one respect more." Nothing strange, if the274 theory be true; but quite unaccountable, if it be not. If I copy a long series of letters of which the last half-dozen are concealed, and if I guess those aright, as is found to be the case when they are afterwards uncovered, this must be because I have made out the import of the inscription. To say, that because I have copied all that I could see, it is nothing strange that I should guess those which I cannot see, would be absurd, without supposing such a ground for guessing. The notion that the discovery of the laws and causes of phenomena is a loose haphazard sort of guessing, which gives "plausible" explanations, accidental coincidences, casual "harmonies," laws, "in some measure analogous" to the true ones, suppositions "tenable" for a time, appears to me to be a misapprehension of the whole nature of science; as it certainly is inapplicable to the case to which it is principally applied by Mr. Mill.

52. There is another kind of evidence of theories, very closely approaching to the verification of untried predictions, and to which, apparently, Mr. Mill does not attach much importance, since he has borrowed the term by which I have described it, Consilience, but has applied it in a different manner (ii. 530, 563, 590). I have spoken, in the Philosophy[281], of the Consilience of Inductions, as one of the Tests of Hypotheses, and have exemplified it by many instances; for example, the theory of universal gravitation, obtained by induction from the motions of the planets, was found to explain also that peculiar motion of the spheroidal earth which produces the Precession of the Equinoxes. This, I have said, was a striking and surprising coincidence which gave the theory a stamp of truth beyond the power of ingenuity to counterfeit. I may compare such occurrences to a case of interpreting an unknown character, in which two different inscriptions, deciphered by different persons, had given the same alphabet. We should,275 in such a case, believe with great confidence that the alphabet was the true one; and I will add, that I believe the history of science offers no example in which a theory supported by such consiliences, had been afterwards proved to be false.

53. Mr. Mill accepts (ii. 21) a rule of M. Comte's, that we may apply hypotheses, provided they are capable of being afterwards verified as facts. I have a much higher respect for Mr. Mill's opinion than for M. Comte's[282]; but I do not think that this rule will be found of any value. It appears to me to be tainted with the vice which I have already noted, of throwing the whole burthen of explanation upon the unexplained word fact—unexplained in any permanent and definite opposition to theory. As I have said, the Newtonian theory is a fact. Every true theory is a fact. Nor does the distinction become more clear by Mr. Mill's examples. "The vortices of Descartes would have been," he says, "a perfectly legitimate hypothesis, if it had been possible by any mode of explanation which we could entertain the hope of possessing, to bring the question whether such vortices exist or not, within the reach of our observing faculties." But this was possible, and was done. The free276 passage of comets through the spaces in which these vortices should have been, convinced men that these vortices did not exist. In like manner Mr. Mill rejects the hypothesis of a luminiferous ether, "because it can neither be seen, heard, smelt, tasted, or touched." It is a strange complaint to make of the vehicle of light, that it cannot be heard, smelt, or tasted. Its vibrations can be seen. The fringes of shadows for instance, show its vibrations, just as the visible lines of waves near the shore show the undulations of the sea. Whether this can be touched, that is, whether it resists motion, is hardly yet clear. I am far from saying there are not difficulties on this point, with regard to all theories which suppose a medium. But there are no more difficulties of this kind in the undulatory theory of light, than there are in Fourier's theory of heat, which M. Comte adopts as a model of scientific investigation; or in the theory of voltaic currents, about which Mr. Mill appears to have no doubt; or of electric atmospheres, which, though

141

generally obsolete, Mr. Mill appears to favour; for though it had been said that we feel such atmospheres, no one had said that they have the other attributes of matter.

VIII. Newton's Vera Causa.—54. Mr. Mill conceives (ii. 17) that his own rule concerning hypotheses coincides with Newton's Rule, that the cause assumed must be a vera causa. But he allows that "Mr. Whewell ... has had little difficulty in showing that his (Newton's) conception was neither precise nor consistent with itself." He also allows that "Mr. Whewell is clearly right in denying it to be necessary that the cause assigned should be a cause already known; else how could we ever become acquainted with new causes?" These points being agreed upon, I think that a little further consideration will lead to the conviction that Newton's Rule of philosophizing will best become a valuable guide, if we understand it as asserting that when the explanation of two or more different kinds of phenomena (as the revolutions of the planets, the fall of a stone, and the precession of the equinoxes,) lead us to the same cause, such a coincidence gives a277 reality to the cause. We have, in fact, in such a case, a Consilience of Inductions.

55. When Mr. Mill condemns me (ii. 24) (using, however, expressions of civility which I gladly acknowledge,) for having recognized no mode of Induction except that of trying hypothesis after hypothesis until one is found which fits the phenomena, I must beg to remind the readers of our works, that Mr. Mill himself allows (i. 363) that the process of finding a conception which binds together observed facts "is tentative, that it consists of a succession of guesses, many being rejected until one at last occurs fit to be chosen." I must remind them also that I have given a Section upon the Tests of Hypotheses, to which I have just referred,—that I have given various methods of Induction, as the Method of Gradation, the Method of Natural Classification, the Method of Curves, the Method of Means, the Method of Least Squares, the Method of Residues: all which I have illustrated by conspicuous examples from the History of Science; besides which, I conceive that what I have said of the Ideas belonging to each science, and of the construction and explication of conceptions, will point out in each case, in what region we are to look for the Inductive Element in order to make new discoveries. I have already ventured to say, elsewhere, that the methods which I have given, are as definite and practical as any others which have been proposed, with the great additional advantage of being the methods by which all great discoveries in science have really been made.

IX. Successive Generalizations.—56. There is one feature in the construction of science which Mr. Mill notices, but to which he does not ascribe, as I conceive, its due importance: I mean, that process by which we not only ascend from particular facts to a general law, but when this is done, ascend from the first general law to others more general; and so on, proceeding to the highest point of generalization. This character of the scientific process was first clearly pointed out by Bacon, and is one of the most noticeable instances of278 his philosophical sagacity. "There are," he says, "two ways, and can be only two, of seeking and finding truth. The one from sense and particulars, takes a flight to the most general axioms, and from these principles and their truth, settled once for all, invents and judges of intermediate axioms. The other method collects axioms from sense and particulars, ascending continuously and by degrees, so that in the end it arrives at the most general axioms:" meaning by axioms, laws or principles. The structure of the most complete sciences consists of several such steps,—floors, as Bacon calls them, of successive generalization; and thus this structure may be exhibited as a kind of scientific pyramid. I have constructed this pyramid in the case of the science of Astronomy[283]: and I am gratified to find that the illustrious Humboldt approves of the design, and speaks of it as executed with complete success[284]. The capability of being exhibited in this form of successive generalizations, arising from particulars upward to some very general law, is the condition of all tolerably perfect sciences; and the steps of the successive generalizations are commonly the most important events in the history of the science.

57. Mr. Mill does not reject this process of generalization; but he gives it no conspicuous place, making it only one of three modes of reducing a law of causation into other laws. "There is," he says (i. 555), "the subsumption of one law under another; ... the gathering up of several laws into one more general law which includes them all. He adds afterwards, that the general law is the sum of the partial ones (i. 557), an expression which appears to me inadequate, for reasons which I have already stated. The general law is not the mere sum of the particular laws. It is, as I have already said, their amount in a new point of279 view. A new conception is introduced; thus, Newton did not merely add together the laws of the motions of the moon and of the planets, and of the satellites, and of the earth; he looked at them altogether as the result of a universal force of mutual gravitation; and therein consisted his generalization. And the like might be pointed out in other cases.

58. I am the more led to speak of Mr. Mill as not having given due importance to this process of successive generalization, by the way in which he speaks in another place (ii. 525) of this doctrine of Bacon. He conceives Bacon "to have been radically wrong when he enunciates, as a universal rule, that induction should proceed from the lowest to the middle principles, and from those to the highest, never reversing that order, and consequently, leaving no room for the discovery of new principles by way of deduction[285] at all."

59. I conceive that the Inductive Table of Astronomy, to which I have already referred, shows that in that science,—the most complete which has yet existed,—the history of the science has gone on, as to its general movement, in accordance with the view which Bacon's sagacity enjoined. The successive generalizations, so far as they were true, were made by successive generations. I conceive also that the Inductive Table of Optics shows the same thing; and this, without taking for granted the truth of the Undulatory Theory; for with regard to all the steps of the progress of the science, lower than that highest one, there is, I conceive, no controversy.

60. Also, the Science of Mechanics, although Mr. Mill more especially refers to it, as a case in which the280 highest generalizations (for example the Laws of Motion) were those earliest ascertained with any scientific exactness, will, I think, on a more careful examination of its history, be found remarkably to confirm Bacon's view. For, in that science, we have, in the first place, very conspicuous examples of the vice of the method pursued by the ancients in flying to the highest generalizations first; as when they made their false distinctions of the laws of natural and violent motions, and of terrestrial and celestial motions. Many erroneous laws of motion were asserted through neglect of facts or want of experiments. And when Galileo and his school had in some measure succeeded in discovering some of the true laws of the motions of terrestrial bodies, they

did not at once assert them as general: for they did not at all apply those laws to the celestial motions. As I have remarked, all Kepler's speculations respecting the causes of the motions of the planets, went upon the supposition that the First Law of terrestrial Motion did not apply to celestial bodies; but that, on the contrary, some continual force was requisite to keep up, as well as to originate, the planetary motions. Nor did Descartes, though he enunciated the Laws of Motion with more generality than his predecessors, (but not with exactness,) venture to trust the planets to those laws; on the contrary, he invented his machinery of Vortices in order to keep up the motions of the heavenly bodies. Newton was the first who extended the laws of terrestrial motion to the celestial spaces; and in doing so, he used all the laws of the celestial motions which had previously been discovered by more limited inductions. To these instances, I may add the gradual generalization of the Third Law of motion by Huyghens, the Bernoullis, and Herman, which I have described in the History[286] as preceding that Period of Deduction, to which the succeeding narrative[287] is appropriated. In Mechanics, then, we have a cardinal example of the historically gradual and successive281 ascent of science from particulars to the most general laws.

61. The Science of Hydrostatics may appear to offer a more favourable example of the ascent to the most general laws, without going through the intermediate particular laws; and it is true, with reference to this science, as I have observed[288], that it does exhibit the peculiarity of our possessing the most general principles on which the phenomena depend, and from which many cases of special facts are explained by deduction; while other cases cannot be so explained, from the want of principles intermediate between the highest and the lowest. And I have assigned, as the reason of this peculiarity, that the general principles of the Mechanics of Fluids were not obtained with reference to the science itself, but by extension from the sister science of the Mechanics of Solids. The two sciences are parts of the same Inductive Pyramid; and having reached the summit of this Pyramid on one side, we are tempted to descend on the other from the highest generality to more narrow laws. Yet even in this science, the best part of our knowledge is mainly composed of inductive laws, obtained by inductive examination of particular classes of facts. The mere mathematical investigations of the laws of waves, for instance, have not led to any results so valuable as the experimental researches of Bremontier, Emy, the Webers, and Mr. Scott Russell. And in like manner in Acoustics, the Mechanics of Elastic Fluids[289], the deductions of mathematicians made on general principles have not done so much for our knowledge, as the cases of vibrations of plates and pipes examined experimentally by Chladni, Savart, Mr. Wheatstone and Mr. Willis. We see therefore, even in these sciences, no reason to slight the wisdom which exhorts us to ascend from particulars to intermediate laws, rather than to hope to deduce these latter better from the more general laws obtained once for all.

282

62. Mr. Mill himself indeed, notwithstanding that he slights Bacon's injunction to seek knowledge by proceeding from less general to more general laws, has given a very good reason why this is commonly necessary and wise. He says (ii. 526), "Before we attempt to explain deductively, from more general laws, any new class of phenomena, it is desirable to have gone as far as is practicable in ascertaining the empirical laws of these phenomena; so as to compare the results of deduction, not with one individual instance

after another, but with general propositions expressive of the points of agreement which have been found among many instances. For," he adds with great justice, "if Newton had been obliged to verify the theory of gravitation, not by deducing from it Kepler's laws, but by deducing all the observed planetary positions which had served Kepler to establish those laws, the Newtonian theory would probably never have emerged from the state of an hypothesis." To which we may add, that it is certain, from the history of the subject, that in that case the hypothesis would never have been framed at all.

X. Mr. Mill's Hope from Deduction.—63. Mr. Mill expresses a hope of the efficacy of Deduction, rather than Induction, in promoting the future progress of Science; which hope, so far as the physical sciences are concerned, appears to me at variance with all the lessons of the history of those sciences. He says (i. 579), "that the advances henceforth to be expected even in physical, and still more in mental and social science, will be chiefly the result of deduction, is evident from the general considerations already adduced:" these considerations being, that the phenomena to be considered are very complex, and are the result of many known causes, of which we have to disentangle the results.

64. I cannot but take a very different view from this. I think that any one, looking at the state of physical science, will see that there are still a vast mass of cases, in which we do not at all know the causes, at least, in their full generality; and that the283 knowledge of new causes, and the generalization of the laws of those already known, can only be obtained by new inductive discoveries. Except by new Inductions, equal, in their efficacy for grouping together phenomena in new points of view, to any which have yet been performed in the history of science, how are we to solve such questions as those which, in the survey of what we already know, force themselves upon our minds? Such as, to take only a few of the most obvious examples—What is the nature of the connexion of heat and light? How does heat produce the expansion, liquefaction and vaporization of bodies? What is the nature of the connexion between the optical and the chemical properties of light? What is the relation between optical, crystalline and chemical polarity? What is the connexion between the atomic constitution and the physical qualities of bodies? What is the tenable definition of a mineral species? What is the true relation of the apparently different types of vegetable life (monocotyledons, dicotyledons, and cryptogamous plants)? What is the relation of the various types of animal life (vertebrates, articulates, radiates, &c.)? What is the number, and what are the distinctions of the Vital Powers? What is the internal constitution of the earth? These, and many other questions of equal interest, no one, I suppose, expects to see solved by deduction from principles already known. But we can, in many of them, see good hope of progress by a large use of induction; including, of course, copious and careful experiments and observations.

65. With such questions before us, as have now been suggested, I can see nothing but a most mischievous narrowing of the field and enfeebling of the spirit of scientific exertion, in the doctrine that "Deduction is the great scientific work of the present and of future ages;" and that "A revolution is peaceably and progressively effecting itself in philosophy the reverse of that to which Bacon has attached his name." I trust, on the contrary, that we have many new laws of nature still to discover; and that our race is destined284 to obtain a sight of wider truths than any we yet discern, including, as cases, the general laws we now know, and obtained from these known laws as they must be, by Induction.

66. I can see, however, reasons for the comparatively greater favour with which Mr. Mill looks upon Deduction, in the views to which he has mainly directed his attention. The explanation of remarkable phenomena by known laws of Nature, has, as I have already said, a greater charm for many minds than the discovery of the laws themselves. In the case of such explanations, the problem proposed is more definite, and the solution more obviously complete. For the process of induction includes a mysterious step, by which we pass from particulars to generals, of which step the reason always seems to be inadequately rendered by any words which we can use; and this step to most minds is not demonstrative, as to few is it given to perform it on a great scale. But the process of explanation of facts by known laws is deductive, and has at every step a force like that of demonstration, producing a feeling peculiarly gratifying to the clear intellects which are most capable of following the process. We may often see instances in which this admiration for deductive skill appears in an extravagant measure; as when men compare Laplace with Newton. Nor should I think it my business to argue against such a preference, unless it were likely to leave us too well satisfied with what we know already, to chill our hope of scientific progress, and to prevent our making any further strenuous efforts to ascend, higher than we have yet done, the mountain-chain which limits human knowledge.

67. But there is another reason which, I conceive, operates in leading Mr. Mill to look to Deduction as the principal means of future progress in knowledge, and which is a reason of considerable weight in the subjects of research which, as I conceive, he mainly has in view. In the study of our own minds and of the laws which govern the history of society, I do not think that it is very likely that we shall hereafter285 arrive at any wider principles than those of which we already possess some considerable knowledge; and this, for a special reason; namely, that our knowledge in such cases is not gathered by mere external observation of a collection of external facts; but acquired by attention to internal facts, our own emotions, thoughts, and springs of action; facts are connected by ties existing in our own consciousness, and not in mere observed juxtaposition, succession, or similitude. How the character, for instance, is influenced by various causes, (an example to which Mr. Mill repeatedly refers, ii. 518, &c.), is an inquiry which may perhaps be best conducted by considering what we know of the influence of education and habit, government and occupation, hope and fear, vanity and pride, and the like, upon men's characters, and by tracing the various effects of the intermixture of such influences. Yet even here, there seems to be room for the discovery of laws in the way of experimental inquiry: for instance, what share race or family has in the formation of character; a question which can hardly be solved to any purpose in any other way than by collecting and classing instances. And in the same way, many of the principles which regulate the material wealth of states, are obtained, if not exclusively, at least most clearly and securely, by induction from large surveys of facts. Still, however, I am quite ready to admit that in Mental and Social Science, we are much less likely than in Physical Science, to obtain new truths by any process which can be distinctively termed Induction; and that in those sciences, what may be called Deductions from principles of thought and action of which we are already conscious, or to which we assent when they are felicitously picked out of our thoughts and put into words, must have a large share; and I may add, that this observation of Mr. Mill appears to me to be important, and, in its present connexion, new.

XI. Fundamental opposition of our doctrines.—68. I have made nearly all the remarks which I now think it of any consequence to make upon Mr. Mill's Logic, so far as it bears upon the doctrines contained in my History and Philosophy. And yet there286 remains still untouched one great question, involving probably the widest of all the differences between him and me. I mean the question whether geometrical axioms, (and, as similar in their evidence to these, all axioms,) be truths derived from experience, or be necessary truths in some deeper sense. This is one of the fundamental questions of philosophy; and all persons who take an interest in metaphysical discussions, know that the two opposite opinions have been maintained with great zeal in all ages of speculation. To me it appears that there are two distinct elements in our knowledge, Experience, without, and the Mind, within. Mr. Mill derives all our knowledge from Experience alone. In a question thus going to the root of all knowledge, the opposite arguments must needs cut deep on both sides. Mr. Mill cannot deny that our knowledge of geometrical axioms and the like, seems to be necessary. I cannot deny that our knowledge, axiomatic as well as other, never is acquired without experience.

69. Perhaps ordinary readers may despair of following our reasonings, when they find that they can only be made intelligible by supposing, on the one hand, a person who thinks distinctly and yet has never seen or felt any external object; and on the other hand, a person who is transferred, as Mr. Mill supposes (ii. 117), to "distant parts of the stellar regions where the phenomena may be entirely unlike those with which we are acquainted," and where even the axiom, that every effect must have a cause, does not hold good. Nor, in truth, do I think it necessary here to spend many words on this subject. Probably, for those who take an interest in this discussion, most of the arguments on each side have already been put forwards with sufficient repetition. I have, in an "Essay on the Fundamental Antithesis of Philosophy," and in some accompanying "Remarks," printed[290] at the end of the second edition of my Philosophy, given my reply to what has been said on this subject, both by Mr. Mill, and by the author of a very able critique on my His287tory and Philosophy which appeared in the Quarterly Review in 1841: and I will not here attempt to revive the general discussion.

70. Perhaps I may be allowed to notice, that in one part of Mr. Mill's work where this subject is treated, there is the appearance of one of the parties to the controversy pronouncing judgment in his own cause. This indeed is a temptation which it is especially difficult for an author to resist, who writes a treatise upon Fallacies, the subject of Mr. Mill's fifth Book. In such a treatise, the writer has an easy way of disposing of adverse opinions by classing them as "Fallacies," and putting them side by side with opinions universally acknowledged to be false. In this way, Mr. Mill has dealt with several points which are still, as I conceive, matters of controversy (ii. 357, &c.).

71. But undoubtedly, Mr. Mill has given his argument against my opinions with great distinctness in another place (i. 319). In order to show that it is merely habitual association which gives to an experimental truth the character of a necessary truth, he quotes the case of the laws of motion, which were really discovered from experiment, but are now looked upon as the only conceivable laws; and especially, what he conceives as "the reductio ad absurdum of the theory of inconceivableness," an opinion which I had ventured to throw out, that if we could conceive the Composition of bodies distinctly, we might be able to

see that it is necessary that the modes of their composition should be definite. I do not think that readers in general will see anything absurd in the opinion, that the laws of Mechanics, and even the laws of the Chemical Composition of bodies, may depend upon principles as necessary as the properties of space and number; and that this necessity, though not at all perceived by persons who have only the ordinary obscure and confused notions on such subjects, may be evident to a mind which has, by effort and discipline, rendered its ideas of Mechanical Causation, Elementary Composition and Difference of Kind, clear and precise. It may easily be, I conceive, that while such necessary288 principles are perceived to be necessary only by a few minds of highly cultivated insight, such principles as the axioms of Geometry and Arithmetic may be perceived to be necessary by all minds which have any habit of abstract thought at all: and I conceive also, that though these axioms are brought into distinct view by a certain degree of intellectual cultivation, they may still be much better described as conditions of experience, than as results of experience:—as laws of the mind and of its activity, rather than as facts impressed upon a mind merely passive.

XII. Absurdities in Mr. Mill's Logic.—72. I will not pursue the subject further: only, as the question has arisen respecting the absurdities to which each of the opposite doctrines leads, I will point out opinions connected with this subject, which Mr. Mill has stated in various parts of his book.

He holds (i. 317) that it is merely from habit that we are unable to conceive the last point of space or the last instant of time. He holds (ii. 360) that it is strange that any one should rely upon the à priori evidence that space or extension is infinite, or that nothing can be made of nothing. He holds (i. 304) that the first law of motion is rigorously true, but that the axioms respecting the lever are only approximately true. He holds (ii. 110) that there may be sidereal firmaments in which events succeed each other at random, without obeying any laws of causation; although one might suppose that even if space and cause are both to have their limits, still they might terminate together: and then, even on this bold supposition, we should no where have a world in which events were casual. He holds (ii. 111) that the axiom, that every event must have a cause, is established by means of an "induction by simple enumeration:" and in like manner, that the principles of number and of geometry are proved by this method of simple enumeration alone. He ascribes the proof (i. 162) of the axiom, "things which are equal to the same are equal to each other," to the fact that this proposition has been perpetually found true and never false. He holds (i. 338) that "In all289 propositions concerning numbers, a condition is implied, without which none of them would be true; and that condition is an assumption which may be false. The condition is that $1 = 1$."

73. Mr. Mill further holds (i. 309), that it is a characteristic property of geometrical forms, that they are capable of being painted in the imagination with a distinctness equal to reality:—that our ideas of forms exactly resemble our sensations: which, it is implied, is not the case with regard to any other class of our ideas;—that we thus may have mental pictures of all possible combinations of lines and angles, which are as fit subjects of geometrical experimentation as the realities themselves. He says, that "we know that the imaginary lines exactly resemble real ones;" and that we obtain this knowledge respecting the characteristic property of the idea of space by experience; though it does not appear how we can compare our ideas with the realities, since we know the realities only by our

148

ideas; or why this property of their resemblance should be confined to one class of ideas alone.

74. I have now made such remarks as appear to me to be necessary, on the most important parts of Mr. Mill's criticism of my Philosophy. I hope I have avoided urging any thing in a contentious manner; as I have certainly written with no desire of controversy, but only with a view to offer to those who may be willing to receive it, some explanation of portions of my previous writings. I have already said, that if this had not have been my especial object, I could with pleasure have noted the passages of Mr. Mill's Logic which I admire, rather than the points in which we differ. I will in a very few words refer to some of these points, as the most agreeable way of taking leave of the dispute.

I say then that Mr. Mill appears to me especially instructive in his discussion of the nature of the proof which is conveyed by the syllogism; and that his doctrine, that the force of the syllogism consists in an inductive assertion, with an interpretation added to it, solves very happily the difficulties which baffle the290 other theories of this subject. I think that this doctrine of his is made still more instructive, by his excepting from it the cases of Scriptural Theology and of Positive Law (i. 260), as cases in which general propositions, not particular facts, are our original data. I consider also that the recognition of Kinds (i. 166) as classes in which we have, not a finite but an inexhaustible body of resemblances among individuals, and as groups made by nature, not by mere definition, is very valuable, as stopping the inroad to an endless train of false philosophy. I conceive that he takes the right ground in his answer to Hume's argument against miracles (ii. 183): and I admire the acuteness with which he has criticized Laplace's tenets on the Doctrine of Chances, and the candour with which he has, in the second edition, acknowledged oversights on this subject made in the first. I think that much, I may almost say all, which he says on the subject of Language, is very philosophical; for instance, what he says (ii. 238) of the way in which words acquire their meaning in common use. I especially admire the acuteness and force with which he has shown (ii. 255) how moral principles expressed in words degenerate into formulas, and yet how the formula cannot be rejected without a moral loss. This "perpetual oscillation in spiritual truths," as he happily terms it, has never, I think, been noted in the same broad manner, and is a subject of most instructive contemplation. And though I have myself refrained from associating moral and political with physical science in my study of the subject, I see a great deal which is full of promise for the future progress of moral and political knowledge in Mr. Mill's sixth Book, "On the Logic of the Moral and Political Sciences." Even his arrangement of the various methods which have been or may be followed in "the Social Science,"—"the Chemical or Experimental Method," "the Geometrical or Abstract Method," "the Physical or Concrete Deductive Method," "the Inverse Deductive or Historical Method," though in some degree fanciful and forced, abounds with valuable suggestions; and his estimate of "the291 interesting philosophy of the Bentham school," the main example of "the geometrical method," is interesting and philosophical. On some future occasion, I may, perhaps, venture into the region of which Mr. Mill has thus essayed to map the highways: for it is from no despair either of the great progress to be made in such truth as that here referred to, or of the effect of philosophical method in arriving at such truth, that I have, in what I have now written, confined myself to the less captivating but more definite part of the subject.

149

CHAPTER XXIII.
Political Economy as an Inductive Science.

(Moral Sciences.)—1. Both M. Comte and Mr. Mill, in speaking of the methods of advancing science, aim, as I have said, at the extension of their methods to moral subjects, and aspire to suggest means for the augmentation of our knowledge of ethical, political, and social truths. I have not here ventured upon a like extension of my conclusions, because I wished to confine my views of the philosophy of discovery to the cases in which all allow that solid and permanent discoveries have been made. Moreover in the case of moral speculations, we have to consider not only observed external facts and the ideas by which they are colligated, but also internal facts, in which the instrument of observation is consciousness, and in which observations and ideas are mingled together, and act and react in a peculiar manner. It may therefore be doubted whether the methods which have been effectual in the discovery of physical theories will not require to be greatly modified, or replaced by processes altogether different, when we would make advances in ethical, political, or social knowledge. In ethics, at least, it seems plain that we must take our starting-point not without but within us. Our mental powers, our affections, our reason, and any other faculties which we have, must be the basis of our convictions. And in this field of knowledge, the very form of our highest propositions is different from what it is in the physical sciences. In Physics we examine what is, in a form more or less general: in Ethics we seek to determine what OUGHT to be, as the highest rule, which is supreme over all293 others. In this case we cannot expect the methods of physical discovery to aid us.

But others of the subjects which I have mentioned, though strongly marked and influenced by this ethical element, are still of a mixed character, and require also observation of external facts of human, individual, and social conduct, and generalizations derived from such observations. The facts of political constitutions and social relations in communities of men, and the histories of such communities, afford large bodies of materials for political and social science; and it seems not at all unlikely that such science may be governed, in its formation and progress, by laws like those which govern the physical sciences, and may be steered clear of errors and directed towards truths by an attention to the forms which error and truth have assumed in the most stable and certain sciences. The different forms of society, and the principal motives which operate upon men regarded in masses, may be classified as facts; and though our consciousness of what we ourselves are and the affections which we ourselves feel are always at work in our interpretations of such facts, yet the knowledge which we thus obtain may lead us to bodies of knowledge which we may call Sciences, and compare with the other sciences as to their form and maxims.

(Political Economy.)—2. Among such bodies of knowledge, I may notice as a specimen, the science of Political Economy, and may compare it with other sciences in the respects which have been referred to.

M. Comte has given a few pages to the discussion of this science of Political Economy[291]; but what he has said amounts only to a few vague remarks on Adam

Smith and Destutt de Tracy; his main object being, it would seem, to introduce his usual formula, and to condemn all that has hitherto been done (with which there is no evidence that he is adequately acquainted) as worthless, because it is "theological," "metaphysical," "literary," and not "positive."

294

Mr. Mill has much more distinctly characterized the plan and form of Political Economy in his system[292]. He regards this science as that which deals with the results which take place in human society in consequence of the desire of wealth. He explains, however, that it is only for the sake of convenience that one of the motives which operate upon man is thus insulated and treated as if it were the only one:—that there are other principles, for instance, the principles on which the progress of population depends, which co-operate with the main principle, and materially modify its results: and he gives reasons why this mode of simplifying the study of social phenomena tends to promote the progress of systematic knowledge.

Instead of discussing these reasons, I will notice the way in which the speculations of political economists have exemplified tendencies to error, and corrections of those tendencies, of the same nature as those which we have already noticed in speaking of other sciences.

(Wages, Profits, and Rent.)—3. We may regard as one of the first important steps in this science, Adam Smith's remark, that the value or price of any article bought and sold consists of three elements, Wages, Profits, and Rent. Some of the most important of subsequent speculations were attempts to determine the laws of each of these three elements. At first it might be supposed that there ought to be added to them a fourth element, Materials. But upon consideration it will be seen that materials, as an element of price, resolves itself into wages and rent; for all materials derive their value from the labour which is bestowed upon them. The iron of the ploughshare costs just what it costs to sink the mine, dig up and smelt the iron. The wood of the frame costs what it costs to cut down the tree, together with the rent of the ground on which it grows.

(Premature Generalizations.)—4. But what determines Wages?—The amount of persons seeking work,295 that is, speaking loosely, the population; and the amount of money which is devoted to the payment of wages. And what determines the population? It was replied,—the means of subsistence. And how does the population tend to increase?—In a geometrical ratio. And how does the subsistence tend to increase?—At most in an arithmetical ratio. And hence it was inferred that the population tends constantly to run beyond the means of subsistence, and will be limited by a threatened deficiency of these means. And the wages paid must be such as to form this limit. And therefore the wages paid will always be such as just to keep up the population in its ordinary state of progress. Here was one general proposition which was gathered from summary observations of society.

Again: as to Rent: Adam Smith had treated Rent as if it were a monopoly price—the result of a monopoly of the land by the landowners. But subsequent writers acutely remarked that land is of various degrees of fertility, and there is some land which barely pays the cultivator, if cultivating it he pay no rent. And rent can be afforded for other land only in so far as it is better than this bad land. And thus, there was obtained another general proposition; that the Rent of good land was just equal to the excess of its produce over the worst cultivable land.

Now these two propositions are examples of a hasty and premature generalization, like that from which the sweeping physical systems of antiquity were derived. They were examples of that process which Francis Bacon calls anticipation; in which we leap at once from a few facts to propositions of the highest generality; and supposing these to be securely established, proceed to draw a body of conclusions from them, and thus frame a system.

And what is the sounder and wiser mode of proceeding in order to obtain a science of such things? We must classify the facts which we observe, and take care that we do not ascribe to the facts in our immediate neighbourhood or specially under our notice, a generality of prevalence which does not belong to296 them. We must proceed by the ladder of Induction, and be sure we have obtained the narrower generalizations, before we aspire to the widest.

(Correction of them by Induction. Rent.)—5. For instance; in the case of the latter of the above two propositions—that Rent is the excess of the produce of good soils over the worst—that is the case in England and Scotland; but is it the case in other countries? Let us see. Why is it the case in England? Because if the rent demanded for good land were more than the excess of the produce over bad land, the farmer would prefer the bad land as more gainful. If the rent demanded for good land were less than the excess, the bad land would be abandoned by the farmer.

But all this goes upon the supposition that the farmer can remove from good land to bad, or from bad to good, or apply his capital in some other way than farming, according as it is more gainful. This is true in England; but is it true all over the world?

By no means. It is true in scarcely any other part of the world. In almost every other part of the world the cultivator is bound to the land, so that he cannot remove himself and his capital from it; and cannot, because he is not satisfied with his position upon it, seek and find a position and a subsistence elsewhere. On the contrary, he is bound by the laws and customs of the country, by constitution, history and character, so that he cannot, or can only with great difficulty, change his plan and mode of life. And thus over great part of the world the fundamental supposition on which rests the above generalization respecting Rent is altogether false.

An able political economist[293] has taken the step, which as we have said, sound philosophy would have prescribed: he has classified the states of society which exist or have existed on the earth, as they bear on this point, the amount of Rent. He has classified the modes in which the produce is, in different countries297 and different stages of society, divided between the cultivator and the proprietor: and he finds that the natural divisions are these:—Serf Rents, that is, labour rents paid by the Cultivator to the Landowner, as in Russia: Métayer Rents, where the produce is divided between the Cultivator and the Landowner, as in Central Europe: Ryot Rents, where a portion of the produce is paid to the Sovereign as Landlord, as in India: Cottier Rents, where a money-rent is paid by a Cultivator who raises his own subsistence from the soil; and Farmers' Rents, where a covenanted Rent is paid by a person employing labourers. In this last case alone is it true that the Rent is equal to the excess of good over bad soils.

The error of the conclusion, in this case, arises from assuming the mobility of capital and labour in cases in which it is not moveable: which is much as if mechanicians had reasoned respecting rigid bodies, supposing them to be fluid bodies.

But the error of method was in not classifying the facts of societies before jumping to a conclusion which was to be applicable to all societies.

(Wages.)—6. And in like manner there is an error of the same kind in the assertion of the other general principles:—that wages are determined by the capital which is forthcoming for the payment of wages; and that population is determined in its progress by wages. For there is a vast mass of population on the surface of the earth which does not live upon wages: and though in England the greater part of the people lives upon wages, in the rest of the world the part that does so is small. And in this case, as in the other, we must class these facts as they exist in different nations, before we can make assertions of any wide generality.

Mr. Jones[294] classed the condition of labourers in different countries in the same inductive manner in which he classed the tenure of land. He pointed out that298 there are three broad distinct classes of them: Unhired Labourers, who cultivate the ground which they occupy, and live on self-produced wages; Paid Dependants, who are paid out of the revenue or income of their employers, as the military retainers and domestic artizans of feudal times in Europe, and the greater part of the people of Asia at the present day; and Hired Labourers, who are paid wages from capital.

This last class, though taken as belonging to the normal condition of society by many political economists, is really the exceptional case, taking the world at large; and no propositions concerning the structure and relations of ranks in society can have any wide generality which are founded on a consideration of this case alone.

(Population.)—7. And again: with regard to the proposition that the progress of population depends merely on the rate of wages, a very little observation of different communities, and of the same communities at different times, will show that this is a very rash and hasty generalization. When wages rise, whether or not population shall undergo a corresponding increase depends upon many other circumstances besides this single fact of the increase of wages. The effect of a rise of wages upon population is affected by the form of the wages, the time occupied by the change, the institutions of the society under consideration, and other causes: and a due classification of the conditions of the society according to these circumstances, is requisite in order to obtain any general proposition concerning the effect of a rise or fall of wages upon the progress of the population.

And thus those precepts of the philosophy of discovery which we have repeated so often, which are so simple, and which seem so obvious, have been neglected or violated in the outset of Political Economy as in so many other sciences:—namely, the precepts

153

that we must classify our facts before we generalize, and seek for narrower generalizations and inductions before we aim at the widest. If these maxims had been obeyed, they would have saved the earlier specu299lators on this subject from some splendid errors; but, on the other hand, it may be said, that if these earlier speculators had not been thus bold, the science could not so soon have assumed that large and striking form which made it so attractive, and to which it probably owes a large part of its progress.

300

CHAPTER XXIV.
Modern German Philosophy[295].

I. Science is the Idealization of Facts.

1. I have spoken, a few chapters back, of the Reaction against the doctrines of the Sensational School in England and France. In Germany also there was a Reaction against these doctrines;—but there, this movement took a direction different from its direction in other countries. Omitting many other names, Kant, Fichte, Schelling and Hegel may be regarded as the writers who mark, in a prominent manner, this Germanic line of speculation. The problem of philosophy, in the way in which they conceived it, may best be explained by reference to that Fundamental Antithesis of which I had occasion to speak in the History of Scientific Ideas[296]. And in order to characterize the steps taken by these modern German philosophers, I must return to what I have said concerning the Fundamental Antithesis.

This Antithesis, as I have there remarked, is stated in various ways:—as the Antithesis of Thoughts and Things; of Ideas and Sensations; of Theory and Facts; of Necessary Truth and Experience; of the Subjective and Objective elements of our knowledge; and in other phrases. I have further remarked that the elements thus spoken of, though opposed, are inseparable. We cannot have the one without the other. We cannot have thoughts without thinking of Things: we cannot have things before us without thinking of them.

301

Further, it has been shown, I conceive, that our knowledge derives from the former of these two elements, namely our Ideas, its form and character of knowledge; our ideas being the necessary Forms of knowledge, while the Matter of our knowledge in each case is supplied by the appropriate perception or outward experience.

Thus our Ideas of Space and Time are the necessary Forms of our geometrical and arithmetical knowledge; and no sensations or experience are needed as the matter of such knowledge, except in so far as sensation and experience are needed to evoke our Ideas in any degree. And hence these sciences are sometimes called Formal sciences. All other Sciences involve, along with the experience and observation appropriate to each, a development of the ideal conditions of knowledge existing in our minds; and I have given the history, both of this development of ideas and of the matter derived from experience, in two former works, the History of Scientific Ideas, and the History of the Inductive Sciences. I have there traced this history through the whole body of the physical sciences.

But though Ideas and Perceptions are thus separate elements in our philosophy, they cannot in fact be distinguished and separated, but are different aspects of the same thing. And the only way in which we can approach to truth is by gradually and successively, in one instance after another, advancing from the perception to the idea; from the fact to the theory.

2. I would now further observe, that in this progression from fact to theory, we advance (when the theory is complete and completely possessed by the mind) from the apprehension of truths as actual to the apprehension of them as necessary; and thus Facts which were originally observed merely as Facts become the consequences of theory, and are thus brought within the domain of Ideas. That which was a part of the objective world becomes also a part of the subjective world; a necessary part of the thoughts of the theorist. And in this way the progress of true theory is the Idealization of Facts.

302

Thus the Progress of Science consists in a perpetual reduction of Facts to Ideas. Portions are perpetually transferred from one side to another of the Fundamental Antithesis: namely, from the Objective to the Subjective side. The Centre or Fulcrum of the Antithesis is shifted by every movement which is made in the advance of science, and is shifted so that the ideal side gains something from the real side.

3. I will proceed to illustrate this Proposition a little further. Necessary Truths belong to the Subjective, Observed Facts to the Objective side of our knowledge. Now in the progress of that exact speculative knowledge which we call Science, Facts which were at a previous period merely Observed Facts, come to be known as Necessary Truths; and the attempts at new advances in science generally introduce the representation of known truths of fact, as included in higher and wider truths, and therefore, so far, necessary.

We may exemplify this progress in the history of the science of Mechanics. Thus the property of the lever, the inverse proportion of the weights and arms, was known as a fact before the time of Aristotle, and known as no more; for he gives many fantastical and inapplicable reasons for the fact. But in the writings of Archimedes we find this fact brought within the domain of necessary truth. It was there transferred from the empirical to the ideal side of the Fundamental Antithesis; and thus a progressive step was made in science. In like manner, it was at first taken by Galileo as a mere fact of experience, that in a falling body, the velocity increases in proportion to the time; but his followers have seen in this the necessary effect of the uniform force of gravity. In like manner, Kepler's empirical Laws were shown by Newton to be necessary results of a central force attracting inversely as the square of the distance. And if it be still, even at present, doubtful whether this is the necessary law of a central force, as some philosophers have maintained that it is, we cannot doubt that if now or hereafter, those philosophers303 could establish their doctrine as certain, they would make an important step in science, in addition to those already made.

155

And thus, such steps in science are made, whenever empirical facts are discerned to be necessary laws; or, if I may be allowed to use a briefer expression, whenever facts are idealized.

4. In order to show how widely this statement is applicable, I will exemplify it in some of the other sciences.

In Chemistry, not to speak of earlier steps in the science, which might be presented as instances of the same general process, we may remark that the analyses of various compounds into their elements, according to the quantity of the elements, form a vast multitude of facts, which were previously empirical only, but which are reduced to a law, and therefore to a certain kind of ideal necessity, by the discovery of their being compounded according to definite and multiple proportions. And again, this very law of definite proportions, which may at first be taken as a law given by experience only, it has been attempted to make into a necessary truth, by asserting that bodies must necessarily consist of atoms, and atoms must necessarily combine in definite small numbers. And however doubtful this Atomic Theory may at present be, it will not be questioned that any chemical philosopher who could establish it, or any other Theory which would produce an equivalent change in the aspect of the science, would make a great scientific advance. And thus, in this Science also, the Progress of Science consists in the transfer of facts from the empirical to the necessary side of the antithesis; or, as it was before expressed, in the idealization of facts.

5. We may illustrate the same process in the Natural History Sciences. The discovery of the principle of Morphology in plants was the reduction of a vast mass of Facts to an Idea; as Schiller said to Göthe when he explained the discovery; although the latter, cherishing a horror of the term Idea,304 which perhaps is quite as common in England as in Germany, was extremely vexed at being told that he possessed such furniture in his mind. The applications of this Principle to special cases, for instance, to Euphorbia by Brown, to Reseda by Lindley, have been attempts to idealize the facts of these special cases.

6. We may apply the same view to steps in Science which are still under discussion;—the question being, whether an advance has really been made in science or not. For instance, in Astronomy, the Nebular Hypothesis has been propounded, as an explanation of many of the observed phenomena of the Universe. If this Hypothesis could be conceived ever to be established as a true Theory, this must be done by its taking into itself, as necessary parts of the whole Idea, many Facts which have already been observed; such as the various form of nebulæ;—many Facts which it must require a long course of years to observe, such as the changes of nebulæ from one form to another;— and many facts which, so far as we can at present judge, are utterly at variance with the Idea, such as the motions of satellites, the relations of the material elements of planets, the existence of vegetable and animal life upon their surfaces. But if all these Facts, when fully studied, should appear to be included in the general Idea of Nebular Condensation according to the Laws of Nature, the Facts so idealized would undoubtedly constitute a very remarkable advance in science. But then, we are to recollect that we are not to suppose that the Facts will agree with the Idea, merely because the Idea, considered by itself, and without carefully attending to the Facts, is a large and striking Idea. And we are

also to recollect that the Facts may be compared with another Idea, no less large and striking; and that if we take into our account, (as, in forming an Idea of the Course of the Universe, we must do,) not only vegetable and animal, but also human life, this other Idea appears likely to take into it a far larger portion of the known Facts, than the Idea of the Nebular Hypothesis.305 The other Idea which I speak of is the Idea of Man as the principal Object in the Creation; to whose sustenance and development the other parts of the Universe are subservient as means to an end; and although, in our attempts to include all known Facts in this Idea, we again meet with many difficulties, and find many trains of Facts which have no apparent congruity with the Idea; yet we may say that, taking into account the Facts of man's intellectual and moral condition, and his history, as well as the mere Facts of the material world, the difficulties and apparent incongruities are far less when we attempt to idealize the Facts by reference to this Idea, of Man as the End of Creation, than according to the other Idea, of the World as the result of Nebular Condensation, without any conceivable End or Purpose. I am now, of course, merely comparing these two views of the Universe, as supposed steps in science, according to the general notion which I have just been endeavouring to explain, that a step in science is some Idealization of Facts.

7. Perhaps it will be objected, that what I have said of the Idealization of Facts, as the manner in which the progress of science goes on, amounts to no more than the usual expressions, that the progress of science consists in reducing Facts to Theories. And to this I reply, that the advantage at which I aim, by the expression which I have used, is this, to remind the reader, that Fact and Theory, in every subject, are not marked by separate and prominent features of difference, but only by their present opposition, which is a transient relation. They are related to each other no otherwise than as the poles of the fundamental antithesis: the point which separates those poles shifts with every advance of science; and then, what was Theory becomes Fact. As I have already said elsewhere, a true Theory is a Fact; a Fact is a familiar Theory. If we bear this in mind, we express the view on which I am now insisting when we say that the progress of science consists in reducing Facts to Theories. But I think306 that speaking of Ideas as opposed to Facts, we express more pointedly the original Antithesis, and the subsequent identification of the Facts with the Idea. The expression appears to be simple and apt, when we say, for instance, that the Facts of Geography are identified with the Idea of globular Earth; the Facts of Planetary Astronomy with the Idea of the Heliocentric system; and ultimately, with the Idea of Universal Gravitation.

8. We may further remark, that though by successive steps in science, successive Facts are reduced to Ideas, this process can never be complete. However the point may shift which separates the two poles, the two poles will always remain. However, far the ideal element may extend, there will always be something beyond it. However far the phenomena may be idealized, there will always remain some which are not idealized, and which are mere phenomena. This also is implied by making our expressions refer to the fundamental antithesis: for because the antithesis is fundamental, its two elements will always be present; the objective as well as the subjective. And thus, in the contemplation of the universe, however much we understand, there must always be something which we do not understand; however far we may trace necessary truths, there must always be things which are to our apprehension arbitrary: however far we may extend the sphere of our internal world, in which we feel power and see light, it must always be surrounded by

our external world, in which we see no light, and only feel resistance. Our subjective being is inclosed in an objective shell, which, though it seems to yield to our efforts, continues entire and impenetrable beyond our reach, and even enlarges in its extent while it appears to give up to us a portion of its substance.

II. Successive German Philosophies.

9. The doctrine of the Fundamental Antithesis of two elements of which the union is involved in all307 knowledge, and of which the separation is the task of all philosophy, affords us a special and distinct mode of criticizing the philosophies which have succeeded each other in the world; and we may apply it to the German Philosophies of which we have spoken.

The doctrine of the Fundamental Antithesis is briefly this:

That in every act of knowledge (1) there are two opposite elements which we may call Ideas and Perceptions; but of which the opposition appears in various other antitheses; as Thoughts and Things, Theories and Facts, Necessary Truths and Experiential Truths; and the like: (2) that our knowledge derives from the former of these elements, namely our Ideas, its form and character as knowledge, our Ideas of space and time being the necessary forms, for instance, of our geometrical and arithmetical knowledge; (3) and in like manner, all our other knowledge involving a development of the ideal conditions of knowledge existing in our minds: (4) but that though ideas and perceptions are thus separate elements in our philosophy, they cannot, in fact, be distinguished and separated, but are different aspects of the same thing; (5) that the only way in which we can approach to truth is by gradually and successively, in one instance after another, advancing from the perception to the idea; from the fact to the theory; from the apprehension of truths as actual to the apprehension of them as necessary. (6) This successive and various progress from fact to theory constitutes the history of science; (7) and this progress, though always leading us nearer to that central unity of which both the idea and the fact are emanations, can never lead us to that point, nor to any measurable proximity to it, or definite comprehension of its place and nature.

10. Now the doctrine being thus stated, successive sentences of the statement contain successive steps of German philosophy, as it has appeared in the series of celebrated authors whom I have named.

Ideas, and Perceptions or Sensations, being regarded as the two elements of our knowledge, Locke, or at308 least the successors of Locke, had rejected the former element, Ideas, and professed to resolve all our knowledge into Sensation. After this philosophy had prevailed for a time, Kant exposed, to the entire conviction of the great body of German speculators, the untenable nature of this account of our knowledge. He taught (one of the first sentences of the above statement) that (2) Our knowledge derives from our Ideas its form and character as knowledge; our Ideas of space and time being, for instance, the necessary forms of our geometrical and arithmetical knowledge. Fichte carried still further this view of our knowledge, as derived from our Ideas, or from its nature as knowledge; and held that (3) all our knowledge is a development of the ideal conditions of knowledge existing in our minds (one of our next following sentences). But

158

when the ideal element of our knowledge was thus exclusively dwelt upon, it was soon seen that this ideal system no more gave a complete explanation of the real nature of knowledge, than the old sensational doctrine had done. Both elements, Ideas and Sensations, must be taken into account. And this was attempted by Schelling, who, in his earlier works, taught (as we have also stated above) that (4) Ideas and Facts are different aspects of the same thing:—this thing, the central basis of truth in which both elements are involved and identified, being, in Schelling's language, the Absolute, while each of the separate elements is subjected to conditions arising from their union. But this Absolute, being a point inaccessible to us, and inconceivable by us, as our philosophy teaches (as above), cannot to any purpose be made the basis of our philosophy: and accordingly this Philosophy of the Absolute has not been more permanent than its predecessors. Yet the philosophy of Hegel, which still has a wide and powerful sway in Germany, is, in the main, a development of the same principle as that of Schelling;—the identity of the idea and the fact; and Hegel's Identity-System, is rather a more methodical and technical exposition of Schelling's Philosophy of the Absolute than a new system. But309 Hegel traces the manifestation of the identity of the idea and fact in the progress of human knowledge; and thus in some measure approaches to our doctrine (above stated), that (5) the way in which we approach to truth is by gradually and successively, in one instance after another, that is, historically, advancing from the perception to the idea, from the fact to the theory: while at the same time Hegel has not carried out this view in any comprehensive or complete manner, so as to show that (6) this process constitutes the history of science: and as with Schelling, his system shows an entire want of the conviction (above expressed as part of our doctrine), (7) that we can never, in our speculations reach or approach to the central unity of which both idea and fact are emanations.

11. This view of the relation of the Sensational School, of the Schools of Kant, Fichte, Schelling, and Hegel, and of the fundamental defects of all, may be further illustrated. It will, of course, be understood that our illustration is given only as a slight and imperfect sketch of these philosophies; but their relation may perhaps become more apparent by the very brevity with which it is stated; and the object of the present chapter is not the detailed criticism of systems, but this very relation of systems to each other.

The actual and the ideal, the external and the internal elements of knowledge, were called by the Germans the objective and the subjective elements respectively. The forms of knowledge and especially space and time, were pronounced by Kant to be essentially subjective; and this view of the nature of knowledge, more fully unfolded and extended to all knowledge, became the subjective ideality of Fichte. But the subjective and the objective are, as we have said, in their ultimate and supreme form, one; and hence we are told of the subjective-objective, a phrase which has also been employed by Mr. Coleridge. Fichte had spoken of the subjective element as the Me, (das Ich); and of the objective element as the Not-me, (das Nicht-Ich); and has deduced the Not-me from the Me. Schelling, on the310 contrary, laboured with great subtlety to deduce the Me from the Absolute which includes both. And this Absolute, or Subjective-objective, is spoken of by Schelling as unfolding itself into endless other antitheses. It was held that from the assumption of such a principle might be deduced and explained the oppositions which, in the contemplation of nature, present themselves at every step, as leading points of general philosophy:—for example, the opposition of matter as passive and active, as dead and

159

organized, as unconscious or conscious; the opposition of individual and species, of will and moral rule. And this antithetical development was carried further by Hegel, who taught that the Absolute Idea developes itself so as to assume qualities, limitations, and seeming oppositions, and then completes the cycle of its development by returning into unity.

12. That there is, in the history of Science, much which easily lends itself to such a formula, the views which I have endeavoured to expound, show and exemplify in detail. But yet the attempts to carry this view into detail by conjecture—by a sort of divination—with little or no attention to the historical progress and actual condition of knowledge, (and such are those which have been made by the philosophers whom I have mentioned,) have led to arbitrary and baseless views of almost every branch of knowledge. Such oppositions and differences as are found to exist in nature, are assumed as the representatives of the elements of necessary antitheses, in a manner in which scientific truth and inductive reasoning are altogether slighted. Thus, this peculiar and necessary antithetical character is assumed to be displayed in attraction and repulsion, in centripetal and centrifugal forces, in a supposed positive and negative electricity, in a supposed positive and negative magnetism; in still more doubtful positive and negative elements of light and heat; in the different elements of the atmosphere, which are, quite groundlessly, assumed to have a peculiar antithetical character: in animal and vegetable life: in the two sexes; in gravity and light.311 These and many others, are given by Schelling, as instances of the radical opposition of forces and elements which necessarily pervades all nature. I conceive that the heterogeneous and erroneous principles involved in these views of the material world show us how unsafe and misleading is the philosophical assumption on which they rest. And the Triads of Hegel, consisting of Thesis, Antithesis, and Union, are still more at variance with all sound science. Thus we are told that matter and motion are determined as inertia, impulsion, fall; that Absolute Mechanics determines itself as centripetal force, centrifugal force, universal gravitation. Light, it is taught, is a secondary determination of matter. Light is the most intimate element of nature, and might be called the Me of nature: it is limited by what we may call negative light, which is darkness.

13. In these rash and blind attempts to construct physical science à priori, we may see how imperfect the Hegelian doctrines are as a complete philosophy. In the views of moral and political subjects the results of such a scheme are naturally less obviously absurd, and may often be for a moment striking and attractive, as is usually the case with attempts to reduce history to a formula. Thus we are told that the State appears under the following determinations:—first as one, substantial, self-included: next, varied, individual, active, disengaging itself from the substantial and motionless unity: next, as two principles, altogether distinct, and placed front to front in a marked and active opposition: then, arising out of the ruins of the preceding, the idea appears afresh, one, identical, harmonious. And the East, Greece, Rome, Germany, are declared to be the historical forms of these successive determinations. Whatever amount of real historical colour there may be for this representation, it will hardly, I think, be accepted as evidence of a profound political philosophy; but on such parts of the subject I shall not here dwell.

14. I may observe that in the series of philosophical systems now described, the two elements of the312 Fundamental Antithesis are alternately dwelt upon in an exaggerated degree, and then confounded. The Sensational School could see in human knowledge

nothing but facts: Kant and Fichte fixed their attention almost entirely upon ideas: Schelling and Hegel assume the identity of the two, (a point we never can reach,) as the origin of their philosophy. The external world in Locke's school was all in all. In the speculations of Kant this external world became a dim and unknown region. Things were acknowledged to be something in themselves, but what, the philosopher could not tell. Besides the phænomenon which we see, Kant acknowledged a noumenon which we think of; but this assumption, for such it is, exercises no influence upon his philosophy.

15. We may for the sake of illustration imagine to ourselves each system of philosophy as a Drama in which Things are the Dramatis Personæ and the Idea which governs the system is the Plot of the drama. In Kant's Drama, Things in themselves are merely a kind of 'Mute Personages,' κωφὰ πρόσωπα, which stand on the stage to be pointed at and talked about, but which do not tell us anything, or enter into the action of the piece. Fichte carries this further, and if we go on with the same illustration, we may say that he makes the whole drama into a kind of Monologue; in which the author tells the story, and merely names the persons who appear. If we would still carry on the image, we may say that Schelling, going upon the principle that the whole of the drama is merely a progress to the Denouement, which denouement contains the result of all the preceding scenes and events, starts with the last scene of the piece; and bringing all the characters on the stage in their final attitudes, would elicit the story from this. While the true mode of proceeding is, to follow the drama Scene by Scene, learning as much as we can of the Action and the Characters, but knowing that we shall not be allowed to see the Denouement, and that to do so is probably not the lot of our species on earth. So far as any philosopher has thus followed the historical progress of313 the grand spectacle offered to the eyes of speculative man, in which the Phenomena of Nature are the Scenes, and the Theory of them the Plot, he has taken the course by which knowledge really has made its advances. But those who have partially done this, have often, like Hegel, assumed that they had divined the whole course and end of the story, and have thus criticised the scenes and the characters in a spirit quite at variance with that by which any real insight into the import of the representation can be obtained.

If it be asked which position we can assign, in this dramatic illustration, to those who hold that all our knowledge is derived from facts only, and who reject the supposition of ideas; we may say that they look on with a belief that the drama has no plot, and that these scenes are improvised without connexion or purpose.

16. I will only offer one more illustration of the relative position of these successive philosophies. Kant compares the change which he introduced into philosophy to the change which Copernicus introduced into astronomical theory. When Copernicus found that nothing could be made of the phenomena of the heavens so long as everything was made to turn round the spectator, he tried whether the matter might not be better explained if he made the spectator turn, and left the stars at rest. So Kant conceives that our experience is regulated by our own faculties, as the phenomena of the heavens are regulated by our own motions. But accepting and carrying out this illustration, we may say that Kant, in explaining the phenomena of the heavens by means of the motions of the earth, has almost forgotten that the planets have their own proper motions, and has given us a system which hardly explains anything besides broadest appearances, such as the annual and daily motions of the sun; and that Fichte appears as if he wished to deduce all

the motions of the planets, as well as of the sun, from the conditions of the spectator;—while Schelling goes to the origin of the system, like Descartes, and is not content to show how the bodies move, without also314 proving that from some assumed original condition, all the movements and relations of the system must necessarily be what they are. It may be that a theory which explains how the planets, with their orbits and accompaniments, have come into being, may offer itself to bold speculators, like those who have framed and produced the nebular hypothesis. But I need not remind my readers either how precarious such a hypothesis is; or, that if it be capable of being considered probable, its proofs must gradually dawn upon us, step by step, age after age: and that a system of doctrine which assumes such a scheme as a certain and fundamental truth, and deduces the whole of astronomy from it, must needs be arbitrary, and liable to the gravest error at every step. Such a precarious and premature philosophy, at best, is that of Schelling and Hegel; especially as applied to those sciences in which, by the past progress of all sure knowledge, we are taught what the real cause and progress of knowledge is: while at the same time we may allow that all these forms of philosophy, since they do recognize the condition and motion of the spectator, as a necessary element in the explanation of the phenomena, are a large advance upon the Ptolemaic scheme—the view of those who appeal to phenomena alone as the source of our knowledge, and say that the sun, the moon, and the planets move as we see them move, and that all further theory is imaginary and fantastical.

315

CHAPTER XXV.
The Fundamental Antithesis as it exists in the Moral World.

1. WE HAVE hitherto spoken of the Fundamental Antithesis as the ground of our speculations concerning the material world, at least mainly. We have indeed been led by the physical sciences, and especially by Biology, to the borders of Psychology. We have had to consider not only the mechanical effects of muscular contraction, but the sensations which the nerves receive and convey:—the way in which sensations become perceptions; the way in which perceptions determine actions. In this manner we have been led to the subject of volition or will[297], and this brings us to a new field of speculation, the moral nature of man; and this moral nature is a matter not only of speculative but of practical interest. On this subject I shall make only a few brief remarks.

2. Even in the most purely speculative view, the moral aspect of man's nature differs from the aspect of the material universe, in this respect, that in the moral world, external events are governed in some measure by the human will. When we speculate concerning the laws of material nature, we suppose that the phenomena of nature follow a course and order which we may perhaps, in some measure, discover and understand, but which we cannot change or control. But when we consider man as an agent, we suppose him able to determine some at least of the events of the external world; and thus, able to determine the actions of other men, and to lay down316 laws for them. He cannot alter the properties of fire and metals, stones and fluids, air and light; but he can use fire and steel so as to compel other men's actions; stone-walls and ocean-shores so as to control other men's motions; gold and gems so as to have a hold on other men's desires; articulate sounds and intelligible symbols so as to direct other men's thoughts and move their will.

There is an external world of Facts; and in this, the Facts are such as he makes them by his Acts.

3. But besides this, there is also, standing over against this external world of Facts, an internal world of Ideas. The Moral Acts without are the results of Moral Ideas within. Men have an Idea of Justice, for instance, according to which they are led to external acts, as to use force, to make a promise, to perform a contract, as individuals; or to make war and peace, to enact laws and to execute them, as a nation.

4. Some such internal moral Idea necessarily exists, along with all properly human actions. Man feels not only pain and anger, but indignation and the sentiment of wrong, which feelings imply a moral idea of right and wrong. Again, what he thinks of as wrong, he tries to prevent; what he deems right, he attempts to realize. The Idea gives a character to the Act; the Act embodies the Idea. In the moral world as in the natural world, the Antithesis is universal and inseparable. It is an Antithesis of inseparable elements. In human action, there is ever involved the Idea of what is right, and the external Act in which this idea is in some measure embodied.

5. But the moral Ideas, such as that of Justice, of Rightness, and the like, are always embodied incompletely in the world of external action. Although men's actions are to a great extent governed by the Ideas of Justice, Rightness and the like; (for it must be recollected that we include in their actions, laws, and the enforcement of laws;) yet there is a large portion of human actions which is not governed by such ideas: (actions which result from mere desire, and violations of law). There is a perpetual Antithesis of317 Ideas and Facts, which is the fundamental basis of moral as of natural philosophy. In the former as in the latter subject, besides what is ideal, there is an Actual which the ideal does not include. This Actual is the region in which the results of mere desire, of caprice, of apparent accident, are found. It is the region of history, as opposed to justice; it is the region of what is, as distinct from what ought to be.

6. Now what I especially wish here to remark, is this;—that the progress of man as a moral being consists in a constant extension of the Idea into the region of Facts. This progress consists in making human actions conform more and more to the moral Ideas of Justice, Rightness, and the like; including in human actions, as we have said, Laws, the enforcement of Laws, and other collective acts of bodies of men. The History of Man as Man consists in this extension of moral Ideas into the region of Facts. It is not that the actual history of what men do has always consisted in such an extension of moral Ideas; for there has ever been, in the actual doings of men, a large portion of facts which had no moral character; acts of desire, deeds of violence, transgressions of acknowledged law, and the like. But such events are not a part of the genuine progress of humanity. They do not belong to the history of man as man, but to the history of man as brute. On the other hand, there are events which belong to the history of man as man, events which belong to the genuine progress of humanity; such as the establishment of just laws; their enforcement; their improvement by introducing into them a fuller measure of moral Ideas. By such means there is a constant progress of man as a moral being. By this realization of moral Ideas there is a constant progress of Humanity.

7. I have made this reflection, because it appears to me to bring into view an analogy between the Progress of Science and the Progress of Man, or of Humanity, in the sense in which I have used the term. In both these lines of Progress, Facts are more and more identified with Ideas. In both, there is a funda318mental Antithesis of Ideas and Facts, and progress consists in a constant advance of the point which separates the two elements of this Antithesis. In both, Facts are constantly won over to the domain of Ideas. But still, there is a difference in the two cases; for in the one case the Facts are beyond our control. We cannot make them other than they are; and all that we can do, if we can do that, is to shape our Ideas so that they shall coincide with the Facts, and still have the manifest connexion which belongs to them as Ideas. In the other case, the Facts are, to a certain extent, in our power. They are what we make them, for they are what we do. In this case, the Facts ought to come towards the Ideas, rather than the Ideas towards the Facts. As we called the former process the Idealization of Facts, we may call this the Realization of Ideas; and the analogy which I have here wished to bring into view may be expressed by saying, that the Progress of Physical Science consists in a constant successive Idealization of Physical Facts; and the Progress of man's Moral Being is a constant successive Realization of Moral Ideas.

8. Thus the necessary co-existence of an objective and a subjective element belongs not only to human knowledge, as was before explained, but also to human action. The objective and the subjective element are inseparable in this case as in the other. We have always the Fact of Positive Law, along with the Idea of Absolute Justice; the Facts of Gain or Loss, along with the Idea of Rights. The Idea of Justice is inseparable from historical facts, for justice gives to each his own, and history determines what that is. We cannot even conceive justice without society, or society without law, and thus in the moral and in the natural world the fundamental antithesis is inseparable, even in thought. The two elements must always subsist; for however far the moral ideas be realized in the world, there will always remain much in the world which is not conformable to moral ideas, even if it were only through its necessary dependence on an unmoral and immoral past. As in the physical world so in the319 moral, however much the ideal sphere expands, it is surrounded by a region which is not conformable to the idea, although in one case the expansion takes place by educing ideas out of facts, in the other, by producing facts from ideas.

I shall hereafter venture to pursue further this train of speculation, but at present I shall make some remarks on writers who may be regarded as the successors amongst ourselves of these German schools of Philosophy.

320

CHAPTER XXVI.
Of the "Philosophy of the Infinite."

In the last Chapter but one I stated that Schelling propounded a Philosophy of the Absolute, the Absolute being the original basis of truth in which the two opposite elements, Ideas and Facts, are identified, and that Hegel also founded his philosophy on the Identity of these two elements. These German philosophies appear to me, as I have ventured to intimate, of small or no value in their bearing on the history of actual science.

164

I have in the history of the sciences noted instances in which these writers seem to me to misconceive altogether the nature and meaning of the facts of scientific history; as where[298] Schelling condemns Newton's Opticks as a fabric of fallacies: and where[299] Hegel says that the glory due to Kepler has been unjustly transferred to Newton. As it appears to me important that English philosophers should form a just estimate of Hegel's capacity of judging and pronouncing on this subject, I will print in the Appendix a special discussion of what he has said respecting Newton's discovery of the law of gravitation.

Recently attempts have been made to explain to English readers these systems of German philosophy, and in these attempts there are some points which may deserve our notice as to their bearing on the philosophy of science. I find some difficulty in discussing these attempts, for they deal much with phrases which appear to me to offer no grasp to man's power of reason. What, for instance, is the Absolute, which occupies a321 prominent place in these expositions? It is, as I have stated, in Schelling, the central basis of truth in which things and thoughts are united and identified. To attempt to reason about such an "Absolute" appears to me to be an entire misapprehension of the power of reason. Again; one of the most eminent of the expositors has spoken of each system of this kind as a Philosophy of the Unconditioned[300]. But what, we must ask, is the Unconditioned? That which is subject to no conditions, is subject to no conditions which distinguish it from any thing else, and so, cannot be a matter of thought. But again; this Absolute or Unconditioned is (if I rightly understand) said to be described also by various other names; unity, identity, substance, absolute cause, the infinite, pure thought, &c. As each of these terms expresses some condition on which the name fixes our thoughts, I cannot understand why they should any of them be called the Unconditioned; and as they express very different thoughts, I cannot understand why they should be called by the same name. From speculations starting from such a point, I can expect nothing but confusion and perplexity; nor can I find that anything else has come of them. They appear to me more barren, and more certain to be barren, of any results which have any place in our real knowledge, than the most barren speculations of the schoolmen of the middle ages: which indeed they much resemble in all their features—their acuteness, their learning, their ambitious aim, and their actual failure.

2. But leaving the Absolute and the Unconditioned, as notions which cannot be dealt with by our reason without being something entirely different from their definitions, we may turn for a moment to another notion which is combined with them by the expositors of whom I speak, and which has some bearing upon our positive science, because it enters into the reasonings of mathematics: I mean the notion of Infinite. Some of those who hold that we can know nothing concerning322 the Absolute and the Unconditioned, (which they pretend to prove, though concerning such words I do not conceive that anything can be true or false,) hold also that the Infinite is in the same condition;—that we can know nothing concerning what is Infinite;—therefore, I presume, nothing concerning infinite space, infinite time, infinite number, or infinite degrees.

To disprove this doctrine, it might be sufficient to point out that there is a vast mass of mathematical science which includes the notion of infinites, and leads to a great body of propositions concerning Infinites. The whole of the infinitesimal calculus depends upon conceiving finite magnitudes divided into an infinite number of parts: these parts are infinitely small, and of these parts there are other infinitesimal parts infinitely smaller still, and so on, as far as we please to go. And even those methods which shun the term infinite, as Newton's method of Ultimate Ratios, the method of Indivisibles, and the method of Exhaustions of the ancient geometers, do really involve the notion of infinite; for they imply a process continued without limit.

3. But perhaps it will be more useful to point out the fallacies of the pretended proofs that we can know nothing concerning Infinity and infinite things.

The argument offered is, that of infinity we have no notion but the negation of a limit, and that from this negative notion no positive result can be deduced.

But to this I reply: It is not at all true that our notion of what is infinite is merely that it is that which has no limit. We must ask further that what? that space? that time? that number?—And if that space, that what kind of space? That line? that surface? that solid space?—And if that line, that line bounded at one end, or not? If that surface, that surface bounded on one, or on two, or on three sides? or on none? However any of these questions are answered, we may still have an infinite space. Till they are answered, we can assert nothing about the space; not because we can assert nothing about infinites; but because we are not told what kind of infinite we are talking of.

323

In reality the definition of an Infinite Quantity is not negative merely, but contains a positive part as well. We assume a quantity of a certain kind which may be augmented by carrying onward its limits in one or more directions: this is a finite quantity of a given kind. We then—when we have thus positively determined the kind of the quantity— suppose the limit in one or more directions to be annihilated, and thus we have an infinite quantity. But in this infinite quantity there remain the positive properties from which we began, as well as the negative property, the negation of a limit; and the positive properties joined with the negative property may and do supply grounds of reasoning respecting the infinite quantity.

4. This is lore so elementary to mathematicians that it appears almost puerile to dwell upon it; but this seems to have been overlooked, in the proof that we can have no knowledge concerning infinites. In such proof it is assumed as quite evident, that all infinites are equal. Yet, as we have seen, infinites may differ infinitely among themselves, both in quantity and in kind. A German writer is quoted[301] for an "ingenious" proof of this kind. In his writings, the opponent is supposed to urge that a line BAC may be made infinite by carrying the extremity C infinitely to the right, and again infinite by carrying the extremity B infinitely to the left; and thus the line infinitely extended both ways would be double of the line infinite on one side only. The supposed reply to this is, that it cannot be so, because one infinite is equal to another: and moreover that what is bounded at one end A, cannot be infinite: both which assumptions are without the smallest ground. That one infinite quantity may be double of another, is just as clear and certain as that one finite quantity may. For instance, if one leaf of the book which the reader has before him were produced infinitely upwards it would be an infinite space, though bounded at the bottom and at both sides. If324 the other leaf were in like manner produced infinitely

166

upwards it would in like manner be infinite; and the two together, though each infinite, would be double of either of them.

5. As I have said, infinite quantities are conceived by conceiving finite quantities increased by the transfer of a certain limit, and then by negativing this limit altogether. And thus an infinite number is conceived by assuming the series 1, 2, 3, 4, and so on, up to a limit, and then removing this limit altogether. And this shows the baselessness of another argument quoted from Werenfels. The opponent asks, Are there in the infinite line an infinite number of feet? Then in the double line there must be twice as many; and thus the former infinite number did not contain all the (possible) unities; (numerus infinitus non omnes habet unitates, sed præter eum concipi possunt totidem unitates, quibus ille careat, eique possunt addi). To which I reply, that the definition of an infinite number is not that it contains all possible unities: but this—that the progress of numeration being begun according to a certain law, goes on without limit. And accordingly it is easy to conceive how one infinite number may be larger than another infinite number, in any proportion. If, for instance, we take, instead of the progression of the natural numbers 1, 2, 3, 4, &c. and the progression of the square numbers 1, 4, 9, 16, &c. any term of the latter series will be greater than the corresponding term of the other series in a ratio constantly increasing, and the infinite term of the one, infinitely greater than the corresponding infinite term of the other.

6. In the same manner we form a conception of infinite time, by supposing time to begin now, and to go on, after the nature of time, without limit; or by going back in thought from the present to a past time, and by continuing this retrogression without limit. And thus we have time infinite a parte ante and a parte post, as the phrase used to run; and time infinite both ways includes both, and is the most complete notion of eternity.

7. Perhaps those who thus maintain that we cannot325 conceive anything infinite, mean that we cannot form to ourselves a definite image of anything infinite. And this of course is true. We cannot form to ourselves an image of anything of which one of the characteristics is that it is, in a certain way, unlimited. But this impossibility does not prevent our reasoning about infinite quantities; combining as elements of our reasoning, the absence of a limit with other positive characters.

8. One of the consequences which is drawn by the assertors of the doctrine that we cannot know anything about Infinity, is that we cannot obtain from science any knowledge concerning God: And I have been the more desirous to show the absence of proof of this doctrine, because I conceive that science does give us some knowledge, though it be very little, of the nature of God: as I shall endeavour to show hereafter.

For instance, I conceive that when we say that God is an eternal Being, this phraseology is not empty and unmeaning. It has been used by the wisest and most thoughtful men in all ages, and, as I conceive, may be used with undiminished, or with increased propriety, after all the light which science and philosophy have thrown upon such declarations. The reader of Newton will recollect how emphatically he uses this expression along with others of a cognate character[302]: "God is eternal and infinite, ... that is, He endures from eternity to eternity, and is present from infinity to infinity.... He is not eternity and infinity, but eternal and infinite. He is not duration and space, but He endures and is present. He endures always, and is present everywhere, and by existing always and everywhere He constitutes duration and space." We shall see shortly that the view to which we are led may be very fitly expressed by this language.

But I will first notice some other aspects of this philosophy.

326

CHAPTER XXVII.
Sir William Hamilton on Inertia and Weight.

In a preceding chapter I have spoken of Sir William Hamilton as the expositor, to English readers, of modern German systems, and especially of the so-called "Philosophy of the Unconditioned." But the same writer is also noticeable as a continuator of the speculations of English and Scottish philosophers concerning primary and secondary qualities; and these speculations bear so far upon the philosophy of science that it is proper to notice them here.

1. In our survey of the sciences, we have spoken of a class which we have termed the Secondary Mechanical Sciences; these being the sciences which explain certain sensible phenomena, as sound, light, and heat, by means of a medium interposed between external bodies and our organs of sense. In these cases, we ascribe to bodies certain qualities: we call them resonant, bright, red or green, hot or cold. But in the sciences which relate to these subjects, we explain these qualities by the figure, size and motions of the parts of the medium which intervenes between the object and the ear, eye, or other sensible organ. And those former qualities, sound, warmth and colour, are called secondary qualities of the bodies; while the latter, figure, size and motion, are called the primary qualities of body.

2. This distinction, in its substance, is of great antiquity. The atomic theory which was set up at an early period of Greek philosophy was an attempt to account for the secondary qualities of bodies by means of their primary qualities. And this is really the scientific ground of the distinction. Those are primary327 qualities or attributes of body by means of which we, in a scientific view, explain and derive their other qualities. But the explanation of the sensible qualities of bodies by means of their operation through a medium has till now been very defective, and is so still. We have to a certain extent theories of Sound, Light and Heat, which reduce these qualities to scales and standards, and in some measure account mechanically for their differences and gradations. But we have as yet no similar theory of Smells and Tastes. Still, we do not doubt that fragrance and flavour are perceived by means of an aerial medium in which odours float, and a fluid medium in which sapid matters are dissolved. And the special odour and flavour which are thus perceived must depend upon the size, figure, motion, number, &c. of the particles thus conveyed to the organs of taste and smell: that is, those secondary qualities, as well as the others, must depend upon the primary qualities of the parts of the medium.

3. In this way the distinction of primary and secondary qualities is definite and precise. But when men attempt to draw the distinction by guess, without any scientific

principle, the separation of the two classes is vague and various. I have, in the History of Scientific Ideas[303], pointed out some of the variations which are to be found on this subject in the writings of philosophers. Sir William Hamilton[304] has given an account of many more which he has compared and analysed with great acuteness. He has shown how this distinction is treated, among others, by the ancient atomists, Leucippus and Democritus, by Aristotle, Galen, Galileo, Descartes, Boyle, Malebranche, Locke, Reid, Stewart, Royer-Collard. He then proceeds to give his own view; which is, that we may most properly divide the qualities of bodies into three classes, which he calls Primary, Secundo-primary, and Secondary. The former he enumerates as 1, Extension; 2, Divisibility; 3, Size; 4, Density or Rarity; 5, Figure;328 6, Incompressibility absolute; 7, Mobility; 8, Situation. The Secundo-primary are Gravity, Cohesion, Inertia, Repulsion. The Secondary are those commonly so called, Colour, Sound, Flavour, Savour, and Tactical Sensation; to which he says may be added the muscular and cutaneous sensation which accompany the perception of the Secundo-primary qualities. "Such, though less directly the result of foreign causes, are Titillation, Sneezing, Horripilation, Shuddering, the feeling of what is called Setting-the-teeth-on-edge, &c."

The Secundo-primary qualities Sir William Hamilton traces in further detail. He explains that with reference to Gravity, bodies are heavy or light. With reference to Cohesion, there are many coordinate pairs, of which he enumerates these:—hard and soft; firm and fluid,—the fluid being subdivided into thick and thin; viscid and friable; tough and brittle; rigid and flexible; fissile and infissile; ductile and inductile; retractile and irretractile; rough and smooth; slippery and tenacious. With reference to Repulsion he gives these qualities:—compressible and incompressible; elastic and inelastic. And with reference to Inertia he mentions only moveable and immoveable.

I do not see what advantage is gained to philosophy by such an enumeration of qualities as this, which, after all, does not pretend to completeness; nor do I see anything either precise or fundamental in such distinctions as that of elasticity, a mode of cohesion, and elasticity, a mode of repulsion. But a question in which our philosophy is really concerned is how far any of these qualities are universal qualities of matter. Sir W. Hamilton holds that they are none of them necessary qualities of matter, and therefore of course not universal, and argues this point at some length. With regard to one of his Secundo-primary qualities, I will make some remarks.

4. Inertia.—In discussing the Ideas which enter into the Mechanical Sciences[305], I have stated that the Idea329 of Force and Resistance to Force, that is, of Force and Matter, are the necessary foundations of those sciences. Force cannot act without matter to act on; Matter cannot exist without Force to keep its parts together and to keep it in its place. But Force acting upon matter may either be Force producing rest, or Force producing motion. If we consider Force producing motion, the motion produced, that is, the velocity produced, must depend upon the quantity of matter moved. It cannot be that the same power, acting in the same way, shall produce the same velocity by pushing a small pebble and a large rock. If this were so, we could have no science on such matters. It must needs be that the same force produces a smaller velocity in the larger body; and this according to some measure of its largeness. The measure of the degree in which the body thus resists this communication of motion is inertia. And the inertia is necessarily supposed to be proportional to the quantity of matter, because it is by this inertia that this

existence and quantity of the matter is measured. If therefore any Science concerning Force and Matter is to exist, matter must have inertia, and the inertia must be proportional to the quantity of matter.

5. Sir W. Hamilton, in opposition to this, says, that we can conceive a body occupying space, and yet without attraction or repulsion for another body, and wholly indifferent to this or that position, in space, to motion and to rest. He infers thence that inertia is not a necessary quality of bodies.

To this I reply, that even if we can conceive such bodies, (which in fact man, living in a world of matter cannot conceive,) at any rate we cannot conceive any science about such bodies. If bodies were indifferent to motion and rest, Forces could not be measured by their effects; nor could be measured or known in any way. Such bodies might float about like clouds, visible to the eye, but intangible, and governed by no laws of motion. But if we have any science about bodies, they must be tangible, and governed by laws of motion. Not, then, from any observed properties of330 bodies, but from the possibility of any science about bodies, does it follow that all bodies have inertia.

6. Gravity.—Reasoning of the same kind may be employed about weight. We can conceive, it is urged, matter without weight. But I reply, we cannot conceive a science which deals with matter that has no weight:—a science, I mean, which deals with the quantity of matter of bodies, as arising from the sum of their elements. For the quantity of matter of bodies is and must be measured by those sensible properties of matter which undergo quantitative addition, subtraction and division, as the matter is added, subtracted, and divided. The quantity of matter cannot be known in any other way. But this mode of measuring the quantity of matter, in order to be true at all, must be universally true. If it were only partially true—if some kinds of matter had weight and others had not—the limits of the mode of measuring matter by weight would be arbitrary: and therefore the whole procedure would be arbitrary, and as a mode of obtaining philosophical truth, altogether futile. But we suppose truth respecting the composition of bodies to be attainable; therefore we must suppose the rule, which is the necessary basis of such truth, to be itself true.

Sir W. Hamilton has replied to these arguments, but, as I conceive, without affecting the force of them. I will repeat here the answer which I have already given[306], and will reprint in the Appendix the Memoir by which his objections were occasioned.

He says, (1), that our reasoning assumes that we must necessarily have it in our power to ascertain the Quantity of Matter; whereas this may be a problem out of the reach of human determination.

To this I reply, that my reasoning does assume that there is a science, or sciences, which make assertions concerning the Quantity of Matter: Mechanics and Chemistry are such sciences. My assertion is, that to make such sciences possible, Quantity of Matter must331 be proportional to Weight. If my opponent deny that Mechanics and Chemistry can exist as science, he may invalidate my proof; but not otherwise.

170

(2) He says that there are two conceivable ways of estimating the Quantity of Matter: by the Space occupied, and by the Weight or Inertia; and that I assume the second measure gratuitously.

To which I reply, that the most elementary steps in Mechanics and in Chemistry contradict the notion that the Quantity of Matter is proportionate to the Space. They proceed necessarily on a distinction between Space and Matter:—between mere Extension and material Substance.

(3) He allows that we cannot make the Extension of a body the measure of the Quantity of Matter, because, he says, we do not know if "the compressing force" is such as to produce "the closest compression." That is, he assumes a compressing force, assumes a "closest compression," assumes a peculiar (and very improbable) atomic hypothesis; and all this, to supply a reason why we are not to believe the first simple principle of Mechanics and Chemistry.

(4) He speaks of "a series of apparent fluids (as Light or its vehicle, the Calorific, the Electro-galvanic, and Magnetic agents) which we can neither denude of their character of substance, nor clothe with the attribute of weight."

To which my reply is, that precisely because I cannot "clothe" these agents with the attribute of Weight, I do "denude them of the character of Substance." They are not substances, but agencies. These Imponderable Agents are not properly called "Imponderable Fluids." This I conceive that I have proved; and the proof is not shaken by denying the conclusion without showing any defect in the reasoning.

(5) Finally, my critic speaks about "a logical canon," and about "a criterion of truth, subjectively necessary and objectively certain;" which matters I shall not waste the reader's time by discussing.

332

CHAPTER XXVIII.
Influence of German Systems of Philosophy in Britain.

The philosophy of Kant, as I have already said, involved a definite doctrine on the subject of the Fundamental Antithesis, and a correction of some of the errors of Locke and his successors. It was not however at first favourably received among British philosophers, and those who accepted it were judged somewhat capriciously and captiously. I will say a word on these points[307].

1. (Stewart)—Dugald Stewart, in his Dissertation on the Progress of the Moral Sciences, repeatedly mentions Kant's speculations, and always unfavourably. In Note I to Part I. of the Dissertation he says, "In our own times, Kant and his followers seem to have thought that they had thrown a strong light on the nature of space and also of time, when they introduced the word form (form of the intellect) as a common term applicable to both. Is not this to revert to the scholastic folly of verbal generalization?" And in Part II. he gives a long and laborious criticism of a portion of Kant's speculations; of which

the spirit may be collected from his describing them as resulting in "the metaphysical conundrum, that the human mind (considered as a noumenon and not as a phenomenon) neither exists in space nor time." And after mentioning Meiners and Herder along with Kant, he adds,333 "I am ashamed to say that in Great Britain the only one of these names which has been much talked of is Kant." And again in Note EE, he translates some portion of the German philosopher, adding, that to the expressions so employed he can attach no meaning.

Stewart, in his criticism of Kant's doctrines, remarks that, in asserting that the human mind possesses, in its own ideas, an element of necessary and universal truth, not derived from experience, Kant had been anticipated by Price, by Cudworth, and even by Plato; to whose Theætetus both Price and Cudworth refer, as containing views similar to their own. And undoubtedly this doctrine of ideas, as indispensable sources of necessary truths, was promulgated and supported by weighty arguments in the Theætetus; and has ever since been held by many philosophers, in opposition to the contrary doctrine, also extensively held, that all truth is derived from experience. But, in pointing out this circumstance as diminishing the importance of Kant's speculations, Stewart did not sufficiently consider that doctrines, fundamentally the same, may discharge a very different office at different periods of the history of philosophy. Plato's Dialogues did not destroy, nor even diminish, the value of Cudworth's "Immutable Morality." Notwithstanding Cudworth's publications, Price's doctrines came out a little afterwards with the air and with the effect of novelties. Cudworth's assertion of ideas did not prevent the rise of Hume's skepticism; and it was Hume's skepticism which gave occasion to Kant's new assertion of necessary and universal truth, and to his examination into the grounds of the possibility and reality of such truth. To maintain such doctrine after the appearance of intermediate speculations, and with reference to them, was very different from maintaining it before; and this is the merit which Kant's admirers claim for him. Nor can it be denied that his writings produced an immense effect upon the mode of treating such questions in Germany; and have had, even in this country, an influence far beyond what Mr. Stewart would have deemed their due.

334

2. (Mr. G. H. Lewes.)—But as injustice has thus been done to Kant by confounding his case with that of his predecessors of like opinions, so on the other hand, injustice has also been done, both to him and those who have followed him in the assertion of ideas, by confounding their case with his. This injustice seems to me to be committed by a writer on the History of Philosophy, who has given an account of the successive schools of philosophy up to our own time;—has assigned to Kant an important and prominent place in the recent history of metaphysics;—but has still maintained that Kant's philosophy, and indeed every philosophy, is and must be a failure. In order to prove this thesis, the author naturally has to examine Kant's doctrines and the reasons assigned for them, and to point out what he conceives to be the fallacy of these arguments. This accordingly he professes to do; but as soon as he has entered upon the argument, he substitutes, as his opponent, for the philosopher of Königsberg, a writer of our own time and country, who does not profess himself a Kantian, who has been repeatedly accused, with whatever justice, of misrepresenting what he has borrowed from Kant, and whose main views are, in the opinion of the writer himself, very different from Kant's. Mr.

Lewes[308], in the chapter entitled "Examination of Kant's Fundamental Principles," after a preliminary statement of the points he intends to consider, says "Now to the question. As Kant confessedly was led to his own system by the speculations of Hume," and so on; and forthwith he introduces the name of Dr. Whewell as the writer whose views he has to criticize, without stating how he connects him with Kant, and goes on arguing against him for a dozen pages to the end of the Chapter.

335

3. It is true, however, that I had adopted some of Kant's views, or at least some of his arguments. The chapters[309] on the Ideas of Space and Time in the Philosophy of the Inductive Sciences, were almost literal translations of chapters in the Kritik der Reinen Vernunft. Yet the author was charged by a reviewer at the time, with explaining these doctrines "in a manner incompatible with the clear views of Emanuel Kant." It appeared to be assumed by the English admirers of the Kantian philosophy, that Kant's views were true and clear in Germany, but became untenable when adopted in England.

4. (Mr. Mansel)—But the most important of my critics on this ground is Mr. Mansel, who has revived the censure of my speculations as not doing justice to the Kantian philosophy. "It is much to be regretted," he says[310], "that Dr. Whewell, who has made good use of Kantian principles in many parts of his Philosophy of the Inductive Sciences," has not more accurately observed Kant's distinction between the necessary laws under which all men think, and the contingent laws under which certain men think of certain things. And further on Mr. Mansel, after giving great praise to the general spirit of the Philosophy of the Inductive Sciences, says, "It is to be regretted that the accuracy of his theory has been in so many instances vitiated by a stumble at the threshold of the Critical Philosophy." Mr. Mansel is, indeed, by much the most zealous English Kantian whose writings I have seen;—among those, I mean, who have brought original powers of philosophical thought to bear upon such subjects; and have not been, as some have been, enslaved by an admiration of German systems, just as bigotted as the contempt of them which others feel. And as Mr.336 Mansel has stated distinctly some of the points in which he conceives that I have erred in deviating from the doctrines of Kant, I should wish to make a few remarks on those points.

5. Kant considers that Space and Time are conditions of perception, and hence sources of necessary and universal truth. Dr. Whewell agrees with Kant in placing in the mind certain sources of necessary truth; he calls these Fundamental Ideas, and reckons, besides Space and Time, others, as Cause, Likeness, Substance, and several more. Mr. Mill, the most recent and able expounder of the opposite doctrine, derives all truths from Observation, and denies that there is such a separate source of truth as Ideas. Mr. Mansel does not agree either with Mr. Mill or Dr. Whewell; he adheres to the original Kantian thesis, that Space and Time are sources of necessary truths, but denies the office to the other Fundamental Ideas of Dr. Whewell. In reading what has been said by Mr. Mill, Mr. Mansel, and other critics, on the subject of what I have called Fundamental Ideas, I am led to perceive that I have expressed myself incautiously, with regard to the identity of character between the first two of these Fundamental Ideas, namely, Space and Time, and the others, as Force, Composition, and the like. And I am desirous of explaining, to those

173

who take an interest in these speculations, how far I claim for the other Fundamental Ideas the same character and attributes as for Space and Time.

6. The special and characteristic property of all the Fundamental Ideas is what I have already mentioned, that they are the mental sources of necessary and universal scientific truths. I call them Ideas, as being something not derived from sensation, but governing sensation, and consequently giving form to our experience;—Fundamental, as being the foundation of knowledge, or at least of Science. And the way in which those Ideas become the foundations of Science is, that when they are clearly and distinctly entertained in the mind, they give rise to inevitable convictions or intuitions, which may be expressed as337 Axioms; and these Axioms are the foundations of Sciences respective of each Idea. The Idea of Space, when clearly possessed, gives rise to geometrical Axioms, and is thus the foundation of the Science of Geometry. The Idea of Mechanical Force, (a modification of the Idea of Cause,) when clearly developed in the mind, gives birth to Axioms which are the foundation of the Science of Mechanics. The Idea of Substance gives rise to the Axiom which is universally accepted,—that we cannot, by any process, (for instance, by chemical processes,) create or destroy matter, but can only combine and separate elements;—and thus gives rise to the Science of Chemistry.

7. Now it may be observed, that in giving this account of the foundation of Science, I lay stress on the condition that the Ideas must be clearly and distinctly possessed. The Idea of Space must be quite clear in the mind, or else the Axioms of Geometry will not be seen to be true: there will be no intuition of their truth; and for a mind in such a state, there can be no Science of Geometry. A man may have a confused and perplexed, or a vacant and inert state of mind, in which it is not clearly apparent to him, that two straight lines cannot inclose a space. But this is not a frequent case. The Idea of Space is much more commonly clear in the minds of men than the other Ideas on which science depends, as Force, or Substance. It is much more common to find minds in which these latter Ideas are not so clear and distinct as to make the Axioms of Mechanics or of Chemistry self-evident. Indeed the examples of a state of mind in which the Ideas of Force or of Substance are so clear as to be made the basis of science, are comparatively few. They are the examples of minds scientifically cultivated, at least to some extent. Hence, though the Axioms of Mechanics or of Chemistry may be, in their own nature, as evident as those of Geometry, they are not evident to so many persons, nor at so early a period of intellectual or scientific culture. And this being the case, it is not surprising that some persons should doubt whether these Axioms are evident338 at all;—should think that it is an error to assert that there exist, in such sciences as Mechanics or Chemistry, Fundamental Ideas, fit to be classed with Space, as being, like it, the origin of Axioms.

In speaking of all the Fundamental Ideas as being alike the source of Axioms when clearly possessed, without dwelling sufficiently upon the amount of mental discipline which is requisite to give the mind this clear possession of most of them; and in not keeping before the reader the different degrees of evidence which, in most minds, the Axioms of different sciences naturally have, I have, as I have said, given occasion to my readers to misunderstand me. I will point out one or two passages which show that this misunderstanding has occurred, and will try to remove it.

8. The character of axiomatic truths seen by intuition is, that they are not only seen to be true, but to be necessary;—that the contrary of them is not only false, but inconceivable. But this inconceivableness depends entirely upon the clearness of the Ideas which the axioms involve. So long as those Ideas are vague and indistinct, the contrary of an Axiom may be assented to, though it cannot be distinctly conceived. It may be assented to, not because it is possible, but because we do not see clearly what is possible. To a person who is only beginning to think geometrically, there may appear nothing absurd in the assertion, that two straight lines may inclose a space. And in the same manner, to a person who is only beginning to think of mechanical truths, it may not appear to be absurd, that in mechanical processes, Reaction should be greater or less than Action; and so, again, to a person who has not thought steadily about Substance, it may not appear inconceivable, that by chemical operations, we should generate new matter, or destroy matter which already exists.

Here then we have a difficulty:—the test of Axioms is that the contrary of them is inconceivable; and yet persons, till they have in some measure studied the subject, do not see this inconceivableness. Hence our339 Axioms must be evident only to a small number of thinkers; and seem not to deserve the name of self-evident or necessary truths.

This difficulty has been strongly urged by Mr. Mill, as supporting his view, that all knowledge of truth is derived from experience. And in order that the opposite doctrine, which I have advocated, may not labour under any disadvantages which really do not belong to it, I must explain, that I do not by any means assert that those truths which I regard as necessary, are all equally evident to common thinkers, or evident to persons in all stages of intellectual development. I may even say, that some of those truths which I regard as necessary, and the necessity of which I believe the human mind to be capable of seeing, by due preparation and thought, are still such, that this amount of preparation and thought is rare and peculiar; and I will willingly grant, that to attain to and preserve such a clearness and subtlety of mind as this intuition requires, is a task of no ordinary difficulty and labour.

9. This doctrine,—that some truths may be seen by intuition, but yet that the intuition of them may be a rare and difficult attainment,—I have not, it would seem, conveyed with sufficient clearness to obviate misapprehension. Mr. Mill has noticed a passage of my Philosophy on this subject, which he has understood in a sense different from that which I intended. Speaking of the two Principles of Chemical Science,—that combinations are definite in kind, and in quantity,—I had tried to elevate myself to the point of view in which these Principles are seen, not only to be true, but to be necessary. I was aware that even the profoundest chemists had not ventured to do this; yet it appeared to me that there were considerations which seemed to show that any other rule would imply that the world was a world on which the human mind could not employ itself in scientific speculation at all. These considerations I ventured to put forwards, not as views which could at present be generally accepted, but as views to which chemical340 philosophy appeared to me to tend. Mr. Mill, not unnaturally, I must admit, supposed me to mean that the two Principles of Chemistry just stated, are self-evident, in the same way and in the same degree as the Axioms of Geometry are so. I afterwards explained that what I meant to do was, to throw out an opinion, that if we could conceive the composition of bodies distinctly, we might be able to see that it is necessary that the

modes of this composition should be definite. This Mr. Mill does not object to[311]: but he calls it a great attenuation of my former opinion; which he understood to be that we, (that is, men in general,) already see, or may see, or ought to see, this necessity. Such a general apprehension of the necessity of definite chemical composition I certainly never reckoned upon; and even in my own mind, the thought of such a necessity was rather an anticipation of what the intuitions of philosophical chemists in another generation would be, than an assertion of what they now are or ought to be; much less did I expect that persons, neither chemists nor philosophers, would already, or perhaps ever, see that a proposition, so recently discovered to be true, is not only true, but necessary.

10. Of the bearing of this view on the question at issue between Mr. Mill and me, I may hereafter speak; but I will now notice other persons who have misunderstood me in the same way.

An able writer in the Edinburgh Review[312] has, in like manner, said, "Dr. Whewell seems to us to have gone much too far in reducing to necessary truths what assuredly the generality of mankind will not feel to be so." It is a fact which I do not at all contest, that the generality of mankind will not feel the Axioms of Chemistry, or even of Mechanics, to be necessary truths. But I had said, not that the generality of mankind would feel this necessity, but (in a passage just before quoted by the Reviewer) that the mind341 under certain circumstances attains a point of view from which it can pronounce mechanical (and other) fundamental truths to be necessary in their nature, though disclosed to us by experience and observation.

Both the Edinburgh Reviewer and Mr. Mansel appear to hold a distinction between the fundamental truths of Geometry, and those of the other subjects which I have classed with them. The latter says, that perhaps metaphysicians may hereafter establish the existence of other subjective conditions of intuitions (or, as I should call them, Fundamental Ideas,) besides Space and Time, but that in asserting such to exist in the science of Mechanics, I certainly go too far: and he gives as an instance my Essay,— "Demonstration that all matter is heavy." I certainly did not expect that the Principles asserted in that Essay would be assented to as readily or as generally as the Axioms of Geometry; but I conceive that I have there proved that Chemical Science, using the balance as one of its implements, cannot admit "imponderable bodies" among its elements. This impossibility will, I think, not only be found to exist in fact, but seen to exist necessarily, by chemists, in proportion as they advance towards general propositions of Chemical Science in which the so-called "imponderable fluids" enter. But even if I be right in this opinion, to how few will this necessity be made apparent, and how slowly will the intuition spread! I am as well aware as my critics, that the necessity will probably never be apparent to ordinary thinkers.

11. Though Mr. Mansel does not acknowledge any subjective conditions of intuition besides Space and Time, he does recognize other kinds of necessity, which I should equally refer to Fundamental Ideas; because they are, no less than Space and Time, the foundations of universal and necessary truths in science. Such are[313] the Principle of Substance;—All Qualities exist in some subject: and the Principle of Causality;—342 Every Event has its Cause. To these Principles he ascribes a "metaphysical necessity," the nature and grounds of which he analyses with great acuteness. But what I have to observe

is, that whatever differences may be pointed out between the grounds of the necessity, in this case of metaphysical necessity, and in that which Mr. Mansel calls mathematical necessity which belongs to the Conditions or Ideas of Space and of Time; still, it is not the less true that the Ideas of Substance and of Cause, do afford a foundation for necessary truths, and that on these truths are built Sciences. That every Change must have a Cause, with the corresponding Axioms,—that the Cause is known by the Effect, and Measured by it,—is the basis of the Science of Mechanics. That there is a Substance to which qualities belong, with the corresponding Axiom,—that we cannot create or destroy Substance, though we may alter Qualities by combining and separating Substances,—is the basis of the Science of Chemistry. And that this doctrine of the Indestructibility of Substance is a primary axiomatic truth, is certain; both because it has been universally taken for granted by men seeking for general truths; and because it is not and cannot be proved by experience[314]. So that I have here, even according to Mr. Mansel's own statement, other grounds besides Space and Time, for necessary truths in Science.

12. Besides mathematical and metaphysical necessity, Mr. Mansel recognizes also a logical necessity. I will not pretend to say that this kind of necessity is exactly represented by any of those Fundamental Ideas which are the basis of Science; but yet I think it will be found that this logical necessity mainly operates through the attribution of Names to things; and that a large portion of its cogency arises from these maxims,—that names must be so imposed that General Propositions shall be possible,—and so that Reasoning shall be possible. Now these maxims are really the343 basis of Natural History, and are so stated in the Philosophy of the Inductive Sciences. The former maxim is the principle of all Classification; and though we have no syllogisms in Natural History, the apparatus of genus, species, differentia, and the like, which was introduced in the analysis of syllogistic reasoning, is really more constantly applied in Natural History than in any other science.

13. Besides the different kinds of necessity which Mr. Mansel thus acknowledges, I do not see why he should not, on his own principles, recognize others; as indeed he appears to me to do. He acknowledges, I think, the distinction of Primary and Secondary qualities; and this must involve him in the doctrine that Secondary Qualities are necessarily perceived by means of a Medium. Again: he would, I think, acknowledge that in organized bodies, the parts exist for a Purpose; and Purpose is an Idea which cannot be inferred by reasoning from facts, without being possessed and applied as an Idea. So that there would, I conceive, exist, in his philosophy, all the grounds of necessary truth which I have termed Fundamental Ideas; only that he would further subdivide, classify, and analyse, the kinds and grounds of this necessity.

In this he would do well; and some of his distinctions and analyses of this kind are, in my judgment, very instructive. But I do not see what objection there can be to my putting together all these kinds of necessity, when my purpose requires it; and, inasmuch as they all are the bases of Science, I may call them by a general name; for instance, Grounds of Scientific Necessity; and these are precisely what I mean by Fundamental Ideas.

That some steady thought, and even some progress in the construction of Science, is needed in order to see the necessity of the Axioms thus introduced, is true, and is repeatedly asserted and illustrated in the History of the Sciences. The necessity of such

Axioms is seen, but it is not seen at first. It becomes clearer and clearer to each person, and clear to one person after another, as the human mind dwells more and344 more steadily on the several subjects of speculation. There are scientific truths which are seen by intuition, but this intuition is progressive. This is the remark which I wish to make in answer to those of my critics who have objected that truths which I have propounded as Axioms, are not evident to all.

14. That the Axioms of Science are not evident to all, is true enough, and too true. Take the Axiom of Substance:—that we may change the condition of a substance in various ways, but cannot destroy it. This has been assumed as evident by philosophers in all ages; but if we ask an ordinary person whether a body can be destroyed by fire, or diminished, will he unhesitatingly reply, that it cannot? It requires some thought to say[315], as the philosopher said, that the weight of the smoke is to be found by subtracting the weight of the ashes from that of the fuel; nay, even when this is said, it appears, at first, rather an epigram than a scientific truth. Yet it is by thinking only, not by an experiment, that, from a happy guess it becomes a scientific truth. And the thought is the basis, not the result, of experimental truths; for which reason I ascribe it to a Fundamental Idea. And so, such truths are the genuine growth of the human mind; not innate, as if they needed not to grow; still less, dead twigs plucked from experience and stuck in from without; not universal, as if they grew up everywhere; but not the less, under favourable circumstances, the genuine growth of the scientific intellect.

15. Not only do I hold that the Axioms, on which the truths of science rest, grow from guesses into Axioms in various ways, and often gradually, and at different periods in different minds, and partially, even in the end; but I conceive that this may be shown by the history of science, as having really happened, with regard to all the most conspicuous of such principles. The scientific insight which enabled discoverers to achieve their exploits, implied that they were among345 the first to acquire an intuitive conviction of the Axioms of their Science: the controversies which form so large a portion of the history of science, arise from the struggles between the clear-sighted and the dimsighted, between those who were forwards and those who were backwards in the progress of ideas; and these controversies have very often ended in diffusing generally a clearness of thought, on the controverted subject, which at first, the few only, or perhaps not even they, possessed. The History of Science consists of the History of Ideas, as well as of the History of Experience and Observation. The latter portion of the subject formed the principal matter of my History of the Inductive Sciences; the former occupied a large portion of the Philosophy of the Inductive Sciences[316]; which, I may perhaps be allowed to explain, is, for the most part, a Historical Work no less than the other; and was written in a great measure, at the same time, and from the same survey of the works of scientific writers.

16. I am aware that the explanation which I have given, may naturally provoke the opponents of the doctrine of scientific necessity to repeat their ordinary fundamental objections, in a form adapted to the expressions which I have used. They may say, the fact that these so-called Axioms thus become evident only during the progress of experience, proves that they are derived from experience: they may, in reply to our image, say, that truths are stuck into the mind by experience, as seeds are stuck into the ground; and that to maintain that they can grow under any other conditions, is to hold the doctrine of

spontaneous generation, which is equally untenable in the intellectual and in the physical world. I shall not however here resume the general discussion; but shall only say briefly in reply, that Axioms,—for instance, this Axiom, that material substances cannot be created or annihilated by any process which we can apply,—though it becomes evident in the progress of experience, cannot be derived346 from experience; for it is a proposition which never has nor can be proved by experience; but which, nevertheless, has been always assumed by men, seeking for general truths, as necessarily true, and as controlling and correcting all possible experience. And with regard to the image of vegetable development, I may say, that as such development implies both inherent forms in the living seed, and nutritive powers in earth and air; so the development of our scientific ideas implies both a formative power, and materials acted on; and that, though the analogy must be very defective, we conceive that we best follow it by placing the formative power in the living mind, and in the external world the materials acted on: while the doctrine that all truth is derived from experience only, appears to reject altogether one of these elements, or to assert the two to be one.

347

CHAPTER XXIX.
Necessary Truth is progressive.
Objections considered.

The doctrine that necessary truth is progressive is a doctrine very important in its bearing upon the nature of the human mind; and, as I conceive, in its theological bearing also. But it is a doctrine to which objections are likely to be made from various quarters, and I will consider some of these objections.

1. Necessary truths, it will be said, cannot increase in number. New ones cannot be added to the old ones. For necessary truths are those of which the necessity is plain and evident to all mankind—to the common sense of man; such as the axioms of geometry. But that which is evident to all mankind must be evident from the first: that which is plain to the common sense of man cannot require scientific discovery: that which is necessarily true cannot require accumulated proof.

To this I reply, that necessary truths require for their apprehension a certain growth and development of the human mind. Though it is seen that they are necessarily true, this is seen only by those who think steadily and clearly, and to think steadily and clearly on any kind of subject, requires time and attention;—requires mental culture. This may be seen even in the case of the axioms of geometry. These axioms are self-evident: but to whom are they self-evident? Not to uncultured savages, or young children; or persons of loose vague habits of thought. To see the truth and necessity of geometrical axioms, we need geometrical culture.

Therefore that any axioms are not evident without patient thought and continued study of the subject, does not disprove their necessity. Principles may be348 axiomatic and necessary, although they require time, and the progress of thought and of knowledge, to bring them to light. And axioms may be thus gradually brought to light by the progress of knowledge.

Nor is it difficult to give examples of such axioms, other than geometrical. There is an axiom which has obtained currency among thoughtful men from the time that man began to speculate about himself and the universe:—E nihilo nil fit: Nothing can be made of nothing. No material substance can be produced or destroyed by natural causes, though its form and consistence may be changed indefinitely. Is not this an axiom? a necessary truth? Yet it is not evident to all men at first, and without mental culture. At first and before habits of steady and consistent thought are formed, men think familiarly of the creation and destruction of matter. Only when the mind has received some philosophical culture does it see the truth and necessity of the axiom of substance, and then it does see it.

And the axioms on which the science of mechanics rests, that the cause is measured by the effects, that reaction is equal and opposite to action, and the like,—are not these evident to a mind cultivated by steady thought on such subjects? and do they not require such culture of the mind in order to see them? Are they not obscure or uncertain to those who are not so cultured, that is to common thinkers: to the general bulk of mankind? Thus then it requires the discipline of the science of mechanics to enable the mind to see the axioms of that science.

And does not this go further, as science and the careful study of the grounds of science go further? To a person well disciplined in mechanical reasoning it has become, not a conclusion, but a principle, that in mechanical action what is gained in power is lost in time: or that in any change, the force gained is equal to the force lost, so that new force cannot be generated, any more than new matter, by natural changes. Is this an axiom? a necessary fundamental truth? It appears so to at least one great thinker and discoverer now349 alive among us. If it do not appear so to us, or not in the same sense, may not this be because we have not yet reached his point of view? May not the conviction which is now his alone become hereafter the conviction of the philosophical world? And whatever the case may be in this instance, have there not been examples of this progress? Did not Galileo and the disciples of Galileo reduce several mechanical principles to the character of necessary truths, after they had by experiment and reasoning discovered them to be actually true? And have we not in these cases so many proofs that necessary truth is progressive, along with the progress of knowledge?

2. But, it will be said, the necessary character claimed for such truths is an illusion. The propositions so brought into view are really established by observation: by the study of external facts: and it is only the effect of habit and familiarity which makes men of science, when they well know them to be true, think them to be necessarily true. They are really the results of experience, as their history shows; and therefore cannot be necessary and à priori truths.

To which I reply: Such principles as I have mentioned,—that material substance cannot be produced or destroyed—that the cause is measured by the effect—that reaction is equal and opposite to action: are not the results of experience, nor can be. No experience can prove them; they are necessarily assumed as the interpretation of experience. They were not proved in the course of scientific investigations, but brought to light as such investigations showed their necessity. They are not the results, but the conditions of experimental sciences. If the Axiom of Substance were not true, and were not assumed, we could not have such a science as Chemistry, that is, we could have no knowledge at all respecting the changes of form of substances. If the Axioms of Mechanics were not true and were not assumed, we could have no science of Mechanics, that is, no knowledge of the laws of force acting on matter. It is not any special results of the science350 in such cases; but the existence, the possibility, of any science, which establishes the necessity of these axioms. They are not the consequences of knowledge, acquired from without, but the internal condition of our being able to know. And when we are to know concerning any new subject contained in the universe, it is not inconceivable nor strange that there should be new conditions of our knowledge.

It is not inconceivable or strange, therefore, that as new sciences are formed, new axioms, the foundations of such sciences, should come into view. As the light of clear and definite knowledge is kindled in successive chambers of the universe, it may disclose, not only the aspect of those new apartments, but also the form and structure of the lamp which man is thus allowed to carry from point to point, and to transmit from hand to hand. And though the space illumined to man's vision may always be small in comparison with the immeasurable abyss of darkness by which it is surrounded, and though the light may be dim and feeble, as well as partial; this need not make us doubt that, so far as we can by the aid of this lamp, we see truly: so far as we discern the necessary laws of the universe, the laws are true, and their truth is rooted in that in which the being of the universe is rooted.

And, to dwell for a moment longer on this image, we may also conceive that all that this lamp—the intellect of man cultivated by science,—does, by the light which it gives, is this—that it dispels a darkness which is dark for man alone, and discloses to him some things in some measure as all things lie in clear and perfect light before the eye of God. To the Divine Mind all the laws of the universe are plain and clear in all their multiplicity, extent and depth. The human mind is capable of seeing some of these laws, though only a few; to some extent, though but a little way; to some depth, though never to the bottom. But the Human Mind, can, in the course of ages and generations, by the long exercise of thought, successfully employed in augmenting knowledge, improve its powers of vision; and may thus come to see351 more laws than at first, to trace their extent more largely, to understand them more thoroughly; and thus the inward intellectual light of man may become broader and broader from age to age, though ever narrow when compared with completeness.

3. Is it strange to any one that inward light, as well as outward knowledge, should thus increase in the course of man's earthly career? that as knowledge extends, the foundations of knowledge should expand? that as man goes on discovering new truths, he should also discover something concerning the conditions of truth? Is it wonderful that as science is progressive the philosophy of science also should be progressive? that as we know more of everything else, we should also come to know more of our powers of knowing?

This does not seem to have been supposed by philosophers in general; or rather, they have assumed that they could come to know more about the powers of knowing by thinking about them, even without taking into account the light thrown upon the nature of knowledge by the progress of knowledge. From Plato downwards, through Aristotle, through the Schoolmen, to Descartes, to Locke, to Kant, Schelling and Hegel, philosophers have been perpetually endeavouring to explore the nature, the foundations, the consequences of our knowledge. But since Plato, scarcely one of them has ever proceeded as if new light were thrown upon knowledge by new knowledge. They have, many or all of them, attempted to establish fundamental truths, some of them new fundamental truths, about the human mind and the nature and conditions of its knowledge. These attempts show that they do not deny or doubt that there may be such new fundamental truths. Such new fundamental truths respecting the human mind and respecting knowledge must be, in many cases at least, (as it will be seen that they are, on examining the systems proposed by the philosophers just mentioned,) seen by their own light to be true. They are new axioms in philosophy. These philosophers therefore, or their disciples, cannot consistently blame us for holding the possibility of new axioms being introduced into philosophy from age352 to age, as there arise philosophers more and more clear-sighted.

4. But though they have no ground for rejecting our new axioms merely because they are new, we may have good ground for doubting the value of their new axioms, that is, of the foundations of their systems; because they are new truths about knowledge gathered by merely exploring the old fields of knowledge. We found our hopes of obtaining a larger view of the constitution of the human mind than the early philosophers had, on this:—that we obtain our view by studying the operation of the human mind since their time; its progress in acquiring a large stock of uncontested truths and in obtaining a wide and real knowledge of the universe. Here are new materials which the ancients had not; and which may therefore justify the hope that we may build our philosophy higher than the ancients did. But modern philosophers who use only the same materials as the ancient philosophers used, have not the same grounds for hope which we have. If they borrow all their examples and illustrations of man's knowledge of the universe, from the condition of the universe as existing in Space and Time, that is, from the geometrical condition of the universe, they may fail to obtain the light which might be obtained if they considered that the universe is also subject to conditions of Substance, of Cause and Effect, of Force and Matter: is filled with Kinds of things, in whose structure we assume Design and Ends; and so on; and if they reflected that these conditions or Ideas are not mere vague notions, but the bases of sciences which all thoughtful persons allow to be certain and real.

It is then, as I have said, from taking advantage of the progressive character which physical science, in the history of man, has been found to possess, that I hope to learn more of the nature and prospects of the human mind and soul, than those can learn who still take their stand on the old limited ground of man's knowledge. The knowledge of Geometry by the Greeks was the starting-point of their sound philosophy. It showed that something might be certainly known, and353 it showed, in some degree, how it was known. It thus refuted the skepticism which was destroying philosophy, and offered specimens of solid truth for the philosopher to analyse. But the Greeks tried to go beyond geometry in their knowledge of the universe. They tried to construct a science of Astronomy—of Harmonics—of Optics—of Mechanics. In the two former subjects, they succeeded to a very considerable extent. The question then arose, What was the philosophical import of these new sciences? What light did they throw on the nature of the universe, on the nature of knowledge, on the nature of the human mind? These questions Plato attempted to answer. He said that the lesson of these new sciences is this:—that the universe is framed upon the Divine Ideas; that man can to a certain extent obtain sight of these Ideas; and that when he does this, he knows concerning the universe. And again, he also put the matter otherwise: there is an Intelligible World, of which the Visible and Sensible world is only a dim image. Science consists in understanding the Intelligible World, which man is to a certain extent able to do, by the nature of his understanding. This was Plato's philosophy, founded upon the progress which human knowledge had made up to his time. Since his time, knowledge, that is science, has made a large additional progress. What is the philosophical lesson to be derived from this progress, and from the new provinces thus added to human knowledge? This is a question which I have tried to answer. I am not aware that any one since Plato has taken this line of speculation;—I mean, has tried to spell out the lesson of philosophy which is taught us, not by one specimen, or a few only, of the knowledge respecting the universe which man has acquired; but by including in his survey all the provinces of human knowledge, and the whole history of each. At any rate, whatever any one else may have done in this way, it seems to me that new inferences remain to be drawn, of the nature of those which Plato drew: and those I here attempt to deduce and to illustrate.

354

CHAPTER XXX.
The Theological Bearing of the Philosophy of Discovery.

That necessary truth is progressive;—that science is the idealization of facts, and that this process goes on from age to age, and advances with the advance of scientific discovery;—these are doctrines which I have endeavoured to establish and to elucidate. If these doctrines are true, they are so important that I may be excused should I return to them again and again, and trace their consequences in various directions. Especially I would examine the bearing of these doctrines upon our religious philosophy. I have hitherto abstained in a great measure from discussing religious doctrines; but such a reserve carried too far must deprive our philosophy of all completeness. No philosophy of science can be complete which is not also a philosophy of the universe; and no philosophy of the universe can satisfy thoughtful men, which does not include a reference to the power by which the universe came to be what it is. Supposing, then, such a reference to be admitted, let us see what aspect our doctrines give to it.

1. (How can there be necessary truths concerning the actual universe?)—In looking at the bearing of our doctrine on the philosophy of the universe, we are met by a difficulty, which is indeed, only a former difficulty under a new aspect. When we are come to the conclusion that science consists of facts idealized, we are led to ask, How this can be? How can facts be idealized? How can that which is a fact of external observation become a result of internal thought? How can that which was known à posteriori become known à355 priori? How can the world of things be identified with the world of thoughts? How can we discover a necessary connexion among mere phenomena?

Or to put the matter otherwise: How is it that the deductions of the intellect are verified in the world of sense? How is it that the truths of science obtained à priori are

183

exemplified in the general rules of facts observed à posteriori? How is it that facts, in science, always do correspond to our ideas?

I have propounded this paradox in various forms, because I wish it to be seen that it is, at first sight, a real, not merely a verbal contradiction, or at least a difficulty. If we can discover the solution of this difficulty in any one form, probably we can transpose the answer so as to suit the other forms of the question.

2. Suppose the case to be as I have stated it; that in some sciences at least, laws which were at first facts of observation come to be seen as necessary truths; and let us see to what this amounts in the several sciences.

It amounts to this: the truths of Geometry, such as we discern them by the exercise of our own thoughts, are always verified in the world of observation. The laws of space, derived from our Ideas, are universally true in the external world.

In the same way, as to number: the laws or truths respecting number, which are deduced from our Idea of Number, are universally true in the external world.

In the same way, as to the science which deals with matter and force: the truths of which I have spoken as derived from Ideas:—that action is equal to reaction; and that causes are measured by their effects;—are universally verified in all the laws of phenomena of the external world, which are disclosed by the science of Mechanics.

In the same way with regard to the composition and resolution of bodies into their elements; the truths derived from our Idea of Matter:—that no composition or resolution can increase or diminish the quantity of matter in the world, and that the properties of compounds are determined by their composition;—are356 truths derived from Ideas of quantity of matter, and of composition and resolution; but these truths are universally verified when we come to the facts of Chemistry.

In the same way it is a truth flowing from the Ideas of the Kinds of things, (as the possible subject of general propositions expressed in language,) that the kinds of things must be definite; and this law is verified whenever we express general propositions in general terms: for instance, when we distinguish species in Mineralogy.

3. This last example may appear to most readers doubtful. I have purposely pursued the enumeration till I came to a doubtful example, because it is, and I conceive always will be, impossible to extend this general view to all the Sciences. On the contrary, this doctrine applies at present to only a very few of the sciences, even in the eyes of those who hold the existence of ideal truths. The doctrine extends at present to a few only of the sciences, even if it extend to one or two besides those which have been mentioned— Geometry, Mechanics, Chemistry, Mineralogy: and though it may hereafter appear that Ideal Truths are possible and attainable for a few other sciences, yet the laws disclosed by sciences which cannot be reduced to ideal elements will, I conceive, always very far outnumber those which can be so reduced. The great body of our scientific knowledge will always be knowledge obtained by mere observation, not knowledge obtained by the use of theories alone.

184

4. The survey of the history and philosophy of the Sciences which we have attempted in previous works enables us to offer a sort of estimate of the relative portions of science which have and which have not thus been idealized. For the Aphorisms[317] which we have collected from that survey, contain Axioms which may be regarded as the Ideal portions of the various sciences; and the inspection of that series of aphorisms will show us to how such a portion of science, any357thing of this axiomatic or ideal character can he applied. These Axioms are the Axioms of Geometry (Aphorism XXVI); of Arithmetic (XXXVI); of Causation (XLVII); of a medium for the sensation of secondary qualities (LVIII), and their measure (LXIX); of Polarity (LXXII); of Chemical Affinity (LXXVI); of Substance (LXXVII); of Atoms (LXXIX).

Have we any axioms in the sciences which succeed these in our survey, as Botany, Zoology, Biology, Palæontology?

There is the Axiom of Symmetry (LXXX); of Kind, (already in some measure spoken of, (LXXXIII)); of Final Cause (CV); of First Cause (CXVI).

5. (Small extent of necessary truth.)—It is easily seen how small a portion of each of these latter sciences is included in these axioms: while, with regard to the sciences first mentioned, the Axioms include, in a manner, the whole of the science. The science is only the consequence of the Axioms. The whole science of Mechanics is only the development of the Axioms concerning action and reaction, and concerning cause and its measures, which I have mentioned as a part of our Ideal knowledge.

In fact, beginning from Geometry and Arithmetic, and going through the sciences of Mechanics, of Secondary Qualities, and of Chemistry, onwards to the sciences which deal with Organized Beings, we find that our ideal truths occupy a smaller and smaller share of the sciences in succession, and that the vast variety of facts and phenomena which nature offers to us, is less and less subject to any rules or principles which we can perceive to be necessary.

But still, that there are principles,—necessary principles, which prevail universally even in these higher parts of the natural sciences,—appears on a careful consideration of the axioms which I have mentioned:—that in symmetrical natural bodies the similar parts are similarly affected;—that every event must have a cause;—that there must be a First Cause, and the like.

6. It being established, then, that in the progress of science, facts are idealized—that à posteriori truths358 become à priori truths;—that the world of things is identified with the world of thoughts to a certain extent;—to an extent which grows larger as we see into the world of things more clearly; the question recurs which I have already asked: How can this be?

How can it be that the world without us is thus in some respects identical with the world within us?—that is our question.

7. (How did things come to be as they are?)—It would seem that we may make a step in the solution of this question, if we can answer this other: How did the world without us and the world within us come to be what they are?

To this question, two very different answers are returned by those who do and those who do not believe in a Supreme Mind or Intelligence, as the cause and foundation of the world.

Those who do not believe that the world has for its cause and foundation a Supreme Intelligence, or who do not connect their philosophy with this belief, would reply to our inquiry, that the reason why man's thoughts and ideas agree with the world is, that they are borrowed from the world; and that the persuasion that these Ideas and truths derived from them have any origin except the world without us, is an illusion.

On this view I shall not now dwell; for I wish to trace out the consequences of the opposite view, that there exists a Supreme Mind, which is the cause and foundation of the universe. Those who hold this, and who also hold that the human mind can become possessed of necessary truths, if they are asked how it is that these necessary truths are universally verified in the material world, will reply, that it is so because the Supreme Creative-Mind has made it so to be:—that the truths which exist or can be generated in man's mind agree with the laws of the universe, because He who has made and sustains man and the universe has caused them to agree:—that our Ideas correspond to the Facts of the world, and the Facts to our Ideas, because our Ideas are given us by the same power359 which made the world, and given so that these can and must agree with the world so made.

8. (View of the Theist).—This, in its general form, would be the answer of the theist, (so we may call him who believes in a Supreme Intelligent Cause of the world and of man,) to the questions which we have propounded—the perplexity or paradox which we have tried to bring into view. But we must endeavour to trace this view—this answer—more into detail.

If a Supreme Intelligence be the cause of the world and of the Laws which prevail among its phenomena, these Laws must exist as Acts of that Intelligence—as Laws caused by the thoughts of the Supreme Mind—as Ideas in the Mind of God. And then the question would be, How we are to conceive these thoughts, these Ideas, to be at the same time Divine and human:—to be at the same time Ideas in the Divine Mind, and necessary truths in the human mind; and this is the question which I would now inquire into.

9. (Is this Platonism?)—To the terms in which the inquiry is now propounded it may be objected that I am taking for granted the Platonic doctrine, that the world is constituted according to the Ideas of the Divine Mind. It may be said that this doctrine is connected with gross extravagancies of speculation and fiction, and has long been obsolete among sound philosophers.

To which I reply, that if such doctrines have been pushed into extravagancies, with them I have nothing to do, nor have I any disposition or wish to revive them. But I do

186

not conceive the doctrine, to the extent to which I have stated it, to be at all obsolete:—that the Cause and Foundation of the Universe is a Divine Mind: and from that doctrine it necessarily follows, that the laws of the Universe are in the Ideas of the Divine Mind.

I would then, as I have said, examine the consequences of this doctrine, in reference to the question of which I have spoken. And in order to do this, it may help us, if we consider separately the bearing of360 this doctrine upon separate portions of our knowledge of the universe;—separately its bearing upon the laws which form the subject-matter of different sciences:—if we take particular human Ideas, and consider what the Divine Ideas must be with regard to each of them.

10. (Idea of Space.)—Let us take, in the first place, the Idea of Space. Concerning this Idea we possess necessary truths; namely, the Axioms of Geometry; and, as necessarily resulting from them, the whole body of Geometry. And our former inquiry, as narrowed within the limits of this Idea, will be, How is it that the truths of Geometry—à priori truths—are universally verified in the observed phenomena of the universe? And the theist's answer which we have given will now assume this form:—This is so because the Supreme Mind has constituted and constitutes the universe according to the Idea of Space. The universe conforms to the Idea of Space, and the Idea of Space exists in the human mind;—is necessarily evoked and awakened in the human mind existing in the universe. And since the Idea of Space, which is a constituent of the universe, is also a constituent of the human mind, the consequences of this Idea in the universe and in the human mind necessarily coincide; that is, the spacial Laws of the universe necessarily coincide with the spacial Science which man elaborates out of his mind.

11. To this it may be objected, that we suppose the Idea of Space in the Divine Mind (according to which Idea, among others, the universe is constituted,) to be identical with the Idea of Space in the human mind; and this, it may be urged, is too limited and material a notion of the Divine Mind to be accepted by a reverent philosophy.

I reply, that I suppose the Divine Idea of Space and the human Idea of Space to coincide, only so far as the human Idea goes; and that the Divine Idea may easily have so much more luminousness and comprehensiveness as Divine Ideas may be supposed to have compared with human. Further, that this Idea of Space, the first of the Ideas on which human science361 is founded, is the most luminous and comprehensive of such Ideas; and there are innumerable other Ideas, the foundations of sciences more or less complete, which are extremely obscure and limited in the human mind, but which must be conceived to be perfectly clear and unlimitedly comprehensive in the Divine Mind. And thus, the distance between the human and the Divine Mind, even as to the views which constitute the most complete of the human sciences, is as great in our view as in any other.

12. That the Idea of Space in the human mind, though sufficiently clear and comprehensive to be the source of necessary truths, is far too obscure and limited to be regarded as identical with the Divine Idea, will be plain to us, if we call to mind the perplexities which the human mind falls into when it speculates concerning space infinite. An Intelligence in which all these perplexities should vanish by the light of the Idea itself, would be infinitely elevated in clearness and comprehensiveness of intellectual vision

above human intelligence, even though its Idea of Space should coincide with the human Idea as far as the human Idea goes.

I do not shrink from saying, therefore, that the Idea of Space which is a constituent of the human mind existing in the universe is, as far as it goes, identical with the Idea of Space which is a constituent of the universe. And this I give as the answer to the question, How it is that the necessary truths of Geometry universally coincide with the relations of the phenomena of the universe? And this doctrine, it is to be remembered, carries us to the further doctrine, that the Idea of Space in the human mind is, so far as it goes, coincident with the Idea of Space in the Divine Mind.

13. (Idea of Time.)—What I have said of the Idea of Space, may be repeated, for the most part, with regard to the Idea of Time; except that the Idea of Time, as such, does not give rise to a large collection of necessary truths, such as the propositions of Geometry. Some philosophers regard Number as a modification362 or derivative of the Idea of Time. If we accept this view, we have, in the Science of Arithmetic, a body of necessary truths which flow from the Idea of Time. But this doctrine, whichever way held, does not bear much on the question with which we are now concerned. That which we do hold is, that the Idea of Time in the human mind is, so far as it goes, coincident with the Idea of Time in the Divine Mind: and that this is the reason why the events of the universe, as contemplated by us, conform to necessary laws of succession: while at the same time we must suppose that all the perplexities in the Idea of Time which embarrass the human mind—the perplexities, for instance, which arise from contemplating a past and a future eternity, are, in the Divine Mind, extinguished in the Light of the Idea itself.

Space and Time have, and have generally been regarded as having, peculiar prerogatives in our speculations concerning the constitution of the universe. We see and perceive all things as subject to the laws of Space and Time; or rather (for the term Law does not here satisfy us), as being and happening in space and in time: and probably most persons will have no repugnance to the doctrine that the Divine Mind, as well as the human, so regards them, and has so constituted them and us that they must be so regarded. Space and Time are human Ideas which include all objects and events, and are the foundation of all human Science. And we can conceive that Space and Time are also Divine Ideas which the Divine Mind causes to include all objects and events, and makes to be the foundation of all existence. So far as these Ideas go, our doctrine is not difficult or new.

14. (Ideas of Force and Matter.)—But what are we to say of the Ideas which come next in the survey of the sciences, Force and Matter? These are human Ideas—the foundations of several sciences—of the mechanical sciences in particular. But are they the foundations of necessary truths? Have we necessary truths respecting Force and Matter? We have endeavoured to prove that we have:—that certain fundamental pro363positions in the Science of Mechanics, although, historically speaking, they were discovered by observation and experience, are yet, philosophically speaking, necessary propositions. And being such, the facts of the universe must needs conform to these propositions; and the reason why they do so, we hold, in this as in the former case, to be, that these Ideas, Force and Matter, are Ideas in the Divine Mind:—Ideas according to which the universe is, by the Divine Cause, constituted and established.

188

15. That Force and Matter are Ideas existing in the Divine Mind, and coincident with the Idea of Force and Matter in the human mind, as far as these go, is a doctrine which is important in our view of the universe in relation to its Cause and Foundation.

These are very comprehensive and fundamental Ideas, and there are certain universal relations among external things which rest upon these Ideas. The two, Force and Matter, are, in a certain way, the necessary antithesis and opposite condition each of the other. Force (that is Mechanical Force, Pressure or Impulse) cannot act without matter to act upon. Matter (that is Body) cannot exist without Force by which it is kept in its place, by which its parts are held together, and by which it excludes every other body from the place which it occupies. We cannot conceive Force without Matter, or Matter without Force; the two are, as Action and Reaction, necessarily co-ordinate and coexistent. In every part of the universe they must be so. In every part of the universe, if there be material objects, there must be Force; if there be Force, there must be material objects.

Our apprehension of this universal necessity arises from our having the Ideas of Force and Matter which are human Ideas. The actuality of this universal antithesis arises from the Ideas of Force and Matter being Ideas in the Divine Mind;—Ideas realized as a part of the fundamental constitution of the universe.

That Force and Matter are thus among the Ideas in the Divine Mind, and that, with them, the Ideas of Force and Matter in the human mind, regarded in their364 most general form, agree so far as they go, is another step in the doctrine which I am trying to unfold. That the Ideas of Force and Matter in the Divine Mind are such as to banish by their own light, innumerable contradictions and perplexities which darken these Ideas in the human mind, is to be supposed: and thus the Divine Mind is infinitely luminous and comprehensive compared with the human mind.

16. (Creation of Matter.)—It may perhaps be urged, as an objection to this doctrine, that it asserts Matter to be a necessary constituent of the universe, and thus involves the assertion of the eternity of Matter. But in reality the doctrine asserts Matter to be eternal, only in the way in which time and space are eternal. Whether we hold that there was a creation before which time and space did not exist,—with the poet who says

Ere Time and Space were Time and Space were not,—
is not essential to our present inquiry. Certainly we cannot conceive such a state, and therefore cannot reason about it. We have no occasion here to speak of Creation, nor have spoken of it. What I have said is, that Space and Time, Force and Matter are universal elements, principles, constituents, of the universe as it is—and necessary Ideas of the human mind existing in that universe. If there ever was a Creation before which Matter did not exist, it was a Creation before which Force did not exist. And in the universe as it is, the two are necessarily co-existent in the human thought because they are co-existent in the Divine Thought which makes the world.

We apply then to Force and Matter the doctrine—the Platonic doctrine, if any one please so to call it,—that the world is constituted according to the Ideas of the Divine

Mind, and that the human mind apprehends the inward and most fundamental relations of the universe by sharing in some measure of those same Ideas.

17. (Platonic Ideas.)—But do we go on with Plato to extend this doctrine of Ideas to all the objects and365 all the aspects of objects which constitute the material universe? Do we say with Plato that there is not only an Idea of a Triangle by conformity to which a figure is a triangle, but an Idea of Gold, by conformity to which a thing is gold, and Idea of a Table, by conformity to which a thing is a table?

We say none of these things. We say nothing which at all approaches to them. We do not say that there is an Idea of a Triangle, the archetype of all triangles; we only say that man has an Idea of Space, which is an Idea of a fundamental reality; and that therefore from this Idea flow real and universal truths—about triangles and other figures. Still less do we say that we have an archetypal Idea of Gold, or of a Metal in general, or of any of the kinds of objects which exist in the world. Here we part company with Plato altogether.

But have we any Ideas at all with regard to objects which we thus speak of as separable into Kinds? We can have knowledge,—even exact and general knowledge, that is, science—with regard to such things—with regard to plants and metals—gold and iron. Do we possess in our minds, with regard to those objects, any Ideas, any universal principles, such as we possess with regard to geometrical figures or mechanical actions? And if so, are those human Ideas verified in the universe, as the Ideas hitherto considered are? and do they thus afford us further examples of Ideas in the human mind which are also Ideas in the Divine Mind, manifested in the constitution of the universe?

18. (Idea of Kinds.)—We answer Yes to these questions, on this ground:—the objects that exist in the world, plants and metals, gold and iron, for example, in order that they may be objects with regard to which we can have any knowledge, must be objects of distinct and definite thought. Plant must differ from metal, gold from iron, in order that we may know anything at all about any of these objects. The differences by which such objects differ need not necessarily be expressed by definitions, as the difference of a triangle and a square are expressed; but there must manifestly366 be fixed and definite differences, in order that we may have any knowledge about them. These Kinds of things must be so far distinct and definite, as to be objects of distinct and definite thought. The Kinds of natural objects must differ, and we must think of things as of different Kinds, in order that we may know anything about natural objects. Living in a world in which we exercise our Intellect upon the natural objects which surround us, we must regard them as distinct from each other in Kind. We must have an Idea of Kinds of natural objects.

19. The Idea of a Kind involves this principle: That where the Kind differs the Properties may differ, but so far as the Kind is the same the Properties contemplated in framing the notion of each Kind are the same. Gold cannot have the distinctive properties of Iron without being Iron.

In the case of human knowledge, each Kind is marked by a word—a name; and the doctrine that the notion of the Kind must be so applied that this same Kind of object shall have the same properties, has been otherwise expressed by saying that Names must be so applied that general propositions may be possible. We must so apply the name of Gold that we may be able to say, gold has a specific gravity of a certain amount and is ductile in a certain degree.

20. But this condition of the names of Kinds,—that they must be such that general propositions about these Kinds of objects shall be possible;—is it a necessary result of the Idea of Kind? And if so, can the Idea of Kind, thus implying the use of language, and a condition depending on the use of language, be an Idea in the Divine as well as in the human mind? Can it be, in this respect, like the Ideas which we have already considered, Space and Time, Force and Matter?

We cannot suppose that the Ideas which exist in the Divine Mind imply, in the Supreme Intelligence, the need of language, like human language. But there is no incongruity in supposing that they imply that which we take as the condition of such language367 as we speak of, namely, distinct thought. There is nothing incongruous in supposing that the Supreme Intelligence regards the objects which exist in the universe as distinct in Kind: and that the Idea of Kind in the human mind agrees with the Idea of Kind in the Divine Mind, as far as it goes. And as we have seen, the Idea of Properties is correlative and coexistent with the Idea of Kind, so that the one changing, the other changes also. There is nothing incongruous in supposing that the Divine Mind manifests in the universe of which it is the Cause and Foundation, these two, its co-ordinate Ideas: and that the human mind sees that these two Ideas are co-ordinate and coexistent, in virtue of its participating in these Ideas of the Divine Mind. The universe is full of things which man perceives do and must differ correspondingly in kind and in properties; and this is so, because the Ideas of various Kinds and various Properties are part of the scheme of the universe in the Divine Mind.

21. That the Ideas of Kinds and Properties as coordinate and interdependent, though common, to a certain extent, to the human and the Divine Mind, are immeasurably more luminous, penetrating and comprehensive in the Divine than in the human mind, is abundantly evident. In fact, though man assents to such axioms as these,—that the Properties of Things depend upon their Kinds, and that the Kinds of Things are determined by their Properties,—yet the nature of connexion of Kinds and Properties is a matter in which man's mind is all but wholly dark, and on which the Divine Mind must be perfectly clear. For in how few cases—if indeed in any one—can we know what is the essence of any Kind;—what is the real nature of the connexion between the character of the Kind and its Properties! Yet on this point we must suppose that the Divine Intellect, which is the foundation of the world, is perfectly clear. Every Kind of thing, every genus and species of object, appears to Him in its essential character, and its properties follow as necessary consequences. He sees the essences of things368 through all time and through all space; while we, slowly and painfully, by observation and experiment, which we cannot idealize or can idealize only in the most fragmentary manner, make out a few of the properties of each Kind of thing. Our Science here is but a drop in the ocean of that truth, which is known to the Divine Mind but kept back from us; but still, that we can know and do know anything, arises from our taking hold of that principle, human as well as Divine, that there are differences of Kinds of things, and corresponding differences of their properties.

191

22. (Idea of Substance.)—I shall not attempt to enumerate all the Ideas which, being thus a part of the foundation of Science in the human mind and of Existence in the universe, are shown to be at the same time Ideas in the Divine and in the human mind. But there is one other of which the necessary and universal application is so uncontested, that it may well serve further to exemplify our doctrine. In all reasonings concerning the composition and resolution of the elements of bodies, it is assumed that the quantity of matter cannot be increased or diminished by anything which we can do to them. We have an Idea of Substance, as something which may have its qualities altered by our operations upon it, but cannot have its quantity changed. And this Idea of Substance is universally verified in the facts of observation and experiment. Indeed it cannot fail to be so; for it regulates and determines the way in which we interpret the facts of observation and experiment. It authorized the philosopher who was asked the weight of a column of smoke to reply, "Subtract the weight of the ashes from that of the fuel, and you have the weight of the smoke:" for in virtue of that idea we assume that, in combustion, or in any other operation, all the substance which is subjected to the operation must exist in the result in some form or other. Now why may we reasonably make this assumption, and thus, as it were, prescribe laws to the universe? Our reply is, Because Substance is one of the Ideas according to which the universe is constituted. The material things369 which make up the universe are substance according to this Idea. They are substance according to this Idea in the Divine Mind, and they are substance according to this Idea in the human mind, because the human mind has this Idea, to a certain extent, in common with the Divine Mind. In this, as in the other cases, the Idea must be immeasurably more clear and comprehensive in the Divine Mind than in the human. The human Idea of substance is full of difficulty and perplexity: as for instance; how a substance can assume successively a solid, fluid and airy form; how two substances can be combined so as entirely to penetrate one another and have new qualities: and the like. All these perplexities and difficulties we must suppose to vanish in the Divine Idea of Substance. But still there remains in the human, as in the Divine Idea, the source and root of the universal truth, that though substances may be combined or separated or changed in form in the processes of nature or of art, no portion of substance can come into being or cease to be.

23. (Idea of Final Cause.)—There is yet one other Idea which I shall mention, though it is one about which difficulties have been raised, since the consideration of such difficulties may be instructive: the Idea of a purpose, or as it is often termed, a Final Cause, in organized bodies. It has been held, and rightly[318], that the assumption of a Final Cause of each part of animals and plants is as inevitable as the assumption of an efficient cause of every event. The maxim, that in organized bodies nothing is in vain, is as necessarily true as the maxim that nothing happens by chance. I have elsewhere[319] shown fully that this Idea is not deduced from any special facts, but is assumed as a law governing all facts in organic nature, directing the researches and interpreting the observations of physiologists. I have also remarked that it is not at variance with that other law, that plants and that animals are constructed upon general plans, of which plans, it may be, we do not see the370 necessity, though we see how wide is their generality. This Idea of a purpose,—of a Final Cause,—then, thus supplied by our minds, is found to be applicable throughout the organic world. It is in virtue of this Idea that we conceive animals and plants as subject to disease; for disease takes place when the parts do not fully answer their purpose; when they do not do what they ought to do. How is it then that we

thus find an Idea which is supplied by our own minds, but which is exemplified in every part of the organic world? Here perhaps the answer will be readily allowed. It is because this Idea is an Idea of the Divine Mind. There is a Final Cause in the constitution of these parts of the universe, and therefore we can interpret them by means of the Idea of Final Cause. We can see a purpose, because there is a purpose. Is it too presumptuous to suppose that we can thus enter into the Ends and Purposes of the Divine Mind? We willingly grant and declare that it would be presumptuous to suppose that we can enter into them to any but a very small degree. They doubtless go immeasurably beyond our mode of understanding or conceiving them. But to a certain extent we can go. We can go so far as to see that they are Ends and Purposes. It is not a vain presumption in us to suppose that we know that the eye was made for seeing and the ear for hearing. In this the most pious of men see nothing impious: the most cautious philosophers see nothing rash. And that we can see thus far into the designs of the Divine Mind, arises, we hold, from this:—that we have an Idea of Design and of Purpose which, so far as it is merely that, is true; and so far, is Design and Purpose in the same sense in the one case and in the other.

I am very far from having exhausted the list of Fundamental Ideas which the human mind possesses and which have been made the foundations of Sciences. Of all such Ideas, I might go on to remark, that they are of universal validity and application in the region of external Facts. In all the cases I might go on to inquire, How is it that man's Ideas, developed in his internal world, are found to coincide universally with371 the laws of the external world? By what necessity, on what ground does this happen? And in all cases I should have had to reply, that this happens, and must happen, because these Ideas of the human mind are also Ideas of the Divine Mind according to which the universe is constituted. Man has these thoughts, and sees them verified in the universe, because God had these thoughts and exemplifies them in the universe.

24. (Human immeasurably inferior to Divine).—But of all these Ideas, I should also have to remark, that the way in which man possesses them is immeasurably obscure and limited in comparison with the way in which God must be supposed to possess them. These human Ideas, though clear and real as far as they go, in every case run into obscurity and perplexity, from which the Ideas of the Divine Mind must be supposed to be free. In every case, man, by following the train of thought involved in each Idea, runs into confusion and seeming contradictions. It may be that by thinking more and more, and by more and more studying the universe, he may remove some of this confusion and solve some of these contradictions. But when he has done in this way all that he can, an immeasurable region of confusion and contradiction will still remain; nor can he ever hope to advance very far, in dispelling the darkness which hangs over the greater part of the universe. His knowledge, his science, his Ideas, extend only so far as he can keep his footing in the shallow waters which lie on the shore of the vast ocean of unfathomable truth.

25. But further, we have not, even so, exhausted our estimate of the immeasurable distance between the human mind and the Divine Mind:—very far from it: we have only spoken of the smallest portion of the region of truth,—that about which we have Sciences and Scientific Ideas. In that region alone do we claim for man the possession of Ideas the clearness of which has in it something divine. But how narrow is the province

of Science compared with the whole domain of human thought! We may enumerate the sciences of which we have been speaking, and which involve372 such Ideas as I have mentioned. How many are they? Geometry, Arithmetic, Chemistry, Classification, Physiology. To these we might have added a few others; as the sciences which deal with Light, Heat, Polarities; Geology and the other Palætiological Sciences; and there our enumeration at present must stop. For we can hardly as yet claim to have Sciences, in the rigorous sense in which we use the term, about the Vital Powers of man, his Mental Powers, his historical attributes, as Language, Society, Arts, Law, and the like. On these subjects few philosophers will pretend to exhibit to us Ideas of universal validity, prevailing through all the range of observation. Yet all these things proceed according to Ideas in the Divine Mind by which the universe, and by which man, is constituted. In such provinces of knowledge, at least, we have no difficulty in seeing or allowing how blind man is with regard to their fundamental and constituent principles; how weak his reason; how limited his view. If on some of the plainest portions of possible knowledge, man have Ideas which may be regarded as coincident to a certain extent with those by which the universe is really constituted; still on by far the largest portion of the things which most concern him, he has no knowledge but that which he derives from experience, and which he cannot put in so general a form as to have any pretensions to rest it upon a foundation of connate Ideas.

26. (Science advances towards the Divine Ideas.)—But there is yet one remark tending somewhat in the opposite direction, which I must make, as a part of the view which I wish to present. Science, in the rigorous sense of the term, involves, we have said, Ideas which to a certain extent agree with the Ideas of the Divine Mind. But science in that sense is progressive; new sciences are formed and old sciences extended. Hence it follows that the Ideas which man has, and which agree with the Ideas of the Divine Mind, may receive additions to their number from time to time. This may seem a bold assertion; yet this is what, with due restriction, we conceive to be373 true. Such Ideas as we have spoken of receive additions, in respect of their manifestation and development. The Ideas, the germ of them at least, were in the human mind before; but by the progress of scientific thought they are unfolded into clearness and distinctness. That this takes place with regard to scientific Ideas, the history of science abundantly shows. The Ideas of Space and Time indeed, were clear and distinct from the first, and accordingly the Sciences of Geometry and Arithmetic have existed from the earliest times of man's intellectual history. But the Ideas upon which the Science of Mechanics depends, having been obscure in the ancient world, are become clear in modern times. The Ideas of Composition and Resolution have only in recent centuries become so clear as to be the basis of a definite science. The Idea of Substance indeed was always assumed, though vaguely applied by the ancients; and the Idea of a Design or End in vital structures is at least as old as Socrates. But the Idea of Polarities was never put forth in a distinct form till quite recently; and the Idea of Successive Causation, as applied in Geology and in the other Palætiological Sciences, was never scientifically applied till modern times: and without attempting to prove the point by enumeration, it will hardly be doubted that many Scientific Ideas are clear and distinct among modern men of science which were not so in the ancient days.

Now all such scientific Ideas are, as I have been urging, points on which the human mind is a reflex of the Divine Mind. And therefore in the progress of science, we obtain,

194

not indeed new points where the human mind reflects the Divine, but new points where this reflection is clear and luminous. We do not assert that the progress of science can bring into existence new elements of truth in the human mind, but it may bring them into view. It cannot add to the characters of Divine origin in the human mind, but it may add to or unfold the proofs of such an origin. And this is what we conceive it does. And though we do not conceive that the Ideas which science thus brings into374 view are the most important of man's thoughts in other respects, yet they may, and we conceive do, supply a proof of the Divine nature of the human mind, which proof is of peculiar cogency. What other proofs may be collected from other trains of human thought, we shall hereafter consider.

27. (Recapitulation.)—This, then, is the argument to which we have been led by the survey of the sciences in which we have been engaged:—That the human mind can and does put forth, out of its natural stores, duly unfolded, certain Ideas as the bases of scientific truths: These Ideas are universally and constantly verified in the universe: And the reason of this is, that they agree with the Ideas of the Divine Mind according to which the universe is constituted and sustained: The human mind has thus in it an element of resemblance to the Divine Mind: To a certain extent it looks upon the universe as the Divine Mind does; and therefore it is that it can see a portion of the truth: And not only can the human mind thus see a portion of the truth, as the Divine Mind sees it: but this portion, though at present immeasurably small, and certain to be always immeasurably small compared with the whole extent of truth which with greater intellectual powers, he might discern, nevertheless may increase from age to age.

This is then, I conceive, one of the results of the progress of scientific discovery—the Theological Result of the Philosophy of Discovery, as it may, I think, not unfitly be called:—That by every step in such discovery by which external facts assume the aspect of necessary consequences of our Ideas, we obtain a fresh proof of the Divine nature of the human mind: And though these steps, however far we may go in this path, can carry us only a very little way in the knowledge of the universe, yet that such knowledge, so far as we do obtain it, is Divine in its kind, and shows that the human mind has something Divine in its nature.

The progress by which external facts assume the aspect of necessary consequences of our Ideas, we have375 termed the idealization of facts; and in this sense we have said, that the progress of science consists in the Idealization of Facts. But there is another way in which the operation of man's mind may be considered—an opposite view of the identification of Ideas with Facts; which we must consider, in order to complete our view of the bearing of the progress of human thought upon the nature of man.

376

CHAPTER XXXI.
Man's Knowledge of God.

1. MAN'S powers and means of knowledge are so limited and imperfect that he can know little concerning God. It is well that men in their theological speculations should

recollect that it is so, and should pursue all such speculations in a modest and humble spirit.

But this humility and modesty defeat their own ends, when they lead us to think that we can know nothing concerning God: for to be modest and humble in dealing with this subject, implies that we know this, at least, that God is a proper object of modest and humble thought.

2. Some philosophers have been led, however, by an examination of man's faculties and of the nature of being, to the conclusion that man can know nothing concerning God. But we may very reasonably doubt the truth of this conclusion. We may ask, How can we know that we can know nothing? If we can know nothing, we cannot even know that.

It is much more reasonable to begin with things that we really do know, and to examine how far such knowledge can carry us, respecting God, as well as anything else. This is the course which we have been following, and its results are very far from being trifling or unimportant.

In thus beginning from what we know, we start from two points, on each of which we have, we conceive, some real and sure knowledge:—namely, mathematical and physical knowledge of the universe without us; and a knowledge of our own moral and personal nature within us.

377

3. (From Nature we learn something of God.)—In pursuing the first line of thought, we are led to reason thus. The universe is governed by certain Ideas: for instance, everything which exists and happens in the universe, exists and happens IN Space and Time. Why is this? It is, we conceive, because God has constituted and constitutes the universe so that it may be so; that is, because the Ideas of Space and of Time are Ideas according to which God has established and upholds the universe.

But we may proceed further in this way, as we have already said. The universe not only exists in space and time, but it has in it substances—material substances: or taking it collectively, Material Substance. Can we know anything concerning this substance? Yes: something we can know; for we know that material substance cannot be brought into being or annihilated by any natural process. We have then an Idea of Substance which is a Law of the universe. How is this?—We reply, that it is because our Idea of Substance is an Idea on which God has established and upholds the universe.

Can we proceed further still? Can we discern any other Ideas according to which the universe is constituted? Yes: as we have already remarked, we can discern several, though as we go on from one to another they become gradually fainter in their light, less cogent in their necessity. We can see that Force as well as Material Substance is an Idea on which the universe is constituted, and that Force and Matter are a necessary and universal antithesis: we can see that the Things which occupy the universe must be of definite Kinds, in order that an intelligent mind may occupy itself about them, and thus that the

Idea of Kind is a constitutive Idea of the universe. We can see that some kinds of things have life, and our Idea of Life is, that every part of a living thing is a means to an End; and thus we recognize End, or Final Cause, as an Idea which prevails throughout the universe, and we recognize this Idea as an Idea according to which God constitutes and upholds the universe.

378

Since we know so much concerning the universe, and since every Law of the universe which is a necessary form of thought about the universe must exist in the Divine Mind, in order that it may find a place in our minds, how can we say that we can know nothing concerning the Divine Mind?

4. (Though but Little.)—But on the other hand, we easily see how little our knowledge is, compared with what we do not know. Even the parts of our knowledge which are the clearest are full of perplexities; and of the Laws of the universe, including living as well as lifeless things, how small a portion do we know at all!

Even the parts of our knowledge which are the clearest, I say, are full of perplexities. Infinite Space and an infinite Past, an infinite Future,—how helplessly our reason struggles with these aspects of our Ideas! And with regard to Substance, how did ingenerable and indestructible substance come into being? And with regard to Matter, how can passive Matter be endued with living force? And with regard to Kinds, how immeasurably beyond our power of knowing are their numbers and their outward differences: still more their internal differences and central essence! And with regard to the Design which we see in the organs of living things, though we can confidently say we see it, how obscurely is it shown, and how much is our view of it disturbed by other Laws and Analogies! And the Life of things, the end to which such Design tends, how full of impenetrable mysteries is it! or rather how entirely a mass of mystery into which our powers of knowledge strive in vain to penetrate!

There is therefore no danger that by following this train of thought we should elevate our view of man too high, or bring down God in our thoughts to the likeness of man. Even if we were to suppose the Idea of the Divine Mind to be of the same kind as the Ideas of the human mind, the very few Ideas of this kind, which man possesses, compared with the whole range of the universe, and the scanty length to which he can follow each, make his knowledge so small and imper379fect, that he has abundant reason to be modest and humble in his contemplations concerning the Intelligence that knows all and constitutes all. He can, as I have already said, wade but a few steps into the margin of the boundless and unfathomable ocean of truth.

5. But the Ideas of the Divine Mind must necessarily be different in kind, as well as in number and extent, from the Ideas of the human mind, on this very account, that they are complete and perfect. The Mind which can conceive all the parts and laws of the universe in all their mutual bearings, fundamental reasons, and remote consequences, must be different in kind, as well as in extent, from the mind which can only trace a few of these parts, and see these laws in a few of their aspects, and cannot sound the whole

197

depth of any of them. The Divine Mind differs from the human, in the way in which we must needs suppose what is Divine to differ from what is human.

6. It has sometimes been said that the Divine Mind differs from the human as the Infinite from the finite. And this has been given as a reason why we cannot know anything concerning God; for we cannot, it is said, know anything concerning the Infinite. Our conception of the Infinite being merely negative, (the negation of a limit,) makes all knowledge about it impossible. But this is not truly said. Our conception of the Infinite is not merely negative. As I have elsewhere remarked, our conception of the Infinite is positive in this way:—that in order to form this conception, we begin to follow a given Idea in a given direction; and then, having thus begun, we suppose that the progress of thought goes on in that direction without limit. To arrive at our Idea of infinite space, for example, we must determine what kind of space we mean,—line, area or solid; and from what origin we begin: and infinite space has different attributes as we take different beginnings in this way.

And so with regard to the kinds of infinity (for there are many) which belong to the Divine Mind. We have a few Ideas which represent the Laws of the380 universe:—as Space, Time, Substance, Force, Matter, Kind, End; of such Ideas the Divine Mind may have an infinite number. These Ideas in the human mind are limited in depth and clearness: in the Divine Mind they must be infinitely clearer than the clearest human Intuition; infinitely more profound than the profoundest human thought. And in this way, and, as we shall see, in other ways also, the Divine Mind infinitely transcends the human mind when most fully instructed and unfolded.

In this way and in other ways also, I say. For we have hitherto spoken of the human mind only as contemplating the external world;—as discerning, to a certain small extent, the laws of the universe. We have spoken of the world of things without: we must now speak of the world within us;—of the world of our thoughts, our being, our moral and personal being.

7. (From ourselves we learn something concerning God.)—We must speak of this: for this is, as I have said, another starting point and another line in which we may proceed from what we know, and see how far our knowledge carries us, and how far it teaches us anything concerning God.

Looking at ourselves, we perceive that we have to act, as well as to contemplate: we are practical as well as speculative beings. And tracing the nature and conditions of our actions, in the depths of our thought we find that there is in the aspect of actions a supreme and inevitable distinction of right and wrong. We cannot help judging of our actions as right and wrong. We acknowledge that there must be such a judgment appropriate to them. We have these Ideas of right and wrong as attributes of actions; and thus we are moral beings.

8. And again: the actions are our actions. We act in this way or that. And we are not mere things, which move and change as they are acted on, but which do not themselves act, as man acts. I am not a Thing but a Person; and the men with whom I act, who act

with me—act in various ways towards me, well or ill—are also persons. Man is a personal being.

381

The Ideas of right and wrong—the moral Ideas of man—are then a part of the scheme of the universe to which man belongs. Could they be this, if they were not also a part of the nature of that Divine Mind which constitutes the universe?—It would seem not: the Moral Law of the universe must be a Law of the Divine Mind, in order that it may be a Law felt and discerned by man.

9. (Objection answered.)—But, it may be objected, the Moral Law of the universe is a Law in a different sense from the Laws of the universe of which we spoke before—the mathematical and physical laws of the universe. Those were laws according to which things are, and events occur: but Moral Laws are Laws according to which men ought to act, and according to which actions ought to be. There is a difference, so that we cannot reason from the human to the Divine Mind in the same manner in this case as in the other.

True: we cannot reason in the same manner. But we can reason still more confidently. For the Law directing what ought to be is the Supreme Law, and the mind which constitutes the Supreme Law is the Supreme Mind, that is, the Divine Mind.

10. That the Moral Law is not verified among men in fact, is not a ground for doubting that it is a Law of the Divine Mind; but it is a ground for inquiring what consequences the Divine Mind has annexed to the violation of the Law; and in what manner the supremacy of the Law will be established in the total course of the history of the universe, including, it may be, the history of other worlds than that in which we now live.

Considering how dimly and imperfectly we see what consequences the Divine Governor has annexed to the violation of the Moral Law, He who sees all these consequences and has provided for the establishment of His Law in the whole history of the human race, must be supposed to be infinitely elevated above man in wisdom;—more even in virtue of this aspect of His nature, than in virtue of that which is derived from the contemplation of the universe.

382

11. Man is a person; and his personality is his highest attribute, or at least, that which makes all his highest attributes possible. And the highest attribute which belongs to the finite minds which exist in the universe must exist also in the Infinite Mind which constitutes the universe as it is. The Divine Mind must reside in a Divine Person. And as man, by his personality, acts in obedience to or in transgression of a moral law, so God, by His Personality, acts in establishing the Law and in securing its supremacy in the whole history of the world.

12. (Creation.)—Acknowledging a Divine Mind which is the foundation and support of the world as it is, constituting and upholding its laws, it may be asked, Does this view point to a beginning of the world? Was there a time when the Divine Mind called into being the world, before non-existent? Was there a Creation of the world?

I do not think that an answer to this question, given either way, affects the argument which I have been urging. The Laws of the Universe discoverable by the human mind, are the Laws of the Divine Mind, whether or not there was a time when these Laws first came into operation, or first produced the world which we see. The argument respecting the nature of the Divine Mind is the same, whether or not we suppose a Creation.

But, in point of fact, every part of our knowledge of the Universe does seem to point to a beginning. Every part of the world has been, so far as we can see, formed by natural causes out of something different from what it now is. The Earth, with its lands and seas, teeming with innumerable forms of living things, has been produced from an earth formed of other lands and seas, occupied with quite different forms of life: and if we go far enough back, from an earth in which there was no life. The stars which we call fixed move and change; the nebulæ in their shape show that they too are moving and changing. The Earth was, some at least hold, produced by the condensation of a nebula. The history of man, as well383 as of others of its inhabitants, points to a beginning. Languages, Arts, Governments, Histories, all seem to have begun from a starting-point, however remote. Indeed not only a beginning, but a beginning at no remote period, appears to be indicated by most of the sciences which carry us backwards in the world's history.

But we must allow, on the other hand, that though all such lines of research point towards a beginning, none of them can be followed up to a beginning. All the lines converge, but all melt away before they reach the point of convergence. As I have elsewhere said[320], in no science has man been able to arrive at a beginning which is homogeneous with the known course of events, though we can often go very far back, and limit the hypotheses respecting the origin. We have, in the impossibility of thus coming to any conclusion by natural reason on the subject of creation, another evidence of the infinitely limited nature of the human mind, when compared with the Creative or Constitutive Divine Mind.

13. (End of the World.)—But if our natural reason, aided by all that science can teach, can tell us nothing respecting the origin and beginning of this world, still less can reason tell us anything with regard to the End of this world. On this subject, the natural sciences are even more barren of instruction than on the subject of Creation. Yet we may say that as the Constitution of the Universe, and its conformity to a Collection of eternal and immutable Ideas as its elements, are not inconsistent with the supposition of a Beginning of the present course of the world, so neither are they inconsistent with the supposition of an End. Indeed it would not be at all impossible that physical inquiries should present the prospect of an End, even more clearly than they afford the retrospect of a Beginning. If, for instance, it should be found that the planets move in a resisting medium which384 constantly retards their velocity, and must finally make them fall in upon the central sun, there would be an end of the earth as to its present state. We cannot

therefore, on the grounds of Science, deny either a Beginning or an End of the present world.

14. But here another order of considerations comes into play, namely, those derived from moral and theological views of the world. On these we must, in conclusion, say a few words.

It is very plain that these considerations may lead us to believe in a view of the Beginning, Middle, and End of the history of the world, very different from anything which the mere physical and natural sciences can disclose to us. And these expressions to which I have been led, the Beginning, the Middle, and the End of the world's history according to theological views, are full of suggestions of the highest interest. But the interest which belongs to these suggestions is of a solemn and peculiar kind; and the considerations to which such suggestions point are better, I think, kept apart from such speculations as those with which I have been concerned in the present volume.

385

CHAPTER XXXII.
Analogies of Physical and Religious Philosophy.

1. ANY assertion of analogy between physical and religious philosophy will very properly be looked upon with great jealousy as likely to be forced and delusive; and it is only in its most general aspects that a sound philosophy on the two subjects can offer any points of resemblance. But in some of its general conditions the discovery of truth in the one field of knowledge and in the other may offer certain analogies, as well as differences, which it may be instructive to notice; and to some such aspects of our philosophy I shall venture to refer.

For the physical sciences—the sciences of observation and speculation—the progress of our exact and scientific knowledge, as I have repeatedly said, consists in reducing the objects and events of the universe to a conformity with Ideas which we have in our own minds:—the Ideas, for instance, of Space, Force, Substance, and the like. In this sense, the intellectual progress of men consists in the Idealization of Facts.

2. In moral subjects, on the other hand, where man has not merely to observe and speculate, but also to act;—where he does not passively leave the facts and events of the world such as they are, but tries actively to alter them and to improve the existing state of things, his progress consists in doing this. He makes a moral advance when he succeeds in doing what he thus attempts:—when he really improves the state of things with which he has to do by removing evil and producing good:—when he makes the state of things, namely, the relations between him and other persons, his acts and their acts, conform more and386 more to Ideas which he has in his own mind:—namely, to the Ideas of Justice, Benevolence, and the like. His moral progress thus consists in the realization of Ideas.

And thus we are led to the Aphorism, as we may call it, that Man's Intellectual Progress consists in the Idealization of Facts, and his Moral Progress consists in the Realization of Ideas.

3. But further, though that progress of science which consists in the idealization of facts may be carried through several stages, and indeed, in the history of science, has been carried through many stages, yet it is, and always must be, a progress exceedingly imperfect and incomplete, when compared with the completeness to which its nature points. Only a few sciences have made much progress; none are complete; most have advanced only a step or two. In none have we reduced all the Facts to Ideas. In all or almost all the unreduced Facts are far more numerous and extensive than those which have been reduced. The general mass of the facts of the universe are mere facts, unsubdued to the rule of science. The Facts are not Idealized. The intellectual progress is miserably scanty and imperfect, and would be so, even if it were carried much further than it is carried. How can we hope that it will ever approach to completeness?

4. And in like manner, the moral progress of man is still more miserably scanty and incomplete. In how small a degree has he in this sense realized his Ideas! In how small a degree has he carried into real effect, and embodied in the relations of society, in his own acts and in those of others with whom he is concerned, the Ideas of Justice and Benevolence and the like! How far from a complete realization of such moral Ideas are the acts of the best men, and the relations of the best forms of society! How far from perfection in these respects is man! and how certain it is that he will always be very far from perfection! Far below even such perfection as he can conceive, he will always be in his acts and feelings. The moral387 progress of man, of each man, and of each society, is, as I have said, miserably scanty and incomplete; and when regarded as the realization of his moral Ideas, its scantiness and incompleteness become still more manifest than before.

Hence we are led to another Aphorism:—that man's progress in the realization of Moral Ideas, and his progress in the Scientific idealization of Facts, are, and always will be, exceedingly scanty and incomplete.

5. But there is another aspect of Ideas, both physical and moral, in which this scantiness and incompleteness vanish. In the Divine Mind, all the physical Ideas are entertained with complete fulness and luminousness; and it is because they are so entertained in the Divine Mind, and it is because the universe is constituted and framed upon them, that we find them verified in every part of the universe, whenever we make our observation of facts and deduce their laws.

In like manner the Moral Ideas exist in the Divine Mind in complete fulness and luminousness; and we are naturally led to believe and expect that they must be exemplified in the moral universe, as completely and universally as the physical laws are exemplified in the physical universe. Is this so? or under what conditions can we conceive this to be?

6. In answering this question, we must consider how far the moral, still more even than the physical Ideas of the Divine Mind, are elevated above our human Ideas; but yet

not so far as to have no resemblance to our corresponding human Ideas; for if this were so, we could not reason about them at all.

In speaking of man's moral Ideas, Benevolence, Justice, and the like, we speak of them as belonging to man's Soul, rather than to his Mind, which we have commonly spoken of as the seat of his physical Ideas. A distinction is thus often made between the intellectual and the moral faculties of man; but on this distinction we here lay no stress. We may speak of man's Mind and Soul, meaning that part of his being in which are all his Ideas, intellectual and moral.

388

And now let us consider the question which has just been asked:—how we can conceive the Divine Benevolence and Justice to be completely and universally realized in the moral world, as the Ideas of Space, Time, &c. are in the physical world?

7. Our Ideas of Benevolence, Justice, and of other Virtues, may be elevated above their original narrowness, and purified from their original coarseness, by moral culture; as our Ideas of Force and Matter, of Substance and Elements, and the like, may be made clear and convincing by philosophical and scientific culture. This appears, in some degree, in the history of moral terms, as the progress of clearness and efficacy in the Idea of the material sciences appears in the history of the terms belonging to such sciences. Thus among the Romans, while they confined their kindly affections within their own class, a stranger was universally an enemy; peregrinus was synonymous with hostis. But at a later period, they regarded all men as having a claim on their kindness; and he who felt and acted on this claim was called humane. This meaning of the word humanity shows the progress (in their Ideas at least) of the virtue which the word humanity designates.

8. And as man can thus rise to a point of view where he sees that man is to be loved as man, so the humane and loving man inevitably assumes that God loves all men; and thus assumes that there is, or may be, a love of man in man's heart, which represents and resembles in kind, however remote in degree, the love of God to man.

But as in man's love of man there are very widely different stages, rising from the narrow love of a savage to his family or his tribe, to the widest and warmest feelings of the most enlightened and loving universal philanthropist;—so must we suppose that there are stages immeasurably wider by which God's love of man is more comprehensive and more tender than any love of man for man. The religious philosopher will fully assent to the expressions of this conviction delivered by pious men in all ages. "The eternal God is389 thy refuge, and beneath thee are the everlasting arms." "When my father and my mother forsake me the Lord taketh me up," is the expression of Divine Love, consistent with philosophy as well as with revelation. But as the Divine Love is more comprehensive and enduring than any human love, so is it in an immeasurably greater degree, more enlightened. It is not a love that seeks merely the pleasure and gratification of its object; that even an enlightened human love does not do. It seeks the good of its objects; and such a good as is the greatest good, to an Intelligence which can embrace all cases, causes, and contingencies. To our limited understanding, evil seems often to be inflicted, and the good of a part seems inconsistent with the good of another part. Our attempts to conceive a Supreme and complete Good provided for all the creatures which exist in the universe, baffle and perplex us, even more than our attempts to conceive infinite space, infinite time, and an infinite chain of causation. But as the most careful attention which we can give to the Ideas of Space, Time, and Causation convinces us that these Ideas are perfectly clear and complete in the Divine Mind, and that our perplexity and confusion on these subjects arise only from the vast distance between the Divine Mind and our human mind, so is it reasonable to suppose the same to be the source of the confusion which we experience when we attempt to determine what most conduces to the good of our fellow-creatures; and when, urged by love to them, we endeavour to promote this good. We can do little of what Infinite Love would do, yet are we not thereby dispensed from seeking in some degree to imitate the working of Divine Love. We can see but little of what Infinite Intelligence sees, and this should be one source of confidence and comfort, when we stumble upon perplexities produced by the seeming mixture of good and evil in the world.

9. But when we ask the questions which have already been stated: Whether this Infinite Divine Love is realized in the world, and if so, How: I conceive that we are irresistibly impelled to reply to the former question,390 that it is: and we then turn to the latter. We are led to assume that there is in God an Infinite Love of man, a creature in a certain degree of a Divine nature. We must, as a consequence of this, assume that the Love of God to man, necessarily is, in the end, and on the whole, completely and fully realized in the history of the world. But what is the complete history of the world! Is it that which consists in the lives of men such as we see them between their birth and their death? If the minds or souls of men are alive after the death of the body, that future life, as well as this present life, belongs to the history of the world;—to that providential history, of which the totality, as we have said, must be governed by Infinite Divine Love. And in addition to all other reasons for believing that the minds and souls of men do thus survive their present life, is this:—that we thus can conceive, what otherwise it is difficult or impossible to conceive, the operation of Infinite Love in the whole of the history of mankind. If there be a Future State in which men's souls are still under the authority and direction of the Divine Governor of the world, all that is here wanting to complete the scheme of a perfect government of Intelligent Love may thus be applied: all seeming and partial evil may be absorbed and extinguished in an ultimate and universal good.

10. The Idea of Justice as belonging to God suggests to us some of the same kind of reflexions as those which we have made respecting the Divine Love. We believe God to be just: otherwise, as has been said, He would not be God. And as we thus, from the nature of our minds and souls, believe God to be just, we must, in this belief, understand Justice according to the Idea which we have of Justice; that is, in some measure, according to the Idea of Justice, as exemplified in human actions and feelings. It would be absurd to combine the two propositions, that we necessarily believe that God is just, and that by just, we mean something entirely different from the common meaning of the word.

But though the Divine Idea of Justice must neces391sarily, in some measure, coincide with our Idea of Justice, we must believe in this, as in other cases, that the Divine Idea is immeasurably more profound, comprehensive, and clear, than the human Idea. Even the human Idea of Justice is susceptible of many and large progressive steps, in the way of clearness, consistency, and comprehensiveness. In the moral history of man this Idea advances from the hard rigour of inflexible written Law to the equitable estimation of the real circumstances of each case; it advances also from the narrow Law of a single community to a larger Law, which includes and solves the conflicts of all such Laws. Further, the administration of human Law is always imperfect, often erroneous, in consequence of man's imperfect knowledge of the facts of each case, and still more, from his ignorance of the designs and feelings of the actors. If the Judge could see into the heart of the person accused, and could himself rise higher and higher in judicial wisdom, he might exemplify the Idea of Justice in a far higher degree than has ever yet been done.

11. But all such advance in the improvement of human Justice must still be supposed to stop immeasurably short of the Divine Justice, which must include a perfect knowledge of all men's actions, and all men's hearts and thoughts; and a universal application of the wisest and most comprehensive Laws. And the difference of the Divine and of the human Idea of Justice may, like the differences of other Divine and human Ideas, include the solution of all the perplexities in which we find ourselves involved when we would trace the Idea to all its consequences. The Divine Idea is immeasurably elevated above the human Idea; in the Divine Idea all inconsistency, defect, and incompleteness vanish, and Justice includes in its administration every man, without any admixture of injustice. This is what we must conceive of the Divine administration, since God is perfectly just.

12. But here, as before, we have another conclusion suggested to us. We are, by the considerations just now spoken of, led to believe that, in the Divine392 administration of the world is an administration of perfect Justice;—that is, such is the Divine Administration in the end and on the whole, taking into account the whole of the providential history of the world. But the course of the world, taking into account only what happens to man in this present life, is not, we may venture to say, a complete and entire administration of justice. It often happens that injustice is successful and triumphant, even in the end, so far as the end is seen here. It happens that wrong is done, and is not remedied or punished. It happens that blameless and virtuous men are subjected to pain, grief, violence, and oppression, and are not protected, extricated, or avenged. In the affairs of this world, the prevalence of injustice and wrong-doing is so apparent, as to be a common subject of complaint: and though the complaint may be exaggerated, and though a calm and comprehensive view may often discern compensating and remedial influences which are not visible at first sight, still we cannot regard the lot of happiness or misery which falls to each man in this world and this life as apportioned according to a scheme of perfect and universal justice, such as in our thoughts we cannot but require the Divine administration to be.

13. Here then we are again led to the same conviction by regarding the Divine administration of the world as the realization of the Divine Justice, to which we were before led by regarding it as the realization of the Divine Love. Since the Idea is not fully or completely realized in man's life in this present world, this present world cannot be the whole of the Divine Administration. To complete the realization of the Idea of Justice, as an element of the Divine Administration, there must be a life of man after his life in this present world. If man's mind and soul, the part of him which is susceptible of happiness and misery, survive this present life, and be still subject to the Divine Administration, the Idea of Divine Justice may still be completely realized, notwithstanding all that here looks

like injustice or defective justice; and it belongs to the Idea of Justice to remedy and com393pensate, not to prevent wrong. And thus by this supposition of a Future State of man's existence, we are enabled to conceive that, in the whole of the Divine Government of the universe, all seeming injustice and wrong may be finally corrected and rectified, in an ultimate and universal establishment of a reign of perfect Righteousness.

14. Admitting the view thus presented, we may again discern a remarkable analogy between what we have called our physical Ideas (those of Space, Time, Cause, Substance, and the like), and our moral Ideas, (those of Benevolence, Justice, &c.). In both classes we must suppose that our human Ideas represent, though very incompletely and at an immeasurable distance, the Divine Ideas. Even our physical Ideas, when pursued to their consequences, are involved in a perplexity and confusion from which the Divine Ideas are free. Our Ideas of Benevolence and Justice are still more full of imperfections and inconsistency, when we would frame them into a complete scheme, and yet from such imperfections and inconsistency we must suppose that the Divine Benevolence and Justice are exempt. Our physical Ideas we find in every case exactly exemplified and realized in the universe, and we account for this by considering that they are the Divine Ideas, on which the universe is constituted. Our moral Ideas, the Ideas of Benevolence and Justice in particular, must also be realized in the universe, as a scheme of Divine Government. But they are not realized in the world as constituted of man living this present life. The Divine Scheme of the world, therefore, extends beyond this present life of man. If we could include in our survey the future life as well as the present life of man, and the future course of the Divine Government, we should have a scheme of the Moral Government of the universe, in which the Ideas of Perfect Benevolence and Perfect Justice are as completely and universally exemplified and realized, as the Ideas of Space, Time, Cause, Substance, and the like, are in the physical universe.

15. There is one other remark bearing upon this394 analogy, which seems to deserve our attention. As I have said in the last chapter, the scheme of the world, as governed by our physical Ideas, seems to point to a Beginning of the world, or at least of the present course of the world: and if we suppose a Beginning, our thoughts naturally turn to an End. But if our physical Ideas point to a Beginning and suggest an End, do our Ideas of Divine Benevolence and Justice in any way lend themselves to this suggestion?—Perhaps we might venture to say that in some degree they do, even to the eye of a mere philosophical reason. Perhaps our reason alone might suggest that there is a progression in the human race, in various moral attributes—in art, in civilization, and even in humanity and in justice, which implies a beginning. And that at any rate there is nothing inconsistent with our Idea of the Divine Government in the supposition that the history of this world has a Beginning, a Middle and an End.

16. If therefore there should be conveyed to us by some channel especially appropriated to the communication and development of moral and religious Ideas, the knowledge that the world, as a scheme of Divine Government, has a Beginning, a Middle, and an End, of a Kind, or at least, invested with circumstances quite different from any which our physical Ideas can disclose to us, there would be, in such a belief, nothing at all inconsistent with the analogies which our philosophy—the philosophy of our Ideas illustrated by the whole progress of science—has impressed upon us. On the grounds of this philosophy, we need find no difficulty in believing that as the visible universe exhibits

the operation of the Divine Ideas of Space, Time, Cause, Substance, and the like, and discloses to us traces of a Beginning of the present mode of operation, so the moral universe exhibits to us the operation of the Divine Benevolence and Justice; and that these Divine attributes wrought in a special and peculiar manner in the Beginning; interposed in a peculiar and special manner in the Middle; and will again act in a peculiar and special manner in395 the End of the world. And thus the conditions of the physical universe, and the Government of the Moral world, are both, though in different ways, a part of the work which God is carrying on from the Beginning of things to the End— opus quod Deus operator a principio usque ad finem.

17. We are led by such analogies as I have been adducing to believe that the whole course of events in which the minds and souls of men survive the present life, and are hereafter subjected to the Divine government in such a way as to complete all that is here deficient in the world's history, is a scheme of perfect Benevolence and Justice. Now, can we discern in man's mind or soul itself any indication of a destiny like this? Are there in us any powers and faculties which seem as if they were destined to immortality? If there be, we have in such faculties a strong confirmation of that belief in the future life of man which has already been suggested to us as necessary to render the Divine government conceivable.

18. According to our philosophy there are powers and faculties which do thus seem fitted to endure, and not fitted to terminate and be extinguished. The Ideas which we have in our minds—the physical Ideas, as we have called them, according to which the universe is constituted,—agree, as far as they go, with the Ideas of the Divine Mind, seen in the constitution of the universe. But these Divine Ideas are eternal and imperishable: we therefore naturally conclude that the human mind which includes such elements, is also eternal and imperishable. Since the mind can take hold of eternal truths, it must be itself eternal. Since it is, to a certain extent, the image of God in its faculties, it cannot ever cease to be the image of God. When it has arrived at a stage in which it sees several aspects of the universe in the same form in which they present themselves to the Divine Mind, we cannot suppose that the Author of the human mind will allow it and all its intellectual light to be extinguished.

19. And our conviction that this extinction of the human mind cannot take place becomes stronger still,396 when we consider that the mind, however imperfect and scanty its discernment of truth may be, is still capable of a vast, and even of an unlimited progress in the pursuit and apprehension of truth. The mind is capable of accepting and appropriating, through the action of its own Ideas, every step in science which has ever been made—every step which shall hereafter be made. Can we suppose that this vast and boundless capacity exists for a few years only, is unfolded only into a few of its simplest consequences, and is then consigned to annihilation? Can we suppose that the wonderful powers which carry man on, generation by generation, from the contemplation of one great and striking truth to another, are buried with each generation? May we not rather suppose that that mind, which is capable of indefinite progression, is allowed to exist in an infinite duration, during which such progression may take place?

20. I propose this argument as a ground of hope and satisfactory reflexion to those who love to dwell on the natural arguments for the Immortality of the Soul. I do not

attempt to follow it into detail. I know too well how little such a cause can gain by obstinate and complicated argumentation, to attempt to urge the argument in that manner: and probably different persons, among those who accept the argument as valid, would give different answers to many questions of detail, which naturally arise out of the acceptance of this argument. I will not here attempt to solve, or even to propound these questions. My main purpose in offering these views and this argument at all, is to give some satisfaction to those who would think it a sad and blank result of this long survey of the nature and progress of science in which we have been so long engaged (through this series of works), that it should in no way lead to a recognition of the Author of that world about which our Science is, and to the high and consolatory hopes which lift man beyond this world. No survey of the universe can be at all satisfactory to thoughtful men, which has not a theological bearing; nor can any view of man's powers and means of know397ing be congenial to such men, which does not recognize an infinite destination for the mind which has an infinite capacity; an eternal being of the Faculty which can take a steady hold of eternal being.

21. And as we may derive such a conviction from our physical Ideas, so too may we no less from our moral Ideas. Our minds apprehend Space and Time and Force and the like, as Ideas which are not dependent on the body; and hence we believe that our minds shall not perish with our bodies. And in the same manner our souls conceive pure Benevolence and perfect Justice, which go beyond the conditions of this mortal life; and hence we believe that our souls have to do with a life beyond this mortal life.

It is more difficult to speak of man's indefinite moral progression even than of his indefinite intellectual progression. Yet in every path of moral speculation we have such a progression suggested to us. We may begin, for instance, with the ordinary feelings and affections of our daily nature:—Love, Hate, Scorn. But when we would elevate the Soul in our imagination, we ascend above these ordinary affections, and take the repulsive and hostile ones as fitted only to balance their own influences. And thus the poet, speaking of a morally poetical nature, describes it:

The Poet in a golden clime was born,
With golden stars above.
He felt the hate of hate, the scorn of scorn,
The love of love.
But the loftier moralist can rise higher than this, and can, and will, reject altogether Hate and Scorn from his view of man's better nature. His description would rather be—

The good man in a loving clime was born,
With loving stars above.
He felt sorrow for hate, pity for scorn,
And love of love.
He would, in his conception of such a character, ascribe to it all the virtues which result from the398 control and extinction of these repulsive and hostile affections:—the virtues of magnanimity, forgivingness, unselfishness, self-devotion, tenderness, sweetness. And these we can conceive in a higher and higher degree, in proportion as our own hearts become tender, forgiving, pure and unselfish. And though in every human stage of such a moral proficiency, we must suppose that there is still some struggle with the remaining

vestiges of our unkind, unjust, angry and selfish affections, we can see no limit to the extent to which this struggle may be successful; no limit to the degree in which these traces of the evil of our nature may be worn out by an enduring practice and habit of our better nature. And when we contemplate a human character which has, through a long course of years, and through many trials and conflicts, made a large progress in this career of melioration, and is still capable, if time be given, of further progress towards moral perfection, is it not reasonable to suppose that He who formed man capable of such progress, and who, as we must needs believe, looks with approval on such progress where made, will not allow the progress to stop when it has gone on to the end of man's short earthly life? Is it not rather reasonable to suppose that the pure and elevated and all-embracing affection, extinguishing all vices and including all virtues, to which the good man thus tends, shall continue to prevail in him as a permanent and ever-during condition, in a life after this?

But can man raise himself to such a stage of moral progress, by his own efforts? Such a progress is an approximation towards the perfection of moral Ideas, and therefore an approximation towards the image of God, in whom that perfection resides: is it not then reasonable to suppose that man needs a Divine Influence to enable him to reach this kind of moral completeness? And is it not also reasonable to suppose that, as he needs such aid, in order that the Idea of his moral progress may be realized, so he will receive such aid from the Divine Power which realizes the Idea of Divine Love in the world; and to do so, must399 realize it in those human souls which are most fitted for such a purpose?

But these questions remind me how difficult, and indeed, how impossible it is to follow such trains of reflexion by the light of philosophy alone. To answer such questions, we need, not Religious Philosophy only, but Religion: and as I do not here venture beyond the domain of philosophy, I must, however abruptly, conclude.

THE END.

[Pg 400]
[Pg 401]

[Pg 402]
[Pg 403]

APPENDIX.

Appendix A.
OF THE PLATONIC THEORY OF IDEAS.

(Cam. Phil. Soc. Nov. 10, 1856.)

Though Plato has, in recent times, had many readers and admirers among our English scholars, there has been an air of unreality and inconsistency about the commendation which most of these professed adherents have given to his doctrines. This appears to be no captious criticism, for instance, when those who speak of him as immeasurably superior in argument to his opponents, do not venture to produce his arguments in a definite form as able to bear the tug of modern controversy;—when they use his own Greek phrases as essential to the exposition of his doctrines, and speak as if these phrases could not be adequately rendered in English;—and when they assent to those among the systems of philosophy of modern times which are the most clearly opposed to the system of Plato. It seems not unreasonable to require, on the contrary, that if Plato is to supply a philosophy for us, it must be a philosophy which can be expressed in our own language;—that his system, if we hold it to be well founded, shall compel us to deny the opposite systems, modern as well as ancient;—and that, so far as we hold Plato's doctrines to be satisfactorily established, we should be able to produce the arguments for them, and to refute the arguments against them. These seem reasonable requirements of the adherents of any philosophy, and therefore, of Plato's.

I regard it as a fortunate circumstance, that we have recently had presented to us an exposition of Plato's philosophy which does conform to those reasonable conditions; and we may discuss this exposition with the less reserve, since its accomplished author, though belonging to this generation, is no longer alive. I refer to the Lectures on the History of Ancient Philosophy, by the late Professor Butler of Dublin. In these Lectures, we find an account of the Platonic Philosophy which shows that the writer had considered it as, what it is, an attempt to solve large problems, which in all ages force themselves upon the notice of thoughtful men. In Lectures VIII. and X., of the Second Series, especially, we have a404 statement of the Platonic Theory of Ideas, which may be made a convenient starting point for such remarks as I wish at present to make. I will transcribe this account; omitting, as I do so, the expressions which Professor Butler uses, in order to present the theory, not as a dogmatical assertion, but as a view, at least not extravagant. For this purpose, he says, of the successive portions of the theory, that one is "not too absurd to be maintained;" that another is "not very extravagant either;" that a third is "surely allowable;" that a fourth presents "no incredible account" of the subject; that a fifth is "no preposterous notion in substance, and no unwarrantable form of phrase." Divested of these modest formulæ, his account is as follows: [Vol. II. p. 117.]

"Man's soul is made to contain not merely a consistent scheme of its own notions, but a direct apprehension of real and eternal laws beyond it. These real and eternal laws are things intelligible, and not things sensible.

"These laws impressed upon creation by its Creator, and apprehended by man, are something distinct equally from the Creator and from man, and the whole mass of them may fairly be termed the World of Things Intelligible.

"Further, there are qualities in the supreme and ultimate Cause of all, which are manifested in His creation, and not merely manifested, but, in a manner—after being brought out of his super-essential nature into the stage of being [which is] below him, but next to him—are then by the causative act of creation deposited in things, differencing them one from the other, so that the things partake of them (μετέχουσι), communicate with them (κοινωνοῦσι).

"The intelligence of man, excited to reflection by the impressions of these objects thus (though themselves transitory) participant of a divine quality, may rise to higher conceptions of the perfections thus faintly exhibited; and inasmuch as these perfections are unquestionably real existences, and known to be such in the very act of contemplation,—this may be regarded as a direct intellectual apperception of them,—a Union of the Reason with the Ideas in that sphere of being which is common to both.

"Finally, the Reason, in proportion as it learns to contemplate the Perfect and Eternal, desires the enjoyment of such contemplations in a more consummate degree, and cannot be fully satisfied, except in the actual fruition of the Perfect itself.

"These suppositions, taken together, constitute the Theory of Ideas."

In remarking upon the theory thus presented, I shall abstain from any discussion of the theological part of it, as a subject which405 would probably be considered as unsuited to the meetings of this Society, even in its most purely philosophical form. But I conceive that it will not be inconvenient, if it be not wearisome, to discuss the Theory of Ideas as an attempt to explain the existence of real knowledge; which Prof. Butler very rightly considers as the necessary aim of this and cognate systems of philosophy[321].

I conceive, then, that one of the primary objects of Plato's Theory of Ideas is, to explain the existence of real knowledge, that is, of demonstrated knowledge, such as the propositions of geometry offer to us. In this view, the Theory of Ideas is one attempt to solve a problem, much discussed in our times, What is the ground of geometrical truth? I do not mean that this is the whole object of the Theory, or the highest of its claims. As I have said, I omit its theological bearings; and I am aware that there are passages in the Platonic Dialogues, in which the Ideas which enter into the apprehension and demonstration of geometrical truths are spoken of as subordinate to Ideas which have a theological aspect. But I have no doubt that one of the main motives to the construction of the Theory of Ideas was, the desire of solving the Problem, "How is it possible that man should apprehend necessary and eternal truths?" That the truths are necessary, makes them eternal, for they do not depend on time; and that they are eternal, gives them at once a theological bearing.

That Plato, in attempting to explain the nature and possibility of real knowledge, had in his mind geometrical truths, as examples of such knowledge is, I think, evident from the general purport of his discourses on such subjects. The advance of Greek geometry into a conspicuous position, at the time when the Heraclitean sect were proving that nothing could be proved and nothing could be known, naturally suggested mathematical truth as the refutation of the skepticism of mere sensation. On the one side it was said, we can know nothing except by our sensations; and that which we observe with our senses is constantly changing; or at any rate, may change at any moment. On the other hand it was said, we do know geometrical truths, and as truly as we know them, that they cannot change. Plato was quite alive to the lesson, and to the importance of this kind of truths. In the Meno and in the Phædo he refers to them, as illustrating the nature of the human mind: in the Republic and the Timæus he again speaks of truths which far transcend anything406 which the senses can teach, or even adequately exemplify. The senses, he argues in the Theætetus, cannot give us the knowledge which we have; the source of it must therefore be in the mind itself; in the Ideas which it possesses. The impressions of sense are constantly varying, and incapable of giving any certainty: but the Ideas on which real truth depends are constant and invariable, and the certainty which arises from these is firm and indestructible. Ideas are the permanent, perfect objects, with which the mind deals when it contemplates necessary and eternal truths. They belong to a region superior to the material world, the world of sense. They are the objects which make up the furniture of the Intelligible World; with which the Reason deals, as the Senses deal each with its appropriate Sensation.

But, it will naturally be asked, what is the Relation of Ideas to the Objects of Sense? Some connexion, or relation, it is plain, there must be. The objects of sense can suggest, and can illustrate real truths. Though these truths of geometry cannot be proved, cannot even be exactly exemplified, by drawing diagrams, yet diagrams are of use in helping ordinary minds to see the proof; and to all minds, may represent and illustrate it. And though our conclusions with regard to objects of sense may be insecure and imperfect, they have some show of truth, and therefore some resemblance to truth. What does this arise from? How is it explained, if there is no truth except concerning Ideas?

To this the Platonist replied, that the phenomena which present themselves to the senses partake, in a certain manner, of Ideas, and thus include so much of the nature of Ideas, that they include also an element of Truth. The geometrical diagram of Triangles and Squares which is drawn in the sand of the floor of the Gymnasium, partakes of the nature of the true Ideal Triangles and Squares, so that it presents an imitation and suggestion of the truths which are true of them. The real triangles and squares are in the mind: they are, as we have said, objects, not in the Visible, but in the Intelligible World. But the Visible Triangles and Squares make us call to mind the Intelligible; and thus the objects of sense suggest, and, in a way, exemplify the eternal truths.

This I conceive to be the simplest and directest ground of two primary parts of the Theory of Ideas;—The Eternal Ideas constituting an Intelligible World; and the Participation in these Ideas ascribed to the objects of the world of sense. And it is plain that so far, the Theory meets what, I conceive, was its primary purpose; it answers the questions, How can we have certain knowledge, though we cannot get it from Sense? and, How can we have407 knowledge, at least apparent, though imperfect, about the world of sense?

But is this the ground on which Plato himself rests the truth of his Theory of Ideas? As I have said, I have no doubt that these were the questions which suggested the Theory; and it is perpetually applied in such a manner as to show that it was held by Plato in this sense. But his applications of the Theory refer very often to another part of it;—to the Ideas, not of Triangles and Squares, of space and its affections; but to the Ideas of Relations—as the Relations of Like and Unlike, Greater and Less; or to things quite different from the things of which geometry treats, for instance, to Tables and Chairs, and other matters, with regard to which no demonstration is possible, and no general truth (still less necessary an eternal truth) capable of being asserted.

I conceive that the Theory of Ideas, thus asserted and thus supported, stands upon very much weaker ground than it does, when it is asserted concerning the objects of thought about which necessary and demonstrable truths are attainable. And in order to devise arguments against this part of the Theory, and to trace the contradictions to which

212

it leads, we have no occasion to task our own ingenuity. We find it done to our hands, not only in Aristotle, the open opponent of the Theory of Ideas, but in works which stand among the Platonic Dialogues themselves. And I wish especially to point out some of the arguments against the Ideal Theory, which are given in one of the most noted of the Platonic Dialogues, the Parmenides.

The Parmenides contains a narrative of a Dialogue held between Parmenides and Zeno, the Eleatic Philosophers, on the one side, and Socrates, along with several other persons, on the other. It may be regarded as divided into two main portions; the first, in which the Theory of Ideas is attacked by Parmenides, and defended by Socrates; the second, in which Parmenides discusses, at length, the Eleatic doctrine that All things are One. It is the former part, the discussion of the Theory of Ideas, to which I especially wish to direct attention at present: and in the first place, to that extension of the Theory of Ideas, to things of which no general truth is possible; such as I have mentioned, tables and chairs. Plato often speaks of a Table, by way of example, as a thing of which there must be an Idea, not taken from any special Table or assemblage of Tables; but an Ideal Table, such that all Tables are Tables by participating in the nature of this Idea. Now the question is, whether there is any force, or indeed any sense, in this assumption; and this question is discussed in the Parmenides. Socrates is there408 represented as very confident in the existence of Ideas of the highest and largest kind, the Just, the Fair, the Good, and the like. Parmenides asks him how far he follows his theory. Is there, he asks, an Idea of Man, which is distinct from us men? an Idea of Fire? of Water? "In truth," replies Socrates, "I have often hesitated, Parmenides, about these, whether we are to allow such Ideas." When Plato had proceeded to teach that there is an Idea of a Table, of course he could not reject such Ideas as Man, and Fire, and Water. Parmenides, proceeding in the same line, pushes him further still. "Do you doubt," says he, "whether there are Ideas of things apparently worthless and vile? Is there an Idea of a Hair? of Mud? of Filth?" Socrates has not the courage to accept such an extension of the theory. He says, "By no means. These are not Ideas. These are nothing more than just what we see them. I have often been perplexed what to think on this subject. But after standing to this a while, I have fled the thought, for fear of falling into an unfathomable abyss of absurdities." On this, Parmenides rebukes him for his want of consistency. "Ah Socrates," he says, "you are yet young; and philosophy has not yet taken possession of you as I think she will one day do--when you will have learned to find nothing despicable in any of these things. But now your youth inclines you to regard the opinions of men." It is indeed plain, that if we are to assume an Idea of a Chair or a Table, we can find no boundary line which will exclude Ideas of everything for which we have a name, however worthless or offensive. And this is an argument against the assumption of such Ideas, which will convince most persons of the groundlessness of the assumption:—the more so, as for the assumption of such Ideas, it does not appear that Plato offers any argument whatever; nor does this assumption solve any problem, or remove any difficulty[322]. Parmenides, then, had reason to say that consistency required Socrates, if he assumed any such Ideas, to assume all. And I conceive his reply to be to this effect; and to be thus a reductio ad absurdum of the Theory of Ideas in this sense. According to the opinions of those who see in the Parmenides an exposition of Platonic doctrines, I believe that Parmenides is conceived in this passage, to suggest to Socrates what is necessary for the completion of the Theory of Ideas. But upon either supposition, I wish409 especially to draw the attention of my readers to the position of superiority in the Dialogue in which Parmenides is here placed with regard to Socrates.

Parmenides then proceeds to propound to Socrates difficulties with regard to the Ideal Theory, in another of its aspects;—namely, when it assumes Ideas of Relations of things; and here also, I wish especially to have it considered how far the answers of Socrates to these objections are really satisfactory and conclusive.

"Tell me," says he (§ 10, Bekker), "You conceive that there are certain Ideas, and that things partaking of these Ideas, are called by the corresponding names;—an Idea of Likeness, things partaking of which are called Like;—of Greatness, whence they are Great: of Beauty, whence they are Beautiful?" Socrates assents, naturally: this being the simple and universal statement of the Theory, in this case. But then comes one of the real difficulties of the Theory. Since the special things participate of the General Idea, has each got the whole of the Idea, which is, of course, One; or has each a part of the Idea? "For," says Parmenides, "can there be any other way of participation than these two?" Socrates replies by a similitude: "The Idea, though One, may be wholly in each object, as the Day, one and the same, is wholly in each place." The physical illustration, Parmenides damages by making it more physical still. "You are ingenious, Socrates," he says, (§ 11) "in making the same thing be in many places at the same time. If you had a number of persons wrapped up in a sail or web, would you say that each of them had the whole of it? Is not the case similar?" Socrates cannot deny that it is. "But in this case, each person has only a part of the whole; and thus your Ideas are partible." To this, Socrates is represented as assenting in the briefest possible phrase; and thus, here again, as I conceive, Parmenides retains his superiority over Socrates in the Dialogue.

There are many other arguments urged against the Ideal Theory by Parmenides. The next is a consequence of this partibility of Ideas, thus supposed to be proved, and is ingenious enough. It is this:

"If the Idea of Greatness be distributed among things that are Great, so that each has a part of it, each separate thing will be Great in virtue of a part of Greatness which is less than Greatness itself. Is not this absurd?" Socrates submissively allows that it is.

And the same argument is applied in the case of the Idea of Equality.

"If each of several things have a part of the Idea of Equality, it will be Equal to something, in virtue of something which is less than Equality."

410

And in the same way with regard to the Idea of Smallness.

"If each thing be small by having a part of the Idea of Smallness, Smallness itself will be greater than the small thing, since that is a part of itself."

These ingenious results of the partibility of Ideas remind us of the ingenuity shown in the Greek geometry, especially the Fifth Book of Euclid. They are represented as not resisted by Socrates (§ 12): "In what way, Socrates, can things participate in Ideas, if they cannot do so either integrally or partibly?" "By my troth," says Socrates, "it does not seem easy to tell." Parmenides, who completely takes the conduct of the Dialogue, then turns to another part of the subject and propounds other arguments. "What do you say to this?" he asks.

"There is an Ideal Greatness, and there are many things, separate from it, and Great by virtue of it. But now if you look at Greatness and the Great things together, since they are all Great, they must be Great in virtue of some higher Idea of Greatness which includes both. And thus you have a Second Idea of Greatness; and in like manner you will have a third, and so on indefinitely."

This also, as an argument against the separate existence of Ideas, Socrates is represented as unable to answer. He replies interrogatively:

"Why, Parmenides, is not each of these Ideas a Thought, which, by its nature, cannot exist in anything except in the Mind? In that case your consequences would not follow."

This is an answer which changes the course of the reasoning: but still, not much to the advantage of the Ideal Theory. Parmenides is still ready with very perplexing arguments. (§ 13.)

"The Ideas, then," he says, "are Thoughts. They must be Thoughts of something. They are Thoughts of something, then, which exists in all the special things; some one thing which the Thought perceives in all the special things; and this one Thought thus involved in all, is the Idea. But then, if the special things, as you say, participate in the Idea, they participate in the Thought; and thus, all objects are made up of Thoughts, and all things think; or else, there are thoughts in things which do not think."

This argument drives Socrates from the position that Ideas are Thoughts, and he moves to another, that they are Paradigms, Exemplars of the qualities of things, to which the things themselves are like, and their being thus like, is their participating in the Idea. But here too, he has no better success. Parmenides argues thus:

"If the Object be like the Idea, the Idea must be like the411 Object. And since the Object and the Idea are like, they must, according to your doctrine, participate in the Idea of Likeness. And thus you have one Idea participating in another Idea, and so on in infinitum." Socrates is obliged to allow that this demolishes the notion of objects partaking in their Ideas by likeness: and that he must seek some other way. "You see then, O Socrates," says Parmenides, "what difficulties follow, if any one asserts the independent existence of Ideas!" Socrates allows that this is true. "And yet," says Parmenides, "you do not half perceive the difficulties which follow from this doctrine of Ideas." Socrates expresses a wish to know to what Parmenides refers; and the aged sage replies by explaining that if Ideas exist independently of us, we can never know anything about them: and that even the Gods could not know anything about man. This argument, though somewhat obscure, is evidently stated with perfect earnestness, and Socrates is represented as giving his assent to it. "And yet," says Parmenides (end of § 18), "if any one gives up entirely the doctrine of Ideas, how is any reasoning possible?"

All the way through this discussion, Parmenides appears as vastly superior to Socrates; as seeing completely the tendency of every line of reasoning, while Socrates is driven blindly from one position to another; and as kindly and graciously advising a young man respecting the proper aims of his philosophical career; as well as clearly pointing out the consequences of his assumptions. Nothing can be more complete than the higher position assigned to Parmenides in the Dialogue.

This has not been overlooked by the Editors and Commentators of Plato. To take for example one of the latest; in Steinhart's Introduction to Hieronymus Müller's translation of Parmenides (Leipzig, 1852), p. 261, he says: "It strikes us, at first, as strange, that Plato here seems to come forward as the assailant of his own doctrine of Ideas. For the difficulties which he makes Parmenides propound against that doctrine are by no means sophistical or superficial, but substantial and to the point. Moreover there is among all these objections, which are partly derived from the Megarics, scarce one which does not appear again in the penetrating and comprehensive argumentations of Aristotle against the Platonic Doctrine of Ideas."

Of course, both this writer and other commentators on Plato offer something as a solution of this difficulty. But though these explanations are subtle and ingenious, they appear to leave no satisfactory or permanent impression on the mind. I must avow that, to me, they appear insufficient and empty; and I cannot help412 believing that the solution is of a more simple and direct kind. It may seem bold to maintain an opinion different from that of so many eminent scholars; but I think that the solution which I offer, will derive confirmation from a consideration of the whole Dialogue; and therefore I shall venture to propound it in a distinct and positive form. It is this:

I conceive that the Parmenides is not a Platonic Dialogue at all; but Antiplatonic, or more properly, Eleatic: written, not by Plato, in order to explain and prove his Theory of Ideas, but by some one, probably an admirer of Parmenides and Zeno, in order to show how strong were his master's arguments against the Platonists and how weak their objections to the Eleatic doctrine.

I conceive that this view throws an especial light on every part of the Dialogue, as a brief survey of it will show. Parmenides and Zeno come to Athens to the Panathenaic festival: Parmenides already an old man, with a silver head, dignified and benevolent in his appearance, looking five and sixty years old: Zeno about forty, tall and handsome. They are the guests of Pythodorus, outside the Wall, in the Ceramicus; and there they are visited by Socrates then young, and others who wish to hear the written discourses of Zeno. These discourses are explanations of the philosophy of Parmenides, which he had delivered in verse.

Socrates is represented as showing, from the first, a disposition to criticize Zeno's dissertation very closely; and without any prelude or preparation, he applies the Doctrine of Ideas to refute the Eleatic Doctrine that All Things are One. (§ 3.) When he had heard to the end, he begged to have the first Proposition of the First Book read again. And then, "How is it, O Zeno, that you say, That if the Things which exist are Many, and not One, they must be at the same time like and unlike? Is this your argument? Or do I misunderstand you?" "No," says Zeno, "you understand quite rightly." Socrates then turns to Parmenides, and says, somewhat rudely, as it seems, "Zeno is a great friend of yours, Parmenides: he shows his friendship not only in other ways, but also in what he writes. For he says the same things which you say, though he pretends that he does not. You say, in your poems, that All Things are One, and give striking proofs: he says that existences are not many, and he gives many and good proofs. You seem to soar above us, but you do not really differ." Zeno takes this sally good-humouredly, and tells him that he pursues the scent with the keenness of a Laconian hound. "But," says he (§ 6), "there really is less of ostentation in my writing than you think. My Essay was merely written as a defence of Parmenides long ago, when I was413 young; and is not a piece of display composed now that I am older. And it was stolen from me by some one; so that I had no choice about publishing it."

Here we have, as I conceive, Socrates already represented as placed in a disadvantageous position, by his abruptness, rude allusions, and readiness to put bad interpretations on what is done. For this, Zeno's gentle pleasantry is a rebuke. Socrates, however, forthwith rushes into the argument; arguing, as I have said, for his own Theory.

"Tell me," he says, "do you not think there is an Idea of Likeness, and an Idea of Unlikeness? And that everything partakes of these Ideas? The things which partake of Unlikeness are unlike. If all things partake of both Ideas, they are both like and unlike; and where is the wonder? (§ 7.) If you could show that Likeness itself was Unlikeness, it would be a prodigy; but if things which partake of these opposites, have both the opposite qualities, it appears to me, Zeno, to involve no absurdity.

"So if Oneness itself were to be shown to be Maniness" (I hope I may use this word, rather than multiplicity) "I should be surprised; but if any one say that I am at the same time one and many, where is the wonder? For I partake of maniness: my right side is different from my left side, my upper from my under parts. But I also partake of Oneness, for I am here One of us seven. So that both are true. And so if any one say that stocks and stones, and the like, are both one and many,—not saying that Oneness is Maniness, nor Maniness Oneness, he says nothing wonderful: he says what all will allow. (§ 8.) If then, as I said before, any one should take separately the Ideas or Essence of Things, as Likeness and Unlikeness, Maniness and Oneness, Rest and Motion, and the like, and then should show that these can mix and separate again, I should be wonderfully surprised, O Zeno: for I reckon that I have tolerably well made myself master of these subjects[323]. I should be much more surprised if any one could show me this contradiction involved in the Ideas themselves; in the object of the Reason, as well as in Visible objects."

It may be remarked that Socrates delivers all this argumentation with the repetitions which it involves, and the vehemence of414 its manner, without waiting for a reply to any of his interrogations; instead of making every step the result of a concession of his opponent, as is the case in the Dialogues where he is represented as triumphant. Every reader of Plato will recollect also that in those Dialogues, the triumph of temper on the part of Socrates is represented as still more remarkable than the triumph of argument. No vehemence or rudeness on the part of his adversaries prevents his calmly following his reasoning; and he parries coarseness by compliment. Now in this Dialogue, it is remarkable that this kind of triumph is given to the adversaries of Socrates. "When Socrates had thus delivered himself," says Pythodorus, the narrator of the conversation, "we thought that Parmenides and Zeno would both be angry. But it was not so. They bestowed entire attention upon him, and often looked at each other, and smiled, as in admiration of Socrates. And when he had ended, Parmenides said: 'O Socrates, what an admirable person you are, for the earnestness with which you reason! Tell me then, Do you then believe the doctrine to which you have been referring;—that there are certain Ideas, existing independent of Things; and that there are, separate from the Ideas, Things which partake of them? And do you think that there is an Idea of Likeness besides the likeness which we have; and a Oneness and a Maniness, and the like? And an Idea of the Right, and the Good, and the Fair, and of other such qualities?'" Socrates says that he does hold this; Parmenides then asks him, how far he carries this doctrine of Ideas, and propounds to him the difficulties which I have already stated; and when Socrates is unable to answer him, lets him off in the kind but patronizing way which I have already described.

To me, comparing this with the intellectual and moral attitude of Socrates in the most dramatic of the other Platonic Dialogues, it is inconceivable, that this representation of Socrates should be Plato's. It is just what Zeno would have written, if he had wished to bestow upon his master Parmenides the calm dignity and irresistible argument which Plato assigns to Socrates. And this character is kept up to the end of the Dialogue. When Socrates (§ 19) has acknowledged that he is at loss which way to turn for his philosophy, Parmenides undertakes, though with kind words, to explain to him by what fundamental error in the course of his speculative habits he has been misled. He says; "You try to make a complete Theory of Ideas, before you have gone through a proper intellectual discipline. The impulse which urges you to such speculations is admirable—is divine. But you must exercise yourself in reasoning which many think trifling, while you are yet415 young; if you do not, the truth will elude your grasp." Socrates asks submissively what is the course of such discipline: Parmenides replies, "The course pointed out by Zeno, as you have heard." And then, gives him some instructions in what manner he is to test any proposed Theory. Socrates is frightened at the laboriousness and obscurity of the process. He says, "You tell me, Parmenides, of an overwhelming course of study; and I do not well comprehend it. Give me an example of such an examination of a Theory." "It is too great a labour," says he, "for one so old as I am." "Well then, you, Zeno," says Socrates, "will you not give us such an example?" Zeno answers, smiling, that they had better get it from Parmenides himself; and joins in the petition of Socrates to him, that he will instruct them. All the company unite in the request. Parmenides compares himself to an aged racehorse, brought to the course after long disuse, and trembling at the risk; but finally consents. And as an example of a Theory to be examined, takes his own Doctrine, that All Things are One, carrying on the Dialogue thenceforth, not with Socrates, but with Aristoteles (not the Stagirite, but afterwards one of the Thirty), whom he chooses as a younger and more manageable respondent.

The discussion of this Doctrine is of a very subtle kind, and it would be difficult to make it intelligible to a modern reader. Nor is it necessary for my purpose to attempt to do so. It is plain that the discussion is intended seriously, as an example of true philosophy; and each step of the process is represented as irresistible. The Respondent

218

has nothing to say but Yes; or No; How so? Certainly; It does appear; It does not appear. The discussion is carried to a much greater length than all the rest of the Dialogue; and the result of the reasoning is summed up by Parmenides thus: "If One exist, it is Nothing. Whether One exist or do not exist, both It and Other Things both with regard to Themselves and to Each other, All and Everyway are and are not, appear and appear not." And this also is fully assented to; and so the Dialogue ends.

I shall not pretend to explain the Doctrines there examined that One exists, or One does not exist, nor to trace their consequences. But these were Formulæ, as familiar in the Eleatic school, as Ideas in the Platonic; and were undoubtedly regarded by the Megaric contemporaries of Plato as quite worthy of being discussed, after the Theory of Ideas had been overthrown. This, accordingly, appears to be the purport of the Dialogue; and it is pursued, as we see, without any bitterness toward Socrates or his disciples; but with a persuasion that they were poor philosophers, conceited talkers, and weak disputants.

416

The external circumstances of the Dialogue tend, I conceive, to confirm this opinion, that it is not Plato's. The Dialogue begins, as the Republic begins, with the mention of a Cephalus, and two brothers, Glaucon and Adimantus. But this Cephalus is not the old man of the Piræus, of whom we have so charming a picture in the opening of the Republic. He is from Clazomenæ, and tells us that his fellow-citizens are great lovers of philosophy; a trait of their character which does not appear elsewhere. Even the brothers Glaucon and Adimantus are not the two brothers of Plato who conduct the Dialogue in the later books of the Republic: so at least Ast argues, who holds the genuineness of the Dialogue. This Glaucon and Adimantus are most wantonly introduced; for the sole office they have, is to say that they have a half-brother Antiphon, by a second marriage of their mother. No such half-brother of Plato, and no such marriage of his mother, are noticed in other remains of antiquity. Antiphon is represented as having been the friend of Pythodorus, who was the host of Parmenides and Zeno, as we have seen. And Antiphon, having often heard from Pythodorus the account of the conversation of his guests with Socrates, retained it in his memory, or in his tablets, so as to be able to give the full report of it which we have in the Dialogue Parmenides[324]. To me, all this looks like a clumsy imitation of the Introductions to the Platonic Dialogues.

I say nothing of the chronological difficulties which arise from bringing Parmenides and Socrates together, though they are considerable; for they have been explained more or less satisfactorily; and certainly in the Theætetus, Socrates is represented as saying that he when very young had seen Parmenides who was very old[325]. Athenæus, however[326], reckons this among Plato's fictions. Schleiermacher gives up the identification and relation of the persons mentioned in the Introduction as an unmanageable story.

I may add that I believe Cicero, who refers to so many of Plato's Dialogues, nowhere refers to the Parmenides. Athenæus does refer to it; and in doing so blames Plato for his coarse imputations on Zeno and Parmenides. According to our view, these are hostile attempts to ascribe rudeness to Socrates or to Plato. Stallbaum acknowledges that Aristotle nowhere refers to this Dialogue.

Appendix B.
ON PLATO'S SURVEY OF THE SCIENCES.

(Cam. Phil. Soc. April 23, 1855.)

A survey by Plato of the state of the Sciences, as existing in his time, may be regarded as hardly less interesting than Francis Bacon's Review of the condition of the Sciences of his time, contained in the Advancement of Learning. Such a survey we have, in the seventh book of Plato's Republic; and it will be instructive to examine what the Sciences then were, and what Plato aspired to have them become; aiding ourselves by the light afforded by the subsequent history of Science.

In the first place, it is interesting to note, in the two writers, Plato and Bacon, the same deep conviction that the large and profound philosophy which they recommended, had not, in their judgment, been pursued in an adequate and worthy manner, by those who had pursued it at all. The reader of Bacon will recollect the passage in the Novum Organon (Lib. I. Aphorism 80) where he speaks with indignation of the way in which philosophy had been degraded and perverted, by being applied as a mere instrument of utility or of early education: "So that the great mother of the Sciences is thrust down with indignity to the offices of a handmaid;—is made to minister to the labours of medicine or mathematics; or again, to give the first preparatory tinge to the immature minds of youth[327]."

In the like spirit, Plato says (Rep. VI. § 11, Bekker's ed.):

"Observe how boldly and fearlessly I set about my explanation of my assertion that philosophers ought to rule the world. For I begin by saying, that the State must begin to treat the study of philosophy in a way opposite to that now practised. Now, those who meddle at all with this study are put upon it when they are children, between the lessons which they receive in the farm-yard and in the shop[328]; and as soon as they have been introduced to the hardest part of the subject, are taken off from it, even those who get the most of philosophy. By the hardest part, I mean, the discussion of principles— Dialectic[329]. And in their succeeding years, if they are willing to listen to a few lectures of those who make philosophy their business, they think they have done great things, as if it were something foreign to the business of life. And as they advance towards old age, with a very few exceptions, philosophy in them is extinguished: extinguished far more completely than the Heraclitean sun, for theirs is not lighted up again, as that is every morning:" alluding to the opinion which was propounded, by way of carrying the doctrine of the unfixity of sensible objects to an extreme; that the Sun is extinguished every night and lighted again in the morning. In opposition to this practice, Plato holds that philosophy should be the especial employment of men's minds when their bodily strength fails.

What Plato means by Dialectic, which he, in the next Book, calls the highest part of philosophy, and which is, I think, what he here means by the hardest part of philosophy, I may hereafter consider: but at present I wish to pass in review the Sciences which he speaks of, as leading the way to that highest study. These Sciences are Arithmetic, Plane Geometry, Solid Geometry, Astronomy and Harmonics.

The view in which Plato here regards the Sciences is, as the instruments of that culture of the philosophical spirit which is to make the philosopher the fit and natural ruler of the perfect State—the Platonic Polity. It is held that to answer this purpose, the mind must be instructed in something more stable than the knowledge supplied by the senses;—a knowledge of objects which are constantly changing, and which therefore can be no real permanent Knowledge, but only Opinion. The real and permanent Knowledge which we thus require is to be found in certain sciences, which deal with truths necessary and universal, as we should now419 describe them: and which therefore are, in Plato's language, a knowledge of that which really is[330].

This is the object of the Sciences of which Plato speaks. And hence, when he introduces Arithmetic, as the first of the Sciences which are to be employed in this mental discipline, he adds (VII. § 8) that it must be not mere common Arithmetic, but a science which leads to speculative truths[331], seen by Intuition[332]; not an Arithmetic which is studied for the sake of buying and selling, as among tradesmen and shopkeepers, but for the sake of pure and real Science[333].

I shall not dwell upon the details with which he illustrates this view, but proceed to the other Sciences which he mentions.

Geometry is then spoken of, as obviously the next Science in order; and it is asserted that it really does answer the required condition of drawing the mind from visible, mutable phenomena to a permanent reality. Geometers indeed speak of their visible diagrams, as if their problems were certain practical processes; to erect a perpendicular; to construct a square: and the like. But this language, though necessary, is really absurd. The figures are mere aids to their reasonings. Their knowledge is really a knowledge not of visible objects, but of permanent realities: and thus, Geometry is one of the helps by which the mind may be drawn to Truth; by which the philosophical spirit may be formed, which looks upwards instead of downwards.

Astronomy is suggested as the Science next in order, but Socrates, the leader of the dialogue, remarks that there is an intermediate Science first to be considered. Geometry treats of plane figures; Astronomy treats of solids in motion, that is, of spheres in motion; for the astronomy of Plato's time was mainly the doctrine of the sphere. But before treating of solids in motion, we must have a science which treats of solids simply. After taking space of two dimensions, we must take space of three dimensions, length, breadth and depth, as in cubes and the like[334]. But such a Science, it is remarked, has not yet been discovered. Plato "notes as420 deficient" this branch of knowledge; to use the expression employed by Bacon on the like occasions in his Review. Plato goes on to say, that the cultivators of such a science have not received due encouragement; and that though scorned and starved by the public, and not recommended by any obvious utility, it has still made great progress, in virtue of its own attractiveness.

221

In fact, researches in Solid Geometry had been pursued with great zeal by Plato and his friends, and with remarkable success. The five Regular Solids, the Tetrahedron or Pyramid, Cube, Octahedron, Dodecahedron and Icosahedron, had been discovered; and the curious theorem, that of Regular Solids there can be just so many, these and no others, was known. The doctrine of these Solids was already applied in a way, fanciful and arbitrary, no doubt, but ingenious and lively, to the theory of the Universe. In the Timæus, the elements have these forms assigned to them respectively. Earth has the Cube: Fire has the Pyramid: Water has the Octahedron: Air has the Icosahedron: and the Dodecahedron is the plan of the Universe itself. This application of the doctrine of the Regular Solids shows that the knowledge of those figures was already established; and that Plato had a right to speak of Solid Geometry as a real and interesting Science. And that this subject was so recondite and profound,—that these five Regular Solids had so little application in the geometry which has a bearing on man's ordinary thoughts and actions,—made it all the more natural for Plato to suppose that these solids had a bearing on the constitution of the Universe; and we shall find that such a belief in later times found a ready acceptance in the minds of mathematicians who followed in the Platonic line of speculation.

Plato next proceeds to consider Astronomy; and here we have an amusing touch of philosophical drama. Glaucon, the hearer and pupil in the Dialogue, is desirous of showing that he has profited by what his instructor had said about the real uses of Science. He says Astronomy is a very good branch of education. It is such a very useful science for seamen and husbandmen and the like. Socrates says, with a smile, as we may suppose: "You are very amusing with your zeal for utility. I suppose you are afraid of being condemned by the good people of Athens for diffusing Useless Knowledge." A little afterwards Glaucon tries to do better, but still with no great success. He says, "You blamed me for praising Astronomy awkwardly: but now I will follow your lead. Astronomy is one of the sciences which you require, because it makes men's minds look upwards, and study things above. Any one can see that." "Well," says Socrates, "perhaps any one can see it421 except me—I cannot see it." Glaucon is surprised, but Socrates goes on: "Your notice of 'the study of things above' is certainly a very magnificent one. You seem to think that if a man bends his head back and looks at the ceiling he 'looks upwards' with his mind as well as his eyes. You may be right and I may be wrong: but I have no notion of any science which makes the mind look upwards, except a science which is about the permanent and the invisible. It makes no difference, as to that matter, whether a man gapes and looks up or shuts his mouth and looks down. If a man merely look up and stare at sensible objects, his mind does not look upwards, even if he were to pursue his studies swimming on his back in the sea."

The Astronomy, then, which merely looks at phenomena does not satisfy Plato. He wants something more. What is it? as Glaucon very naturally asks.

Plato then describes Astronomy as a real science (§ 11). "The variegated adornments which appear in the sky, the visible luminaries, we must judge to be the most beautiful and the most perfect things of their kind: but since they are mere visible figures, we must suppose them to be far inferior to the true objects; namely, those spheres which, with their real proportions of quickness and slowness, their real number, their real figures, revolve and carry luminaries in their revolutions. These objects are to be apprehended by reason and mental conception, not by vision." And he then goes on to say that the varied figures which the skies present to the eye are to be used as diagrams to assist the study of that higher truth; just as if any one were to study geometry by means of beautiful diagrams constructed by Dædalus or any other consummate artist.

Here then, Plato points to a kind of astronomical science which goes beyond the mere arrangement of phenomena: an astronomy which, it would seem, did not exist at the time when he wrote. It is natural to inquire, whether we can determine more precisely what kind of astronomical science he meant, and whether such science has been brought into existence since his time.

He gives us some further features of the philosophical astronomy which he requires. "As you do not expect to find in the most exquisite geometrical diagrams the true evidence of quantities being equal, or double, or in any other relation: so the true astronomer will not think that the proportion of the day to the month, or the month to the year, and the like, are real and immutable things. He will seek a deeper truth than these. We must treat Astronomy, like Geometry, as a series of problems suggested by visible things.422 We must apply the intelligent portion of our mind to the subject."

Here we really come in view of a class of problems which astronomical speculators at certain periods have proposed to themselves. What is the real ground of the proportion of the day to the month, and of the month to the year, I do not know that any writer of great name has tried to determine: but to ask the reason of these proportions, namely, that of the revolution of the earth on its axis, of the moon in its orbit, and of the earth in its orbit, are questions just of the same kind as to ask the reason of the proportion of the revolutions of the planets in their orbits, and of the proportion of the orbits themselves. Now who has attempted to assign such reasons?

Of course we shall answer, Kepler: not so much in the Laws of the Planetary motions which bear his name, as in the Law which at an earlier period he thought he had discovered, determining the proportion of the distances of the several Planets from the Sun. And, curiously enough, this solution of a problem which we may conceive Plato to have had in his mind, Kepler gave by means of the Five Regular Solids which Plato had brought into notice, and had employed in his theory of the Universe given in the Timæus.

Kepler's speculations on the subject just mentioned were given to the world in the Mysterium Cosmographicum published in 1596. In his Preface, he says "In the beginning of the year 1595 I brooded with the whole energy of my mind on the subject of the Copernican system. There were three things in particular of which I pertinaciously sought the causes; why they are not other than they are: the number, the size, and the motion of the orbits." We see how strongly he had his mind impressed with the same thought which Plato had so confidently uttered: that there must be some reason for those proportions in the scheme of the Universe which appear casual and vague. He was confident at this period that he had solved two of the three questions which haunted him;—that he could account for the number and the size of the planetary orbits. His account was given in this way.—"The orbit of the Earth is a circle; round the sphere to which this circle belongs describe a dodecahedron; the sphere including this will give the orbit of Mars. Round

223

Mars inscribe a tetrahedron; the circle including this will be the orbit of Jupiter. Describe a cube round Jupiter's orbit; the circle including this will be the orbit of Saturn. Now inscribe in the Earth's orbit an icosahedron: the circle inscribed in it will be the orbit of Venus. Inscribe an octahedron in the orbit of Venus; the circle inscribed in it will be Mercury's orbit. This is423 the reason of the number of the planets;" and also of the magnitudes of their orbits.

These proportions were only approximations; and the Rule thus asserted has been shown to be unfounded, by the discovery of new Planets. This Law of Kepler has been repudiated by succeeding Astronomers. So far, then, the Astronomy which Plato requires as a part of true philosophy has not been brought into being. But are we thence to conclude that the demand for such a kind of Astronomy was a mere Platonic imagination?—was a mistake which more recent and sounder views have corrected? We can hardly venture to say that. For the questions which Kepler thus asked, and which he answered by the assertion of this erroneous Law, are questions of exactly the same kind as those which he asked and answered by means of the true Laws which still fasten his name upon one of the epochs of astronomical history. If he was wrong in assigning reasons for the number and size of the planetary orbits, he was right in assigning a reason for the proportion of the motions. This he did in the Harmonice Mundi, published in 1619: where he established that the squares of the periodic times of the different Planets are as the cubes of their mean distances from the central Sun. Of this discovery he speaks with a natural exultation, which succeeding astronomers have thought well founded. He says: "What I prophesied two and twenty years ago as soon as I had discovered the five solids among the heavenly bodies; what I firmly believed before I had seen the Harmonics of Ptolemy; what I promised my friends in the title of this book (On the perfect Harmony of the celestial motions), which I named before I was sure of my discovery; what sixteen years ago I regarded as a thing to be sought; that for which I joined Tycho Brahe, for which I settled in Prague, for which I devoted the best part of my life to astronomical contemplations; at length I have brought to light, and have recognized its truth beyond my most sanguine expectations." (Harm. Mundi, Lib. V.)

Thus the Platonic notion, of an Astronomy which deals with doctrines of a more exact and determinate kind than the obvious relations of phænomena, may be found to tend either to error or to truth. Such aspirations point equally to the five regular solids which Kepler imagined as determining the planetary orbits, and to the Laws of Kepler in which Newton detected the effect of universal gravitation. The realities which Plato looked for, as something incomparably more real than the visible luminaries, are found, when we find geometrical figures, epicycles and eccentrics, laws of motion424 and laws of force, which explain the appearances. His Realities are Theories which account for the Phenomena, Ideas which connect the Facts.

But, is Plato right in holding that such Realities as these are more real than the Phenomena, and constitute an Astronomy of a higher kind than that of mere Appearances? To this we shall, of course, reply that Theories and Facts have each their reality, but that these are realities of different kinds. Kepler's Laws are as real as day and night; the force of gravity tending to the Sun is as real as the Sun; but not more so. True Theories and Facts are equally real, for true Theories are Facts, and Facts are familiar Theories. Astronomy is, as Plato says, a series of Problems suggested by visible Things;

and the Thoughts in our own minds which bring the solutions of these Problems, have a reality in the Things which suggest them.

But if we try, as Plato does, to separate and oppose to each other the Astronomy of Appearances and the Astronomy of Theories, we attempt that which is impossible. There are no Phenomena which do not exhibit some Law; no Law can be conceived without Phenomena. The heavens offer a series of Problems; but however many of these Problems we solve, there remain still innumerable of them unsolved; and these unsolved Problems have solutions, and are not different in kind from those of which the extant solution is most complete.

Nor can we justly distinguish, with Plato, Astronomy into transient appearances and permanent truths. The theories of Astronomy are permanent, and are manifested in a series of changes: but the change is perpetual just because the theory is permanent. The perpetual change is the permanent theory. The perpetual changes in the positions and movements of the planets, for instance, manifest the permanent machinery: the machinery of cycles and epicycles, as Plato would have said, and as Copernicus would have agreed; while Kepler, with a profound admiration for both, would have asserted that the motions might be represented by ellipses, more exactly, if not more truly. The cycles and epicycles, or the ellipses, are as real as space and time, in which the motions take place. But we cannot justly say that space and time and motion are more real than the bodies which move in space and time, or than the appearances which these bodies present.

Thus Plato, with his tendency to exalt Ideas above Facts,—to find a Reality which is more real than Phenomena,—to take hold of a permanent Truth which is more true than truths of observation,—425 attempts what is impossible. He tries to separate the poles of the Fundamental Antithesis, which, however antithetical, are inseparable.

At the same time, we must recollect that this tendency to find a Reality which is something beyond appearance, a permanence which is involved in the changes, is the genuine spring of scientific discovery. Such a tendency has been the cause of all the astronomical science which we possess. It appeared in Plato himself, in Hipparchus, in Ptolemy, in Copernicus, and most eminently in Kepler; and in him perhaps in a manner more accordant with Plato's aspirations when he found the five Regular Solids in the Universe, than when he found there the Conic Sections which determine the form of the planetary orbits. The pursuit of this tendency has been the source of the mighty and successful labours of succeeding astronomers: and the anticipations of Plato on this head were more true than he himself could have conceived.

When the above view of the nature of true astronomy has been proposed, Glaucon says:

"That would be a task much more laborious than the astronomy now cultivated." Socrates replies: "I believe so: and such tasks must be undertaken, if our researches are to be good for anything."

225

After Astronomy, there comes under review another Science, which is treated in the same manner. It is presented as one of the Sciences which deal with real abstract truth; and which are therefore suited to that development of the philosophic insight into the highest truth, which is here Plato's main object. This Science is Harmonics, the doctrine of the mathematical relations of musical sounds. Perhaps it may be more difficult to explain to a general audience, Plato's views on this than on the previous subjects: for though Harmonics is still acknowledged as a Science including the mathematical truths to which Plato here refers, these truths are less generally known than those of geometry or astronomy. Pythagoras is reported to have been the discoverer of the cardinal proposition in this Mathematics of Music:—namely, that the musical notes which the ear recognizes as having that definite and harmonious relation which we call an octave, a fifth, a fourth, a third, have also, in some way or other, the numerical relation of 2 to 1, 3 to 2, 4 to 3, 5 to 4. I say "some way or other," because the statements of ancient writers on this subject are physically inexact, but are right in the essential point, that those simple numerical ratios are characteristic of the most marked harmonic relations. The numerical ratios really represent the rate of vibration of the air when those harmonics426 are produced. This perhaps Plato did not know: but he knew or assumed that those numerical ratios were cardinal truths in harmony: and he conceived that the exactness of the ratios rested on grounds deeper and more intellectual than any testimony which the ear could give. This is the main point in his mode of applying the subject, which will be best understood by translating (with some abridgement) what he says. Socrates proceeds:

(§ 11 near the end.) "Motion appears in many aspects. It would take a very wise man to enumerate them all: but there are two obvious kinds. One which appears in astronomy, (the revolutions of the heavenly bodies,) and another which is the echo of that[335]. As the eyes are made for Astronomy, so are the ears made for the motion which produces Harmony[336]: and thus we have two sister sciences, as the Pythagoreans teach, and we assent.

(§ 12.) "To avoid unnecessary labour, let us first learn what they can tell us, and see whether anything is to be added to it; retaining our own view on such subjects: namely this:—that those whose education we are to superintend—real philosophers—are never to learn any imperfect truths:—anything which does not tend to that point (exact and permanent truth) to which all our knowledge ought to tend, as we said concerning astronomy. Now those who cultivate music take a very different course from this. You may see them taking immense pains in measuring musical notes and intervals by the ear, as the astronomers measure the heavenly motions by the eye.

"Yes, says Glaucon, they apply their ears close to the instrument, as if they could catch the note by getting near to it, and talk of some kind of recurrences[337]. Some say they can distinguish an interval, and that this is the smallest possible interval, by which others are to be measured; while others say that the two notes are identical: both parties alike judging by the ear, not by the intellect.

"You mean, says Socrates, those fine musicians who torture their notes, and screw their pegs, and pinch their strings, and speak of the resulting sounds in grand terms of art. We will leave them, and address our inquiries to our other teachers, the Pythagoreans."

226

The expressions about the small interval in Glaucon's speech appear to me to refer to a curious question, which we know was discussed among the Greek mathematicians. If we take a keyed427 instrument, and ascend from a key note by two octaves and a third, (say from A1 to C3) we arrive at the same nominal note, as if we ascend four times by a fifth (A1 to E1, E1 to B2, B2 to F2, F2 to C3). Hence one party might call this the same note. But if the Octaves, Fifths, and Third be perfectly true intervals, the notes arrived at in the two ways will not be really the same. (In the one case, the note is $\frac{1}{2} \times \frac{1}{2} \times \frac{4}{5}$; in the other $\frac{2}{3} \times \frac{2}{3} \times \frac{2}{3} \times \frac{2}{3}$; which are $\frac{1}{5}$ and 16/81, or in the ratio of 81 to 80). This small interval by which the two notes really differ, the Greeks called a Comma, and it was the smallest musical interval which they recognized. Plato disdains to see anything important in this controversy; though the controversy itself is really a curious proof of his doctrine, that there is a mathematical truth in Harmony, higher than instrumental exactness can reach. He goes on to say:

"The musical teachers are defective in the same way as the astronomical. They do indeed seek numbers in the harmonic notes, which the ear perceives: but they do not ascend from them to the Problem, What are harmonic numbers and what are not, and what is the reason of each[338]?" "That", says Glaucon, "would be a sublime inquiry."

Have we in Harmonics, as in Astronomy, anything in the succeeding History of the Science which illustrates the tendency of Plato's thoughts, and the value of such a tendency?

It is plain that the tendency was of the same nature as that which induced Kepler to call his work on Astronomy Harmonice Mundi; and which led to many of the speculations of that work, in which harmonical are mixed with geometrical doctrines. And if we are disposed to judge severely of such speculations, as too fanciful for sound philosophy, we may recollect that Newton himself seems to have been willing to find an analogy between harmonic numbers and the different coloured spaces in the spectrum.

But I will say frankly, that I do not believe there really exists any harmonical relation in either of these cases. Nor can the problem proposed by Plato be considered as having been solved since his time, any further than the recurrence of vibrations, when their ratios are so simple, may be easily conceived as affecting the ear in a peculiar manner. The imperfection of musical scales, which the comma indicates, has not been removed; but we may say that, in the case of this problem, as in the other ultimate Platonic problems, the duplication of the cube and the quadrature of the circle, the428 impossibility of a solution has been already established. The problem of a perfect musical scale is impossible, because no power of 2 can be equal to a power of 3; and if we further take the multiplier 5, of course it also cannot bring about an exact equality. This impossibility of a perfect scale being recognized, the practical problem is what is the system of temperament which will make the scale best suited for musical purposes; and this problem has been very fully discussed by modern writers.

429

Appendix BB.

ON PLATO'S NOTION OF DIALECTIC.

(Cam. Phil. Soc. May 7, 1855.)

The survey of the sciences, arithmetic, plane geometry, solid geometry, astronomy and harmonics—which is contained in the seventh Book of the Republic (§ 6-12), and which has been discussed in the preceding paper, represents them as instruments in an education, of which the end is something much higher—as steps in a progression which is to go further. "Do you not know," says Socrates (§ 12), "that all this is merely a prelude to the strain which we have to learn?" And what that strain is, he forthwith proceeds to indicate. "That these sciences do not suffice, you must be aware: for—those who are masters of such sciences—do they seem to you to be good in dialectic? δεινοὶ διαλεκτικοὶ εἶναι;"

"In truth, says Glaucon, they are not, with very few exceptions, so far as I have fallen in with them."

"And yet, said I, if persons cannot give and receive a reason, they cannot attain that knowledge which, as we have said, men ought to have."

Here it is evident that "to give and to receive a reason," is a phrase employed as coinciding, in a general way at least, with being "good in dialectic;" and accordingly, this is soon after asserted in another form, the verb being now used instead of the adjective. "It is dialectic discussion τὸ διαλέγεσθαι, which executes the strain which we have been preparing." It is further said that it is a progress to clear intellectual light, which corresponds to the progress of bodily vision in proceeding from the darkened cave described in the beginning of the Book to the light of day. This progress, it is added, of course you call Dialectic διαλεκτικήν.

Plato further says, that other sciences cannot properly be called sciences. They begin from certain assumptions, and give us only the consequences which follow from reasoning on such assumptions. But these assumptions they cannot prove. To do so is not in the province of each science. It belongs to a higher science: to the430 science of Real Existences. You call the man Dialectical, who requires a reason of the essence of each thing[339].

And as Dialectic gives an account of other real existences, so does it of that most important reality, the true guide of Life and of Philosophy, the Real Good. He who cannot follow this through all the windings of the battle of Life, knows nothing to any purpose. And thus Dialectic is the pinnacle, the top stone of the edifice of the sciences[340].

Dialectic is here defined or described by Plato according to the subject with which it treats, and the object with which it is to be pursued: but in other parts of the Platonic Dialogues, Dialectic appears rather to imply a certain method of investigation;—to describe the form rather than the matter of discussion; and it will perhaps be worth while to compare these different accounts of Dialectic.

(Phædrus.) One of the cardinal passages on this Point is in the Phædrus, and may be briefly quoted. Phædrus, in the Dialogue which bears his name, appears at first as an admirer of Lysias, a celebrated writer of orations, the contemporary of Plato. In order to expose this writer's style of composition as frigid and shallow, a specimen of it is given, and Socrates not only criticises this, but delivers, as rival compositions, two discourses on the same subject. Of these discourses, given as the inspiration of the moment, the first is animated and vigorous; the second goes still further, and clothes its meaning in a gorgeous dress of poetical and mythical images. Phædrus acknowledges that his favourite is outshone; and Socrates then proceeds to point out that the real superiority of his own discourse consists in its having a dialectical structure, beneath its outward aspect of imagery and enthusiasm. He says: (§ 109, Bekker. It is to be remembered that the subject of all the discourses was Love, under certain supposed conditions.)

"The rest of the performance may be taken as play: but there were, in what was thus thrown out by a random impulse, two features, of which, if any one could reduce the effect to an art, it would be a very agreeable and useful task.

"What are they? Phædrus asks.

"In the first place, Socrates replies, the taking a connected view of the scattered elements of a subject, so as to bring them into one431 Idea; and thus to give a definition of the subject, so as to make it clear what we are speaking of; as was then done in regard to Love. A definition was given of it, what it is: whether the definition was good or bad, at any rate there was a definition. And hence, in what followed, we were able to say what was clear and consistent with itself.

"And what, Phædrus asks, was the other feature?

"The dividing the subject into kinds or elements, according to the nature of the thing itself:—not breaking its natural members, like a bad carver who cannot hit the joint. So the two discourses which we have delivered, took the irrational part of the mind, as their common subject; and as the body has two different sides, the right and the left, with the same names for its parts; so the two discourses took the irrational portion of man; and the one took the left-hand portion, and divided this again, and again subdivided it, till, among the subdivisions, it found a left-handed kind of Love, of which nothing but ill was to be said. While the discourse that followed out the right-hand side of phrenzy, (the irrational portion of man's nature,) was led to something which bore the name of Love like the other, but which is divine, and was praised as the source of the greatest blessing."

"Now I," Socrates goes on to say, "am a great admirer of these processes of division and comprehension, by which I endeavour to speak and to think correctly. And if I can find any one who is able to see clearly what is by nature reducible to one and manifested in many elements, I follow his footsteps as a divine guide. Those who can do this, I call—whether rightly or not, God knows—but I have hitherto been in the habit of calling them dialectical men."

229

It is of no consequence to our present purpose whether either of the discourses of Socrates in the Phædrus, or the two together, as is here assumed, do contain a just division and subdivision of that part of the human soul which is distinguishable from Reason, and do thus exhibit, in its true relations, the affection of Love. It is evident that division and subdivision of this kind is here presented as, in Plato's opinion, a most valuable method; and those who could successfully practise this method are those whom he admires as dialectical men. This is here his Dialectic.

(Sophistes.) We are naturally led to ask whether this method of dividing a subject as the best way of examining it, be in any other part of the Platonic Dialogues more fully explained than it is in the Phædrus; or whether any rules are given for this kind of Dialectic.

432

To this we may reply, that in the Dialogue entitled The Sophist, a method of dividing a subject, in order to examine it, is explained and exemplified with extraordinary copiousness and ingenuity. The object proposed in that Dialogue is, to define what a Sophist is; and with that view, the principal speaker, (who is represented as an Eleatic stranger,) begins by first exemplifying what is his method of framing a definition, and by applying it to define an Angler. The course followed, though it now reads like a burlesque of philosophical methods, appears to have been at that time a bona fide attempt to be philosophical and methodical. It proceeds thus:

"We have to inquire concerning Angling. Is it an Art? It is. Now what kind of art? All art is an art of making or an art of getting: (Poietic or Ktetic.) It is Ktetic. Now the art of getting, is the art of getting by exchange or by capture: (Metabletic or Chirotic.) Getting by capture is by contest or by chase: (Agonistic or Thereutic.) Getting by chase is a chase of lifeless or of living things: (the first has no name, the second is Zootheric.) The chase of living things is the chase of land animals or of water animals: (Pezotheric or Enygrotheric.) Chase of water animals is of birds or of fish: (Ornithothereutic and Halieutic.) Chase of fish is by inclosing or by striking them: (Hercotheric or Plectic.) We strike them by day with pointed instruments, or by night, using torches: (hence the division Ankistreutic and Pyreutic.) Of Ankistreutic, one kind consists in spearing the fish downwards from above, the other in twitching them upwards from below: (these two arts are Triodontic and Aspalieutic.) And thus we have, what we sought, the notion and the description of angling: namely that it is a Ktetic, Chirotic, Thereutic, Zootheric, Enygrotheric, Halieutic, Plectic, Ankistreutic, Aspalieutic Art."

Several other examples are given of this ingenious mode of definition, but they are all introduced with reference to the definition of the Sophist. And it will further illustrate this method to show how, according to it, the Sophist is related to the Angler.

The Sophistical Art is an art of getting, by capture, living things, namely men. It is thus a Ktetic, Chirotic, Thereutic art, and so far agrees with that of the Angler. But here the two arts diverge, since that of the Sophist is Pezotheric, that of the Angler Enygrotheric. To determine the Sophist still more exactly, observe that the chase of land animals is either of tame animals (including man) or of wild animals: (Hemerotheric and

Agriotheric.) The chase of tame animals is either by violence, (as kidnapping, tyranny, and war in general,) or by persuasion, (as by the arts of speech;) that is, it is Biaiotheric or Pithanurgic. The art of persuasion is a private or433 a public proceeding: (Idiothereutic or Demosiothereutic.) The art of private persuasion is accompanied with the giving of presents, (as lovers do,) or with the receiving of pay: (thus it is Dorophoric or Mistharneutic.) To receive pay as the result of persuasion, is the course, either of those who merely earn their bread by supplying pleasure, namely flatterers, whose art is Hedyntic; or of those who profess for pay to teach virtue. And who are they? Plainly the Sophists. And thus Sophistic is that kind of Ktetic, Chirotic, Thereutic, Zootheric, Pezotheric, Hemerotheric, Pithanurgic, Idiothereutic, Mistharneutic art, which professes to teach virtue, and takes money on that account.

The same process is pursued along several other lines of inquiry: and at the end of each of them the Sophist is detected, involved in a number of somewhat obnoxious characteristics. This process of division it will be observed, is at every step bifurcate, or as it is called, dichotomous. Applied as it is in these examples, it is rather the vehicle of satire than of philosophy. Yet, I have no doubt that this bifurcate method was admired by some of the philosophers of Plato's time, as a clever and effective philosophical invention. We may the more readily believe this, inasmuch as one of the most acute persons of our own time, who has come nearer than any other to the ancient heads of sects in the submission with which his followers have accepted his doctrines, has taken up this Dichotomous Method, and praised it as the only philosophical mode of dividing a subject. I refer to Mr. Jeremy Bentham's Chrestomathia (published originally in 1816), in which this exhaustive bifurcate method, as he calls it, was applied to classify sciences and arts, with a view to a scheme of education. How exactly the method, as recommended by him, agrees with the method illustrated in the Sophist, an examination of any of his examples will show. Thus to take Mineralogy as an example: according to Bentham, Ontology is Cœnoscopic or Idioscopic: the Idioscopic is Somatoscopic or Pneumatoscopic; the Somatoscopic is Pososcopic or Poioscopic: Poioscopic is Physiurgoscopic or Anthropurgoscopic: Physiurgoscopic is Uranoscopic or Epigeoscopic: Epigeoscopic is Abioscopic or Embioscopic. And thus Mineralogy is the Science Idioscopic, Somatoscopic, Poioscopic, Physiurgoscopic, Epigeoscopic, Abioscopic: inasmuch as it is the science which regards bodies, with reference to their qualities,—bodies, namely, the works of nature, terrestrial, lifeless.

I conceive that this bifurcate method is not really philosophical or valuable: but that is not our business here. What we have to consider is whether this is what Plato meant by the term Dialectic.

The general description of Dialectic in the Sophistes agrees very434 closely with that quoted from the Phædrus, that it is the separation of a subject according to its natural divisions.

Thus, see in the Sophist the passage § 83: "To divide a subject according to the kinds of things, so as neither to make the same kind different nor different kinds identical, is the office of the Dialectical Science." And this is illustrated by observing that it is the office of the science of Grammar to determine what letters may be combined and what may not; it is the office of the science of Music to determine what sounds differing as acute and grave, may be combined, and what may not: and in like manner it is the office of the science of Dialectic to determine what kinds may be combined in one subject and what may not. And the proof is still further explained.

In many of the Platonic Dialogues, the Dialectic which Socrates is thus represented as approving, appears to include the form of Dialogue, as well as the subdivision of the subject into its various branches. Socrates is presented as attaching so much importance to this form, that in the Protagoras (§ 65) he rises to depart, because his opponent will not conform to this practice. And generally in Plato, Dialectic is opposed to Rhetoric, as a string of short questions and answers to a continuous dissertation.

Xenophon also seems to imply (Mem. IV. 5, 11) that Socrates included in his notion of Dialectic the form of Dialogue as well as the division of the subject.

But that the method of close Dialogue was not called Dialectic by the author of the Sophist, we have good evidence in the work itself. Among other notions which are analysed by the bifurcate division here exhibited, is that of getting by contest (Agonistic, previously given as a division of Ktetic). Now getting by contest may be by peaceful trial of superiority, or by fight: (Hamilletic or Machelic). The fight may be of body against body, or of words against words: these may be called Biastic and Amphisbetic. The fight of words about right and wrong, may be by long discourses opposed to each other, as in judicial cases; or by short questions and answers: the former may be called Dicanic, the latter Antilogic. Of these colloquies, about right and wrong, some are natural and spontaneous, others artificial and studied: the former need no special name; the latter are commonly called Eristic. Of Eristic colloquies, some are a source of expense to those who hold them, some of gain: that is, they are Chrematophthoric or Chrematistic: the former, the occupation of those who talk for pleasure's and for company's sake, is Adoleschic, wasteful garrulity; the latter, that of those who talk for the sake of gain, is Sophistic.435 And thus Sophistic is an art Eristic, which is part of Antilogic, which is part of Amphisbetic, which is part of Agonistic, which is part of Chirotic, which is a part of Ktetic. (§ 23.)

We may notice here an indication that satire rather than exact reason directs these analyses; in that Sophistic, which was before a part of the thereutic branch of chirotic and ktetic, is here a part of the other branch, agonistic.

But the remark which I especially wish to make here is, that the art of discussing points of right and wrong by short questions and answers, being here brought into view, is not called Dialectic, which we might have expected; but Antilogic. It would seem therefore that the Author of the Sophist did not understand by Dialectic such a process as Socrates describes in Xenophon; (Mem. IV. 5, 11, 12;) where he says it was called Dialectic, because it was followed by persons dividing things into their kinds in conversation: (κοινῇ βουλεύεσθαι διαλέγοντας:)or such as the Socrates of Plato insisted upon in the Protagoras and the Gorgias. Of the two elements which the Dialectical Process of Socrates implied, Division of the subject and Dialogue, the author of the Sophistes does not claim the name of Dialectic for either, and seems to reject it for the second.

But without insisting upon the name, are we to suppose that the Dichotomous Method of the Sophistes Dialogue, (I may add of the Politicus, for the method is the same in this Dialogue also,) is the method of division of a subject according to its natural members, of which Plato speaks in the Phædrus?

If the Sophistes be the work of Plato, the answer is difficult either way. If this method be Plato's Dialectic, how came he to omit to say so there? how came he even to seem to deny it? But on the other hand, if this dichotomous division be a different process from the division called Dialectic in the Phædrus, had Plato two methods of division of a subject? and yet has he never spoken of them as two, or marked their distinction?

This difficulty would be removed if we were to adopt the opinion, to which others, on other grounds, have been led, that the Sophistes, though of Plato's time, is not Plato's work. The grounds of this opinion are,—that the doctrines of the Sophistes are not Platonic: (the doctrine of Ideas is strongly impugned and weakly defended:) Socrates is not the principal speaker, but an Eleatic stranger: and there is, in the Dialogue, none of the dramatic character which we generally have in Plato. The Dialogue seems to be the work of some Eleatic opponent of Plato, rather than his.

(Rep. B. VII.) But we can have no doubt that the Phædrus436 contains Plato's real view of the nature of Dialectic, as to its form; let us see how this agrees with the view of Dialectic, as to its matter and object, given in the seventh Book of the Republic.

According to Plato, Real Existences are the objects of the exact sciences (as number and figure, of Arithmetic and Geometry). The things which are the objects of sense transitory phenomena, which have no reality, because no permanence. Dialectic deals with Realities in a more general manner. This doctrine is everywhere inculcated by Plato, and particularly in this part of the Republic. He does not tell us how we are to obtain a view of the higher realities, which are the objects of Dialectic: only he here assumes that it will result from the education which he enjoins. He says (§ 13) that the Dialectic Process (ἡ διαλεκτικὴ μέθοδος) alone leads to true science: it makes no assumptions, but goes to First Principles, that its doctrines may be firmly grounded: and thus it purges the eye of the soul, which was immersed in barbaric mud, and turns it upward; using for this purpose the aid of the sciences which have been mentioned. But when Glaucon inquires about the details of this Dialectic, Socrates says he will not then answer the inquiry. We may venture to say, that it does not appear that he had any answer ready.

Let us consider for a moment what is said about a philosophy rendering a reason for the First Principles of each Science, which the Science itself cannot do. That there is room for such a branch of philosophy in some sciences, we easily see. Geometry, for instance, proceeds from Axioms, Definitions and Postulates; but by the very nature of these terms, does not prove these First Principles. These—the Axioms, Definitions and Postulates,— are, I conceive, what Plato here calls the Hypotheses upon which Geometry proceeds, and for which it is not the business of Geometry to render a reason. According to him, it is the business of "Dialectic" to give a just account of these "Hypotheses." What then is Dialectic?

(Aristotle.) It is, I think, well worthy of remark, that Aristotle, giving an account in many respects different from that of Plato, of the nature of Dialectic, is still led in the same manner to consider Dialectic as the branch of philosophy which renders a reason for First Principles. In the Topics, we have a distinction drawn between reasoning demonstrative, and reasoning dialectical: and the distinction is this:—(Top. I. 1) that demonstration is by syllogisms from true first principles, or from true deductions from such principles; and that the Dialectical Syllogism is that which syllogizes from probable propositions (ἠξ ἠνδόξων). And he adds that437 probable propositions are those which are accepted by all, or by the greatest part, or by the wise. In the next chapter, he speaks of the uses of Dialectic, which, he says, are three, mental discipline, debates, and philosophical science. And he adds (Top. I. 2, 6) that it is also useful with reference to the First Principles in each Science: for from the appropriate Principles of each science we cannot deduce anything concerning First Principles, since these principles are the beginning of reasoning. But from the probable principles in each province of science we must reason concerning First Principles: and this is either the peculiar office of Dialectic, or the office most appropriate to it; for it is a process of investigation, and must lead to the Principles of all methods.

That a demonstrative science, as such, does not explain the origin of its own First Principles, is undoubtedly true. Geometry does not undertake to give a reason for the Axioms, Definitions, and Postulates. This has been attempted, both in ancient and in modern times, by the Metaphysicians. But the Metaphysics employed on such subjects has not commonly been called Dialectic. The term has certainly been usually employed rather as describing a Method, than as determining the subject of investigation. Of the Faculty which apprehends First Principles, both according to Plato and to Aristotle, I will hereafter say a few words.

The object of the dichotomous process pursued in the Sophistes, and its result in each case, is a Definition. Definition also was one of the main features of the inquiries pursued by Socrates, Induction being the other; and indeed in many cases Induction was a series of steps which ended in Definition. And Aristotle also taught a peculiar method, the object and result of which was the construction of Definitions:—namely his Categories. This method is one of division, but very different from the divisions of the Sophistes. His method begins by dividing the whole subject of possible inquiry into ten heads or Categories—Substance, Quantity, Quality, Relation, Place, Time, Position, Habit, Action, Passion. These again are subdivided: thus Quality is Habit or Disposition, Power, Affection, Form. And we have an example of the application of this method to the construction of a Definition in the Ethics; where he determines Virtue to be a Habit with certain additional limitations.

Thus the Induction of Socrates, the Dichotomy of the Eleatics, the Categories of Aristotle, may all be considered as methods by which we proceed to the construction of Definitions. If, by any method, Plato could proceed to the construction of a Definition, or rather of an Idea, of the Absolute Realities on which First Principles depend, such a method would correspond with the notion of438 Dialectic in the Republic. And if it was a method of division like the Eleatic or Aristotelic, it would correspond with the notion of Dialectic in the Phædrus.

That Plato's notion, however, cannot have been exactly either of these is, I think, plain. The colloquial method of stimulating and testing the progress of the student in Dialectic is implied, in the sequel of this discussion of the effect of scientific study. And the method of Dialogue, as the instrument of instruction, being thus supposed, the continuation of the account in the Republic, implies that Plato expected persons to be made dialectical by the study of the exact sciences in a comprehensive spirit. After insisting on Geometry and other sciences, he says (Rep. VII. § 16): "The synoptical man is dialectical; and he who is not the one, is not the other."

But, we may ask, does a knowledge of sciences lead naturally to a knowledge of Ideas, as absolute realities from which First Principles flow? And supposing this to be true, as the Platonic Philosophy supposes, is the Idea of the Good, as the source of moral truths, to be thus attained to? That it is, is the teaching of Plato, here and elsewhere; but have the speculations of subsequent philosophers in the same direction given any confirmation of this lofty assumption?

In reply to this inquiry, I should venture to say, that this assumption appears to be a remnant of the Socratic doctrine from which Plato began his speculations, that Virtue is a kind of knowledge; and that all attempts to verify the assumption have failed. What Plato added to the Socratic notion was, that the inquiry after The Good, the Supreme Good, was to be aided by the analogy or suggestions of those sciences which deal with necessary and eternal truths; the supreme good being of the nature of those necessary and eternal truths. This notion is a striking one, as a suggestion, but it has always failed, I think, in the attempts to work it out. Those who in modern times, as Cudworth and Samuel Clarke, have supposed an analogy between the necessary truths of Geometry and the truths of Morality, though they have used the like expressions concerning the one and the other class of truths, have failed to convey clear doctrines and steady convictions to their readers; and have now, I believe, few or no followers.

The result of our investigation appears to be, that though Plato added much to the matter by means of which the mind was to be improved and disciplined in its research after Principles and Definitions, he did not establish any form of Method according439 to which the inquiry must be conducted, and by which it might be aided. The most definite notion of Dialectic still remained the same with the original informal view which Socrates had taken of it, as Xenophon tells us, (Mem. IV. 5, 11) when he says: "He said that Dialectic (τὸ διαλέγεσθαι) was so called because it is an inquiry pursued by persons who take counsel together, separating the subjects considered according to their kinds (διαλέγοντας). He held accordingly that men should try to be well prepared for such a process, and should pursue it with diligence: by this means, he thought, they would become good men, fitted for responsible offices of command, and truly dialectical" (διαλέκτικωτάτους). And this is, I conceive, the answer to Mr. Grote's interrogatory exclamation (Vol. VIII. p. 577): "Surely the Etymology here given by Xenophon or Socrates of the word (διαλέγεσθαι) cannot be considered as satisfactory." The two notions, of investigatory Dialogue, and Distribution of notions according to their kinds, which are thus asserted to be connected in etymology, were, among the followers of Socrates, connected in fact; the dialectic dialogue was supposed to involve of course the dialectic division of the subject.

Appendix C.
OF THE INTELLECTUAL POWERS ACCORDING TO PLATO.

(Cam. Phil. Soc. Nov. 10, 1856.)

In the Seventh Book of Plato's Republic, we have certain sciences described as the instruments of a philosophical and intellectual education; and we have a certain other intellectual employment spoken of, namely, Dialectic, as the means of carrying the mind beyond these sciences, and of enabling it to see the sources of those truths which the sciences assume as their first principles. These points have been discussed in the two preceding papers. But this scheme of the highest kind of philosophical education proceeds upon a certain view of the nature and degrees of knowledge, and of the powers by which we know; which view had been presented in a great measure in the Sixth Book; this view I shall now attempt to illustrate.

To analyse the knowing powers of man is a task so difficult, that we need not be surprised if there is much obscurity in this portion of Plato's writings. But as a reason for examining what he has said, we must recollect that if there be in it anything on this subject which was true then, it is true still; and also, that if we know any truth on that subject now, we shall find something corresponding to that truth in the best speculations of sagacious ancient writers, like Plato. It may therefore be worth while to discuss the Platonic doctrines on this matter, and to inquire how they are to be expressed in modern phraseology.

Plato's doctrine will perhaps be most clearly understood, if we begin by considering the diagram by which he illustrates the different degrees of knowledge[341]. He sets out from the distinction of visible and intelligible things. There are visible objects, squares and triangles, for instance; but these are not the squares and triangles about which the Geometer reasons. The exactness of his reasoning does not depend on the exactness of his diagrams. He441 reasons from certain mental squares and triangles, as he conceives and understands them. "Thus there are visible and there are intelligible things. There is a visible and an intelligible world[342]: and there are two different regions about which our knowledge is concerned. Now take a line divided into two unequal segments to represent these two regions: and again, divide each segment in the same ratio. The parts of each segment are to represent differences of clearness and distinctness, and in the visible world these parts are things and images. By images I mean shadows, and reflections in water, and in polished bodies; and by things, I mean that of which these images are the resemblances; as animals, plants, things made by man. This difference corresponds to the difference of Knowledge and mere Opinion; and the Opinable is to the Knowable as the Image to the Reality."

This analogy is assented to by Glaucon; and thus there is assumed a ground for a further construction of the diagram.

"Now," he says, "we have to divide the segment which represents Intelligible Things in the same way in which we have divided that which represents Visible Things. The one part must represent the knowledge which the mind gets by dealing as it were with images, and by reasoning downwards from Principles; the other that which it has by dealing with the Ideas themselves, and going to First Principles.

"The one part depends upon assumptions or hypotheses[343], the other is unhypothetical or absolute truth.

"One kind of Intelligible Things, then, is Conceptions; for instance, geometrical conceptions of figures, by means of which we reason downwards, assuming certain First Principles.

"Now the other kind of Intelligible Things is this:—that which the Reason includes in virtue of its power of reasoning, when it442 regards the assumptions of the Sciences as, what they are, assumptions only; and uses them as occasions and starting points, that from these it may ascend to the absolute, (ἀνυπόθετον, unhypothetical,) which does not depend upon assumption, but is the origin of scientific truth. The Reason takes hold of this first principle of truth; and availing itself of all the connections and relations of this principle, it proceeds to the conclusion; using no sensible image in doing this, but contemplating the Ideas alone; and with these Ideas the process begins, goes on, and terminates."

This account of the matter will probably seem to require at least further explanation; and that accordingly is acknowledged in the Dialogue itself. Glaucon says:

"I apprehend your meaning in a certain degree, but not very clearly, for the matter is somewhat abstruse. You wish to prove that the knowledge which, by the Reason, we acquire, of Real Existence and Intelligible Things, is of a higher degree of certainty than the knowledge which belongs to what are commonly called Sciences. Such sciences, you say, have certain assumptions for their bases; and these assumptions are, by the students of such sciences, apprehended, not by Sense (that is, the Bodily Senses), but by a Mental Operation,—by Conception. But inasmuch as such students ascend no higher than the assumptions, and do not go to the First Principles of Truth, they do not seem to you to have true knowledge—intuitive insight—Nous—on the subject of their reasonings, though the subjects are intelligible, along with their principle. And you call this habit and practice of the Geometers and others by the name Conception, not Intuition[344]; taking Conception to be something between Opinion on the one side, and Intuitive Insight on the other."

"You have explained it well, said I. And now consider the four sections (of the line) of which we have spoken, as corresponding to four affections in the mind. Intuition, the highest; Conception, the next; the third, Belief; and the fourth, Conjecture (from likenesses); and arrange them in order, so that they may have more or less of certainty, as their objects have more or less of truth[345].

443

"I understand, said he. I agree to what you say, and I arrange them as you direct."

And so the Sixth Book ends: and the Seventh Book opens with the celebrated image of the Cave, in which men are confined, and see all external objects only by the shadows which they cast on the walls of their prison. And this imperfect knowledge of things is to the true vision of them, which is attained by those who ascend to the light of day, as the ordinary knowledge of men is to the knowledge attainable by those whose minds are purged and illuminated by a true philosophy.

Confining ourselves at present to the part of Plato's speculations which we have mentioned, namely, the degrees of knowledge, and the division of our knowing faculties, we may understand, and may in a great degree accept, Plato's scheme. We have already (in the preceding papers) seen that, by the knowledge of real things, he means, in the first place, the knowledge of universal and necessary truths, such as Geometry and the other exact sciences deal with. These we call sciences of Demonstration; and we are in the habit of contrasting the knowledge which constitutes such sciences with the knowledge obtained by the Senses, by Experience or mere Observation. This distinction of Demonstrative and Empirical knowledge is a cardinal point in Plato's scheme also; the former alone being allowed to deserve the name of Knowledge, and the latter being only Opinion. The Objects with which Demonstration deals may be termed Conceptions, and the objects with which Observation or Sense has to do, however much speculation may reduce them to mere Sensations, are commonly described as Things. Of these Things, there may be Shadows or Images, as Plato says; and as we may obtain a certain kind of knowledge, namely Opinion or Belief, by seeing the Things themselves, we may obtain an inferior kind of Opinion or Belief by seeing their Images, which kind of opinion we may for the moment call Conjecture. Whether then we regard the distinctions of knowledge itself or of the objects of it, we have three terms before us.

If we consider the kinds of knowledge, they are
Demonstration: Belief: Conjecture.
If the objects of this knowledge, they are
Conceptions: Things: Images.
444

But in each of these Series, the first term is evidently wanting: for Demonstration supposes Principles to reason from. Conceptions suppose some basis in the mind which gives them their evidence. What then is the first term in each of these two Series?

The Principles of Demonstration must be seen by Intuition.

Conceptions derive their properties from certain powers or attributes of the mind which we may term Ideas.

Therefore the two series are

Intuition: Demonstration: Belief: Conjecture.
Ideas: Conceptions: Things: Images.

238

Plato further teaches that the two former terms in each Series belong to the Intelligible, the two latter to the Visible World: and he supposes that the ratio of these two primary segments of the line is the same as the ratio in which each segment is divided[346].

In using the term Ideas to describe the mental sources from which Conceptions derive their validity in demonstration, I am employing a phraseology which I have already introduced in the Philosophy of the Inductive Sciences. But independently altogether of this, I do not see what other term could be employed to denote the mental objects, attributes, or powers, whatever they be, from which Conceptions derive their evidence, as Demonstrative Truths derive their evidence from Intuitive Truths.

That the Scheme just presented is Plato's doctrine on this subject, I do not conceive there can be any doubt. There is a little want of precision in his phraseology, arising from his mixing together the two series. In fact, his final series

Noësis: Dianoia: Pistis: Eikasia;

is made by putting in the second place, instead of Demonstration, which is the process pursued, or Science, which is the knowledge obtained, Conception, which is the object with which the mind deals. Such deviations from exact symmetry and correlation in speaking of the faculties of the mind, are almost unavoidable in every language. And there is yet another source of such inaccuracies of language; for we have to speak, not only of the process of acquiring knowledge, and of the objects with which the mind deals, but of the Faculties of the mind which are thus employed. Thus Intuition is the Process; Ideas are the445 Object, in the first term of our series. The Faculty also we may call Intuition; but the Greek offers a distinction. Noësis is the Process of Intuition; but the Faculty is Nous. If we wish to preserve this distinction in English, what must we call the Faculty? I conceive we must call it the Intuitive Reason, a term well known to our older philosophical writers[347]. Again: taking the second term of the series, Demonstration is the process, Science, the result; and Conceptions are the objects with which the mind deals. But what is the Faculty thus employed? What is the Faculty employed in Demonstration? The same philosophical writers of whom I spoke would have answered at once, the Discursive Reason; and I do not know that, even now, we can suggest any better term. The Faculty employed in acquiring the two lower kinds of knowledge, the Faculty which deals with Things and their Images is, of course, Sense, or Sensation.

The assertion of a Faculty of the mind by which it apprehends Truth, which Faculty is higher than the Discursive Reason, as the Truth apprehended by it is higher than mere Demonstrative Truth, agrees (as it will at once occur to several of my readers) with the doctrine taught and insisted upon by the late Samuel Taylor Coleridge. And so far as he was the means of inculcating this doctrine, which, as we see, is the doctrine of Plato, and I might add, of Aristotle, and of many other philosophers, let him have due honour. But in his desire to impress the doctrine upon men's minds, he combined it with several other tenets, which will not bear examination. He held that the two Faculties by which these two kinds of truth are apprehended, and which, as I have said, our philosophical writers call the Intuitive Reason and the Discursive Reason, may be called, and ought to be called, respectively, The Reason and The Understanding; and that the second of these is of the nature of the Instinct of animals, so as to be something intermediate between Reason and

Instinct. These opinions, I may venture to say, are altogether erroneous. The Intuitive Reason and the Discursive Reason are not, by any English writers, called the Reason and the Understanding; and accordingly, Coleridge has had to alter all the passages, namely, those taken from Leighton, Harrington, and Bacon, from which his exposition proceeds. The Understanding is so far from being especially the Discursive or446 Reasoning Faculty, that it is, in universal usage, and by our best writers, opposed to the Discursive or Reasoning Faculty. Thus this is expressly declared by Sir John Davis in his poem On the Immortality of the Soul. He says, of the soul,

> When she rates things, and moves from ground to ground,
> The name of Reason (Ratio) she acquires from this:
> But when by reason she truth hath found,
> And standeth fixt, she Understanding is.

Instead of the Reason being fixed, and the Understanding discursive, as Mr. Coleridge says, the Reason is distinctively discursive; that is, it obtains conclusions by running from one point to another. This is what is meant by Discursus; or, taking the full term, Discursus Rationis, Discourse of Reason. Understanding is fixed, that is, it dwells upon one view of a subject, and not upon the steps by which that view is obtained. The verb to reason, implies the substantive, the Reason, though it is not coextensive with it: for as I have said, there is the Intuitive Reason as well as the Discursive Reason. But it is by the Faculty of Reason that we are capable of reasoning; though undoubtedly the practice or the pretence of reasoning may be carried so far as to seem at variance with reason in the more familiar sense of the term; as is the case also in French. Moliere's Crisale says (in the Femmes Savantes),

> Raisonner est l'emploi de toute ma maison,
> Et le raisonnement en bannit la Raison.

If Mr. Coleridge's assertion were true, that the Understanding is the discursive and the Reason the fixed faculty, we should be justified in saying that The Understanding is the faculty by which we reason, and the Reason is the faculty by which we understand. But this is not so.

Nor is the Understanding of the nature of Instinct, nor does it approach nearer than the Reason to the nature of Instinct, but the contrary. The Instincts of animals bear a very obscure resemblance to any of man's speculative Faculties; but so far as there is any such resemblance, Instinct is an obscure image of Reason, not of Understanding. Animals are said to act as if they reasoned, rather than as if they understood. The verb understand is especially applied to man as distinguished from animals. Mr. Coleridge tells a tale from Huber, of certain bees which, to prevent a piece of honey from falling, balanced it by their weight, while they built a pillar to support it. They did this by Instinct, not understanding what they did; men, doing the same, would have understood what they were doing. Our Translation of the Scriptures, in making447 it the special distinction of man and animals, that he has Understanding and they have not, speaks quite consistently with good philosophy and good English.

Mr. Coleridge's object in his speculations is nearly the same as Plato's; namely, to declare that there is a truth of a higher kind than can be obtained by mere reasoning; and also to claim, as portions of this higher truth, certain fundamental doctrines of Morality.

Among these, Mr. Coleridge places the Authority of Conscience, and Plato, the Supreme Good. Mr. Coleridge also holds, as Plato held, that the Reason of man, in its highest and most comprehensive form, is a portion of a Supreme and Universal Reason; and leads to Truth, not in virtue of its special attributes in each person, but by its own nature.

Many of the opinions which are combined with these doctrines, both in Plato and in Coleridge, are such as we should, I think, find it impossible to accept, upon a careful philosophical examination of them; but on these I shall not here dwell.

I will only further observe, that if any one were to doubt whether the term Νοῦς is rightly rendered Intuitive Reason, we may find proof of the propriety of such a rendering in the remarkable discussion concerning the Intellectual Virtues, which we have in the Sixth Book of the Nicomachean Ethics. It can hardly be questioned that Aristotle had in his mind, in writing that passage, the doctrines of Plato, as expounded in the passage just examined, and similar passages. Aristotle there says that there are five Intellectual Virtues, or Faculties by which the Mind aims at Truth in asserting or denying:—namely, Art, Science, Prudence, Wisdom, Nous. In this enumeration, passing over Art, Prudence, and Wisdom, as virtues which are mainly concerned from practical life, we have, in the region of speculative Truth, a distinction propounded between Science and Nous: and this distinction is further explained (c. 6) by the remarks that Science reasons with Principles; and that these Principles cannot be given by Science, because Science reasons from them; nor by Art, nor Prudence, for these are conversant with matters contingent, not with matters demonstrable; nor can the First Principles of the Reasonings of Science be given by Wisdom, for Wisdom herself has often to reason from Principles. Therefore the First Principles of Demonstrative Reasoning must be given by a peculiar Faculty, Nous. As we have said, Intuitive Reason is the most appropriate English term for this Faculty.

The view thus given of that higher kind of Knowledge which Plato and Aristotle place above ordinary Science, as being the Knowledge of and Faculty of learning First Principles, will enable448 us to explain some expressions which might otherwise be misunderstood. Socrates, in the concluding part of this Sixth Book of the Republic, says, that this kind of knowledge is "that of which the Reason (λόγος) takes hold, in virtue of its power of reasoning[348]." Here we are plainly not to understand that we arrive at First Principles by reasoning: for the very opposite is true, and is here taught;—namely, that First Principles are not what we reason to, but what we reason from. The meaning of this passage plainly is, that First Principles are those of which the Reason takes hold in virtue of its power of reasoning;—they are the conditions which must exist in order to make any reasoning possible:—they are the propositions which the Reason must involve implicitly, in order that we may reason explicitly;—they are the intuitive roots of the dialectical power.

In accordance with the views now explained, Plato's Diagram may be thus further expanded. The term ιδέα is not used in this part of the Republic; but, as is well known, occurs in its peculiar Platonic sense in the Tenth Book.

Intelligible World. νοητον. Visible World. ορατον.
Object   Ideas

ἰδέαι	Conceptions
διάνοια	Things
ζῶα κ.τ.λ.	Images
εἰκίνες	
Process	Intuition
νἰησις	Demonstration
ἐπιστήμη	Belief
πίστις	Conjecture
εἰκασία	
Faculty	Intuitive Reason
νοῦς	Discursive Reason
λόγος	Sensation
αἴσθησις	
449	

Appendix D.
CRITICISM OF ARISTOTLE'S ACCOUNT OF INDUCTION.

(Cam. Phil. Soc. Feb. 11, 1850.)

The Cambridge Philosophical Society has willingly admitted among its proceedings not only contributions to science, but also to the philosophy of science; and it is to be presumed that this willingness will not be less if the speculations concerning the philosophy of science which are offered to the Society involve a reference to ancient authors. Induction, the process by which general truths are collected from particular examples, is one main point in such philosophy: and the comparison of the views of Induction entertained by ancient and modern writers has already attracted much notice. I do not intend now to go into this subject at any length; but there is a cardinal passage on the subject in Aristotle's Analytics, (Analyt. Prior. II. 25) which I wish to explain and discuss. I will first translate it, making such emendations as are requisite to render it intelligible and consistent, of which I shall afterwards give an account.

I will number the sentences of this chapter of Aristotle in order that I may afterwards be able to refer to them readily.

§ 1. "We must now proceed to observe that we have to examine not only syllogisms according to the aforesaid figures,—syllogisms logical and demonstrative,—but also rhetorical syllogisms,—and, speaking generally, any kind of proof by which belief is influenced, following any method.

§ 2. "All belief arises either from Syllogism or from Induction: [we must now therefore treat of Induction.]

§ 3. "Induction, and the Inductive Syllogism, is when by means of one extreme term we infer the other extreme term to be true of the middle term.

242

§ 4. "Thus if A, C, be the extremes, and B the mean, we have to show, by means of C, that A is true of B.

450

§ 5. "Thus let A be long-lived; B, that which has no gall-bladder; and C, particular long-lived animals, as elephant, horse, mule.

§ 6. "Then every C is A, for all the animals above named are long-lived.

§ 7. "Also every C is B, for all those animals are destitute of gall-bladder.

§ 8. "If then B and C are convertible, and the mean (B) does not extend further than extreme (C), it necessarily follows that every B is A.

§ 9. "For it was shown before, that, if any two things be true of the same, and if either of them be convertible with the extreme, the other of the things predicated is true of the convertible (extreme).

§ 10. "But we must conceive that C consists of a collection of all the particular cases; for Induction is applied to all the cases.

§ 11. "But such a syllogism is an inference of a first truth and immediate proposition.

§ 12. "For when there is a mean term, there is a demonstrative syllogism through the mean; but when there is not a mean, there is proof by Induction.

§ 13. "And in a certain way, Induction is contrary to Syllogism; for Syllogism proves, by the middle term, that the extreme is true of the third thing: but Induction proves, by means of the third thing, that the extreme is true of the mean.

§ 14. "And Syllogism concluding by means of a middle term is prior by nature and more usual to us; but the proof by Induction, is more luminous."

I think that the chapter, thus interpreted, is quite coherent and intelligible; although at first there seems to be some confusion, from the author sometimes saying that Induction is a kind of Syllogism, and at other times that it is not. The amount of the doctrine is this.

When we collect a general proposition by Induction from particular cases, as for instance, that all animals destitute of gall-bladder (acholous), are long-lived, (if this proposition were true, of which hereafter,) we may express the process in the form of a Syllogism, if we will agree to make a collection of particular cases our middle term, and assume that the proposition in which the second extreme term occurs is convertible. Thus the known propositions are

Elephant, horse, mule, &c., are long-lived.

243

Elephant, horse, mule, &c., are acholous.
451

But if we suppose that the latter proposition is convertible, we shall have these propositions:

Elephant, horse, mule, &c., are long-lived.
All acholous animals are elephant, horse, mule, &c.,
from whence we infer, quite rigorously as to form,

All acholous animals are long-lived.
This mode of putting the Inductive inference shows both the strong and the weak point of the illustration of Induction by means of Syllogism. The strong point is this, that we make the inference perfect as to form, by including an indefinite collection of particular cases, elephant, horse, mule, &c., in a single term, C. The Syllogism then is

All C are long-lived.
All acholous animals are C.
Therefore all acholous animals are long-lived.
The weak point of this illustration is, that, at least in some instances, when the number of actual cases is necessarily indefinite, the representation of them as a single thing involves an unauthorized step. In order to give the reasoning which really passes in the mind, we must say

Elephant, horse, &c., are long-lived.
All acholous animals are as elephant, horse, &c.,
Therefore all acholous animals are long-lived.
This "as" must be introduced in order that the "all C" of the first proposition may be justified by the "C" of the second.

This step is, I say, necessarily unauthorized, where the number of particular cases is indefinite; as in the instance before us, the species of acholous animals. We do not know how many such species there are, yet we wish to be able to assert that all acholous animals are long-lived. In the proof of such a proposition, put in a syllogistic form, there must necessarily be a logical defect; and the above discussion shows that this defect is the substitution of the proposition, "All acholous animals are as elephant, &c.," for the converse of the experimentally proved proposition, "elephant, &c., are acholous."

In instances in which the number of particular cases is limited, the necessary existence of a logical flaw in the syllogistic translation of the process is not so evident. But in truth, such a flaw exists in all cases of Induction proper: (for Induction by mere enumeration can hardly be called Induction). I will, however, consider for a moment the instance of a celebrated proposition which has often been taken as an example of Induction, and in which the number of particular cases is, or at least is at present supposed to be, limited. Kepler's laws, for instance the law that the planets describe ellipses,452 may be regarded as examples of Induction. The law was inferred, we will suppose, from an examination of the orbits of Mars, Earth, Venus. And the syllogistic illustration which Aristotle gives, will, with the necessary addition to it, stand thus,

244

Mars, Earth, Venus describe ellipses.
Mars, Earth, Venus are planets.
Assuming the convertibility of this last proposition, and its universality, (which is the necessary addition in order to make Aristotle's syllogism valid) we say

All the planets are as Mars, Earth, Venus.
Whence it follows that all the planets describe ellipses.

If, instead of this assumed universality, the astronomer had made a real enumeration, and had established the fact of each particular, he would be able to say

Saturn, Jupiter, Mars, Earth, Venus, Mercury, describe ellipses.

Saturn, Jupiter, Mars, Earth, Venus, Mercury are all the planets.

And he would obviously be entitled to convert the second proposition, and then to conclude that

All the planets describe ellipses.
But then, if this were given as an illustration of Induction by means of syllogism, we should have to remark, in the first place, that the conclusion that "all the planets describe ellipses," adds nothing to the major proposition, that "S., J., M., E., V., m., do so." It is merely the same proposition expressed in other words, so long as S., J., M., E., V., m., are supposed to be all the planets. And in the next place we have to make a remark which is more important; that the minor, in such an example, must generally be either a very precarious truth, or, as appears in this case, a transitory error. For that the planets known at any time are all the planets, must always be a doubtful assertion, liable to be overthrown to-night by an astronomical observation. And the assertion, as received in Kepler's time, has been overthrown. For Saturn, Jupiter, Mars, Earth, Venus, Mercury, are not all the planets. Not only have several new ones been discovered at intervals, as Uranus, Ceres, Juno, Pallas, Vesta, but we have new ones discovered every day; and any conclusion depending upon this premiss that A, B, C, D, E, F, G, H, to Z are all the planets, is likely to be falsified in a few years by the discovery of A´, B´, C´, &c. If, therefore, this were the syllogistic analysis of Induction, Kepler's discovery rested upon a false proposition; and even if the analysis were now made conformable to our present knowledge, that induction, analysed as above, would still453 involve a proposition which to-morrow may show to be false. But yet no one, I suppose, doubts that Kepler's discovery was really a discovery—the establishment of a scientific truth on solid grounds; or, that it is a scientific truth for us, notwithstanding that we are constantly discovering new planets. Therefore the syllogistic analysis of it now discussed (namely, that which introduces simple enumeration as a step) is not the right analysis, and does not represent the grounds of the Inductive Truth, that all the planets describe ellipses.

It may be said that all the planets discovered since Kepler's time conform to his law, and thus confirm his discovery. This we grant: but they only confirm the discovery, they do not make it; they are not its groundwork. It was a discovery before these new cases were known; it was an inductive truth without them. Still, an objector might urge, if any one of these new planets had contradicted the law, it would have overturned the discovery. But this is too boldly said. A discovery which is so precise, so complex (in the phenomena which it explains), so supported by innumerable observations extending through space and time, is not so easily overturned. If we find that Uranus, or that Encke's comet, deviates from Kepler's and Newton's laws, we do not infer that these laws must be false; we say that there must be some disturbing cause in these cases. We seek, and we find these disturbing causes: in the case of Uranus, a new planet; in the case of Encke's comet, a resisting medium. Even in this case therefore, though the number of particulars is limited, the Induction was not made by a simple enumeration of all the particulars. It was made from a few cases, and when the law was discerned to be true in these, it was extended to all; the conversion and assumed universality of the proposition that "these are planets," giving us the proposition which we need for the syllogistic exhibition of Induction, "all the planets are as these."

I venture to say further, that it is plain, that Aristotle did not regard Induction as the result of simple enumeration. This is plain, in the first place, from his example. Any proposition with regard to a special class of animals, cannot be proved by simple enumeration: for the number of particular cases, that is, of animal species in the class, is indefinite at any period of zoological discovery, and must be regarded as infinite. In the next place, Aristotle says (§ 10 of the above extract), "We must conceive that C consists of a collection of all the particular cases; for induction is applied to all the cases." We must conceive (νοεῖν) that C in the major, consists of all the cases, in order that the conclusion may be true of all the cases; but we cannot observe all the cases. But the evident proof that Aristotle does not contemplate in this chapter an Induction by sim454ple enumeration, is the contrast in which he places Induction and Syllogism. For Induction by simple enumeration stands in no contrast to Syllogism. The Syllogism of such Induction is quite logical and conclusive. But Induction from a comparatively small number of particular cases to a general law, does stand in opposition to Syllogism. It gives us a truth,—a truth which, as Aristotle says (§ 14), is more luminous than a truth proved syllogistically, though Syllogism may be more natural and usual. It gives us (§ 11) immediate propositions, obtained directly from observation, and not by a chain of reasoning: "first truths," the principles from which syllogistic reasonings may be deduced. The Syllogism proves by means of a middle term (§ 13) that the extreme is true of a third thing: thus, (acholous being the middle term):

Acholous animals are long-lived:
All elephants are acholous animals:
Therefore all elephants are long-lived.
But Induction proves by means of a third thing (namely, particular cases) that the extreme is true of the mean; thus (acholous, still being the middle term)

Elephants are long-lived:
Elephants are acholous animals:
Therefore acholous animals are long-lived.
It may be objected, such reasoning as this is quite inconclusive: and the answer is, that this is precisely what we, and as I believe, Aristotle, are here pointing out. Induction is inconclusive as reasoning. It is not reasoning: it is another way of getting at truth. As we have seen, no reasoning can prove such an inductive truth as this, that all planets describe

246

ellipses. It is known from observation, but it is not demonstrated. Nevertheless, no one doubts its universal truth, (except, as aforesaid, when disturbing causes intervene). And thence, Induction is, as Aristotle says, opposed to syllogistic reasoning, and yet is a means of discovering truth: not only so, but a means of discovering primary truths, immediately derived from observation.

I have elsewhere taught that all Induction involves a Conception of the mind applied to facts. It may be asked whether this applies in such a case as that given by Aristotle. And I reply, that Aristotle's instance is a very instructive example of what I mean. The Conception which is applied to the facts in order to make the induction possible is the want of the gall-bladder;—and Aristotle supplies us with a special term for this conception; acholous[349]. But,455 it may be said, that the animals observed, the elephant, horse, mule, &c., are acholous, is a mere fact of observation, not a Conception. I reply that it is a Selected Fact, a fact selected and compared in several cases, which is what we mean by a Conception. That there is needed for such selection and comparison a certain activity of the mind, is evident; but this also may become more clear by dwelling a little further on the subject. Suppose that Aristotle, having a desire to know what class of animals are long-lived, had dissected for that purpose many animals; elephants, horses, cows, sheep, goats, deer and the like. How many resemblances, how many differences, must he have observed in their anatomy! He was very likely long in fixing upon any one resemblance which was common to all the long-lived. Probably he tried several other characters, before he tried the presence and absence of the gall-bladder:—perhaps, trying such characters, he found them succeed for a few cases, and then fail in others, so that he had to reject them as useless for his purpose. All the while, the absence of the gall-bladder in the long-lived animals was a fact: but it was of no use to him, because he had not selected it and drawn it forth from the mass of other facts. He was looking for a mean term to connect his first extreme, long-lived, with his second, the special cases. He sought this middle term in the entrails of the many animals which he used as extremes: it was there, but he could not find it. The fact existed, but it was of no use for the purpose of Induction, because it did not become a special Conception in his mind. He considered the animals in various points of view, it may be, as ruminant, as horned, as hoofed, and the contrary; but not as acholous and the contrary. When he looked at animals in that point of view,—when he took up that character as the ground of distinction, he forthwith imagined that he found a separation of long-lived and short-lived animals. When that Fact became a Conception, he obtained an inductive truth, or, at any rate, an inductive proposition.

He obtained an inductive proposition by applying the Conception acholous to his observation of animals. This Conception divided them into two classes; and these classes were, he fancied, long-lived and short-lived respectively. That it was the Conception, and not the Fact which enabled him to obtain his inductive proposition, is further plain from this, that the supposed Fact is not a fact. Acholous animals are not longer-lived than others. The presence or absence of the gall-bladder is no character of longevity. It is true, that in one familiar class of animals, the herbivorous kind, there is a sort of first seeming of the truth of Aristotle's asserted rule: for the horse and mule which have not the gall-bladder are456 longer-lived than the cow, sheep, and goat, which have it. But if we pursue the investigation further, the rule soon fails. The deer-tribe that want the gall-bladder are not longer-lived than the other ruminating animals which have it. And as a conspicuous evidence of the falsity of the rule, man and the elephant are perhaps, for their size, the longest-lived animals, and of these, man has, and the elephant has not, the organ in question. The inductive proposition, then, is false; but what we have mainly to consider is, where the fallacy enters, according to Aristotle's analysis of Induction into Syllogism. For the two premisses are still true; that elephants, &c., are long-lived; and that elephants, &c., are acholous. And it is plain that the fallacy comes in with that conversion and generalization of the latter proposition, which we have noted as necessary to Aristotle's illustration of Induction. When we say "All acholous animals are as elephants, &c.," that is, as those in their biological conditions, we say what is not true. Aristotle's condition (§ 8) is not complied with, that the middle term shall not extend beyond the extreme. For the character acholous does extend beyond the elephant and the animals biologically resembling it; it extends to deer, &c., which are not like elephants and horses, in the point in question. And thus, we see that the assumed conversion and generalization of the minor proposition, is the seat of the fallacy of false Inductions, as it is the seat of the peculiar logical character of true Inductions.

As true Inductive Propositions cannot be logically demonstrated by syllogistic rules, so they cannot be discovered by any rule. There is no formula for the discovery of inductive truth. It is caught by a peculiar sagacity, or power of divination, for which no precepts can be given. But from what has been said, we see that this sagacity shows itself in the discovery of propositions which are both true, and convertible in the sense above explained. Both these steps may be difficult. The former is often very laborious: and when the labour has been expended, and a true proposition obtained, it may turn out useless, because the proposition is not convertible. It was a matter of great labour to Kepler to prove (from calculation of observations) that Mars moves elliptically. Before he proved this, he had tried to prove many similar propositions:—that Mars moved according to the "bisection of the eccentricity,"—according to the "vicarious hypothesis,"—according to the "physical hypothesis,"—and the like; but none of these was found to be exactly true. The proposition that Mars moves elliptically was proved to be true. But still, there was the question, Is it convertible? Do all the planets move as Mars moves? This was proved, (suppose,) to be 457 true, for the Earth and Venus. But still the question remains, Do all the planets move as Mars, Earth, Venus, do? The inductive generalizing impulse boldly answers, Yes, to this question; though the rules of Syllogism do not authorize the answer, and though there remain untried cases. The inductive Philosopher tries the cases as fast as they occur, in order to confirm his previous conviction; but if he had to wait for belief and conviction till he had tried every case, he never could have belief or conviction of such a proposition at all. He is prepared to modify or add to his inductive truth according as new cases and new observations instruct him; but he does not fear that new cases or new observations will overturn an inductive proposition established by exact comparison of many complex and various phenomena.

Aristotle's example offers somewhat similar reflections. He had to establish a proposition concerning long-lived animals, which should be true, and should be susceptible of generalized conversion. To prove that the elephant, horse and mule are destitute of gall-bladder required, at least, the labour of anatomizing those animals in the seat of that organ. But this labour was not enough; for he would find those animals to agree in many other things besides in being acholous. He must have selected that character somewhat at a venture. And the guess was wrong, as a little more labour would have shown him; if for instance he had dissected deer: for they are acholous, and yet short-lived. A trial of this kind would have shown him that the extreme term, acholous, did extend beyond the mean, namely, animals such as elephant, horse, mule; and therefore, that the conversion was not allowable, and that the Induction was untenable. In truth, there is no relation between bile and longevity[350], and this example given by Aristotle of generalization from induction is an unfortunate one.

458

In discussing this passage of Aristotle, I have made two alterations in the text, one of which is necessary on account of the fact; the other on account of the sense. In the received text, the particular examples of long-lived animals given are man, horse, and mule (ἐφ' ᾧ δὲ Γ, τὸ καθέκαστον μακρόβιον, οἷον ἄνθρωπος, καὶ ἵππος, καὶ ἡμίονος). And it is afterwards said that all these are acholous: (ἀλλὰ καὶ τὸ Β, τὸ μὴ ἔχον χολὴν, παντὶ ὑπάρχει τῷ Γ). But man has a gall-bladder: and the fact was well known in Aristotle's time, for instance, to Hippocrates; so that it is not likely that Aristotle would have made the mistake which the text contains. But at any rate, it is a mistake; if not of the transcriber, of Aristotle; and it is impossible to reason about the passage, without correcting the mistake. The substitution of ἔλεφας for ἄνθρωπος makes the reasoning coherent; but of course, any other acholous long-lived animal would do so equally well.

The other emendation which I have made is in § 6. In the received text § 6 and 7 stand thus:

6. Then every C is A, for every acholous animal is long-lived

(τῷ δὴ Γ ὅλῳ ὑπάρχει τὸ Α, πᾶν γὰρ τὸ ἄχολον μακρόβιον).

7. Also every C is B, for all C is destitute of bile.

Whence it may be inferred, says Aristotle, under certain conditions, that every B is A (τὸ Α τῷ Β ὑπάρχειν) that is, that every acholous animal is long-lived. But this conclusion is, according to the common reading, identical with the major premiss; so that the passage is manifestly corrupt. I correct it by substituting for ἄχολον, Γ; and thus reading πᾶν γὰρ τὸ Γ μακρόβιον "for every C is long-lived:" just as in the parallel sentence, 7, we have ἀλλὰ καὶ τὸ Β, τὸ μὴ ἔχον χολην, παντὶ ὑπάρχει τῷ Γ. In this way the reasoning becomes quite clear. The corrupt substitution of ἄχολον for Γ may have been made in various ways; which I need not suggest. As my business is with the sense of the passage, and as it makes no sense without the change, and very good sense with it, I cannot hesitate to make the emendation. And these emendations being made, Aristotle's view of the nature and force of Induction becomes, I think, perfectly clear and very instructive.

459

ADDITIONAL NOTE.

I take the liberty of adding to this Memoir the following remarks, for which I am indebted to Mr.Edleston, Fellow of Trinity College.

Several of the earlier editions of Aristotle have γ instead of ἄχολον in the passage referred to in the above paper: ex. gr.

(1) The edition printed at Basle, 1539 (after Erasmus): "τὸ γ."

(2) Basil (Erasmus) 1550. "τὸ γ."

(3) Burana's Latin version, Venet. 1552, has "omne enim C longævum."

(4) Sylburg, Francf. 1587 "τὸ γ" is printed in brackets thus: "[τὸ γ] τὸ ἄχολον."

(5) So also in Casaubon's edition, 1590.

(6) Casaub. 1605 "τὸ γ," (though the Latin version has "vacans bile;") not "[τὸ γ] τὸ ἄχολον," as the edition of 1590.

(7) In the edition printed Aurel. Allobr. 1607, "[τὸ γ] τὸ ἄχολον," as in (4) and (5).

(8) Du Val's editions, Paris, 1619, 1629, 1654 "τὸ γ," though in Pacius's translation in the adjacent column we find "vacans bile."

(9) In the critical notes to Waitz's edition of the Organon (Lips. 1844) it is stated that "post ἄχολον del. γ. n," implying apparently, that in the MS. marked n, the letter γ, which had been originally written after ἄχολον, had been erased.

The following passages throw light upon the question whether ἄνθρωπος ought or ought not to be retained in the passage discussed in the Memoir.

(A) Aristot. De Animalibus Histor. II. 15, 9 (Bekk.), τῶν μὲν ζωοτόκων καὶ τετραπόδων ἔλαφος οὐκ ἔχει [χολήν] οὐδὲ πρόξ, ἔτι δὲ ἵππος, ὀρεύς, ὄνος, φώκη καὶ τῶν ὑῶν ἔνιοι.... Ἔχει δὲ καὶ ὁ ἐλέφας τὸ ἧπαρ ἄχολον μέν, κ.τ.λ.

(B) Conf. Ib. I. 17, 10, 11. (In the beginning of Chap. 16, he says that the external μόρια of man are γνώριμα, "τὰ δ' ἐντὸς τοὐναντίον. Ἄγνωστα γάρ ἐστι μάλιστα τὰ τῶν ἀνθρώπων, ὥστε δεῖ πρὸς τὰ τῶν ἄλλων μόρια ζώων ἀνάγοντας σκοπεῖν," ...)

(C) Id De Part. Animal. IV. 2, 2. τὰ μὲν γὰρ ὅλως οὐκ ἔχει χολήν, οἷον ἵππος καὶ ὀρεύς καὶ ονος καὶ ἔλαφος καὶ πρόξ.....460 Ἐν δὲ τοῖς γένεσι τοῖς αὐτοῖς τὰ μὲν ἔχειν φαίνεται, τὰ δ' οὐκ ἔχειν, οἷον ἐν τῷ τῶν μυῶν. Τούτων δ' ἐστὶ καὶ ὁ ἄνθρωπος· ἔνιοι μὲν γὰρ φαίνονται ἔχοντες χολὴν ἐπὶ του ἥπατος, ἔνιοι δ' οὐκ ἔχοντες. Διο καὶ γίνεται ἀμφισβήτησις περὶ ὅλου τοῦ γένους· οἱ γὰρ ἐντυχόντες ὁποτερωσοῦν ἔχουσι περὶ πάντων ὑπολαμβάνουσιν ὡς ἁπάντων ἐχόντων.....

(D) Ib. § 11. Διὸ καὶ χαριέστατα λέγουσι τῶν ὦρχαίων ὁι φάσκοντες αἴτιον εἶναι τοῦ πλείω ζῆν χρόνον το μὴ ἔχειν χολήν, βλέψαντες ἐπὶ τὰ μωνυχα καὶ τὰς ελαφους· ταῦτα γὰρ ἄχολά τε καὶ ζῇ πολὺν χρόνον. Ἔτι δὲ καὶ τὰ μὴ ἑωραμένα ὑπ' ἐκείνων ὅτι οὐκ ἔχει χολήν, οἷον δελφις καὶ κάμηλος, καὶ ταῦτα τυγχάνει μακρόβια ὄντα. Εὔλογον γάρ, κ.τ.λ.

(E) The elephant and man are mentioned together as long-lived animals (De Long. et Brev. Vitæ, IV. 2, and De Generat. Animal. IV. 10, 2.)

The following is the import of these passages:

(A) "Of viviparous quadrupeds, the deer, roe, horse, mule, ass, seal, and some of the swine have not the gall-bladder....

The elephant also has the liver without gall-bladder, &c."

(B) "The external parts of man are well known: the internal parts are far from being so. The parts of man are in a great measure unknown; so that we must judge concerning them by reference to the analogy of other animals...."

(C) "Some animals are altogether destitute of gall-bladder, as the horse, the mule, the ass, the deer, the roe.... But in some kinds it appears that some have it, and some have it not, as the mice kind. And among these is man; for some men appear to have a gall-bladder on the liver, and some not to have one. And thus there is a doubt as to the species in general; for those who have happened to examine examples of either kind, hold that all the cases are of that kind."

(D) Those of the ancients speak most plausibly, who say that the absence of the gall-bladder is the cause of long life; looking at animals with uncloven hoof, and deer: for these are destitute of gall-bladder, and live a long time. And further, those animals in which the ancients had not the opportunity of ascertaining that they have not the gall-bladder, as the dolphin, and the camel, are also long-lived animals."

461

It appears, from these passages, that Aristotle was aware that some persons had asserted man to have a gall-bladder, but that he also conceived this not to be universally true. He may have inclined to the opinion, that the opposite case was the more usual, and may have written ἄνθρωπος in the passage which I have been discussing. Another mistake of his is the reckoning deer among long-lived animals.

It appears probable, from the context of the passages (C) and (D), that the conjecture of a connexion between absence of the gall-bladder and length of life was suggested by some such notion as this:—that the gall, from its bitterness, is the cause of irritation, mental and bodily, and that irritation is adverse to longevity. The opinion is ascribed to "the ancients," not claimed by Aristotle as his own.

462

Appendix E.
ON THE FUNDAMENTAL ANTITHESIS OF PHILOSOPHY.

(Cam. Phil. Soc. Feb. 5, 1844.)

1. ALL persons who have attended in any degree to the views generally current of the nature of reasoning are familiar with the distinction of necessary truths and truths of experience; and few such persons, or at least few students of mathematics, require to have this distinction explained or enforced. All geometricians are satisfied that the geometrical truths with which they are conversant are necessarily true: they not only are true, but they must be true. The meaning of the terms being understood, and the proof being gone through, the truth of the proposition must be assented to. That parallelograms upon the same base and between the same parallels are equal;—that angles in the same segment are equal;—these are propositions which we learn to be true by demonstrations deduced from definitions and axioms; and which, when we have thus learnt them, we see could not be otherwise. On the other hand, there are other truths which we learn from experience; as for instance, that the stars revolve round the pole in one day; and that the moon goes through her phases from full to full again in thirty days. These truths we see to be true; but we know them only by experience. Men never could have discovered them without looking at the stars and the moon; and having so learnt them, still no one will pretend to say that they are necessarily true. For aught we can see, things might have been otherwise; and if we had been placed in another part of the solar system, then, according to the opinions of astronomers, experience would have presented them otherwise.

2. I take the astronomical truths of experience to contrast with the geometrical necessary truths, as being both of a familiar definite sort; we may easily find other examples of both kinds of truth. The truths which regard numbers are necessary truths. It is a necessary truth, that 27 and 38 are equal to 65; that half the sum463 of two numbers added to half their difference is equal to the greater number. On the other hand, that sugar will dissolve in water; that plants cannot live without light; and in short, the whole body of our knowledge in chemistry, physiology, and the other inductive sciences, consists of truths of experience. If there be any science which offer to us truths of an ambiguous kind, with regard to which we may for a moment doubt whether they are necessary or experiential, we will defer the consideration of them till we have marked the distinction of the two kinds more clearly.

3. One mode in which we may express the difference of necessary truths and truths of experience, is, that necessary truths are those of which we cannot distinctly conceive the contrary. We can very readily conceive the contrary of experiential truths. We can conceive the stars moving about the pole or across the sky in any kind of curves with any velocities; we can conceive the moon always appearing during the whole month as a luminous disk, as she might do if her light were inherent and not borrowed. But we cannot conceive one of the parallelograms on the same base and between the same parallels larger than the other; for we find that, if we attempt to do this, when we separate the parallelograms into parts, we have to conceive one triangle larger than another, both having all their parts equal; which we cannot conceive at all, if we conceive the triangles

252

distinctly. We make this impossibility more clear by conceiving the triangles to be placed so that two sides of the one coincide with two sides of the other; and it is then seen, that in order to conceive the triangles unequal, we must conceive the two bases which have the same extremities both ways, to be different lines, though both straight lines. This it is impossible to conceive: we assent to the impossibility as an axiom, when it is expressed by saying, that two straight lines cannot inclose a space; and thus we cannot distinctly conceive the contrary of the proposition just mentioned respecting parallelograms.

4. But it is necessary, in applying this distinction, to bear in mind the terms of it;— that we cannot distinctly conceive the contrary of a necessary truth. For in a certain loose, indistinct way, persons conceive the contrary of necessary geometrical truths, when they erroneously conceive false propositions to be true. Thus, Hobbes erroneously held that he had discovered a means of geometrically doubling the cube, as it is called, that is, finding two mean proportionals between two given lines; a problem which cannot be solved by plane geometry. Hobbes not only proposed a construction for this purpose, but obstinately maintained that it464 was right, when it had been proved to be wrong. But then, the discussion showed how indistinct the geometrical conceptions of Hobbes were; for when his critics had proved that one of the lines in his diagram would not meet the other in the point which his reasoning supposed, but in another point near to it; he maintained, in reply, that one of these points was large enough to include the other, so that they might be considered as the same point. Such a mode of conceiving the opposite of a geometrical truth, forms no exception to the assertion, that this opposite cannot be distinctly conceived.

5. In like manner, the indistinct conceptions of children and of rude savages do not invalidate the distinction of necessary and experiential truths. Children and savages make mistakes even with regard to numbers; and might easily happen to assert that 27 and 38 are equal to 63 or 64. But such mistakes cannot make such arithmetical truths cease to be necessary truths. When any person conceives these numbers and their addition distinctly, by resolving them into parts, or in any other way, he sees that their sum is necessarily 65. If, on the ground of the possibility of children and savages conceiving something different, it be held that this is not a necessary truth, it must be held on the same ground, that it is not a necessary truth that 7 and 4 are equal to 11; for children and savages might be found so unfamiliar with numbers as not to reject the assertion that 7 and 4 are 10, or even that 4 and 3 are 6, or 8. But I suppose that no persons would on such grounds hold that these arithmetical truths are truths known only by experience.

6. Necessary truths are established, as has already been said, by demonstration, proceeding from definitions and axioms, according to exact and rigorous inferences of reason. Truths of experience are collected from what we see, also according to inferences of reason, but proceeding in a less exact and rigorous mode of proof. The former depend upon the relations of the ideas which we have in our minds: the latter depend upon the appearances or phenomena, which present themselves to our senses. Necessary truths are formed from our thoughts, the elements of the world within us; experiential truths are collected from things, the elements of the world without us. The truths of experience, as they appear to us in the external world, we call Facts; and when we are able to find among our ideas a train which will conform themselves to the apparent facts, we call this a Theory.

7. This distinction and opposition, thus expressed in various forms; as Necessary and Experiential Truth, Ideas and Senses,465 Thoughts and Things, Theory and Fact, may be termed the Fundamental Antithesis of Philosophy; for almost all the discussions of philosophers have been employed in asserting or denying, explaining or obscuring this antithesis. It may be expressed in many other ways; but is not difficult, under all these different forms, to recognize the same opposition: and the same remarks apply to it under its various forms, with corresponding modifications. Thus, as we have already seen, the antithesis agrees with that of Reasoning and Observation: again, it is identical with the opposition of Reflection and Sensation: again, sensation deals with Objects; facts involve Objects, and generally all things without us are Objects:—Objects of sensation, of observation. On the other hand, we ourselves who thus observe objects, and in whom sensation is, may be called the Subjects of sensation and observation. And this distinction of Subject and Object is one of the most general ways of expressing the fundamental antithesis, although not yet perhaps quite familiar in English. I shall not scruple however to speak of the Subjective and Objective element of this antithesis, where the expressions are convenient.

8. All these forms of antithesis, and the familiar references to them which men make in all discussions, show the fundamental and necessary character of the antithesis. We can have no knowledge without the union, no philosophy without the separation, of the two elements. We can have no knowledge, except we have both impressions on our senses from the world without, and thoughts from our minds within:—except we attend to things, and to our ideas;—except we are passive to receive impressions, and active to compare, combine, and mould them. But on the other hand, philosophy seeks to distinguish the impressions of our senses from the thoughts of our minds;—to point out the difference of ideas and things;—to separate the active from the passive faculties of our being. The two elements, sensations and ideas, are both requisite to the existence of our knowledge, as both matter and form are requisite to the existence of a body. But philosophy considers the matter and the form separately. The properties of the form are the subject of geometry, the properties of the matter are the subject of chemistry or mechanics.

9. But though philosophy considers these elements of knowledge separately, they cannot really be separated, any more than can matter and form. "We cannot exhibit matter without form, or form without matter; and just as little can we exhibit sensations without ideas, or ideas without sensations;—the passive or the active faculties of the mind detached from each other.

466

In every act of my knowledge, there must be concerned the things whereof I know, and thoughts of me who know: I must both passively receive or have received impressions, and I must actively combine them and reason on them. No apprehension of things is purely ideal: no experience of external things is purely sensational. If they be conceived as things, the mind must have been awakened to the conviction of things by sensation: if they be conceived as things, the expressions of the senses must have been bound together by conceptions. If we think of any thing, we must recognize the existence both of thoughts and of things. The fundamental antithesis of philosophy is an antithesis of inseparable elements.

10. Not only cannot these elements be separately exhibited, but they cannot be separately conceived and described. The description of them must always imply their relation; and the names by which they are denoted will consequently always bear a relative significance. And thus the terms which denote the fundamental antithesis of philosophy cannot be applied absolutely and exclusively in any case. We may illustrate this by a consideration of some of the common modes of expressing the antithesis of which we speak. The terms Theory and Fact are often emphatically used as opposed to each other: and they are rightly so used. But yet it is impossible to say absolutely in any case, This is a Fact and not a Theory; this is a Theory and not a Fact, meaning by Theory, true Theory. Is it a fact or a theory that the stars appear to revolve round the pole? Is it a fact or a theory that the earth is a globe revolving round its axis? Is it a fact or a theory that the earth revolves round the sun? Is it a fact or a theory that the sun attracts the earth? Is it a fact or a theory that a loadstone attracts a needle? In all these cases, some persons would answer one way and some persons another. A person who has never watched the stars, and has only seen them from time to time, considers their circular motion round the pole as a theory, just as he considers the motion of the sun in the ecliptic as a theory, or the apparent motion of the inferior planets round the sun in the zodiac. A person who has compared the measures of different parts of the earth, and who knows that these measures cannot be conceived distinctly without supposing the earth a globe, considers its globular form a fact, just as much as the square form of his chamber. A person to whom the grounds of believing the earth to revolve round its axis and round the sun, are as familiar as the grounds for believing the movements of the mail-coaches in this country, conceives the former events to be facts, just as steadily as the latter.467 And a person who, believing the fact of the earth's annual motion, refers it distinctly to its mechanical course, conceives the sun's attraction as a fact, just as he conceives as a fact the action of the wind which turns the sails of a mill. We see then, that in these cases we cannot apply absolutely and exclusively either of the terms, Fact or Theory. Theory and Fact are the elements which correspond to our Ideas and our Senses. The Facts are facts so far as the Ideas have been combined with the sensations and absorbed in them: the Theories are Theories so far as the Ideas are kept distinct from the sensations, and so far as it is considered as still a question whether they can be made to agree with them. A true Theory is a fact, a Fact is a familiar theory.

In like manner, if we take the terms Reasoning and Observation; at first sight they appear to be very distinct. Our observation of the world without us, our reasonings in our own minds, appear to be clearly separated and opposed. But yet we shall find that we cannot apply these terms absolutely and exclusively. I see a book lying a few feet from me: is this a matter of observation? At first, perhaps, we might be inclined to say that it clearly is so. But yet, all of us, who have paid any attention to the process of vision, and to the mode in which we are enabled to judge of the distance of objects, and to judge them to be distant objects at all, know that this judgment involves inferences drawn from various sensations;—from the impressions on our two eyes;—from our muscular sensations; and the like. These inferences are of the nature of reasoning, as much as when we judge of the distance of an object on the other side of a river by looking at it from different points, and stepping the distance between them. Or again: we observe the setting sun illuminate a gilded weathercock; but this is as much a matter of reasoning as when we observe the phases of the moon, and infer that she is illuminated by the sun. All observation involves inferences, and inference is reasoning.

11. Even the simplest terms by which the antithesis is expressed cannot be applied: ideas and sensations, thoughts and things, subject and object, cannot in any case be applied absolutely and exclusively. Our sensations require ideas to bind them together, namely, ideas of space, time, number, and the like. If not so bound together, sensations do not give us any apprehension of things or objects. All things, all objects, must exist in space and in time—must be one or many. Now space, time, number, are not sensations or things. They are something different from, and opposed to sensations and things. We have termed them ideas. It may be said they are relations of things, or of sensations. But468 granting this form of expression, still a relation is not a thing or a sensation; and therefore we must still have another and opposite element, along with our sensations. And yet, though we have thus these two elements in every act of perception, we cannot designate any portion of the act as absolutely and exclusively belonging to one of the elements. Perception involves sensation, along with ideas of time, space, and the like; or, if any one prefers the expression, involves sensations along with the apprehension of relations. Perception is sensation, along with such ideas as make sensation into an apprehension of things or objects.

12. And as perception of objects implies ideas, as observation implies reasoning; so, on the other hand, ideas cannot exist where sensation has not been: reasoning cannot go on when there has not been previous observation. This is evident from the necessary order of development of the human faculties. Sensation necessarily exists from the first moments of our existence, and is constantly at work. Observation begins before we can suppose the existence of any reasoning which is not involved in observation. Hence, at whatever period we consider our ideas, we must consider them as having been already engaged in connecting our sensations, and as modified by this employment. By being so employed, our ideas are unfolded and defined, and such development and definition cannot be separated from the ideas themselves. We cannot conceive space without boundaries or forms; now forms involve sensations. We cannot conceive time without events which mark the course of time; but events involve sensations. We cannot conceive number without conceiving things which are numbered; and things imply sensations. And the forms, things, events, which are thus implied in our ideas, having been the objects of sensation constantly in every part of our life, have modified, unfolded and fixed our ideas, to an extent which we cannot estimate, but which we must suppose to be essential to the processes which at present go on in our minds. We cannot say that objects create ideas; for to perceive objects we must already have ideas. But we may say, that objects and the constant perception of objects have so far modified our ideas, that we cannot, even in thought, separate our ideas from the perception of objects.

We cannot say of any ideas, as of the idea of space, or time, or number, that they are absolutely and exclusively ideas. We cannot conceive what space, or time, or number would be in our minds, if we had never perceived any thing or things in space or time. We cannot conceive ourselves in such a condition as never to have perceived any thing or things in space or time. But, on the other469 hand, just as little can we conceive ourselves becoming acquainted with space and time or numbers as objects of sensation. We cannot

256

reason without having the operations of our minds affected by previous sensations; but we cannot conceive reasoning to be merely a series of sensations. In order to be used in reasoning, sensation must become observation; and, as we have seen, observation already involves reasoning. In order to be connected by our ideas, sensations must be things or objects, and things or objects already include ideas. And thus, as we have said, none of the terms by which the fundamental antithesis is expressed can be absolutely and exclusively applied.

13. I now proceed to make one or two remarks suggested by the views which have thus been presented. And first I remark, that since, as we have just seen, none of the terms which express the fundamental antithesis can be applied absolutely and exclusively, the absolute application of the antithesis in any particular case can never be a conclusive or immoveable principle. This remark is the more necessary to be borne in mind, as the terms of this antithesis are often used in a vehement and peremptory manner. Thus we are often told that such a thing is a Fact and not a Theory, with all the emphasis which, in speaking or writing, tone or italics or capitals can give. "We see from what has been said, that when this is urged, before we can estimate the truth, or the value of the assertion, we must ask to whom is it a fact? what habits of thought, what previous information, what ideas does it imply, to conceive the fact as a fact? Does not the apprehension of the fact imply assumptions which may with equal justice be called theory, and which are perhaps false theory? in which case, the fact is no fact. Did not the ancients assert it as a fact, that the earth stood still, and the stars moved? and can any fact have stronger apparent evidence to justify persons in asserting it emphatically than this had? These remarks are by no means urged in order to show that no fact can be certainly known to be true; but only to show that no fact can be certainly shown to be a fact merely by calling it a fact, however emphatically. There is by no means any ground of general skepticism with regard to truth involved in the doctrine of the necessary combination of two elements in all our knowledge. On the contrary, ideas are requisite to the essence, and things to the reality of our knowledge in every case. The proportions of geometry and arithmetic are examples of knowledge respecting our ideas of space and number, with regard to which there is no room for doubt. The doctrines of astronomy are examples of truths not less certain respecting the external world.

470

14. I remark further, that since in every act of knowledge, observation or perception, both the elements of the fundamental antithesis are involved, and involved in a manner inseparable even in our conceptions, it must always be possible to derive one of these elements from the other, if we are satisfied to accept, as proof of such derivation, that one always co-exists with and implies the other. Thus an opponent may say, that our ideas of space, time, and number, are derived from our sensations or perceptions, because we never were in a condition in which we had the ideas of space and time, and had not sensations or perceptions. But then, we may reply to this, that we no sooner perceive objects than we perceive them as existing in space and time, and therefore the ideas of space and time are not derived from the perceptions. In the same manner, an opponent may say, that all knowledge which is involved in our reasonings is the result of experience; for instance, our knowledge of geometry. For every geometrical principle is presented to us by experience as true; beginning with the simplest, from which all others are derived by

257

processes of exact reasoning. But to this we reply, that experience cannot be the origin of such knowledge; for though experience shows that such principles are true, it cannot show that they must be true, which we also know. We never have seen, as a matter of observation, two straight lines inclosing a space; but we venture to say further, without the smallest hesitation, that we never shall see it; and if any one were to tell us that, according to his experience, such a form was often seen, we should only suppose that he did not know what he was talking of. No number of acts of experience can add to the certainty of our knowledge in this respect; which shows that our knowledge is not made up of acts of experience. We cannot test such knowledge by experience; for if we were to try to do so, we must first know that the lines with which we make the trial are straight; and we have no test of straightness better than this, that two such lines cannot inclose a space. Since then, experience can neither destroy, add to, nor test our axiomatic knowledge, such knowledge cannot be derived from experience. Since no one act of experience can affect our knowledge, no numbers of acts of experience can make it.

15. To this a reply has been offered, that it is a characteristic property of geometric forms that the ideas of them exactly resemble the sensations; so that these ideas are as fit subjects of experimentation as the realities themselves; and that by such experimentation we learn the truth of the axioms of geometry. I might very reasonably ask those who use this language to explain how a471 particular class of ideas can be said to resemble sensations; how, if they do, we can know it to be so; how we can prove this resemblance to belong to geometrical ideas and sensations; and how it comes to be an especial characteristic of those. But I will put the argument in another way. Experiment can only show what is, not what must be. If experimentation on ideas shows what must be, it is different from what is commonly called experience.

I may add, that not only the mere use of our senses cannot show that the axioms of geometry must be true, but that, without the light of our ideas, it cannot even show that they are true. If we had a segment of a circle a mile long and an inch wide, we should have two lines inclosing a space; but we could not, by seeing or touching any part of either of them, discover that it was a bent line.

16. That mathematical truths are not derived from experience is perhaps still more evident, if greater evidence be possible, in the case of numbers. We assert that 7 and 8 are 15. We find it so, if we try with counters, or in any other way. But we do not, on that account, say that the knowledge is derived from experience. We refer to our conceptions of seven, of eight, and of addition, and as soon as we possess these conceptions distinctly, we see that the sum must be fifteen. We cannot be said to make a trial, for we should not believe the apparent result of the trial if it were different. If any one were to say that the multiplication table is a table of the results of experience, we should know that he could not be able to go along with us in our researches into the foundations of human knowledge; nor, indeed, to pursue with success any speculations on the subject.

17. Attempts have also been made to explain the origin of axiomatic truths by referring them to the association of ideas. But this is one of the cases in which the word association has been applied so widely and loosely, that no sense can be attached to it. Those who have written with any degree of distinctness on the subject, have truly taught, that the habitual association of the ideas leads us to believe a connexion of the things: but

they have never told us that this association gave us the power of forming the ideas. Association may determine belief, but it cannot determine the possibility of our conceptions. The African king did not believe that water could become solid, because he had never seen it in that state. But that accident did not make it impossible to conceive it so, any more than it is impossible for us to conceive frozen quicksilver, or melted diamond, or liquefied air; which we may never have seen, but have no difficulty in conceiving. If there were a tropical philosopher really incapable of conceiving water solidified,472 he must have been brought into that mental condition by abstruse speculations on the necessary relations of solidity and fluidity, not by the association of ideas.

18. To return to the results of the nature of the Fundamental Antithesis. As by assuming universal and indissoluble connexion of ideas with perceptions, of knowledge with experience, as an evidence of derivation, we may assert the former to be derived from the latter, so might we, on the same ground, assert the latter to be derived from the former. We see all forms in space; and we might hence assert all forms to be mere modifications of our idea of space. We see all events happen in time; and we might hence assert all events to be merely limitations and boundary-marks of our idea of time. We conceive all collections of things as two or three, or some other number: it might hence be asserted that we have an original idea of number, which is reflected in external things. In this case, as in the other, we are met at once by the impossibility of this being a complete account of our knowledge. Our ideas of space, of time, of number, however distinctly reflected to us with limitations and modifications, must be reflected, limited and modified by something different from themselves. We must have visible or tangible forms to limit space, perceived events to mark time, distinguishable objects to exemplify number. But still, in forms, and events, and objects, we have a knowledge which they themselves cannot give us. For we know, without attending to them, that whatever they are, they will conform and must conform to the truths of geometry and arithmetic. There is an ideal portion in all our knowledge of the external world; and if we were resolved to reduce all our knowledge to one of its two antithetical elements, we might say that all our knowledge consists in the relation of our ideas. Wherever there is necessary truth, there must be something more than sensation can supply: and the necessary truths of geometry and arithmetic show us that our knowledge of objects in space and time depends upon necessary relations of ideas, whatever other element it may involve.

19. This remark may be carried much further than the domain of geometry and arithmetic. Our knowledge of matter may at first sight appear to be altogether derived from the senses. Yet we cannot derive from the senses our knowledge of a truth which we accept as universally certain;—namely, that we cannot by any process add to or diminish the quantity of matter in the world. This truth neither is nor can be derived from experience; for the experiments which we make to verify it pre-suppose its truth. When the philosopher was asked what was the weight of smoke, he bade473 the inquirer subtract the weight of the ashes from the weight of the fuel. Every one who thinks clearly of the changes which take place in matter, assents to the justice of this reply: and this, not because any one had found by trial that such was the weight of the smoke produced in combustion, but because the weight lost was assumed to have gone into some other form of matter, not to have been destroyed. When men began to use the balance in chemical analysis, they did not prove by trial, but took for granted, as self-evident, that the weight

of the whole must be found in the aggregate weight of the elements. Thus it is involved in the idea of matter that its amount continues unchanged in all changes which take place in its consistence. This is a necessary truth: and thus our knowledge of matter, as collected from chemical experiments, is also a modification of our idea of matter as the material of the world incapable of addition or diminution.

20. A similar remark may be made with regard to the mechanical properties of matter. Our knowledge of these is reduced, in our reasonings, to principles which we call the laws of motion. These laws of motion, as I have endeavoured to show[351], depend upon the idea of Cause, and involve necessary truths, which are necessarily implied in the idea of cause;—namely, that every change of motion must have a cause—that the effect is measured by the cause;—that reaction is equal and opposite to action. These principles are not derived from experience. No one, I suppose, would derive from experience the principle, that every event must have a cause. Every attempt to see the traces of cause in the world assumes this principle. I do not say that these principles are anterior to experience; for I have already, I hope, shown, that neither of the two elements of our knowledge is, or can be, anterior to the other. But the two elements are co-ordinate in the development of the human mind; and the ideal element may be said to be the origin of our knowledge with the more propriety of the two, inasmuch as our knowledge is the relation of ideas. The other element of knowledge, in which sensation is concerned, and which embodies, limits, and defines the necessary truths which express the relations of our ideas, may be properly termed experience; and I have, in the discussion just quoted, endeavoured to show how the principles concerning mechanical causation, which I have just stated, are, by observation and experiment, limited and defined, so that they become the laws of motion.474 And thus we see that such knowledge is derived from ideas, in a sense quite as general and rigorous, to say the least, as that in which it is derived from experience.

21. I will take another example of this; although it is one less familiar, and the consideration of it perhaps a little more difficult and obscure. The objects which we find in the world, for instance, minerals and plants, are of different kinds; and according to their kinds, they are called by various names, by means of which we know what we mean when we speak of them. The discrimination of these kinds of objects, according to their different forms and other properties, is the business of chemistry and botany. And this business of discrimination, and of consequent classification, has been carried on from the first periods of the development of the human mind, by an industrious and comprehensive series of observations and experiments; the only way in which any portion of the task could have been effected. But as the foundation of all this labour, and as a necessary assumption during every part of its progress, there has been in men's minds the principle, that objects are so distinguishable by resemblances and differences, that they may be named, and known by their names. This principle is involved in the idea of a Name; and without it no progress could have been made. The principle may be briefly stated thus:—Intelligible Names of kinds are possible. If we suppose this not to be so, language can no longer exist, nor could the business of human life go on. If instead of having certain definite kinds of minerals, gold, iron, copper and the like, of which the external forms and characters are constantly connected with the same properties and qualities, there were no connexion between the appearance and the properties of the object;—if what seemed externally iron might turn out to resemble lead in its hardness;

and what seemed to be gold during many trials, might at the next trial be found to be like copper; not only all the uses of these minerals would fail, but they would not be distinguishable kinds of things, and the names would be unmeaning. And if this entire uncertainty as to kind and properties prevailed for all objects, the world would no longer be a world to which language was applicable. To man, thus unable to distinguish objects into kinds, and call them by names, all knowledge would be impossible, and all definite apprehension of external objects would fade away into an inconceivable confusion. In the very apprehension of objects as intelligibly sorted, there is involved a principle which springs within us, contemporaneous, in its efficacy, with our first intelligent perception of the kinds of things of which the world475 consists. We assume, as a necessary basis of our knowledge, that things are of definite kinds; and the aim of chemistry, botany, and other sciences is to find marks of these kinds; and along with these, to learn their definitely-distinguished properties. Even here, therefore, where so large a portion of our knowledge comes from experience and observation, we cannot proceed without a necessary truth derived from our ideas, as our fundamental principle of knowledge.

22. What the marks are, which distinguish the constant differences of kinds of things (definite marks, selected from among many unessential appearances), and what their definite properties are, when they are so distinguished, are parts of our knowledge to be learnt from observation, by various processes; for instance, among others, by chemical analysis. We find the differences of bodies, as shown by such analysis, to be of this nature:—that there are various elementary bodies, which, combining in different definite proportions, form kinds of bodies definitely different. But, in arriving at this conclusion, we introduce a new idea, that of Elementary Composition, which is not extracted from the phenomena, but supplied by the mind, and introduced in order to make the phenomena intelligible. That this notion of elementary composition is not supplied by the chemical phenomena of combustion, mixture, &c. as merely an observed fact, we see from this; that men had in ancient times performed many experiments in which elementary composition was concerned, and had not seen the fact. It never was truly seen till modern times; and when seen, it gave a new aspect to the whole body of known facts. This idea of elementary composition, then, is supplied by the mind, in order to make the facts of chemical analysis and synthesis intelligible as analysis and synthesis. And this idea being so supplied, there enters into our knowledge along with it a corresponding necessary principle;—That the elementary composition of a body determines its kind and properties. This is, I say, a principle assumed, as a consequence of the idea of composition, not a result of experience; for when bodies have been divided into their kinds, we take for granted that the analysis of a single specimen may serve to determine the analysis of all bodies of the same kind: and without this assumption, chemical knowledge with regard to the kinds of bodies would not be possible. It has been said that we take only one experiment to determine the composition of any particular kind of body, because we have a thousand experiments to determine that bodies of the same kind have the same composition. But this is not so. Our belief in the principle that bodies of the same kind have the same composition is not established476 by experiments, but is assumed as a necessary consequence of the ideas of Kind and of Composition. If, in our experiments, we found that bodies supposed to be of the same kind had not the same composition, we should not at all doubt of the principle just stated, but conclude at once that the bodies were not of the same kind;—that the marks by which the kinds are distinguished had been wrongly stated. This is what has very frequently happened in the

course of the investigations of chemists and mineralogists. And thus we have it, not as an experiential fact, but as a necessary principle of chemical philosophy, that the Elementary Composition of a body determines its Kind and Properties.

23. How bodies differ in their elementary composition, experiment must teach us, as we have already said, that experiment has taught us. But as we have also said, whatever be the nature of this difference, kinds must be definite, in order that language may be possible: and hence, whatever be the terms in which we are taught by experiment to express the elementary composition of bodies, the result must be conformable to this principle, That the differences of elementary composition are definite. The law to which we are led by experiment is, that the elements of bodies continue in definite proportions according to weight. Experiments add other laws; as for instance, that of multiple proportions in different kinds of bodies composed of the same elements; but of these we do not here speak.

24. We are thus led to see that in our knowledge of mechanics, chemistry, and the like, there are involved certain necessary principles, derived from our ideas, and not from experience. But to this it may be objected, that the parts of our knowledge in which these principles are involved has, in historical fact, all been acquired by experience. The laws of motion, the doctrine of definite proportions, and the like, have all become known by experiment and observation; and so far from being seen as necessary truths, have been discovered by long-continued labours and trials, and through innumerable vicissitudes of confusion, error, and imperfect truth. This is perfectly true: but does not at all disprove what has been said. Perception of external objects and experience, experiment and observation are needed, not only, as we have said, to supply the objective element of all knowledge—to embody, limit, define, and modify our ideas; but this intercourse with objects is also requisite to unfold and fix our ideas themselves. As we have already said, ideas and facts can never be separated. Our ideas cannot be exercised and developed in any other form than in their combination with facts, and therefore the trials, corrections, controversies, by477 which the matter of our knowledge is collected, is also the only way in which the form of it can be rightly fashioned. Experience is requisite to the clearness and distinctness of our ideas, not because they are derived from experience, but because they can only be exercised upon experience. And this consideration sufficiently explains how it is that experiment and observation have been the means, and the only means, by which men have been led to a knowledge of the laws of nature. In reality, however, the necessary principles which flow from our ideas, and which are the basis of such knowledge, have not only been inevitably assumed in the course of such investigations, but have been often expressly promulgated in words by clear-minded philosophers, long before their true interpretation was assigned by experiment. This has happened with regard to such principles as those above mentioned; That every event must have a cause; That reaction is equal and opposite to action; That the quantity of matter in the world cannot be increased or diminished: and there would be no difficulty in finding similar enunciations of the other principles above mentioned;—That the kinds of things have definite differences, and that these differences depend upon their elementary composition. In general, however, it may be allowed, that the necessary principles which are involved in those laws of nature of which we have a knowledge become then only clearly known, when the laws of nature are discovered which thus involve the necessary ideal element.

25. But since this is allowed, it may be further asked, how we are to distinguish between the necessary principle which is derived from our ideas, and the law of nature which is learnt by experience. And to this we reply, that the necessary principle may be known by the condition which we have already mentioned as belonging to such principles: ... that it is impossible distinctly to conceive the contrary. We cannot conceive an event without a cause, except we abandon all distinct idea of cause; we cannot distinctly conceive two straight lines inclosing space; and if we seem to conceive this, it is only because we conceive indistinctly. We cannot conceive 5 and 3 making 7 or 9; if a person were to say that he could conceive this, we should know that he was a person of immature or rude or bewildered ideas, whose conceptions had no distinctness. And thus we may take it as the mark of a necessary truth, that we cannot conceive the contrary distinctly.

26. If it be asked what is the test of distinct conception (since it is upon the distinctness of conception that the matter depends), we may consider what answer we should give to this question if it were asked with regard to the truths of geometry. If we doubted478 whether anyone had these distinct conceptions which enable him to see the necessary nature of geometrical truth, we should inquire if he could understand the axioms as axioms, and could follow, as demonstrative, the reasonings which are founded upon them. If this were so, we should be ready to pronounce that he had distinct ideas of space, in the sense now supposed. And the same answer may be given in any other case. That reasoner has distinct conceptions of mechanical causes who can see the axioms of mechanics as axioms, and can follow the demonstrations derived from them as demonstrations. If it be said that the science, as presented to him, may be erroneously constructed; that the axioms may not be axioms, and therefore the demonstrations may be futile, we still reply, that the same might be said with regard to geometry: and yet that the possibility of this does not lead us to doubt either of the truth or of the necessary nature of the propositions contained in Euclid's Elements. We may add further, that although, no doubt, the authors of elementary books maybe persons of confused minds, who present as axioms what are not axiomatic truths; yet that in general, what is presented as an axiom by a thoughtful man, though it may include some false interpretation or application of our ideas, will also generally include some principle which really is necessarily true, and which would still be involved in the axiom, if it were corrected so as to be true instead of false. And thus we still say, that if in any department of science a man can conceive distinctly at all, there are principles the contrary of which he cannot distinctly conceive, and which are therefore necessary truths.

27. But on this it may be asked, whether truth can thus depend upon the particular state of mind of the person who contemplates it; and whether that can be a necessary truth which is not so to all men. And to this we again reply, by referring to geometry and arithmetic. It is plain that truths may be necessary truths which are not so to all men, when we include men of confused and perplexed intellects; for to such men it is not a necessary truth that two straight lines cannot inclose a space, or that 14 and 17 are 31. It need not be wondered at, therefore, if to such men it does not appear a necessary truth that reaction is equal and opposite to action, or that the quantity of matter in the world cannot be increased or diminished. And this view of knowledge and truth does not make it depend upon the state of mind of the student, any more than geometrical knowledge

and geometrical truth, by the confession of all, depend upon that state. We know that a man cannot have any knowledge of geometry without so much of attention to the matter of the science, and so much of care in the479 management of his own thoughts, as is requisite to keep his ideas distinct and clear. But we do not, on that account, think of maintaining that geometrical truth depends merely upon the state of the student's mind. We conceive that he knows it because it is true, not that it is true because he knows it. We are not surprised that attention and care and repeated thought should be requisite to the clear apprehension of truth. For such care and such repetition are requisite to the distinctness and clearness of our ideas: and yet the relations of these ideas, and their consequences, are not produced by the efforts of attention or repetition which we exert. They are in themselves something which we may discover, but cannot make or change. The idea of space, for instance, which is the basis of geometry, cannot give rise to any doubtful propositions. What is inconsistent with the idea of space cannot be truly obtained from our ideas by any efforts of thought or curiosity; if we blunder into any conclusion inconsistent with the idea of space, our knowledge, so far as this goes, is no knowledge: any more than our observation of the external world would be knowledge, if, from haste or inattention, or imperfection of sense, we were to mistake the object which we see before us.

28. But further: not only has truth this reality, which makes it independent of our mistakes, that it must be what is really consistent with our ideas; but also, a further reality, to which the term is more obviously applicable, arising from the principle already explained, that ideas and perceptions are inseparable. For since, when we contemplate our ideas, they have been frequently embodied and exemplified in objects, and thus have been fixed and modified; and since this compound aspect is that under which we constantly have them before us, and free from which they cannot be exhibited; our attempts to make our ideas clear and distinct will constantly lead us to contemplate them as they are manifested in those external forms in which they are involved. Thus in studying geometrical truth, we shall be led to contemplate it as exhibited in visible and tangible figures;—not as if these could be sources of truth, but as enabling us more readily to compare the aspects which our ideas, applied to the world of objects, may assume. And thus we have an additional indication of the reality of geometrical truth, in the necessary possibility of its being capable of being exhibited in a visible or tangible form. And yet even this test by no means supersedes the necessity of distinct ideas, in order to a knowledge of geometrical truth. For in the case of the duplication of the cube by Hobbes, mentioned above, the diagram which he drew made two points appear to coincide, which did not really,480 and by the nature of our idea of space, coincide; and thus confirmed him in his error.

Thus the inseparable nature of the Fundamental Antithesis of Ideas and Things gives reality to our knowledge, and makes objective reality a corrective of our subjective imperfections in the pursuit of knowledge. But this objective exhibition of knowledge can by no means supersede a complete development of the subjective condition, namely, distinctness of ideas. And that there is a subjective condition, by no means makes knowledge altogether subjective, and thus deprives it of reality; because, as we have said, the subjective and the objective elements are inseparably bound together in the fundamental antithesis.

29. It would be easy to apply these remarks to other cases, for instance, to the case of the principle we have just mentioned, that the differences of elementary composition of different kinds of bodies must be definite. We have stated that this principle is necessarily true;—that the contrary proposition cannot be distinctly conceived. But by whom? Evidently, according to the preceding reasoning, by a person who distinctly conceives Kinds, as marked by intelligible names, and Composition, as determining the kinds of bodies. Persons new to chemical and classificatory science may not possess these ideas distinctly; or rather, cannot possess them distinctly; and therefore cannot apprehend the impossibility of conceiving the opposite of the above principle; just as the schoolboy cannot apprehend the impossibility of the numbers in his multiplication table being other than they are. But this inaptitude to conceive, in either case, does not alter the necessary character of the truth: although, in one case, the truth is obvious to all except schoolboys and the like, and the other is probably not clear to any except those who have attentively studied the philosophy of elementary compositions. At the same time, this difference of apprehension of the truth in different persons does not make the truth doubtful or dependent upon personal qualifications; for in proportion as persons attain to distinct ideas, they will see the truth; and cannot, with such ideas, see anything as truth which is not truth. When the relations of elements in a compound become as familiar to a person as the relations of factors in a multiplication table, he will then see what are the necessary axioms of chemistry, as he now sees the necessary axioms of arithmetic.

30. There is also one other remark which I will here make. In the progress of science, both the elements of our knowledge are constantly expanded and augmented. By the exercise of observation and experiment, we have a perpetual accumulation of facts, the481 materials of knowledge, the objective element. By thought and discussion, we have a perpetual development of man's ideas going on: theories are framed, the materials of knowledge are shaped into form; the subjective element is evolved; and by the necessary coincidence of the objective and subjective elements, the matter and the form, the theory and the facts, each of these processes furthers and corrects the other: each element moulds and unfolds the other. Now it follows, from this constant development of the ideal portion of our knowledge, that we shall constantly be brought in view of new Necessary Principles, the expression of the conditions belonging to the Ideas which enter into our expanding knowledge. These principles, at first dimly seen and hesitatingly asserted, at last become clearly and plainly self-evident. Such is the case with the principles which are the basis of the laws of motion. Such may soon be the case with the principles which are the basis of the philosophy of chemistry. Such may hereafter be the case with the principles which are to be the basis of the philosophy of the connected and related polarities of chemistry, electricity, galvanism, magnetism. That knowledge is possible in these cases, we know; that our knowledge may be reduced to principles, gradually more simple, we also know; that we have reached the last stage of simplicity of our principles, few cultivators of the subject will be disposed to maintain; and that the additional steps which lead towards very simple and general principles will also lead to principles which recommend themselves by a kind of axiomatic character, those who judge from the analogy of the past history of science will hardly doubt. That the principles thus axiomatic in their form, do also express some relation of our ideas, of which experiment and observation have given a true and real interpretation, is the doctrine which I have here attempted to establish and illustrate in the most clear and undoubted of the existing sciences; and the evidence of this doctrine in those cases seems to be unexceptionable,

and to leave no room to doubt that such is the universal type of the progress of science. Such a doctrine, as we have now seen, is closely connected with the views here presented of the nature of the Fundamental Antithesis of Philosophy, which I have endeavoured to illustrate.

482

Appendix F.
REMARKS ON A REVIEW OF THE PHILOSOPHY OF THE INDUCTIVE SCIENCES.

Trinity Lodge, April 11th, 1844.

My Dear Herschel,

Being about to send you a copy of a paper on a philosophical question just printed in the Transactions of our Cambridge Society, I am tempted to add, as a private communication, a few Remarks on another aspect of the same question. These Remarks I think I may properly address to you. They will refer to an Article in the Quarterly Review for June, 1841, respecting my History and Philosophy of the Inductive Sciences; and without assigning any other reason, I may say that the interest I know you to take in speculations on such subjects makes me confident that you will give a reasonable attention to what I may have to say on the subject of that Article. With the Reviewal itself, I am so far from having any quarrel, that when it appeared I received it as affording all that I hoped from Public Criticism. The degree and the kind of admiration bestowed upon my works by a writer so familiar with science, so comprehensive in his views, and so equitable in his decisions, as the Reviewer manifestly was, I accepted as giving my work a stamp of acknowledged value which few other hands could have bestowed.

You may perhaps recollect, however, that the Reviewer dissented altogether from some of the general views which I had maintained, and especially from a general view which is also, in the main, that presented in the accompanying Memoir, namely, that, besides Facts, Ideas are an indispensable source of our knowledge; that Ideas are the ground of necessary truth; that the Idea of Space, in particular, is the ground of the necessary truths of geometry. This question, and especially as limited to the last form, will be the subject of my Remarks in the first place; and I wish to consider the Reviewer's objections with the respect which their subtlety and depth of thought well deserve.

483

The Reviewer makes objections to the account which I have given of the source whence geometrical truth derives its characters of being necessary and universal; but he is not one of those metaphysicians who deny those characters to the truths of geometry. He allows in the most ample manner that the truths of geometry are necessary. The question between us therefore is from what this character is derived. The Reviewer prefers, indeed, to have it considered that the question is not concerning the necessity, but, as he says, the universality of these truths; or rather, the nature and grounds of our conviction of their universality. He might have said, with equal justice, the nature and grounds of our conviction of their necessity. For his objection to the term necessity in this case—"that all the propositions about realities are necessarily true, since every reality must be consistent with itself," (p. 206)—does not apply to our conviction of necessity, since we may not be able to see what are the properties of real things; and therefore may have no conviction of their necessity. It may be a necessary property of salt to be soluble, but we see no such necessity; and therefore the assertion of such a property is not one of the necessary truths with which we are here concerned. But to turn back to the necessary or universal truths of geometry, and the ground of those attributes: The main difference between the Author and the Reviewer is brought into view, when the Reviewer discusses the general argument which I had used, in order to show that truths which we see to be necessary and universal cannot be derived from experience. The argument is this,—

"Experience must always consist of a limited number of observations; and however numerous these may be, they can show nothing with regard to the infinite number of cases in which the experiment has not been made.... Truths can only be known to be general, not universal, if they depend upon experience alone. Experience cannot bestow that universality which she herself cannot have; nor that necessity of which she has no comprehension." (Phil. i. pp. 60, 61.)

Here is that which must be considered as the cardinal argument on this subject. It is therefore important to attend to the answer which the Reviewer makes to it. He says,—

"We conceive that a full answer to this argument is afforded by the nature of the inductive propensity,—by the irresistible impulse of the mind to generalize ad infinitum, when nothing in the nature of limitation or opposition offers itself to the imagination; and by our involuntary application of the law of continuity to fill up, by the same ideal substance of truth, every interval which uncontra484dicted experience may have left blank in our inductive conclusion." (p. 207.)

Now here we have two rival explanations of the same thing,—the conviction of the universality of geometrical truths. The one explanation is, that this universality is imposed upon such truths by their involving a certain element, derived from the universal mode of activity of the mind when apprehending such truths, which element I have termed an Idea. The other explanation is, that this universality arises from the inductive propensity—from the irresistible impulse to generalize ad infinitum—from the involuntary application of the law of continuity—from the filling up all intervals with the same ideal substance of truth.

With regard to these two explanations, I may observe, that so far as they are thus stated they do not necessarily differ. They both agree in expressing this; that the ground of the universality of geometrical truths is a certain law of the mind's activity, which determines its procedure when it is concerned in apprehending the external world. One explanation says, that we impress upon the external world the relations of our ideas, and thus believe more than we see,—the other says, that we have an irresistible impulse to introduce into our conviction a relation between what we do observe and what we do not, namely, to generalize ad infinitum from what we do see. One explanation says, that we perceive all external objects as included in absolute ideal space,—the other, that we fill up the intervals of the objects which we perceive with the same ideal substance of truth.

Both sets of expressions may perhaps be admissible; and if admitted, may be understood as expressing the same opinions, or opinions which have much in common. The Author's expressions have the advantage, which ought to belong to them, as the expressions employed in a systematic work, of being fixed expressions, technical phrases, intentionally selected, uniformly and steadily employed whenever the occasion recurs. The Reviewer's expressions are more lively and figurative, and such as well become an occasional composition; but hardly such as could be systematically applied to the subject in a regular treatise. We could not, as a standard and technical phrase, talk of filling up the intervals of observation with the same ideal substance of truth; and the inevitable impulse to generalize would hardly sufficiently express that we generalize according to a certain idea, namely, the idea of space. Perhaps that which is suggested to us as the common import of the two sets of expressions may be conveyed by some other phrase, in a manner free from the objections which lie against both the Author's and the Critic's terms. Perhaps485 the mental idea governing our experience, and the irresistible impulse to generalize our observation, may both be superseded by our speaking of a law of the mind's activity, which is really implied in both. There operates, in observing the external world, a law of the mind's activity, by which it connects its observations; and this law of the mind's activity may be spoken of either as the idea of space, or as the irresistible impulse to generalize the relations of space which it observes. And this expression—the laws of the mind's activity—thus opposed to that merely passive function by which the mind receives the impressions of sense, may be applied to other ideas as well as to the idea of space, and to the impulse to generalize in other truths as well as those of geometry.

So far, it would seem, that the Author and the Critic may be brought into much nearer agreement than at first seemed likely, with regard to the grounds of the necessity and universality in our knowledge. But even if we adopt this conciliatory suggestion, and speak of the necessity and universality of certain truths as arising from the laws of the mind's activity, we cannot, without producing great confusion, allow ourselves to say, as the Critic says, that these truths are thus derived from experience, or from observation. It will, I say, be found fatal to all philosophical precision of thought and language, to say that the fundamental truths of geometry, the axioms, with the conviction of their necessary truth, are derived from experience. Let us take any axiomatic truth of geometry, and ask ourselves if this is not so.

It is, for example, an axiom in geometry that if a straight line cut one of two parallel straight lines, it must cut the other also. Is this truth derived or derivable from observation of actual parallel lines, and a line cutting them, exhibited to our senses? Let those who say that we do acquire this truth by observation, imagine to themselves the mode in which the observation must be made. We have before us two parallel straight lines, and we see that a straight line which cuts the one cuts the other also. We see this again in another case, it may be the angles and the distances being different, and in a third, and in a fourth; and so on; and generalizing, we are irresistibly led to believe the assertion to be universally true. But can any one really imagine this to be the mode in which we arrive at this truth? "We see," says this explanation, "two parallel straight lines, cut by a third." But how do we know that the observed lines are parallel? If we apply any test of parallelism, we must assume some property of parallels, and thus involve some axiom on the subject, which we have no more right to assume than the one now under consideration. We should thus destroy our486 explanation as an account of the mode of

268

arriving at independent geometrical axioms. But probably those who would give such an explanation would not do this. They would not suppose that in observing this property of parallels we try by measurement whether the lines are parallel. They would say, I conceive, that we suppose lines to be parallel, and that then we see that the straight line which cuts the one must cut the other. That when we make this supposition, we are persuaded of the truth of the conclusion, is certain. But what I have to remark is, that this being so, the conclusion is the result, not of observation, but of the hypothesis. The geometrical truth here spoken of, after this admission, no longer flows from experience, but from supposition. It is not that we ascertain the lines to be parallel, and then find that they have this property: but we suppose the lines to be parallel, and therefore they have this property. This is not a truth of experience.

This, it may be said, is so evident that it cannot have been overlooked by a very acute reasoner, such as you describe your Critic to be. What, it may be asked, is the answer which he gives to so palpable an objection as this? How does he understand his assertion that we learn the truth of geometrical axioms from experience (p. 208), so as to make it tenable on his own principles? What account does he give of the origin of such axioms which makes them in any sense to be derived from experience?

In justice to the Reviewer's fairness (which is unimpeachable throughout his argumentation) it must be stated that he does give an account in which he professes to show how this is done. And the main step of his explanation consists in introducing the conception of direction, and unity of direction. He says (p. 208), "The unity of direction, or that we cannot march from a given point by more than one path direct to the same object, is a matter of practical experience, long before it can by possibility become matter of abstract thought." We might ask here, as in the former case, how this can be a matter of experience, except we have some independent test of directness? and we might demand to know what this test is. Or do we not rather, here as in the other case, suppose the directness of the path; and is not the singleness of the direct path a consequence, not of its observed form, but of its hypothetical directness; and thus by no means a result of experience? But we may put our remark upon this deduction of the geometrical axiom in another form. We generalize, it is said, the observations which we have made ever since we were born. But this term "generalize" is far too vague to pass for an explanation, without being itself explained. We are impelled to believe that to be true in general487 which we see to be true in particular. But how do we see any truth? How do we pick out any proposition with respect to a diagram which we see before us? We see in particular, and state in general, some truth respecting straight lines, or parallel lines, or concerning direction. But where do we find the conception of straightness, or parallelism, or direction? These conceptions are not upon the surface of things. The child does not, from his birth, see straightness and parallelism so as to know that he sees them. How then does his experience bear upon a proposition in which these conceptions are involved? It is said that it is a matter of experience long before it is a matter of abstract thought. But how can there be any experience by which we learn these properties of a straight line, till our thoughts are at least so abstract as to conceive what straightness is? If it be said that this conception grows with our experience, and is gradually unfolded with our unfolding materials of knowledge, so as to give import and significance to them: I need make no objection to such a statement, except this—that this power of unfolding out of the mind conceptions which give meaning to our experience, is something in addition to the mere

269

employment of our senses upon the external world. It is what I have called the ideal part of our knowledge. It implies, not only an impulse to generalize from experience, but also an impulse to form conceptions by which generalization is possible. It requires, not only that nothing should oppose the tendency, but that the direction in which the tendency is to operate should be determined by the laws of the mind's activity; by an internal, not by an external agency.

One main ground on which the Reviewer is disposed to quarrel with and reject several of the expressions used in the Philosophy;—such as that space is an idea, a form of our perception, and the like,—is this; that such expressions appear to deprive the external world of its reality; to make it, or at least most of its properties, a creation of the observing mind. He quotes the following argument which is urged in the Philosophy, in order to prove that space is not a notion obtained from experience: "Experience gives us information concerning things without us, but our apprehending them as without us takes for granted their existence in space. Experience acquaints us with the form, position, magnitude, &c. of particular objects, but that they have form, position, magnitude, pre-supposes that they are in space." From this statement he altogether dissents. No, says he, "the reason why we apprehend things as without us is that they are without us. We take for granted that they exist in space, because they do so exist, and because such their existence is488 a matter of direct perception, which can neither be explained in words nor contravened in imagination: because, in short, space is a reality, and not a mere matter of convention or imagination."

Now, if by calling space an idea, we suggest any doubt of its reality and of the reality of the external world, we certainly run the risk of misleading our readers; for the external world is real if anything be real: the bodies which exist in space are things, if things are anywhere to be found. That bodies do exist in space, and that that is the reason why we apprehend them as existing in space, I readily grant. But I conceive that the term Idea ought not to suggest any such doubt of the reality of the knowledge in which it is involved. Ideas are always, in our knowledge, conjoined with facts. Our real knowledge is knowledge, because it involves ideas, real, because it involves facts. We apprehend things as existing in space because they do so exist: and our idea of space enables us so to observe them, and so to conceive them.

But we want, further, a reason why, apprehending them as they are, we also apprehend, that in certain relations they could not be otherwise (that two straight linear objects could not inclose a space, for instance). This circumstance is no way accounted for by saying that we apprehend them as they are; and is, I presume to say, inexplicable, except by supposing that it arises from some property of the observing mind:—an Idea, as I have termed it,—an irresistible Impulse to generalize, as the Reviewer expresses it. Or, as I have suggested, we may adopt a third phrase, a Law of the mind's activity: and in order that no question may remain, whether we ascribe reality to the objects and relations which we observe, we may describe it as "a Law of the mind's activity in apprehending what is." And thus the real existence of the object, and the ideal element which our apprehension of it introduces, would both be clearly asserted.

I am ready to use expressions which recognize the reality of space and other external things more emphatically than those expressions which I have employed in the

Philosophy, if expressions can be found which, while they do this, enable us to explain the possibility of knowledge, and to analyze the structure of truth. It is, indeed, extremely difficult to find, in speaking of this subject, expressions which are satisfactory. The reality of the objects which we perceive is a profound, apparently an insoluble problem[352]. We cannot but suppose that existence is something different from our know489ledge of existence:—that which exists, does not exist merely in our knowing that it does:—truth is truth whether we know it or not. Yet how can we conceive truth, otherwise than as something known? How can we conceive things as existing, without conceiving them as objects of perception? Ideas and Things are constantly opposed, yet necessarily co-existent. How they are thus opposite and yet identical, is the ultimate problem of all philosophy. The successive phases of philosophy have consisted in separating and again uniting these two opposite elements; in dwelling sometimes upon the one and sometimes upon the other, as the principal or original or only element; and then in discovering that such an account of the state of the case was insufficient. Knowledge requires ideas. Reality requires things. Ideas and things co-exist. Truth is, and is known. But the complete explanation of these points appears to be beyond our reach. At least it is not necessary for the purposes of our philosophy. The separation of ideas and sensations in order to discover the conditions of knowledge is our main task. How ideas and sensations are united so as to form things, does not so immediately concern us.

I have stated that we may, without giving up any material portion of the Philosophy of Science to which I have been led, express the conclusions in other phraseology; and that instead of saying that all our knowledge involves certain Fundamental Ideas, the sources from which all universal truth is derived, we may say that there are certain Laws of Mental Activity according to which alone all the real relations of things are apprehended. If this alteration in the phraseology will make the doctrines more generally intelligible or acceptable, there is no reason why it should not be adopted. But I may remark, that a main purpose of the Philosophy was not merely to prove that there are such Fundamental Ideas or Laws of mental activity, but to enumerate those of them which are involved in the existing sciences; and to state the fundamental truths to which the fundamental ideas lead. This was the task which was attempted; and if this have been executed with any tolerable success, it may perhaps be received as a contribution to the philosophy of science, of which the value is not small, in whatever terms it be expressed. And this enumeration of fundamental ideas, and of truths derived from them, must have something to correspond to it, in any other mode of expressing that view of the nature of knowledge which we are led to adopt. If instead of Fundamental Ideas, we speak of Impulses of generalization, or of Laws of mental activity, we must still distinguish such Impulses, or such Laws, according to the distinctions of ideas to which the490 survey of science led us. We shall thus have a series of groups of Laws, or of classes of generalizing Impulses, corresponding to the series of Fundamental Ideas already given. If we employ the language of the Reviewer, we shall have one generalizing Impulse which suggests relations of Space; another which directs us to properties of Numbers; another which deals with Time; another with Cause: another which groups objects according to Likeness; another which suggests a purpose as a necessary relation among them; to which may be added, even while we confine ourselves to the physical sciences, several others, as may be seen in the Philosophy. Now when the fundamental conditions and elements of truth are thus arranged into groups, it is not a matter of so much consequence to decide whether each group shall be said to be bound together by an idea or by an impulse of generalization; as it is to see that, if this happen in virtue of ideas, here are so many distinct ideas which enter into the structure of science, and give universality to its matter; and again, if this happen in virtue of an irresistible impulse of generalization in each case, we have so many different kinds of impulses of generalization. The main purpose in the Philosophy was to analyze scientific truth into its conditions and elements; and I did not content myself with saying that those elements are Sensations and Ideas; the Ideas being that element which makes universal knowledge conceivable and possible. I went further: I enumerated the Ideas which thus enter into science. I showed that in the sciences which I passed in review, the most acute and profound inquirers had taken for granted that certain truths in each science are of universal and necessary validity, and I endeavoured to select the idea in which this universality and necessity resided, and to separate it from all other ideas involved in other sciences. If therefore it be thought better to say that those principles in each science upon which, as upon the axioms in geometry, the universality and necessity of scientific truth depends, are arrived at, not by ideas, but by an irresistible impulse of generalization, those who employ such phraseology, if they make a classification of such impulses corresponding to my classification of ideas, will still adopt the greater part of my philosophy, altering only the phraseology. Or if, as I suggested, instead of "Fundamental Ideas," we use the phrase "Laws of Mental Activity," then our primary intellectual Code—the Constitution of our minds, as it may be termed—will consist of a Body of Laws of which the Titles correspond with the Fundamental Ideas of the Philosophy.

My object was, from the writings of the most sagacious and profound philosophers who have laboured on each science, to extract491 such a code, such a constitution. If I have in any degree succeeded in this, the result must have a reality and a value independently of all forms of expression. Still I do not think that any language can ever serve for such legislation, in which the two elements of truth are not distinguished. Even if we adopt the phraseology which I have just employed, we shall have to recollect that Law and Fact must be kept distinct, and that the Constitution has its Principles as well as its History.

But I will not longer detain you by seeking other modes of expressing the Fundamental Antithesis to which the accompanying Memoir refers. The Remarks which I here send you were written three years ago, on the appearance of the Review which I have quoted. If I succeed in obtaining for them a few minutes' attention from you and a few other friends, I shall be glad that they have been preserved.

I am, my dear Herschel,

always truly yours,

W. WHEWELL.

P.S. I have abstained from sending you a large portion of my Remarks as originally written. I had gone on to show that, in my Philosophy, I had not only enumerated and analyzed a great number of different Fundamental Ideas which belong to the different existing sciences, but that I had also shown in what manner these ideas enter into their respective sciences; namely, by the statement or use of Axioms, which involve the ideas, and which form the basis of each science when systematically exhibited. A number of these Axioms belonging to most of the physical sciences, are stated in the Philosophy. I might have added also that I have attempted to classify the historical steps by which such Axioms are brought into view and applied. But it is not necessary to dwell upon these points, in order to illustrate the difference and the agreement between the Reviewer and me.

Sir John F. W. Herschel, Bart. &c.

492

Appendix G.
OF THE TRANSFORMATION OF HYPOTHESES IN THE HISTORY OF SCIENCE.

(Cam. Phil. Soc. May 19, 1851.)

1. THE history of science suggests the reflection that it is very difficult for the same person at the same time to do justice to two conflicting theories. Take for example the Cartesian hypothesis of vortices and the Newtonian doctrine of universal gravitation. The adherents of the earlier opinion resisted the evidence of the Newtonian theory with a degree of obstinacy and captiousness which now appears to us quite marvellous: while on the other hand, since the complete triumph of the Newtonians, they have been unwilling to allow any merit at all to the doctrine of vortices. It cannot but seem strange, to a calm observer of such changes, that in a matter which depends upon mathematical proofs, the whole body of the mathematical world should pass over, as in this and similar cases they seem to have done, from an opinion confidently held, to its opposite. No doubt this must be, in part, ascribed to the lasting effects of education and early prejudice. The old opinion passes away with the old generation: the new theory grows to its full vigour when its congenital disciples grow to be masters. John Bernoulli continues a Cartesian to the last; Daniel, his son, is a Newtonian from the first. Newton's doctrines are adopted at once in England, for they are the solution of a problem at which his contemporaries have been labouring for years. They find no adherents in France, where Descartes is supposed to have already explained the constitution of the world; and Fontenelle, the secretary of the Academy of Sciences at Paris, dies a Cartesian seventy years after the publication of Newton's Principia. This is, no doubt, a part of the explanation of the pertinacity with which opinions are held, both before and after a scientific revolution: but this is not the whole, nor perhaps the most instructive aspect of the subject. There is another feature in the change,493 which explains, in some degree, how it is possible that, in subjects, mainly at least mathematical, and therefore claiming demonstrative evidence, mathematicians should hold different and even opposite opinions. And the object of the present paper is to point out this feature in the successions of theories, and to illustrate it by some prominent examples drawn from the history of science.

2. The feature to which I refer is this; that when a prevalent theory is found to be untenable, and consequently, is succeeded by a different, or even by an opposite one, the change is not made suddenly, or completed at once, at least in the minds of the most tenacious adherents of the earlier doctrine; but is effected by a transformation, or series of

273

transformations, of the earlier hypothesis, by means of which it is gradually brought nearer and nearer to the second; and thus, the defenders of the ancient doctrine are able to go on as if still asserting their first opinions, and to continue to press their points of advantage, if they have any, against the new theory. They borrow, or imitate, and in some way accommodate to their original hypothesis, the new explanations which the new theory gives, of the observed facts; and thus they maintain a sort of verbal consistency; till the original hypothesis becomes inextricably confused, or breaks down under the weight of the auxiliary hypotheses thus fastened upon it, in order to make it consistent with the facts.

This often-occurring course of events might be illustrated from the history of the astronomical theory of epicycles and eccentrics, as is well known. But my present purpose is to give one or two brief illustrations of a somewhat similar tendency from other parts of scientific history; and in the first place, from that part which has already been referred to, the battle of the Cartesian and Newtonian systems.

3. The part of the Cartesian system of vortices which is most familiarly known to general readers is the explanation of the motions of the planets by supposing them carried round the sun by a kind of whirlpool of fluid matter in which they are immersed: and the explanation of the motions of the satellites round their primaries by similar subordinate whirlpools, turning round the primary, and carried, along with it, by the primary vortex. But it should be borne in mind that a part of the Cartesian hypothesis which was considered quite as important as the cosmical explanation, was the explanation which it was held to afford of terrestrial gravity. Terrestrial gravity was asserted to arise from the motion of the vortex of subtle matter which revolved round the earth's axis and filled the surrounding space. It was maintained that by the rotation of494 such a vortex, the particles of the subtle matter would exert a centrifugal force, and by virtue of that force, tend to recede from the center: and it was held that all bodies which were near the earth, and therefore immersed in the vortex, would be pressed towards the center by the effort of the subtle matter to recede from the center[353].

These two assumed effects of the Cartesian vortices—to carry bodies in their stream, as straws are carried round by a whirlpool, and to press bodies to the center by the centrifugal effort of the whirling matter—must be considered separately, because they were modified separately, as the progress of discussion drove the Cartesians from point to point. The former effect indeed, the dragging force of the vortex, as we may call it, would not bear working out on mechanical principles at all; for as soon as the law of motion was acknowledged (which Descartes himself was one of the loudest in proclaiming), that a body in motion keeps all the motion which it has, and receives in addition all that is impressed upon it; as soon, in short, as philosophers rejected the notion of an inertness in matter which constantly retards its movements,—it was plain that a planet perpetually dragged onwards in its orbit by a fluid moving quicker than itself, must be perpetually accelerated; and therefore could not follow those constantly-recurring cycles of quicker and slower motion which the planets exhibit to us.

The Cartesian mathematicians, then, left untouched the calculation of the progressive motion of the planets; and, clinging to the assumption that a vortex would produce a tendency of bodies to the center, made various successive efforts to construct

274

their vortices in such a manner that the centripetal forces produced by them should coincide with those which the phenomena required, and therefore of course, in the end, with those which the Newtonian theory asserted.

In truth, the Cartesian vortex was a bad piece of machinery for producing a central force: from the first, objections were made to the sufficiency of its mechanism, and most of these objections were very unsatisfactorily answered, even granting the additional machinery which its defenders demanded. One formidable objection was soon started, and continued to the last to be the torment of the Cartesians. If terrestrial gravity, it was urged, arise from the centrifugal force of a vortex which revolves about the earth's axis, terrestrial gravity ought to act in planes perpendicular to the495 earth's axis, instead of tending to the earth's center. This objection was taken by James Bernoulli[354], and by Huyghens[355] not long after the publication of Descartes's Principia. Huyghens (who adopted the theory of vortices with modifications of his own) supposes that there are particles of the fluid matter which move about the earth in every possible direction, within the spherical space which includes terrestrial objects; and that the greater part of these motions being in spherical surfaces concentric with the earth, produces a tendency towards the earth's center.

This was a procedure tolerably arbitrary, but it was the best which could be done. Saurin, a little later[356], gave nearly the same solution of this difficulty. The solution, identifying a vortex of some kind with a central force, made the hypothesis of vortices applicable wherever central forces existed; but then, in return, it deprived the image of a vortex of all that clearness and simplicity which had been its first great recommendation.

But still there remained difficulties not less formidable. According to this explanation of gravity, since the tendency of bodies to the earth's center arose from the superior centrifugal force of the whirling matter which pushed them inward as water pushes a light body upward, bodies ought to tend more strongly to the center in proportion as they are less dense. The rarest bodies should be the heaviest; contrary to what we find.

Descartes's original solution of this difficulty has a certain degree of ingenuity. According to him (Princip. IV. 23) a terrestrial body consists of particles of the third element, and the more it has of such particles, the more it excludes the parts of the celestial matter, from the revolution of which matter gravity arises; and therefore the denser is the terrestrial body, and the heavier it will be.

But though this might satisfy him, it could not satisfy the mathematicians who followed him, and tried to reduce his system to calculation on mechanical principles. For how could they do this, if the celestial matter, by the operation of which the phenomena of force and motion were produced, was so entirely different from ordinary matter, which alone had supplied men with experimental496 illustrations of mechanical principles? In order that the celestial matter, by its whirling, might produce the gravity of heavy bodies, it was mechanically necessary that it must be very dense; and dense in the ordinary sense of the term; for it was by regarding density in the ordinary sense of the term that the mechanical necessity had been established.

The Cartesians tried to escape this result (Huyghens, Pesanteur, p. 161, and John Bernoulli, Nouvelles Pensées, Art. 31) by saying that there were two meanings of density and rarity; that some fluids might be rare by having their particles far asunder, others, by having their particles very small though in contact. But it is difficult to think that they could, as persons well acquainted with mechanical principles, satisfy themselves with this distinction; for they could hardly fail to see that the mechanical effect of any portion of fluid depends upon the total mass moved, not on the size of its particles.

Attempts made to exemplify the vortices experimentally only showed more clearly the force of this difficulty. Huyghens had found that certain bodies immersed in a whirling fluid tended to the center of the vortex. But when Saulmon[357] a little later made similar experiments, he had the mortification of finding that the heaviest bodies had the greatest tendency to recede from the axis of the vortex. "The result is," as the Secretary of the Academy (Fontenelle) says, "exactly the opposite of what we could have wished, for the [Cartesian] system of gravity: but we are not to despair; sometimes in such researches disappointment leads to ultimate success."

But, passing by this difficulty, and assuming that in some way or other a centripetal force arises from the centrifugal force of the vortex, the Cartesian mathematicians were naturally led to calculate the circumstances of the vortex on mechanical principles; especially Huyghens, who had successfully studied the subject of centrifugal force. Accordingly, in his little treatise on the Cause of Gravitation (p. 143), he calculates the velocity of the fluid matter of the vortex, and finds that, at a point in the equator, it is 17 times the velocity of the earth's rotation.

It may naturally be asked, how it comes to pass that a stream of fluid, dense enough to produce the gravity of bodies by its centrifugal force, moving with a velocity 17 times that of the earth (and therefore moving round the earth in 85 minutes), does not sweep497 all terrestrial objects before it. But to this Huyghens had already replied (p. 137), that there are particles of the fluid moving in all directions, and therefore that they neutralize each other's action, so far as lateral motion is concerned.

And thus, as early as this treatise of Huyghens, that is, in three years from the publication of Newton's Principia, a vortex is made to mean nothing more than some machinery or other for producing a central force. And this is so much the case, that Huyghens commends (p. 165), as confirming his own calculation of the velocity of his vortex, Newton's proof that at the Moon's orbit the centripetal force is equal to the centrifugal; and that thus, this force is less than the centripetal force at the earth's surface in the inverse proportion of the squares of the distances.

John Bernoulli, in the same manner, but with far less clearness and less candour, has treated the hypothesis of vortices as being principally a hypothetical cause of central force. He had repeated occasions given him of propounding his inventions for propping up the Cartesian doctrine, by the subjects proposed for prizes by the Paris Academy of Sciences; in which competition Cartesian speculations were favourably received. Thus the subject of the Prize Essays for 1730 was, the explanation of the Elliptical Form of the planetary orbits and of the Motion of their Aphelia, and the prize was assigned to John Bernoulli, who gave the explanation on Cartesian principles. He explains the elliptical figure, not as

Descartes himself had done, by supposing the vortex which carries the planet round the sun to be itself squeezed into an elliptical form by the pressure of contiguous vortices; but he supposes the planet, while it is carried round by the vortex, to have a limited oscillatory motion to and from the center, produced by its being originally, not at the distance at which it would float in equilibrium in the vortex, but above or below that point. On this supposition, the planet would oscillate to and from the center, Bernoulli says, like the mercury when deranged in a barometer: and it is evident that such an oscillation, combined with a motion round the center, might produce an oval curve, either with a fixed or with a moveable aphelion. All this however merely amounts to a possibility that the oval may be an ellipse, not to a proof that it will be so; nor does Bernoulli advance further.

It was necessary that the vortices should be adjusted in such a manner as to account for Kepler's laws; and this was to be done by making the velocity of each stratum of the vortex depend in a suitable manner on its radius. The Abbé de Molières attempted this on the supposition of elliptical vortices, but could not reconcile498 Kepler's first two laws, of equal elliptical areas in equal times, with his third law, that the squares of the periodic times are as the cubes of the mean distances[358]. Bernoulli, with his circular vortices, could accommodate the velocities at different distances so that they should explain Kepler's laws. He pretended to prove that Newton's investigations respecting vortices (in the ninth Section of the Second Book of the Principia) were mechanically erroneous; and in truth, it must be allowed that, besides several arbitrary assumptions, there are some errors of reasoning in them. But for the most part, the more enlightened Cartesians were content to accept Newton's account of the motions and forces of the solar system as part of their scheme; and to say only that the hypothesis of vortices explained the origin of the Newtonian forces; and that thus theirs was a philosophy of a higher kind. Thus it is asserted (Mém. Acad. 1734), that M. de Molières retains the beautiful theory of Newton entire, only he renders it in a sort less Newtonian, by disentangling it from attraction, and transferring it from a vacuum into a plenum. This plenum, though not its native region, frees it from the need of attraction, which is all the better for it. These points were the main charms of the Cartesian doctrine in the eyes of its followers;—the getting rid of attractions, which were represented as a revival of the Aristotelian "occult qualities," "substantial forms," or whatever else was the most disparaging way of describing the bad philosophy of the dark ages[359];—and the providing some material intermedium, by means of which a body may affect another at a distance; and thus avoid the reproach urged against the Newtonians, that they made a body act where it was not. And we are the less called upon to deny that this last feature in the Newtonian theory was a difficulty, inasmuch as Newton himself was never499 unwilling to allow that gravity might be merely an effect produced by some ulterior cause.

With such admissions on the two sides, it is plain that the Newtonian and Cartesian systems would coincide, if the hypothesis of vortices could be modified in such a way as to produce the force of gravitation. All attempts to do this, however, failed: and even John Bernoulli, the most obstinate of the mathematical champions of the vortices, was obliged to give them up. In his Prize Essay for 1734, (on the Inclinations of the Planetary Orbits[360],) he says (Art. VIII.), "The gravitation of the Planets towards the center of the Sun and the weight of bodies towards the center of the earth has not, for its cause, either the attraction of M. Newton, or the centrifugal force of the matter of the vortex according to M. Descartes;" and he then goes on to assert that these forces are produced by a perpetual torrent of matter tending to the center on all sides, and carrying all bodies with it. Such a hypothesis is very difficult to refute. It has been taken up in more modern times by Le Sage[361], with some modifications; and may be made to account for the principal facts of the universal gravitation of matter. The great difficulty in the way of such a hypothesis is, the overwhelming thought of the whole universe filled with torrents of an invisible but material and tangible substance, rushing in every direction in infinitely prolonged straight lines and with immense velocity. Whence can such matter come, and whither can it go? Where can be its perpetual and infinitely distant fountain, and where the ocean into which it pours itself when its infinite course is ended? A revolving whirlpool is easily conceived and easily supplied; but the central torrent of Bernoulli, the infinite streams of particles of Le Sage, are an explanation far more inconceivable than the thing explained.

But however the hypothesis of vortices, or some hypothesis substituted for it, was adjusted to explain the facts of attraction to a center, this was really nearly all that was meant by a vortex500 or a "tourbillon," when the system was applied. Thus in the case of the last act of homage to the Cartesian theory which the French Academy rendered in the distribution of its prizes, the designation of a Cartesian Essay in 1741 (along with three Newtonian ones) as worthy of a prize for an explanation of the Tides; the difference of high and low water was not explained, as Descartes has explained it, by the pressure, on the ocean, of the terrestrial vortex, forced into a strait where it passes under the Moon; but the waters were supposed to rise towards the Moon, the terrestrial vortex being disturbed and broken by the Moon, and therefore less effective in forcing them down. And in giving an account of a Tourmaline from Ceylon (Acad. Sc. 1717), when it has been ascertained that it attracts and repels substances, the writer adds, as a matter of course, "It would seem that it has a vortex." As another example, the elasticity of a body was ascribed to vortices between its particles: and in general, as I have said, a vortex implied what we now imply by speaking of a central force.

4. In the same manner vortices were ascribed to the Magnet, in order to account for its attractions and repulsions. But we may note a circumstance which gave a special turn to the hypothesis of vortices as applied to this subject, and which may serve as a further illustration of the manner in which a transition may be made from one to the other of two rival hypotheses.

If iron filings be brought near a magnet, in such a manner as to be at liberty to assume the position which its polar action assigns to them; (for instance, by strewing them upon a sheet of paper while the two poles of the magnet are close below the paper;) they will arrange themselves in certain curves, each proceeding from the N. to the S. pole of the magnet, like the meridians in a map of the globe. It is easily shown, on the supposition of magnetic attraction and repulsion, that these magnetic curves, as they are termed, are each a curve whose tangent at every point is the direction of a small line or particle, as determined by the attraction and repulsion of the two poles. But if we suppose a magnetic vortex constantly to flow out of one pole and into the other, in streams which follow such curves, it is evident that such a vortex, being supposed to exercise material pressure and impulse, would arrange the iron filings in corresponding streams, and would thus produce the phenomenon which I have described. And the hypothesis of central torrents of Bernoulli or Le Sage which I have referred to, would, in its application to magnets, really become this hypothesis of a magnetic vortex, if we further suppose that the matter of the torrents which proceed to one pole and from the 501 other, mingles its streams, so as at each point to produce a stream in the resulting direction. Of course we shall have to suppose two sets of magnetic torrents;—a boreal torrent, proceeding to the north pole, and from the south pole of a magnet; and an austral torrent proceeding to the south and from the north pole:—and with these suppositions, we make a transition from the hypothesis of attraction and repulsion, to the Cartesian hypothesis of vortices, or at least, torrents, which determine bodies to their magnetic positions by impulse.

Of course it is to be expected that, in this as in the other case, when we follow the hypothesis of impulse into detail, it will need to be loaded with so many subsidiary hypotheses, in order to accommodate it to the phenomena, that it will no longer seem tenable. But the plausibility of the hypothesis in its first application cannot be denied:— for, it may be observed, the two opposite streams would counteract each other so as to produce no local motion, only direction. And this case may put us on our guard against other suggestions of forces acting in curve lines, which may at first sight appear to be discerned in magnetic and electric phenomena. Probably such curve lines will all be found to be only resulting lines, arising from the direct action and combination of elementary attraction and repulsion.

5. There is another case in which it would not be difficult to devise a mode of transition from one to the other of two rival theories; namely, in the case of the emission theory and the undulation theory of Light. Indeed several steps of such a transition have already appeared in the history of optical speculation; and the conclusive objection to the emission theory of light, as to the Cartesian theory of vortices, is, that no amount of additional hypotheses will reconcile it to the phenomena. Its defenders had to go on adding one piece of machinery after another, as new classes of facts came into view, till it became more complex and unmechanical than the theory of epicycles and eccentrics at its worst period. Otherwise, as I have said, there was nothing to prevent the emission theory from migrating into the undulatory theory, and as the theory of vortices did into the theory of attraction. For the emissionists allow that rays may interfere; and that these interferences may be modified by alternate fits in the rays; now these fits are already a kind of undulation. Then again the phenomena of polarized light show that the fits or undulations must have a transverse character: and there is no reason why emitted rays should not be subject to fits of transverse modification as well as to any other fits. In short, we may add to the emitted rays 502 of the one theory, all the properties which belong to the undulations of the other, and thus account for all the phenomena on the emission theory; with this limitation only, that the emission will have no share in the explanation, and the undulations will have the whole. If, instead of conceiving the universe full of a stationary ether, we suppose it to be full of etherial particles moving in every direction; and if we suppose, in the one case and in the other, this ether to be susceptible of undulations proceeding from every luminous point; the results of the two hypotheses will be the same; and all we shall have to say is, that the supposition of the emissive motion of the particles is superfluous and useless.

6. This view of the manner in which rival theories pass into one another appears to be so unfamiliar to those who have only slightly attended to the history of science, that I have thought it might be worth while to illustrate it by a few examples.

It might be said, for instance, by such persons[362], "Either the planets are not moved by vortices, or they do not move by the law by which heavy bodies fall. It is impossible that both opinions can be true." But it appears, by what has been said above, that the Cartesians did hold both opinions to be true; and one with just as much reason as the other, on their assumptions. It might be said in the same manner, "Either it is false that the planets are made to describe their orbits by the above quasi-Cartesian theory of Bernoulli, or it is false that they obey the Newtonian theory of gravitation." But this would be said quite erroneously; for if the hypothesis of Bernoulli be true, it is so because it agrees in its result with the theory of Newton. It is not only possible that both opinions may be true, but it is certain that if the first be so, the second is. It might be said again, "Either the planets describe their orbits by an inherent virtue, or according to the Newton theory." But this again would be erroneous, for the Newtonian doctrine decided nothing as to whether the force of gravitation was inherent or not. Cotes held that it was, though Newton strongly protested against being supposed to hold such an opinion. The word inherent is no part of the physical theory, and will be asserted or denied according to our metaphysical views of the essential attributes of matter and force.

Of course, the possibility of two rival hypotheses being true, one of which takes the explanation a step higher than the other, is not affected by the impossibility of two contradictory asser503tions of the same order of generality being both true. If there be a new-discovered comet, and if one astronomer asserts that it will return once in every twenty years, and another, that it will return once in every thirty years, both cannot be right. But if an astronomer says that though its interval was in the last instance 30 years, it will only be 20 years to the next return, in consequence of perturbation and resistance, he may be perfectly right.

And thus, when different and rival explanations of the same phenomena are held, till one of them, though long defended by ingenious men, is at last driven out of the field by the pressure of facts, the defeated hypothesis is transformed before it is extinguished. Before it has disappeared, it has been modified so as to have all palpable falsities squeezed out of it, and subsidiary provisions added, in order to reconcile it with the phenomena. It has, in short, been penetrated, infiltrated, and metamorphosed by the surrounding medium of truth, before the merely arbitrary and erroneous residuum has been finally ejected out of the body of permanent and certain knowledge.

504

Appendix H.
ON HEGEL'S CRITICISM OF NEWTON'S PRINCIPIA.

(Cam. Phil. Soc. May 21, 1849.)

The Newtonian doctrine of universal gravitation, as the cause of the motions which take place in the solar system, is so entirely established in our minds, and the fallacy of all the ordinary arguments against it is so clearly understood among us, that it would undoubtedly be deemed a waste of time to argue such questions in this place, so far as physical truth is concerned. But since in other parts of Europe, there are teachers of philosophy whose reputation and influence are very great, and who are sometimes referred to among our own countrymen as the authors of new and valuable views of truth, and who yet reject the Newtonian opinions, and deny the validity of the proofs commonly given of them, it may be worth while to attend for a few minutes to the declarations of such teachers, as a feature in the present condition of European philosophy. I the more readily assume that the Cambridge Philosophical Society will not think a communication on such a subject devoid of interest, in consequence of the favourable reception which it has given to philosophical speculations still more abstract, which I have on previous occasions offered to it. I will therefore proceed to make some remarks on the opinions concerning the Newtonian doctrine of gravitation, delivered by the celebrated Hegel, of Berlin, than whom no philosopher in modern, and perhaps hardly any even in ancient times, has had his teaching received with more reverential submission by his disciples, or been followed by a more numerous and zealous band of scholars bent upon diffusing and applying his principles.

The passages to which I shall principally refer are taken from one of his works which is called the Encyclopædia (Encyklopädie), of which the First Part is the Science of Logic, the Second, the Philosophy of Nature, the Third, the Philosophy of Spirit. The Second Part,505 with which I am here concerned, has for an aliter title, Lectures on Natural Philosophy (Vorlesungen über Natur-philosophie), and would through its whole extent offer abundant material for criticism, by referring it to principles with which we are here familiar: but I shall for the present confine myself to that part which refers to the subject which I have mentioned, the Newtonian Doctrine of Gravitation, § 269, 270, of the work. Nor shall I, with regard to this part, think it necessary to give a continuous and complete criticism of all the passages bearing upon the subject; but only such specimens, and such remarks thereon, as may suffice to show in a general manner the value and the character of Hegel's declarations on such questions. I do not pretend to offer here any opinion upon the value and character of Hegel's philosophy in general: but I think it not unlikely that some impression on that head may be suggested by the examination, here offered, of some points in which we can have no doubt where the truth lies; and I am not at all persuaded that a like examination of many other parts of the Hegelian Encyclopædia, would not confirm the impression which we shall receive from the parts now to be considered.

Hegel both criticises the Newtonian doctrines, or what he states as such; and also, not denying the truth of the laws of phenomena which he refers to, for instance Kepler's laws, offers his own proof of these laws. I shall make a few brief remarks on each of these portions of the pages before me. And I would beg it to be understood that where I may happen to put my remarks in a short, and what may seem a peremptory form, I do so for the sake of saving time; knowing that among us, upon subjects so familiar, a few words will suffice. For the same reason, I shall take passages from Hegel, not in the order in which they occur, but in the order in which they best illustrate what I have to say. I shall do Hegel no injustice by this mode of proceeding: for I will annex a faithful translation, so far as I can make one, of the whole of the passages referred to, with the context.

No one will be surprised that a German, or indeed any lover of science, should speak with admiration of the discovery of Kepler's laws, as a great event in the history of Astronomy, and a glorious distinction to the discoverer. But to say that the glory of the discovery of the proof of these laws has been unjustly transferred from Kepler to Newton, is quite another matter. This is what Hegel says (a)[363]. And we have to consider the reasons which he assigns for saying so.

506

He says (b) that "it is allowed by mathematicians that the Newtonian Formula maybe derived from the Keplerian laws," and hence he seems to infer that the Newtonian law is not an additional truth. That is, he does not allow that the discovery of the cause which produces a certain phenomenal law is anything additional to the discovery of the law itself.

"The Newtonian formula may be derived from the Keplerian law." It was professedly so derived; but derived by introducing the Idea of Force, which Idea and its consequences were not introduced and developed till after Kepler's time.

"The Newtonian formula may be derived from the Keplerian law." And the Keplerian law may be derived, and was derived, from the observations of the Greek astronomers and their successors; but was not the less a new and great discovery on that account.

But let us see what he says further of this derivation of the Newtonian "formula" from the Keplerian Law. It is evident that by calling it a formula, he means to imply, what he also asserts, that it is no new law, but only a new form (and a bad one) of a previously known truth.

How is the Newtonian "formula," that is, the law of the inverse squares of the central force, derived from the Keplerian law of the cubes of the distances proportional to the squares of the times? This, says Hegel, is the "immediate derivation." (c).—By Kepler's law, A being the distance and T the periodic time, $A3/T2$ is constant. But Newton calls $A/T2$ universal gravitation; whence it easily follows that gravitation is inversely as $A2$.

This is Hegel's way of representing Newton's proof. Reading it, any one who had never read the Principia might suppose that Newton defined gravitation to be $A/T2$. We, who have read the Principia, know that Newton proves that in circles, the central force (not the universal gravitation) is as $A/T2$: that he proves this, by setting out from the idea of force, as that which deflects a body from the tangent, and makes it describe a curved line: and that in this way, he passes from Kepler's laws of mere motion to his own law of Force.

But Hegel does not see any value in this. Such a mode of treating the subject he says (i) "offers to us a tangled web, formed of the Lines of the mere geometrical construction, to which a507 physical meaning of independent forces is given." That a measure of forces is found in such lines as the sagitta of the arc described in a given time, (not such a

282

meaning arbitrarily given to them,) is certainly true, and is very distinctly proved in Newton, and in all our elementary books.

But, says Hegel, as further showing the artificial nature of the Newtonian formulæ, (h) "Analysis has long been able to derive the Newtonian expression and the laws therewith connected out of the Form of the Keplerian Laws;" an assertion, to verify which he refers to Francœur's Mécanique. This is apparently in order to show that the "lines" of the Newtonian construction are superfluous. We know very well that analysis does not always refer to visible representations of such lines: but we know too, (and Francœur would testify to this also,) that the analytical proofs contain equivalents to the Newtonian lines. We, in this place, are too familiar with the substitution of analytical for geometrical proofs, to be led to suppose that such a substitution affects the substance of the truth proved. The conversion of Newton's geometrical proofs of his discoveries into analytical processes by succeeding writers, has not made them cease to be discoveries: and accordingly, those who have taken the most prominent share in such a conversion, have been the most ardent admirers of Newton's genius and good fortune.

So much for Newton's comparison of the Forces in different circular orbits, and for Hegel's power of understanding and criticising it. Now let us look at the motion in different parts of the same elliptical orbit, as a further illustration of the value of Hegel's criticism. In an elliptical orbit the velocity alternately increases and diminishes. This follows necessarily from Kepler's law of the equal description of the areas, and so Newton explains it. Hegel, however, treats of this acceleration and retardation as a separate fact, and talks of another explanation of it, founded upon Centripetal and Centrifugal Force (o). Where he finds this explanation, I know not; certainly not in Newton, who in the second and third section of the Principia explains the variation of the velocity in a quite different manner, as I have said; and nowhere, I think, employs centrifugal force in his explanations. However, the notion of centrifugal as acting along with centripetal force is introduced in some treatises, and may undoubtedly be used with perfect truth and propriety. How far Hegel can judge when it is so used, we may see from what he says of the confusion produced by such an explanation, which is, he says, a maximum. In the first place, he speaks of the motion being uniformly accelerated and retarded in508 an elliptical orbit, which, in any exact use of the word uniformly, it is not. But passing by this, he proceeds to criticise an explanation, not of the variable velocity of the body in its orbit, but of the alternate access and recess of the body to and from the center. Let us overlook this confusion also, and see what is the value of his criticism on the explanation. He says (p), "according to this explanation, in the motion of a planet from the aphelion to the perihelion, the centrifugal is less than the centripetal force; and in the perihelion itself the centripetal force is supposed suddenly to become greater than the centrifugal;" and so, of course, the body re-ascends to the aphelion.

Now I will not say that this explanation has never been given in a book professing to be scientific; but I have never seen it given; and it never can have been given but by a very ignorant and foolish person. It goes upon the utterly unmechanical supposition that the approach of a body to the center at any moment depends solely upon the excess of the centripetal over the centrifugal force; and reversely. But the most elementary knowledge of mechanics shows us that when a body is moving obliquely to the distance from the center, it approaches to or recedes from the center in virtue of this obliquity, even if no force at all act. And the total approach to the center is the approach due to this cause, plus the approach due to the centripetal force, minus the recess due to the centrifugal force. At the aphelion, the centripetal is greater than the centrifugal force; and hence the motion becomes oblique; and then, the body approaches to the center on both accounts, and approaches on account of the obliquity of the path even when the centrifugal has become greater than the centripetal force, which it becomes before the body reaches the perihelion. This reasoning is so elementary, that when a person who cannot see this, writes on the subject with an air of authority, I do not see what can be done but to point out the oversight and leave it.

But there is, says Hegel (q), another way of explaining the motion by means of centripetal and centrifugal forces. The two forces are supposed to increase and decrease gradually, according to different laws. In this case, there must be a point where they are equal, and in equilibrio; and this being the case, they will always continue equal, for there will be no reason for their going out of equilibrium.

This, which is put as another mode of explanation, is, in fact, the same mode; for, as I have already said, the centrifugal force, which is less than the centripetal at the aphelion, becomes the greater of the two before the perihelion; and there is an intermediate position, at which the two forces are equal. But at this point, is there no509 reason why, being equal, the forces should become unequal? Reason abundant: for the body, being there, moves in a line oblique to the distance, and so changes its distance; and the centripetal and centrifugal force, depending upon the distance by different laws, they forthwith become unequal.

But these modes of explanation, by means of the centripetal and centrifugal forces and their relation, are not necessary to Newton's doctrine, and are nowhere used by Newton; and undoubtedly much confusion has been produced in other minds, as well as Hegel's, by speaking of the centrifugal force, which is a mere intrinsic geometrical result of a body's curvilinear motion round a center, in conjunction with centripetal force, which is an extrinsic force, acting upon the body and urging it to the center. Neither Newton, nor any intelligent Newtonian, ever spoke of the centripetal and centrifugal force as two distinct forces both extrinsic to the motion, which Hegel accuses them of doing. (n)

I have spoken of the third and second of Kepler's laws; of Newton's explanations of them, and of Hegel's criticism. Let us now, in the same manner, consider the first law, that the planets move in ellipses. Newton's proof that this was the result of a central force varying inversely as the square of the distance, was the solution of a problem at which his contemporaries had laboured in vain, and is commonly looked upon as an important step. "But," says Hegel, (d) "the proof gives a conic section generally, whereas the main point which ought to be proved is, that the path of the body is an ellipse only, not a circle or any other conic section." Certainly if Newton had proved that a planet cannot move in a circle, (which Hegel says he ought to have done), his system would have perplexed astronomers, since there are planets which move in orbits hardly distinguishable from circles, and the variation of the extremity from planet to planet shows that there is nothing to prevent the excentricity vanishing and the orbit becoming a circle.

"But," says Hegel again, (e) "the conditions which make the path to be an ellipse rather than any other conic section, are empirical and extraneous;—the supposed casual strength of the impulsion originally received." Certainly the circumstances which determine the amount of excentricity of a planet's orbit are derived from experience, or rather, observation. It is not a part of Newton's system to determine à priori what the excentricity of a planet's orbit must be. A system that professes to do this will undoubtedly be one very different from his. And as our knowledge of the excentricity is derived from observation, it is, in that sense, empirical and casual. The strength of the original impulsion is a510 hypothetical and impartial way of expressing this result of observation. And as we see no reason why the excentricity should be of any certain magnitude, we see none why the fraction which expresses the excentricity should not become as large as unity, that is, why the orbit should not become a parabola; and accordingly, some of the bodies which revolve about the same appear to move in orbits of this form: so little is the motion in an ellipse, as Hegel says, (f) "the only thing to be proved."

But Hegel himself has offered proof of Kepler's laws, to which, considering his objections to Newton's proofs, we cannot help turning with some curiosity.

And first, let us look at the proof of the Proposition which we have been considering, that the path of a planet is necessarily an ellipse. I will translate Hegel's language as well as I can; but without answering for the correctness of my translation, since it does not appear to me to conform to the first condition of translation, of being intelligible. The translation however, such as it is, may help us to form some opinion of the validity and value of Hegel's proofs as compared with Newton's. (r)

"For absolutely uniform motion, the circle is the only path.... The circle is the line returning into itself in which all the radii are equal; there is, for it, only one determining quantity, the radius.

"But in free motion, the determination according to space and to time come into view with differences. There must be a difference in the spatial aspect in itself, and therefore the form requires two determining quantities. Hence the form of the path returning into itself is an ellipse."

Now even if we could regard this as reasoning, the conclusion does not in the smallest degree follow. A curve returning into itself and determined by two quantities, may have innumerable forms besides the ellipse; for instance, any oval form whatever, besides that of the conic section.

But why must the curve be a curve returning into itself? Hegel has professed to prove this previously (m) from "the determination of particularity and individuality of the bodies in general, so that they have partly a center in themselves, and partly at the same time their center in another." Without seeking to find any precise meaning in this, we may ask whether it proves the impossibility of the orbits with moveable apses, (which do not return into themselves,) such as the planets (affected by perturbations) really do describe, and such as we know that bodies must describe in all cases, except when the force varies exactly as the square of the 511 distance? It appears to do so: and it proves this impossibility of known facts at least as much as it proves anything.

Let us now look at Hegel's proof of Kepler's second law, that the elliptical sectors swept by the radius vector are proportional to the time. It is this: (s).

"In the circle, the arc or angle which is included by the two radii is independent of them. But in the motion [of a planet] as determined by the conception, the distance from the center and the arc run over in a certain time must be compounded in one determination, and must make out a whole. This whole is the sector, a space of two dimensions. And hence the arc is essentially a Function of the radius vector; and the former (the arc) being unequal, brings with it the inequality of the radii."

As was said in the former case, if we could regard this as reasoning, it would not prove the conclusion, but only, that the arc is some function or other of the radii.

Hegel indeed offers (t) a reason why there must be an arc involved. This arises, he says, from "the determinateness [of the nature of motion], at one while as time in the root, at another while as space in the square. But here the quadratic character of the space is, by the returning of the line of motion into itself, limited to a sector."

Probably my readers have had a sufficient specimen of Hegel's mode of dealing with these matters. I will however add his proof of Kepler's third law, that the cubes of the distances are as the squares of the times.

Hegel's proof in this case (u) has a reference to a previous doctrine concerning falling bodies, in which time and space have, he says, a relation to each other as root and square. Falling bodies however are the case of only half-free motion, and the determination is incomplete.

"But in the case of absolute motion, the domain of free masses, the determination attains its totality. The time as the root is a mere empirical magnitude: but as a component of the developed Totality, it is a Totality in itself: it produces itself, and therein has a reference to itself. And in this process, Time, being itself the dimensionless element, only comes to a formal identity with itself and reaches the square: Space, on the other hand, as a positive external relation, comes to the full dimensions of the conception of space, that is, the cube. The Realization of the two conceptions (space and time) preserves their original difference. This is the third Keplerian law, the relation of the Cubes of the distances to the squares of the times."

512

"And this," he adds, (v) with remarkable complacency, "represents simply and immediately the reason of the thing:—while on the contrary, the Newtonian Formula, by means of which the Law is changed into a Law for the Force of Gravity, shows the distortion and inversion of Reflexion, which stops half-way."

I am not able to assign any precise meaning to the Reflexion, which is here used as a term of condemnation, applicable especially to the Newtonian doctrine. It is repeatedly applied in the same manner by Hegel. Thus he says, (g) "that what Kepler expresses in a simple and sublime manner in the form of Laws of the Celestial Motions, Newton has metamorphosed into the Reflexion-Form of the Force of Gravitation."

Though Hegel thus denies Newton all merit with regard to the explanation of Kepler's laws by means of the gravitation of the planets to the sun, he allows that to the Keplerian Laws Newton added the Principle of Perturbations (k). This Principle he accepts to a certain extent, transforming the expression of it after his peculiar fashion. "It lies," he says, (l) "in this: that matter in general assigns a center for itself: the collective bodies of the system recognise a reference to their sun, and all the individual bodies, according to the relative positions into which they are brought by their motions, form a momentary relation of their gravity towards each other."

This must appear to us a very loose and insufficient way of stating the Principle of Perturbations, but loose as it is, it recognises that the Perturbations depend upon the gravity of the planets one to another, and to the sun. And if the Perturbations depend upon these forces, one can hardly suppose that any one who allows this will deny that the primary undisturbed motions depend upon these forces, and must be explained by means of them; yet this is what Hegel denies.

It is evident, on looking at Hegel's mode of reasoning on such subjects, that his views approach towards those of Aristotle and the Aristotelians; according to which motions were divided into natural and unnatural;—the celestial motions were circular and uniform in their nature;—and the like. Perhaps it may be worth while to show how completely Hegel adheres to these ancient views, by an extract from the additions to the Articles on Celestial Motions, made in the last edition of the Encyclopædia. He says (w),

"The motion of the heavenly bodies is not a being pulled this way and that, as is imagined (by the Newtonians). They go along, as the ancients said, like blessed gods. The celestial conformity is513 not such a one as has the principle of rest or motion external to itself. It is not right to say because a stone is inert, and the whole earth consists of stones, and the other heavenly bodies are of the same nature as the earth, therefore the heavenly bodies are inert. This conclusion makes the properties of the whole the same as those of the part. Impulse, Pressure, Resistance, Friction, Pulling, and the like, are valid only for other than celestial matter."

There can be no doubt that this is a very different doctrine from that of Newton.

I will only add to these specimens of Hegel's physics, a specimen of the logic by which he refutes the Newtonian argument which has just been adduced; namely, that the celestial bodies are matter, and that matter, as we see in terrestrial matter, is inert. He says (x),

"Doubtless both are matter, as a good thought and a bad thought are both thoughts; but the bad one is not therefore good, because it is a thought."

APPENDIX TO THE MEMOIR ON HEGEL'S CRITICISM OF NEWTON'S PRINCIPIA.

Hegel. Encyclopædia (2nd Ed. 1827), Part XI. p. 250.

C. Absolute Mechanics.

§ 269.

Gravitation is the true and determinate conception of material Corporeity, which (Conception) is realized to the Idea (zur Idee). General Corporeity is separable essentially into particular Bodies, and connects itself with the Element of Individuality or subjectivity, as apparent (phenomenal) presence in the Motion, which by this means is immediately a system of several Bodies.

Universal gravitation must, as to itself, be recognised as a profound thought, although it was principally as apprehended in the sphere of Reflexion that it eminently attracted notice and confidence on account of the quantitative determinations therewith connected, and was supposed to find its confirmation in Experiments (Erfahrung) pursued from the Solar System down to the phenomena514 of Capillary Tubes.—But Gravitation contradicts immediately the Law of Inertia, for in virtue of it (Gravitation) matter tends out of itself to the other (matter).—In the Conception of Weight, there are, as has been shown, involved the two elements—Self-existence, and Continuity, which takes away self-existence. These elements of the Conception, however, experience a fate, as particular forces, corresponding to Attractive and Repulsive Force, and are thereby apprehended in nearer determination, as Centripetal and Centrifugal Force, which (Forces) like weight, act upon Bodies, independent of each other, and are supposed to come in contact accidentally in a third thing, Body. By this means, what there is of profound in the thought of universal weight is again reduced to nothing; and Conception and Reason cannot make their way into the doctrine of absolute motion, so long as the so highly-prized discoveries of Forces are dominant there. In the conclusion which contains the Idea of Weight, namely, [contains this Idea] as the Conception which, in the case of motion, enters into external Reality through the particularity of the Bodies, and at the same time into this [Reality] and into their Ideality and self-regarding Reflexion, (Reflexion-in-sich), the rational identity and inseparability of the elements is involved, which at other times are represented as independent. Motion itself, as such, has only its meaning and existence in a system of several bodies, and those, such as stand in relation to each other according to different determinations.

§ 270.

As to what concerns bodies in which the conception of gravity (weight) is realized free by itself, we say that they have for the determinations of their different nature the elements (momente) of their conception. One [conception of this kind] is the universal center of the abstract reference [of a body] to itself. Opposite to this [conception] stands the immediate, extrinsic, centerless Individuality, appearing as Corporeity similarly independent. Those [Bodies] however which are particular, which stand in the

288

determination of extrinsic, and at the same time of intrinsic relation, are centers for themselves, and [also] have a reference to the first as to their essential unity.

The Planetary Bodies, as the immediately concrete, are in their existence the most complete. Men are accustomed to take the Sun as the most excellent, inasmuch as the understanding prefers the abstract to the concrete, and in like manner the fixed stars are esteemed higher than the Bodies515 of the Solar System. Centerless Corporeity, as belonging to externality, naturally separates itself into the opposition of the lunar and the cometary Body. The laws of absolutely free motion, as is well known, were discovered by Kepler;—a discovery of immortal fame. Kepler has proved these laws in this sense, that for the empirical data he found their general expression. Since then, it has become a common way of (a)speaking to say that Newton first found out the proof of these Laws. It has rarely happened that fame has been more unjustly transferred from the first discoverer to another person. On this subject I make the following remarks.

1. That it is allowed by Mathematicians that the Newtonian Formulæ may be derived from the Keplerian Laws. (b)The completely immediate derivation is this: In the third (c)Keplerian Law, A^3/T^2 is the constant quantity. This being put as $A.A^2/T^2$ and calling, with Newton, A/T^2 universal Gravitation, his expression of the effect of gravity in the reciprocal ratio of the square of the distances is obvious.

(d)2. That the Newtonian proof of the Proposition that a body subjected to the Law of Gravitation moves about the central body in an Ellipse, gives a Conic Section generally, while the main Proposition which ought to be proved is that the fall of such a Body is not a Circle or any other Conic Section, but an Ellipse only. Moreover, there are objections which may be made against this proof in itself (Princ. Math. I. 1. Sect. II. Prop. 1); and although it is the foundation of the Newtonian Theory, analysis has no longer any need of it. The conditions which in the sequel make the path of the Body to a determinate Conic Section, are referred to an empirical circumstance, namely, a particular position of the Body at a determined moment of time, and the casual strength of an (f)impulsion which it is supposed to have received originally; so that the circumstance which makes the Curve be an Ellipse, which alone ought to be the thing proved, is extraneous to the Formula.

3. That the Newtonian Law of the so-called Force of Gravitation is in like manner only proved from experience by Induction.

(g)The sum of the difference is this, that what Kepler expressed in a simple and sublime manner in the Form of Laws516 of the Celestial Motions, Newton has metamorphosed into the Reflection-Form of the Force of Gravitation. If the Newtonian Form has not only its convenience but its necessity in reference to the analytical method, this is only a difference (h)of the mathematical formulæ; Analysis has long been able to derive the Newtonian expression, and the Propositions therewith connected, out of the Form of the Keplerian Laws; (on this subject I refer to the elegant exposition in (i)Francœur's Traité Elém. de Mécanique, Liv. II. Ch. xi. n. 4.)—The old method of so-called proof is conspicuous as offering to us a tangled web, formed of the Lines of the mere geometrical construction, to which a physical meaning of independent Forces is given; and of empty Reflexion-determinations of the already mentioned Accelerating

289

Force and Vis Inertiæ, and especially of the relation of the so-called gravitation itself to the centripetal force and centrifugal force, and so on.

The remarks which are here made would undoubtedly have need of a further explication to show how well founded they are: in a Compendium, propositions of this kind which do not agree with that which is assumed, can only have the shape of assertions. Indeed, since they contradict such high authorities, they must appear as something worse, as presumptuous assertions. I will not, on this subject, support myself by saying, by the bye, that an interest in these subjects has occupied me for 25 years; but it is more precisely to the purpose to remark, that the distinctions and determinations which Mathematical Analysis introduces, and the course which it must take according to its method, is altogether different from that which a physical reality must have. The Presuppositions, the Course, and the Results, which the Analysis necessarily has and gives, remain quite extraneous to the considerations which determine the physical value and the signification of those determinations and of that course. To this it is that attention should be directed. We have to do with a consciousness relative to the deluging of physical Mechanics with an inconceivable (unsäglichen) Metaphysic, which—contrary to experience and conception—has those mathematical determinations alone for its source.

It is recognized that what Newton—besides the foundation of the analytical treatment, the development of which, by the bye, has of itself rendered superfluous, or indeed rejected much which belonged to Newton's essential Principles and glory—has added to the Keplerian Laws is the Principle of517 Perturbations,—a Principle whose importance we may here accept thus far (hier in sofern anzuführen ist); namely, so (k)far as it rests upon the Proposition that the so-called attraction is an operation of all the individual parts of bodies, as being material. (l)It lies in this, that matter in general assigns a center for itself (sich das centrum setzt), and the figure of the body is an element in the determination of its place; that collective bodies of the system recognize a reference to their Sun (sich ihre Sonne setzen), but also the individual bodies themselves, according to the relative position with regard to each other into which they come by their general motion, form a momentary relation of their gravity (schwere) towards each other, and are related to each other not only in abstract spatial relations, but at the same time assign to themselves a joint center, which however is again resolved [into the general center] in the universal system.

As to what concerns the features of the path, to show how the fundamental determinations of Free Motion are connected with the Conception, cannot here be undertaken in a satisfactory and detailed manner, and must therefore be left to its fate. The proof from reason of the quantitative determinations of free motion can only rest upon the determinations of Conceptions of space and time, the elements whose relation (intrinsic not extrinsic) motion is.

(m)That, in the first place, the motion in general is a motion returning into itself, is founded on the determination of particularity and individuality of the bodies in general (§ 269), so that partly they have a center in themselves, and partly at the same time their center in another. These are the determinations of Conceptions which form the basis of the false representatives (n)of Centripetal Force and Centrifugal Force, as if each of these were self-existing, extraneous to the other, and independent of it; and as if they only came

290

in contact in their operations and consequently externally. They are, as has already been mentioned, the Lines which must be drawn for the mathematical determinations, transformed into physical realities.

Further, this motion is uniformly accelerated, (and—as returning into itself—in turn uniformly retarded). In motion as free, Time and Space enter as different things which are to make themselves effective in the determination of the motion (o)(§ 266, note). In the so-called Explanation of the uniformly accelerated and retarded motion, by means of the alternate518 decrease and increase of the magnitude of the Centripetal Force and Centrifugal Force, the confusion which the assumption of such independent Forces produces is at its greatest (p)height. According to this explanation, in the motion of a Planet from the Aphelion to the Perihelion, the centrifugal is less than the centripetal force, and on the contrary, in the Perihelion itself, the centrifugal force is supposed to become greater than the centripetal. For the motion from the Perihelion to the Aphelion, this representation makes the forces pass into the opposite relation in the same manner. It is apparent that such a sudden conversion of the preponderance which a force has obtained over another, into an inferiority to the other, cannot be anything taken out of the nature of Forces. On the contrary it must be concluded, that a preponderance which one Force has obtained over another must not only be preserved, but must go onwards to the complete annihilation of the other Force, and the motion must either, by the Preponderance of the Centripetal Force, proceed till it ends in rest, that is, in the Collision of the Planet with the Central Body, or till by the Preponderance of the Centrifugal (q)Force it ends in a straight line. But now, if in place of the suddenness of the conversion, we suppose a gradual increase of the Force in question, then, since rather the other Force ought to be assumed as increasing, we lose the opposition which is assumed for the sake of the explanation; and if the increase of the one is assumed to be different from that of the other, (which is the case in some representations,) then there is found at the mean distance between the apsides a point in which the Forces are in equilibrio. And the transition of the Forces out of Equilibrium is a thing just as little without any sufficient reason as the aforesaid suddenness of inversion. And in the whole of this kind of explanation, we see that the mode of remedying a bad mode of dealing with a subject leads to newer and greater confusion.—A similar confusion makes its appearance in the explanation of the phænomenon that the pendulum oscillates more slowly at the equator. This phænomenon is ascribed to the Centrifugal Force, which it is asserted must then be greater; but it is easy to see that we may just as well ascribe it to the augmented gravity, inasmuch as that holds the pendulum more strongly to the perpendicular line of rest.

519

§ 240.

(r)And now first, as to what concerns the Form of the Path, the Circle only can be conceived as the path of an absolutely uniform motion. Conceivable, as people express it, no doubt it is, that an increasing and diminishing motion should take place in a circle. But this conceivableness or possibility means only an abstract capability of being represented, which leaves out of sight that Determinate Thing on which the question turns.

The Circle is the line returning into itself in which all the radii are equal, that is, it is completely determined by means of the radius. There is only one Determination, and that is the whole Determination.

But in free motion, in which the Determinations according to space and according to time come into view with Differences, in a qualitative relation to each other, this Relation appears in the spatial aspect as a Difference thereof in itself, which therefore requires two Determinations. Hereby the Form of the path returning into itself is essentially an Ellipse.

(s)The abstract Determinations which produces the circle appears also in this way, that the arc or angle which is included by two Radii is independent of them, a magnitude with regard to them completely empirical. But since in the motion as determined by the Conception, the distance from the center, and the arc which is run over in a certain time, must be comprehended in one determinateness, [and] make out a whole, this is the sector, a space-determination of two dimensions: in this way, the arc is essentially a Function of the Radius Vector; and the former (the arc) being unequal, brings with it the inequality of the Radii. That the determination with regard to the space by means of the time appears as a Determination of two Dimensions,—as a Superficies-Determination,—agrees (t)with what was said before (§ 266) respecting Falling Bodies, with regard to the exposition of the same Determinateness, at one while as Time in the root, at another while as Space in the Square. Here, however, the Quadratic character of the space is, by the returning of the Line of motion into itself, limited to a Sector. These are, as may be seen, the general principles on which the Keplerian Law, that in equal times equal sectors are cut off, rests.

This Law becomes, as is clear, only the relation of the arc to the Radius Vector, and the Time enters there as the abstract520 Unity, in which the different Sectors are compared, because as Unity it is the Determining Element. But the further relation is that of the Time, not as Unity, but as a Quantity in general,—as the time of Revolution—to the magnitude of the Path, or, what is the same thing, the distance from the center. As Root and Square, we saw that Time and Space had a relation to each other, in the case of Falling Bodies, the case of half-free motion—because that [motion] is determined on one side by the conception, on the other by external [conditions]. But in the case of absolute motion—the domain (u)of free masses—the determination attains its Totality. The Time as the Root is a mere empirical magnitude; but as a component (moment) of the developed Totality, it is a Totality in itself,—it produces itself, and therein has a reference to itself; as the Dimensionless Element in itself, it only comes to a formal identity with itself, the Square; Space, on the other hand, as the positive Distribution (aussereinander) [comes] to the Dimension of the Conception, the Cube. Their (v)Realization preserves their original difference. This is the third Keplerian Law, the relation of the Cubes of the Distances to the Squares of the Times;—a Law which is so great on this account, that it represents so simply and immediately Reason as belonging to the thing: while on the contrary the Newtonian Formula, by means of which the Law is changed into a Law for the Force of Gravity, shows the Distortion, Perversion and Inversion of Reflexion which stops half-way.

Additions to new Edition. § 269.

The center has no sense without the circumference, nor the circumference without the center. This makes all physical hypotheses vanish which sometimes proceed from the center, sometimes from the particular bodies, and sometimes assign this, sometimes that, as the original [cause of motion] ... It is silly (läppisch) to suppose that the centrifugal force, as a tendency to fly off in a Tangent, has been produced by a lateral projection, a projectile force, an impulse which they have retained ever since they set out on their journey (von Haus aus). Such casualty of the motion produced by external causes belongs to inert matter; as when a stone fastened to a thread which is thrown transversely tries to fly from the thread. We are not to talk in this way of Forces. If we will speak of Force, there is one Force, whose elements521 do not draw bodies to different sides as if they were two (w)Forces. The motion of the heavenly bodies is not a being pulled this way or that, such as is thus imagined; it is free motion: they go along, as the ancients said, as blessed Gods (sie gehen als selige Götter einher). The celestial corporeity is not such a one as has the principle of rest or motion external to itself. Because stone is inert, and all the earth consists of stones, and the other heavenly bodies are of the same nature,—is a conclusion which makes the properties of the whole the same as those of the part. Impulse, Pressure, Resistance, Friction, Pulling, and the like, are valid only for (x)an existence of matter other than the celestial. Doubtless that which is common to the two is matter, as a good thought and a bad thought are both thoughts; but the bad one is not therefore good, because it is a thought.

522

Appendix K.
DEMONSTRATION THAT ALL MATTER IS HEAVY.

(Cam. Phil. Soc. Feb. 22, 1841.)

The discussion of the nature of the grounds and proofs of the most general propositions which the physical sciences include, belongs rather to Metaphysics than to that course of experimental and mathematical investigation by which the sciences are formed. But such discussions seem by no means unfitted to occupy the attention of the cultivators of physical science. The ideal, as well as the experimental side of our knowledge must be carefully studied and scrutinized, in order that its true import may be seen; and this province of human speculation has been perhaps of late unjustly depreciated and neglected by men of science. Yet it can be prosecuted in the most advantageous manner by them only: for no one can speculate securely and rightly respecting the nature and proofs of the truths of science without a steady possession of some large and solid portions of such truths. A man must be a mathematician, a mechanical philosopher, a natural historian, in order that he may philosophize well concerning mathematics, and mechanics, and natural history; and the mere metaphysician who without such preparation and fitness sets himself to determine the grounds of mathematical or mechanical truths, or the principles of classification, will be liable to be led into error at every step. He must speculate by means of general terms, which he will not be able to use as instruments of discovering and conveying philosophical truth, because he cannot, in his own mind, habitually and familiarly, embody their import in special examples.

Acting upon such views, I have already laid before the Philosophical Society of Cambridge essays on such subjects as I here refer to; especially a memoir "On the Nature of the Truth of the Laws of Motion," which was printed by the Society in its Transactions.523 This memoir appears to have excited in other places, notice of such a kind as to show that the minds of many speculative persons are ready for and inclined towards the discussion of such questions. I am therefore the more willing to bring under consideration another subject of a kind closely related to the one just mentioned.

The general questions which all such discussions suggest, are (in the existing phase of English philosophy) whether certain proposed scientific truths, (as the laws of motion,) be necessary truths; and if they are necessary, (which I have attempted to show that in a certain sense they are,) on what ground their necessity rests. These questions may be discussed in a general form, as I have elsewhere attempted to show. But it may be instructive also to follow the general arguments into the form which they assume in special cases; and to exhibit, in a distinct shape, the incongruities into which the opposite false doctrine leads us, when applied to particular examples. This accordingly is what I propose to do in the present memoir, with regard to the proposition stated at the head of this paper, namely, that all matter is heavy.

At first sight it may appear a doctrine altogether untenable to assert that this proposition is a necessary truth: for, it may be urged, we have no difficulty in conceiving matter which is not heavy; so that matter without weight is a conception not inconsistent with itself; which it must be if the reverse were a necessary truth. It may be added, that the possibility of conceiving matter without weight was shown in the controversy which ended in the downfall of the phlogiston theory of chemical composition; for some of the reasoners on this subject asserted phlogiston to be a body with positive levity instead of gravity, which hypothesis, however false, shows that such a supposition is possible. Again, it may be said that weight and inertia are two separate properties of matter: that mathematicians measure the quantity of matter by the inertia, and that we learn by experiment only that the weight is proportional to the inertia; Newton's experiments with pendulums of different materials having been made with this very object.

I proceed to reply to these arguments. And first, as to the possibility of conceiving matter without weight, and the argument thence deduced, that the universal gravity of matter is not a necessary truth, I remark, that it is indeed just, to say that we cannot even distinctly conceive the contrary of a necessary truth to be true; but that this impossibility can be asserted only of those perfectly distinct conceptions which result from a complete develop524ment of the fundamental idea and its consequences. Till we reach this stage of development, the obscurity and indistinctness may prevent our perceiving absolute contradictions, though they exist. We have abundant store of examples of this, even in geometry and arithmetic; where the truths are universally allowed to be necessary, and where the relations which are impossible, are also inconceivable, that is, not conceivable distinctly. Such relations, though not distinctly conceivable, still often appear conceivable and possible, owing to the indistinctness of our ideas. Who, at the first outset of his geometrical studies, sees any impossibility in supposing the side and the diagonal of a square to have a common measure? Yet they can be rigorously proved to be incommensurable, and therefore the attempt distinctly to conceive a common measure of them must fail. The attempts at the geometrical duplication of the cube, and the supposed solutions, (as that of Hobbes,) have involved absolute contradictions; yet this has not prevented their being long and obstinately entertained by men, even of minds acute and clear in other respects. And the same might be shewn to be the case in arithmetic. It is plain, therefore, that we cannot, from the supposed possibility of conceiving matter without weight, infer that the contrary may not be a necessary truth.

Our power of judging, from the compatibility or incompatibility of our conceptions, whether certain propositions respecting the relations of ideas are true or not, must depend entirely, as I have said, upon the degree of development which such ideas have undergone in our minds. Some of the relations of our conceptions on any subject are evident upon the first steady contemplation of the fundamental idea by a sound mind: these are the axioms of the subject. Other propositions may be deduced from the axioms by strict logical reasoning. These propositions are no less necessary than the axioms, though to common minds their evidence is very different. Yet as we become familiar with the steps by which these ulterior truths are deduced from the axioms, their truth also becomes evident, and the contrary becomes inconceivable. When a person has familiarized himself with the first twenty-six propositions of Euclid, and not till then, it becomes evident to him, that parallelograms on the same base and between the same parallels are equal; and he cannot even conceive the contrary. When he has a little further cultivated his geometrical powers, the equality of the square on the hypothenuse of a right-angled triangle to the squares on the sides, becomes also evident; the steps by which it is demonstrated being so familiar to the mind as to be apprehended without a conscious act. And thus, the contrary of a necessary525 truth cannot be distinctly conceived; but the incapacity of forming such a conception is a condition which depends upon cultivation, being intimately connected with the power of rapidly and clearly perceiving the connection of the necessary truth under consideration with the elementary principles on which it depends. And thus, again, it may be that there is an absolute impossibility of conceiving matter without weight; but then, this impossibility may not be apparent, till we have traced our fundamental conceptions of matter into some of their consequences.

The question then occurs, whether we can, by any steps of reasoning, point out an inconsistency in the conception of matter without weight. This I conceive we may do, and this I shall attempt to show.

The general mode of stating the argument is this:—the quantity of matter is measured by those sensible properties of matter which undergo quantitative addition, subtraction and division, as the matter is added, subtracted and divided. The quantity of matter cannot be known in any other way. But this mode of measuring the quantity of matter, in order to be true at all, must be universally true. If it were only partially true, the limits within which it is to be applied would be arbitrary; and therefore the whole procedure would be arbitrary, and, as a method of obtaining philosophical truth, altogether futile.

We may unfold this argument further. Let the contrary be supposed, of that which we assert to be true: namely, let it be supposed that while all other kinds of matter are heavy (and of course heavy in proportion to the quantity of matter), there is one kind of matter which is absolutely destitute of weight; as, for instance, phlogiston, or any other element. Then where this weightless element (as we may term it) is mixed with weighty elements, we shall have a compound, in which the weight is no longer proportional to the quantity of matter. If, for example, 2 measures of heavy matter unite with one measure of phlogiston, the weight is as 2, and the quantity of matter as 3. In all such cases, therefore, the weight ceases to be the measure of the quantity of matter. And as the proportion of the weighty and the weightless matter may vary in innumerable degrees in such compounds, the weight affords no criterion at all of the quantity of matter in them. And the smallest admixture of the weightless element is sufficient to prevent the weight from being taken as the measure of the quantity of matter.

But on this hypothesis, how are we to distinguish such compounds from bodies consisting purely of heavy matter? How are526 we to satisfy ourselves that there is not, in every body, some admixture, small or great, of the weightless element? If we call this element phlogiston, how shall we know that the bodies with which we have to do are, any of them, absolutely free from phlogiston?

We cannot refer to the weight for any such assurance; for by supposition the presence and absence of phlogiston makes no difference in the weight. Nor can any other properties secure us at least from a very small admixture; for to assert that a mixture of 1 in 100 or 1 in 10 of phlogiston would always manifest itself in the properties of the body, must be an arbitrary procedure, till we have proved this assertion by experiment: and we cannot do this till we have learnt some mode of measuring the quantities of matter in bodies and parts of bodies; which is exactly what we question the possibility of, in the present hypothesis.

Thus, if we assume the existence of an element, phlogiston, devoid of weight, we cannot be sure that every body does not contain some portion of this element; while we see that if there be an admixture of such an element, the weight is no longer any criterion of the quantity of matter. And thus we have proved, that if there be any kind of matter which is not heavy, the weight can no longer avail us, in any case or to any extent, as a measure of the quantity of matter.

I may remark, that the same conclusion is easily extended to the case in which phlogiston is supposed to have absolute levity; for in that case, a certain mixture of phlogiston and of heavy matter would have no weight, and might be substituted for phlogiston in the preceding reasoning.

I may remark, also, that the same conclusion would follow by the same reasoning, if any kind of matter, instead of being void of weight, were heavy, indeed, but not so heavy, in proportion to its quantity of matter, as other kinds.

On all these hypotheses there would be no possibility of measuring quantity of matter by weight at all, in any case, or to any extent.

But it may be urged, that we have not yet reduced the hypothesis of matter without weight to a contradiction; for that mathematicians measure quantity of matter, not by weight, but by the other property, of which we have spoken, inertia.

To this I reply, that, practically speaking, quantity of matter is always measured by weight, both by mechanicians and chemists: and as we have proved that this procedure is utterly insecure in all cases, on the hypothesis of weightless matter, the practice rests upon a conviction that the hypothesis is false. And yet the practice is universal. Every experimenter measures quantity of matter527 by the balance. No one has ever thought of measuring quantity of matter by its inertia practically: no one has constructed a measure of quantity of matter in which the matter produces its indications of quantity by its motion. When we have to take into account the inertia of a body, we inquire what its weight is, and assume this as the measure of the inertia; but we never take the contrary course, and ascertain the inertia first in order to determine by that means the weight.

But it may be asked, Is it not then true, and an important scientific truth, that the quantity of matter is measured by the inertia? Is it not true, and proved by experiment, that the weight is proportional to the inertia? If this be not the result of Newton's experiments mentioned above, what, it may be demanded, do they prove?

To these questions I reply: It is true that quantity of matter is measured by the inertia, for it is true that inertia is as the quantity of matter. This truth is indeed one of the laws of motion. That weight is proportional to inertia is proved by experiment, as far as the laws of motion are so proved: and Newton's experiments prove one of the laws of motion, so far as any experiments can prove them, or are needed to prove them.

That inertia is proportional to weight, is a law equivalent to that law which asserts, that when pressure produces motion in a given body, the velocity produced in a given time is as the pressure. For if the velocity be as the pressure, when the body is given, the velocity will be constant if the inertia also be as the pressure. For the inertia is understood to be that property of bodies to which, ceteris paribus, the velocity impressed is inversely proportional. One body has twice as much inertia as another, if, when the same force acts upon it for the same time, it acquires but half the velocity. This is the fundamental conception of inertia.

In Newton's pendulum experiments, the pressure producing motion was a certain resolved part of the weight, and was proportional to the weight. It appeared by the experiments, that whatever were the material of which the pendulum was formed, the rate of oscillation was the same; that is, the velocity acquired was the same. Hence the inertia of the different bodies must have been in each case as the weight: and thus this assertion is true of all different kinds of bodies.

Thus it appears that the assertion, that inertia is universally proportional to weight, is equivalent to the law of motion, that the velocity is as the pressure. The conception of inertia (of which, as we have said, the fundamental conception is, that the velocity528 impressed is inversely proportional to the inertia,) connects the two propositions so as to make them identical.

Hence our argument with regard to the universal gravity of matter brings us to the above law of motion, and is proved by Newton's experiments in the same sense in which that law of motion is so proved.

Perhaps some persons might conceive that the identity of weight and inertia is obvious at once; for both are merely resistance to motion;—inertia, resistance to all motion (or change of motion)—weight, resistance to motion upwards.

But there is a difference in these two kinds of resistance to motion. Inertia is instantaneous, weight is continuous resistance. Any momentary impulse which acts upon a free body overcomes its inertia, for it changes its motion; and this change once effected, the inertia opposes any return to the former condition, as well as any additional change. The inertia is thus overcome by a momentary force. But the weight can only be overcome by a continuous force like itself. If an impulse act in opposition to the weight, it may for a moment neutralize or overcome the weight; but if it be not continued, the weight resumes its effect, and restores the condition which existed before the impulse acted.

But weight not only produces rest, when it is resisted, but motion, when it is not resisted. Weight is measured by the reaction which would balance it; but when unbalanced, it produces motion, and the velocity of this motion increases constantly. Now what determines the velocity thus produced in a given time, or its rate of increase? What determines it to have one magnitude rather than another? To this we must evidently reply, the inertia. When weight produces motion, the inertia is the reaction which makes the motion determinate. The accumulated motion produced by the action of unbalanced weight is as determinate a condition as the equilibrium produced by balanced weight. In both cases the condition of the body acted on is determined by the opposition of the action and reaction.

Hence inertia is the reaction which opposes the weight, when unbalanced. But by the conception of action and reaction, (as mutually determining and determined,) they are measured by each other: and hence the inertia is necessarily proportional to the weight.

But when we have reached this conclusion, the original objection may be again urged against it. It may be said, that there must be some fallacy in this reasoning, for it proves a state of things to be necessary when we can so easily conceive a contrary state of things.529 Is it denied, the opponent may ask, that we can readily imagine a state of things in which bodies have no weight? Is not the uniform tendency of all bodies in the same direction not only not necessary, but not even true? For they do in reality tend, not with equal forces in parallel lines, but to a center with unequal forces, according to their position: and we can conceive these differences of intensity and direction in the force to be greater than they really are; and can with equal ease suppose the force to disappear altogether.

To this I reply, that certainly we may conceive the weight of bodies to vary in intensity and direction, and by an additional effort of imagination, may conceive the weight to vanish: but that in all these suppositions, even in the extreme one, we must suppose the rule to be universal. If any bodies have weight, all bodies must have weight. If the direction of weight be different in different points, this direction must still vary according to the law of continuity; and the same is true of the intensity of the weight. For if this were not so, the rest and motion, the velocity and direction, the permanence and change of bodies, as to their mechanical condition, would be arbitrary and incoherent: they would not be subject to mechanical ideas; that is, not to ideas at all: and hence these conditions of objects would in fact be inconceivable. In order that the universe may be possible, that is, may fall under the conditions of intelligible conceptions, we must be able to conceive a body at rest. But the rest of bodies (except in the absolute negation of all force) implies the equilibrium of opposite forces. And one of these opposite forces must be a general force, as weight, in order that the universe may be governed by general conditions. And this general force, by the conception of force, may produce motion, as well as equilibrium; and this motion again must be determined, and determined by general conditions; which cannot be, except the communication of motion be regulated by an inertia proportional to the weight.

But it will be asked, Is it then pretended that Newton's experiment, by which it was intended to prove inertia proportional to weight, does really prove nothing but what may be demonstrated à priori? Could we know, without experiment, that all bodies,—gold, iron, wood, cork,—have inertia proportional to their weight? And to this we reply, that experiment holds the same place in the establishment of this, as of the other fundamental doctrines of mechanics. Intercourse with the external world is requisite for developing our ideas; measurement of phenomena is needed to fix our conceptions and to render them precise: but the result of our530 experimental studies is, that we reach a position in which our convictions do not rest upon experiment. We learn by observation truths of which we afterwards see the necessity. This is the case with the laws of motion, as I have repeatedly endeavoured to show. The same will appear to be the case with the proposition, that bodies of different kinds have their inertia proportional to their weight.

For bodies of the same kind have their inertia proportional to their weight, both quantities being proportional to the quantity of matter. And if we compress the same quantity of matter into half the space, neither the weight nor the inertia is altered, because these depend on the quantity of matter alone. But in this way we obtain a body of twice the density; and in the same manner we obtain a body of any other density. Therefore whatever be the density, the inertia is proportional to the quantity of matter. But the mechanical relations of bodies cannot depend upon any difference of kind, except a difference of density. For if we suppose any fundamental difference of mechanical nature in the particles or component elements of bodies, we are led to the same conclusion, of arbitrary, and therefore impossible, results, which we deduced from this supposition with regard to weight. Therefore all bodies of different density, and hence, all bodies whatever, must have their inertia proportional to their weight.

Hence we see, that the propositions, that all bodies are heavy, and that inertia is proportional to weight, necessarily follow from those fundamental ideas which we unavoidably employ in all attempts to reason concerning the mechanical relations of bodies. This conclusion may perhaps appear the more startling to many, because they have been accustomed to expect that fundamental ideas and their relations should be self-evident at our first contemplation of them. This, however, is far from being the case, as I have already shown. It is not the first, but the most complete and developed condition of our conceptions which enables us to see what are axiomatic truths in each province of human speculation. Our fundamental ideas are necessary conditions of knowledge, universal forms of intuition, inherent types of mental development; they may even be termed, if any one chooses, results of connate intellectual tendencies; but we cannot term them innate ideas, without calling up a large array of false opinions. For innate ideas were considered as capable of composition, but by no means of simplification: as most perfect in their original condition; as to be found, if any where, in the most uneducated and most uncultivated minds; as the same in all ages, nations, and stages of intellectual culture;531 as capable of being referred to at once, and made the basis of our reasonings, without any special acuteness or effort: in all which circumstances the Fundamental Ideas of which we have spoken, are opposed to Innate Ideas so understood.

I shall not, however, here prosecute this subject. I will only remark, that Fundamental Ideas, as we view them, are not only not innate, in any usual or useful sense, but they are not necessarily ultimate elements of our knowledge. They are the results of our analysis so far as we have yet prosecuted it; but they may themselves subsequently be analysed. It may hereafter appear, that what we have treated as different Fundamental Ideas have, in fact, a connexion, at some point below the structure which we erect upon them. For instance, we treat of the mechanical ideas of force, matter, and the like, as distinct from the idea of substance. Yet the principle of measuring the quantity of matter by its weight, which we have deduced from mechanical ideas, is applied to determine the substances which enter into the composition of bodies. The idea of substance supplies the axiom, that the whole quantity of matter of a compound body is equal to the sum of the quantities of matter of its elements. The mechanical ideas of force and matter lead us to infer that the quantity both of the whole and its parts must be measured by their weights. Substance may, for some purposes, be described as that to which properties belong; matter in like manner may be described as that which resists force. The former involves the Idea of permanent Being; the latter, the Idea of Causation. There may be some elevated point of view from which these ideas may be seen to run together. But even if this be so, it will by no means affect the validity of reasonings founded upon these notions, when duly determined and developed. If we once adopt a view of the nature of knowledge which makes necessary truth possible at all, we need be little embarrassed by finding how closely connected different necessary truths are; and how often, in exploring towards their roots, different branches appear to spring from the same stem.

END OF THE APPENDIX.

532

Cambridge:
PRINTED BY C. J. CLAY, M.A.
AT THE UNIVERSITY PRESS.
1a

WORKS BY
WILLIAM WHEWELL, D.D. F.R.S.
MASTER OF TRINITY COLLEGE, CAMBRIDGE.

HISTORY OF THE INDUCTIVE SCIENCES. Third and Cheaper Edition. Three Volumes, Small Octavo, 24s.

HISTORY OF SCIENTIFIC IDEAS, being the First Part of a Third Edition of the "Philosophy of the Inductive Sciences," with Additions. Two Volumes, 14s.

NOVUM ORGANON RENOVATUM; being the Second Part of a Third Edition of the "Philosophy of the Inductive Sciences." With large Additions. 7s.

INDICATIONS OF THE CREATOR: Theological Extracts from the "History and the Philosophy of the Inductive Sciences." Second Edition. 5s. 6d.

ELEMENTS OF MORALITY, INCLUDING POLITY. Third Edition, with a Supplement. Two Volumes, 15s.

LECTURES ON SYSTEMATIC MORALITY. 7s. 6d.

2a

LECTURES ON THE HISTORY OF MORAL PHILOSOPHY IN ENGLAND. 8s.

OF A LIBERAL EDUCATION IN GENERAL, and with Particular Reference to the Studies of the University of Cambridge. Parts I. and II., in One Volume, 7s. 6d. Part III., sewed, 2s.

ON THE PRINCIPLES OF ENGLISH UNIVERSITY EDUCATION. Second Edition. 5s.

COLLEGE CHAPEL SERMONS. 10s. 6d.

NOTES ON GERMAN CHURCHES. Third Edition. 12s.

THE MECHANICAL EUCLID. Fifth Edition. 5s.

THE MECHANICS OF ENGINEERING. 9s.

THE DOCTRINE OF LIMITS. Octavo, 9s.

CONIC SECTIONS. 2s. 6d.

EDITED BY DR. WHEWELL.

BUTLER'S THREE SERMONS ON HUMAN NATURE, and a Dissertation on Virtue; with a Preface and Syllabus. Third Edition. 3s. 6d.

BUTLER'S SIX SERMONS ON MORAL SUBJECTS. With Preface and Syllabus. 3s. 6d.

LONDON: JOHN W. PARKER AND SON, WEST STRAND.

3a

New Books and New Editions,
Published by John W. Parker and Son, West Strand.

History of England, from the Fall of Wolsey to the Death of Elizabeth. Fifth and Sixth Volumes, containing the Reigns of Edward the Sixth and Mary. By J. Anthony Froude. In the Press.

A Second Edition of the First Four Volumes, containing the Reign of Henry VIII. 2l. 14s.

History of England, during the Reign of George the Third. By W. Massey, M.P. Vols. I. and II. 12s. each. The Third Volume in the Press.

History of Civilization in England. By Henry Thomas Buckle. The First Volume. Octavo. Second Edition. 21s.

Friends in Council. Second Series. The Second Edition. Two Volumes. 14s.

Friends in Council. First Series. New Edition. Two Volumes. 9s.

On Liberty. By John Stuart Mill. The Second Edition. 7s. 6d.

The Recreations of a Country Parson; Essays Parochial, Architectural, Æsthetical, Moral, Social, and Domestic. Being a Selection from the Contributions of A. K. H. B. to "Fraser's Magazine." 9s.

4a

Major Hodson's Twelve Years of a Soldier's Life in India. Edited by his Brother, the Rev. George H. Hodson, M.A. Fellow of Trinity College, Cambridge. Third Edition, with Additions, and a Portrait, 10s. 6d.

The Saint's Tragedy. By Charles Kingsley, Chaplain in Ordinary to the Queen. The Third Edition. Foolscap Octavo. 5s.

On the Classification and Geographical Distribution of Mammalia: On the Gorilla, On the Extinction and Transmutation of Species. By Richard Owen, F.R.S. Octavo. 5s.

The Odes of Horace. Translated into English Verse, with a Life and Notes. By Theodore Martin. 7s. 6d.

Arundines Cami. Edited by the Rev. Henry Drury, M.A. Canon of Salisbury, Chaplain to the House of Commons. The Fifth and Cheaper Edition.

The New Cratylus. By J. W. Donaldson, D.D. Classical Examiner in the University of London. The Third Edition, Revised throughout and considerably Enlarged. 20s.

Night Lessons from Scripture. Compiled by the Author of 'Amy Herbert.' Demy, Red Edges. 3s.

Paley's Evidences of Christianity. With Annotations by the Archbishop of Dublin. Octavo. 9s.

Paley's Moral Philosophy. With Annotations by the Archbishop of Dublin. Octavo. 7s.

The Good News of God. Sermons by Charles Kingsley, Chaplain in Ordinary to the Queen. The Second Edition. 6s.

5a

Sermons on the Atonement and other Subjects, preached before the University of Cambridge. By E. Harold Browne, M.A. Norrisian Professor of Divinity in the University; Canon of Exeter. Octavo. 5s.

An Exposition of the Thirty-nine Articles, Historical and Doctrinal. By Professor Harold Browne. Fourth Edition. Octavo, 16s.

Critical and Grammatical Commentary on St. Paul's Epistle to the Ephesians. By Charles J. Ellicott, B.D. Professor of Divinity, King's College, London. The Second Edition, Enlarged. 8s. 6d.

Lately Published:

I. Galatians. Second Edition, Enlarged. 8s. 6d.
II. Pastoral Epistles. Second Edition. In the Press.
III. Philippians, Colossians, and Philemon. 10s. 6d.
IV. Thessalonians. 7s. 6d.
Peloponnesus: Notes of Study and Travel. By W. G. Clark, M.A. Fellow and Tutor of Trinity College, Cambridge. 10s. 6d.

Revolutions in English History. By Robert Vaughan, D.D. The First Volume, Revolutions of Race. 15s.

History of the Literature of Ancient Greece. From the Manuscripts of the late Professor K. O. Müller. The first half of the Translation by the Right Hon. Sir George Cornewall Lewis, Bart. M.P. The remainder of the Translation, and the Completion of the Work, by John William Donaldson, D.D. Three Volumes, Octavo. 36s. The new portion separately, Two Volumes, 20s.

Soldiers and their Science. By Captain Brabazon, R.A. 7s.

Essays written in the Intervals of Business. The Seventh Edition. 2s. 6d.

Companions of My Solitude. The Fifth Edition. 3s. 6d.

6a

On the Study of Words. By Richard Chenevix Trench, D.D. Dean of Westminster. The Ninth Edition, Revised and Enlarged. 4s.

A Select Glossary of English Words used formerly in Senses different from their Present. By Richard Chenevix Trench, D.D. Dean of Westminster. The Second Edition, Revised and Improved. 4s.

Intellectual Education, and its Influence on the Character and Happiness of Women. By Emily Shirreff. Octavo. 10s.

The Cloister Life of the Emperor Charles the Fifth. By William Stirling, M.P. The Third Edition. 8s.

Man and His Dwelling Place. An Essay towards the Interpretation of Nature. 9s.

Dissertations and Discussions, Political, Philosophical and Historical. By John Stuart Mill. Two Volumes. Octavo. 24s.

Of the Plurality of Worlds. An Essay. The Fifth Edition. 6s.

Bacon's Essays. With Annotations by the Archbishop of Dublin. The Fourth Edition. 10s. 6d.

Extracts from Jean Paul Richter. Translated by Lady Chatterton. 3s. 6d.

Shipwrecks of the Royal Navy. By W. O. S. Gilly. With Preface by the Rev. Dr. Gilly. The Third Edition. 5s.

The Kingdom and People of Siam; with a Narrative of the Mission to that Country. By Sir John Bowring, F.R.S. Two Volumes, with Illustrations and Map. 32s.

7a

The Spanish Conquest in America, and its Relation to the History of Slavery, and to the Government of Colonies. By Arthur Helps. Octavo. Volumes I. II. 28s. Volume III. 16s.

Notes on Hospitals. By Florence Nightingale. The Second Edition. 5s.

The Mediterranean; A Memoir Historical, Geographical, and Nautical. By Admiral W. H. Smyth, D.C.L., F.R.S. Octavo. 15s.

Lectures on Astronomy. By Henry Moseley, M.A., F.R.S. Canon of Bristol. The Fourth Edition. 3s. 6d.

Elements of Chemistry. By William Allen Miller, M.D., F.R.S. Professor of Chemistry, King's College, London. Complete in Three Parts, with numerous Illustrations. £2. 6s. 6d.

Manual of Human Microscopic Anatomy. By Albert Kölliker. With 289 Illustrations. Octavo.

Lectures on the Principles and Practice of Physic. By Thomas Watson, M D. Physician Extraordinary to the Queen. Fourth Edition, revised. Two Volumes. Octavo. 34s.

Anatomy, Descriptive and Surgical. By Henry Gray, F.R.S. Lecturer on Anatomy at St. George's Hospital. With 363 large Woodcuts, from Original Drawings. Royal Octavo, 782 pages. 28s.

Practical Geodesy: Chain Surveying, Surveying Instruments, Levelling, Trigonometry, and Mining; Maritime, Estate, Parochial, and Railroad Surveying. By Butler Williams, C.E. The Third Edition, revised. Octavo. 8s. 6d.

8a

Manual of Geographical Science. Part the Second, Descriptive Geography, containing

Ancient Geography, by the Rev. W. L. Bevan, M.A. Vicar of Hay, Brecon.

Maritime Discovery and Modern Geography, by the Rev. C. G. Nicolay, F.R.G.S.

With Copious Index. Octavo. 15s.

The First Part, Octavo, 10s. 6d. contains:

Mathematical Geography, by M. O'Brien, M.A.
Physical Geography, by D. T. Ansted, M.A., F.R.S.
Chartography, by J. Jackson, F.R.S.
Geographical Terminology, by Rev. C. G. Nicolay.
The Institutes of Justinian; with English Introduction, Translation, and Notes. By Thomas C. Sandars, M.A. late Fellow of Oriel College, Oxford. The Second Edition, revised. Octavo. 15s.

Principles of Political Economy. By John Stuart Mill. Fourth Edition. Two Volumes. Octavo. 30s.

The Senses and the Intellect. The Emotions and the Will: completing a Systematic Exposition of the Human Mind. By Alexander Bain, M.A., Examiner in Logic and Moral Philosophy in the University of London. Octavo. 15s. each.

Babrii Fabulæ Æsopeæ, e Codice Manuscripto Partem Secundam nunc primum edidit Georgius Cornewall Lewis, A.M., Ædis Christi, in Universitate Oxoniensi, Alumnus Honorarius. 3s. 6d.

Babrii Fabulæ Æsopeæ, cum Fabularum deperditarum Fragmentis, recensuit et breviter illustravit Georgius Cornewall Lewis, M.A. 5s. 6d.

9a

The Choephoræ of Æschylus; with Notes. By John Conington, M.A. Professor of Latin, Oxford. 6s.

Notes upon Thucydides. By John G. Sheppard, M.A. Head Master of Kidderminster School, and Lewis Evans, M.A. Head Master of Sandbach School. Books I. and II. 8s.

The Ethics of Aristotle. By Sir Alexander Grant, Bart., M.A. The First Volume, the Essays, 8s. 6d. The Second Volume, Books I.—VI., with Notes, 12s.

The Politics of Aristotle; with Introduction, Essays, Notes, and Index. By R. Congreve, M.A. 16s.

Platonis Philebus; with Introduction, and Notes, Critical and Explanatory. By Charles Badham, D.D., Head Master of Birmingham and Edgbaston Proprietary School. 5s.

Phædrus, Lysis, and Protagoras of Plato, literally translated. By J. Wright, M.A. 4s. 6d.

The Greek Testament; with Notes, Grammatical and Exegetical. By W. Webster, M.A., of King's College, London; and W. F. Wilkinson, M.A., Vicar of St. Werburgh, Derby. Volume I., containing the Four Gospels and the Acts of the Apostles, 20s.

Synonyms of the New Testament. By R. Chenevix Trench, D.D. Dean of Westminster. Fourth Edition. 5s.

Select Private Orations of Demosthenes; with English Notes. By C. T. Penrose, M.A. 4s.

10a

The Frogs of Aristophanes; with English Notes. By Rev. H. P. Cookesley, M.A. 7s.

Aristophanes. Edited, with Notes and Index, by H. A. Holden, M.A., Head Master of Ipswich School. 15s.

⁂ The Plays separately, 1s. each; Notulæ Criticæ and Onomasticon. 4s.

Greek Verses of Shrewsbury School; with Account of the Iambic Metre, and Exercises in Greek Tragic Senarii. Edited by Dr. Kennedy, Head Master. 8s.

Antigone of Sophocles, in Greek and English; with Notes. By Dr. Donaldson. 9s.

Agamemnon of Æschylus, in Greek and English; with Notes. By J. Conington, M.A. 7s. 6d.

Æschylus translated into English Verse; with Notes, Life of Æschylus, and Discourse on Greek Tragedy. By J. S. Blackie, Professor of Greek, Edinburgh. Two Volumes, 46s.

The Alcestis of Euripides; with Notes. By J. H. Monk, D.D., Bishop of Gloucester and Bristol. 4s. 6d.

Pindar; with Notes. By Dr. Donaldson. 16s.

Homeric Ballads. The Text, with Translation in Verse, and Notes. By Dr. Maginn. 6s.

Müller's Dissertations on the Eumenides of Æschylus. Second Edition. 6s. 6d.

C. Cornelii Taciti Opera ad Codices Antiquissimos commentario critico edidit Franciscus Ritter, Professor Bonnensis. Four Volumes, Octavo. 28s.

11a

Propertius; with English Notes. By F. A. Paley, Editor of "Æschylus." Octavo. 10s. 6d.

Plautus: Aulularia; with Notes. By J. Hildyard, B.D. 7s. 6d.

Plautus: Menæchmei; with Notes. By J. Hildyard, B.D. 7s. 6d.

Longer Exercises in Latin Prose Composition; with a Commentary and Remarks on the best mode of forming a correct Latin Style. By Dr. Donaldson. 6s. 6d.

Elements of Logic. By Richard Whately, Archbishop of Dublin. Crown 8vo. 4s. 6d. Octavo. 10s. 6d.

Elements of Rhetoric. By Archbishop Whately. Crown 8vo. 4s. 6d. Octavo. 10s. 6d.

System of Logic, Ratiocinative and Inductive. By John Stuart Mill. Fourth Edition. Two Volumes, Octavo. 25s.

An Historical and Explanatory Treatise on the Book of Common Prayer. By W. G. Humphry, B.D., late Fellow of Trinity College, Cambridge. Second Edition, enlarged. 7s. 6d.

Churchman's Guide: A Copious Index of Sermons and other Works, by eminent Church of England Divines; digested and arranged according to their subjects. By J. Forster, M.A. Octavo. 7s.

On Public Reading: Garrick's Mode of Reading the Liturgy; with Notes, and a Discourse on Public Reading. By R. Cull, Tutor in Elocution. 5s. 6d.

The Churchman's Theological Dictionary. By Robert Eden, M.A., Chaplain to the Bishop of Norwich. Demy 12mo. 5s.

LONDON: JOHN W. PARKER AND SON, WEST STRAND.

12a

Annotated Edition of the English Poets,
WITH INTRODUCTIONS, NOTES, AND MEMOIRS,
Historical, Biographical and Critical,
BY ROBERT BELL.

In Volumes, 2s. 6d. EACH, BOUND IN CLOTH.

ANCIENT POEMS, BALLADS, AND SONGS OF THE PEASANTRY. 2s. 6d.

GREENE AND MARLOWE. 2s. 6d.

EARLY BALLADS ILLUSTRATIVE OF HISTORY, TRADITIONS, AND CUSTOMS. 2s. 6d.

BEN JONSON. 2s. 6d.

CHAUCER. Eight Volumes, 20s.

BUTLER. Three Volumes, 7s. 6d.

THOMSON. Two Volumes, 5s.

DRYDEN. Three Volumes, 7s. 6d.

SHAKSPEARE. 2s. 6d.

COWPER. Three Volumes. 7s. 6d.

SURREY, MINOR CONTEMPORANEOUS POETS, AND BUCKHURST. 2s. 6d.

SONGS FROM THE DRAMATISTS; from the first regular Comedy to the close of the 18th Century. 2s. 6d.

WYATT. 2s. 6d.

OLDHAM. 2s. 6d.

WALLER. 2s. 6d.

London: JOHN W. PARKER AND SON, West Strand.

FOOTNOTES:

1Metaph. xii. 4.

2 Diog. Laert. Vit. Plat.

3 T. ii. p. 16, c, d. ed. Bekker, t. v. p. 437.

4 See the remarks on this phrase in the next chapter.

5Hist. Ind. Sc. b. iii. c. ii.

6 This matter is further discussed in the Appendix, Essay A.

7 These matters are further discussed in the Appendix, Essay B.

8 See Appendix, Essay B.

9Hist. Ind. Sc. b. ii. Additions to 3rd Ed.

10 See these views further discussed in the Appendix, Essay C.

11Metaph. xii. 4.

12Hist. Ind. Sc. b. i. c. iii. sect. 2.

13Analyt. Prior. i. 30.

14Analyt. Post. i. 18.

15Analyt. Prior. ii. 23, περι της επαγωγης.

16Analyt. Post. ii. 19.

17 But the best reading seems to be not ἕν τι but ἔτι: and the clause must be rendered "both to perceive and to retain the perception in the mind." This correction does not disturb the general sense of the passage, that the first principles of science are obtained by finding the One in the Many.

18Analyt. Post. i. 34.

19Ibid. ii. 19.

20Analyt. Prior. ii. 25.

21 See on this subject Appendix, Essay D.

22 See the chapter on Certain Characteristics of Scientific Induction in the Phil. Ind. Sc. or in the Nov. Org. Renov.

23Phil. Ind. Sc. b. viii. c. i. art. 11, or Hist. Sc. Id. b. viii.

24 B. i. c. xi. sect. 2.

25 B. iii. c. i. sect. 9.

26De Cælo, ii. 13.

27Ibid. ii. 10.

28 xii. 8.

29 B. xvi. c. vi.

30On the Classification of Mammalia, &c.: a Lecture delivered at Cambridge, May 10, 1859, p. 3.

31 B. i. c. xi.

32History of Scientific Ideas, and Novum Organum Renovatum.

33 The remainder of this chapter is new in the present edition.

34Hist. of Greece, Part ii. chap. 68.

35De Antiqua Medicina, c. 20.

36 Lib. i. c. 9.

37De Elem. i. 6.

38 In former editions I have not done justice to this passage.

39Hist. Ind. Sc. Addition to Introduction in Third Edition.

40 Lib. i. Fast.

41Hist. Nat. i. 75.

42Quæst. Nat. vii. 25.

43Quæst. Nat. vii. 30, 31.

44Ibid. iii. 7.

45Hist. Ind. Sc. b. iii. c. iv. sect. 8.

46Ibid. b. ix. c. ii.

47 See Hist. Ind. Sc. b. iv. c. i.

48 See the opinion of Aquinas, in Degerando, Hist. Com. des Syst. iv. 499; of Duns Scotus, ibid. iv. 523.

49Liber Excerptionum, Lib. i. c. i.

50Tr. Ex. Lib. i. c. vii.

51 Tenneman, viii. 461.

52Mores Catholici, or Ages of Faith, viii. p. 247.

53 Tenneman, viii. 460.

54 If there were any doubt on this subject, we might refer to the writers who afterwards questioned the supremacy of Aristotle, and who with one voice assert that an infallible authority had been claimed for him. Thus Laurentius Valla: "Quo minus ferendi sunt recentes Peripatetici, qui nullius sectæ hominibus interdicunt libertate ab Aristotele dissentiendi, quasi sophos hic, non philosophus." Pref. in Dial. (Tenneman, ix. 29.) So Ludovicus Vives: "Sunt ex philosophis et ex theologis qui non solum quo Aristoteles pervenit extremum esse aiunt naturæ, sed quâ pervenit eam rectissimam esse omnium et certissimam in natura viam." (Tenneman, ix. 43.) We might urge too, the evasions practised by philosophical Reformers, through fear of the dogmatism to which they had to submit; for example, the protestation of Telesius at the end of the Proem to his work, De Rerum Natura: "Nec tamen, si quid eorum quæ nobis posita sunt, sacris literis, Catholicæve ecclesiæ decretis non cohæreat, tenendum id, quin penitus rejiciendum asseveramus contendimusque. Neque enim humana modo ratio quævis, sed ipse etiam sensus illis posthabendus, et si illis non congruat, abnegandus omnino et ipse etiam est sensus."

55Ages of Faith, viii. 247: to the author of which I am obliged for this quotation.

56 Algazel. See Hist. Ind. Sc. b. iv. c. i.

57 Tenneman, viii. 830.

58 Degerando, iv. 535.

59 Leibnitz's expressions are, (Op. t. vi. p. 16): "Quand j'étais jeune, je prenois quelque a l'Art de Lulle, mais je crus y entrevoir bien des défectuosités, dont j'ai dit quelque chose dans un petit Essai d'écolier intitulé De Arte Combinatoria, publié en 1666, et qui a été réimprimé après malgré moi. Mais comme je ne méprise rien facilement, excepté les arts divinatoires que ne sont que des tromperies toutes pures, j'ai trouvé quelque chose d'estimable encore dans l'Art de Lulle."

60Works, vii. 296.

61Fratris Rogeri Bacon, Ordinis Minorum, Opus Majus, ad Clementem Quartum, Pontificem Romanum, ex MS. Codice Dubliniensi cum aliis quibusdam collato, nunc primum edidit S. Jebb, M.D. Londini, 1733.

62Opus Majus, Præf.

63 Contents of Roger Bacon's Opus Majus.

Part I. On the four causes of human ignorance:—Authority, Custom, Popular Opinion, and the Pride of supposed Knowledge.

Part II. On the source of perfect wisdom in the Sacred Scripture.

Part III. On the Usefulness of Grammar.

Part IV. On the Usefulness of Mathematics.

(1) The necessity of Mathematics in Human Things (published separately as the Specula Mathematica).

(2) The necessity of Mathematics in Divine Things.—1o. This study has occupied holy men: 2o. Geography: 3o. Chronology: 4o. Cycles; the Golden Number, &c.: 5o. Natural Phenomena, as the Rainbow: 6o. Arithmetic: 7o. Music.

(3) The necessity of Mathematics in Ecclesiastical Things. 1o. The Certification of Faith: 2o. The Correction of the Calendar.

(4) The necessity of Mathematics in the State.—1o. Of Climates: 2o. Hydrography: 3o. Geography: 4o. Astrology.

Part V. On Perspective (published separately as Perspectiva).

(1) The organs of vision.

(2) Vision in straight lines.

(3) Vision reflected and refracted.

(4) De multiplicatione specierum (on the propagation of the impressions of light, heat, &c.)

Part VI. On Experimental Science.

64Op. Maj. p. 1.

65Ibid. p. 2.

66Ibid. p. 10.

67 I will give a specimen. Opus Majus, c. viii. p. 35: "These two kinds of philosophers, the Ionic and Italic, ramified through many sects and various successors, till they came to the doctrine of Aristotle, who corrected and changed the propositions of all his predecessors, and attempted to perfect philosophy. In the [Italic] succession, Pythagoras, Archytas Tarentinus and Timæus are most prominently mentioned. But the principal philosophers, as Socrates, Plato, and Aristotle, did not descend from this line, but were Ionics and true Greeks, of whom the first was Thales Milesius.... Socrates, according to Augustine in his 8th book, is related to have been a disciple of Archelaus. This Socrates is called the father of the great philosophers, since he was the master of Plato and Aristotle, from whom all the sects of philosophers descended.... Plato, first learning what Socrates and Greece could teach, made a laborious voyage to Egypt, to Archytas of Tarentum and Timæus, as says Jerome to Paulinus. And this Plato is, according to holy men, preferred to all philosophers, because he has written many excellent things concerning God, and morality, and a future life, which agree with the divine wisdom of God. And Aristotle was born before the death of Socrates, since he was his hearer for three years, as we read in the life of Aristotle.... This Aristotle, being made the master of Alexander the Great, sent two thousand men into all regions of the earth, to search out the nature of things, as Pliny relates in the 8th book of his Naturalia, and composed a thousand books, as we read in his life."

68Ibid. p. 36.

69Autonomaticè.

70Op. Maj. p. 46.

71 See Pref. to Jebb's edition. The passages, there quoted, however, are not extracts from the Opus Majus, but (apparently) from the Opus Minus (MS. Cott. Tib. c. 5.) "Si haberem potestatem supra libros Aristotelis, ego facerem omnes cremari; quia non est nisi temporis amissio studere in illis, et causa erroris, et multiplicatio ignorantiæ ultra id quod valeat explicari.... Vulgus studentum cum capitibus suis non habet unde excitetur ad aliquid dignum, et ideo languet et asininat circa male translata, et tempus et studium amittit in omnibus et expensas."

72 Part ii.

73 Parts iv. v. and vi.

74 Op. Maj. p. 476.

75 Op. Maj. p. 15.

76 Ibid. p. 445, see also p. 448. "Scientiæ aliæ sciunt sua principia invenire per experimenta, sed conclusiones per argumenta facta ex principiis inventis. Si vero debeant habere experientiam conclusionum suarum particularem et completam, tunc oportet quod habeant per adjutorium istius scientiæ nobilis (experimentalis)."

77 Op. Maj. p. 60.

78 Ibid. p. 64.

79 "Veritates magnificas in terminis aliarum scientiarum in quas per nullam viam possunt illæ scientiæ, hæc sola scientiarum domina speculativarum, potest dare." Op. Maj. p. 465.

80 One of the ingredients of a preparation here mentioned, is the flesh of a dragon, which it appears is used as food by the Ethiopians. The mode of preparing this food cannot fail to amuse the reader. "Where there are good flying dragons, by the art which they possess, they draw them out of their dens, and have bridles and saddles in readiness, and they ride upon them, and make them bound about in the air in a violent manner, that the hardness and toughness of the flesh may be reduced, as boars are hunted and bulls are baited before they are killed for eating." Op. Maj. p. 470.

81 Op. Maj. p. 473.

82 Quoted by Jebb, Pref. to Op. Maj.

83 Mosheim, Hist. iii. 161.

84 Op. Maj. p. 57.

85 Mosheim, iii. 161.

86 Gratian published the Decretals in the twelfth century; and the Canon and Civil Law became a regular study in the universities soon afterwards.

87 Tenneman, ix. 4.

88 Tenneman, ix. 25.

89 "Jam nobis manifestum est terram istam in veritate moveri," &c.—De Doctâ Ignorantiâ, lib. ii. c. xii.

90 De Doct. Ignor. lib. i. c. i.

91 De Conjecturis, lib. i. c. iii. iv.

92 Born in 1433.

93 Born 1529, died 1597.

94 Aristoteles Exotericus, p. 50.

95 Tiraboschi, t. vii. pt. ii. p. 411.

96 "Franciscus Patricius, novam veram integram de universis conditurus philosophiam, sequentia uti verissima prænuntiare est ausus. Prænunciata ordine persecutus, divinis oraculis, geometricis rationibus, clarissimisque experimentis comprobavit.

Ante primum nihil,
Post primum omnia,
A principio omnia," &c.
His other works are Panaugia, Pancosmia, Dissertations Peripateticæ.

97 Tiraboschi, t. vii. pt. ii. p. 411.

98 Dissert. Perip. t. ii. lib. v. sub fin.

99 Tenneman, ix. 148.

100 Tenneman, ix. 167.

101 Ibid. 158.

102 Agrippa, De Occult. Phil. lib. i. c. l.

103 Written in 1526.

104 Philip Aurelius Theophrastus Bombastus von Hohenheim, also called Paracelsus Eremita, born at Einsiedlen in Switzerland, in 1493.

105 Hist. Sc. Id. b. ix. c. 2. sect. 1. The Mystical School of Biology.

106 Tenneman, ix. 221.

107 Tenneman, ix. 265.

108 Bernardini Telesii Consentini De Rerum Natura juxta propria Principia.

109 I take this account from Tenneman: this Proem was omitted in subsequent editions of Telesius, and is not in the one which I have consulted. Tenneman, Gesch. d. Phil. ix. 280.

110 Proem.

111 "De Principiis atque Originibus secundum fabulas Cupidinis et Cœli: sive Parmenidis et Telesii et præcipuè Democriti Philosophia tractata in Fabula de Cupidine."

112 "Talia sunt qualia possunt esse ea quæ ab intellectu sibi permisso, nec ab experimentis continenter et gradatim sublevato, profecta videntur."

113 Thom. Campanella de Libris propriis, as quoted in Tenneman, ix. 291.

114 Economisti Italiani, t. i. p. xxxiii.

115 Tenneman, ix. 305.

116 Hist. Ind. Sc. b. xvi. c. iii. sect. 2.

117 Ibid. b. xvii. c. ii. sect. 1.

118 Quæst. Peripat. i. 1.

119 Tenneman, ix. 108.

120 Hist. Ind. Sc. b. v. c. iii. sect. 2.

121 Tenneman, ix. 420. "Quæcunque ab Aristotele dicta essent commenticia esse." Freigius, Vita Petri Rami, p. 10.

122 Rami, Animadv. Aristot. i. iv.

123 See Hist. Ind. Sc. b. iv. c. iv. sect. 4.

124 Tenneman, ix. 230.

125 Ibid. 108.

126 Tenneman, ix. 246.

127 Melancthon, De Anima, p. 207, quoted in Tenneman, ix. 121.

128 His works have never been published, and exist in manuscript in the library of the Institute at Paris. Some extracts were published by Venturi, Essai sur les Ouvrages de Leonard da Vinci. Paris, 1797.

129 Leonardo died in 1520, at the age of 78.

130 Paul III. in 1543.

131Hist. Ind. Sc. b. v. c. ii.

132 Born 1537, died 1619.

133Hist. Ind. Sc. b. xvii. c. ii. sect. 1.

134 Fabricius, De Motu Locali, p. 182.

135 p. 199.

136Speculationum Liber, p. 195.

137Ibid. p. 169.

138 Gulielmi Gilberti, Colcestriensis, Medici Londinensis, De Magnete, Magneticisque Corporibus, et de Magno Magnete Tellure, Physiologia Nova, plurimis et Argumentis et Experimentis demonstrata.

139Hist. Ind. Sc. b. xii. c. i.

140 Pref.

141De Magnete, lib. vi. c. 3, 4.

142Nov. Org. b. i.

143 B. i. Aph. 64.

144 Vol. ix. 185.

145De Magnete, p. 60.

146 B. iii. c. 4.

147Nov. Org. b. ii. Aph. 48.

148 Drinkwater's Life of Galileo, p. 18.

149Life of Galileo, p. 9.

150Hist. Ind. Sc. b. vi. c. ii. sect. 5.

151Life of Galileo, p. 29.

152Ibid. p. 33.

317

153Il Saggiatore, ii. 247.

154Il Saggiatore, ii. 200.

155Ibid. i. 501.

156Hist. Ind. Sc. b. vi. c. ii. sect. 2.

157Hist. Ind. Sc. b. vi. c. ii. sect. 4.

158Ibid. b. v. c. iv. sect. 1.

159De Stell. Mart. p. iv. c. 51 (1609); Drinkwater's Kepler, p. 33.

160 Published 1604. Hist. Ind. Sc. b. ix. c. ii.

161Hist. Ind. Sc. b. v. c. iv. sect. i.

162Hist. Ind. Sc. b. vii. c. vi. sect 1.

163De Stell. Mart. p. 11. c. 19.

164Hist. Ind. Sc. b. ii. c. iv. sect. 6.

165Ibid. sect. 8.

166 Montucla, i. 566.

167De Augm. lib. iv. c. 1.

168 And in other passages: thus, "Ego enim buccinator tantum pugnam non ineo." Nov. Org. lib. iv. c. i.

169 Lib. 1. Aphor. 78 et seq.

170Aug. Sc. Lib. iii. c. 4. p. 194. So in other places, as Nov. Org. i. Aph. 104. "De scientiis tum demum bene sperandum est quando per scalam veram et per gradus continuos, et non intermissos aut hiulcos a particularibus ascendetur ad axiomata minora, et deinde ad media, alia aliis superiora, et postremo demum ad generalissima."

171Nov. Org. 1. Aph. 22.

172Ib. Aph. 20.

173 1 Ax. 15.

174Nov. Org. lib. ii. Aph. 19.

175Inst. Mag. par. iii. (vol. viii. p. 244).

176Hist. Ind. Sc. b. x. c. i.

177Ib. c. iv.

178Nov. Org. lib. i. Aph. 61.

179Nov. Org. lib. ii. Aph. 10.

180 Aph. 11.

181 Aph. 15, p. 105.

182 Page 110.

183 Herschel, On the Study of Nat. Phil. Art. 192.

184Nov. Org. lib. i. Aph. 40.

185Nov. Org. lib. i. Ax. 103.

186Edinb. Rev. No. cxxxii. p. 65.

187Ib.

188 Pref. to the Nat. Hist. i. 243.

189Nov. Org. lib. i. Aph. 19.

190Ibid. lib. i. Aph. 20.

191 Aph. 27.

192Ib. 28.

193 Aph. 104. So Aph. 105. "In constituendo axiomate forma inductionis alia quam adhuc in usu fuit excogitanda est," &c.

194Ep. ad P. Fulgentium. Op. x. 330.

195Nov. Org. i. Aph. 113.

196 See the motto to Kant's Kritik der Reinen Vernunft.

197Œuvres Philosophiques de Bacon, &c. par M. N. Bouillet, 3 Tomes.

Examen de la Philosophie de Bacon ((Euvres Posthumes du Comte J. de Maistre).

Bacon, sa Vie, son Temps, sa Philosophie, par Charles de Remusat.

Histoire de la Vie et des Ouvrages de François Bacon, par J. B. de Vaugelles.

Franz Baco von Verulam, von Kuno Fischer.

The Works of Francis Bacon, collected and edited by James Spedding, Robert Leslie Ellis, and Douglas Denon Heath.

198 Note to Aph. xviii.

199 Pref. to the Parasceue, Vol. i. p. 382.

200 Anatomical Exercitations concerning the Generation of Living Creatures, 1653. Preface.

201 He used similar expressions in conversation. George Ent, who edited his Generation of Animals, visited him, "at that time residing not far from the city; and found him very intent upon the perscrutation of nature's works, and with a countenance as cheerful, as mind unperturbed; Democritus-like, chiefly searching into the cause of natural things." In the course of conversation the writer said, "It hath always been your choice about the secrets of Nature, to consult Nature herself." "'Tis true," replied he; "and I have constantly been of opinion that from thence we might acquire not only the knowledge of those less considerable secrets of Nature, but even a certain admiration of that Supreme Essence, the Creator. And though I have ever been ready to acknowledge, that many things have been discovered by learned men of former times; yet do I still believe that the number of those which remain yet concealed in the darkness of impervestigable Nature is much greater. Nay, I cannot forbear to wonder, and sometimes smile at those, who persuade themselves, that all things were so consummately and absolutely delivered by Aristotle, Galen, or some other great name, as that nothing was left to the superaddition of any that succeeded."

202 Lib. i. c. 2, 3.

203 Anal. Post. ii.

204 Pars iii. p. 45.

205 See Hist. Ind. Sc. b. vi. c. ii.

206 Cap. i. ii.

207 Hist. Ind. Sc. b. ix. c. ii.

208 Meteorum, c. viii. p. 187.

209 Mackintosh, Dissertation on Ethical Science.

210Hist. Ind. Sc. b. vii. c. i.

211 Castelli, Torricelli, Viviani, Baliani, Gassendi, Mersenne, Borelli, Cavalleri.

212De Plenitudine Mundi, in qua defenditur Cartesiana Philosophia contra sententias Francisci Baconi, Th. Hobbii et Sethi Wardi.

213 Bacon's Works, vol. ii. 111.

214Hist. Ind. Sc. b. vii. c. i.

215Nov. Org. lib. ii. Aph. 2.

216Ib. lib. ii. Aph. 45.

217Optics, qu. 31, near the end.

218 Qu. 28.

219Hist. Ind. Sc. b. v. and b. vii.

220Optics, qu. 31.

221History of Ideas, b. iii. c. x.

222Ibid. b. iii. c. ix. x. xi.

223Opticks, qu. 31.

224Nov. Org. l. ii. Aph. 2. "Licet enim in natura nihil existet præter corpora individua, edentia actus puros individuos ex lege; in doctrinis tamen illa ipsa lex, ejusque inquisitio, et inventio, et explicatio, pro fundamento est tam ad sciendum quam ad operandum. Eam autem legem, ejusque paragraphos, formarum nomine intelligimus; præsertim cum hoc vocabulum invaluerit, et familiariter occurrat."

Aph. 17. "Eadem res est forma calidi vel forma luminis, et lex calidi aut lex luminis."

225Essay, b. xi. c. iv. sect. 3.

226Ibid. c. xiii. sect. 22.

227History of Ideas, b. iii. c. iii. Modern Opinions respecting the Idea of Cause.

228Ibid. b. i. c. iv.

229Langue des Calculs, p. 1.

321

230Grammaire, p. xxxvi.

231 Since the selection and construction of terms is thus a matter of so much consequence in the formation of science, it is proper that systematic rules, founded upon sound principles, should be laid down for the performance of this operation. Some such rules are accordingly suggested in b. iv. of the Nov. Org. Ren.

232Disc. Prélim. p. viii.

233 Helvetius Sur l'Homme, c. xxiii.

234 P. xiii.

235 See Mr.Sharpe's Essays.

236 Price's Essays, p. 16.

237 P. 18.

238 Reid, Essays on the Powers of the Human Mind, iii. 31.

239 Stewart, Outlines of Moral Phil. p. 138.

240 Whately, Polit. Econ. p. 76.

241 Cousin, Fragmens Philosophiques, i. 53.

242Ibid. i. 67.

243 See also the vigorous critique of Locke's Essay, by Lemaistre, Soirées de St. Petersbourg.

244 Ampère, Essai, p. 210.

245Kritik der Reinen Vernunft, Pref. p. xv.

246 The sensational system never acquired in Germany the ascendancy which it obtained in England and France; but I am compelled here to pass over the history of philosophy in Germany, except so far as it affects ourselves.

247 i. p. 14.

248 i. p. 7.

249Hist. Ind. Sc. b. xi. c. vii.

250 P. 15.

251 P. 16.

252 M. Comte's statement is so entirely at variance with the fact that I must quote it here. (Phil. Pos. vol. i. p. 705.)

"Le second théorème général de dynamique consiste dans le célèbre et important principe des aires, dont le première idée est due à Kepler, qui découvrit et démontra forte simplement cette propriété pour le cas du mouvement d'une molecule unique, ou en d'autres terms, d'un corps dont tous les points se meuvent identiquement. Kepler établit, par les considérations les plus élémentaires, qui si la force accélératrice totale dont une molecule est animée tend constamment vers un point fixé, le rayon vecteur du mobile décrit autour de ce point des aires égales en temps egaux, de telle sorte que l'aire décrite au bout d'un temps quelconque croît proportionellement à ce temps. Il fit voir en outre que réciproquement, si une semblable relation a été vérifiée dans le mouvement d'un corps par rapport à un certain point, c'est une preuve suffisante de l'action sur le corps d'un force dirigée sans cesse vers ce point."

There is not a trace of the above propositions in the work De Stellâ Martis, which contains Kepler's discovery of his law, nor, I am convinced, in any other of Kepler's works. He is everywhere constant to his conceptions of the magnetic virtue residing in the sun, by means of which the sun, revolving on his axis, carries the planets round with him. M. Comte's statement so exactly expresses Newton's propositions, that one is led to suspect some extraordinary mistake, by which what should have been said of the one was transferred to the other.

253 Vol. ii. p. 433.

254 Vol. ii. 640.

255 I venture to offer this problem;—to express the laws of the phenomena of diffraction without the hypothesis of undulations;—as a challenge to any one who holds such hypothesis to be unphilosophical.

256 ii. p. 641.

257 ii. p. 673.

258 Hist. Ind. Sc. ii. 489, b. x. c. i.

259 ii. p. 561.

260 i. 50.

261 i. 41.

262 ii. 433.

263Phil. Pos. ii. 392-398.

264 [A System of Logic, Ratiocinative and Inductive, being a connected view of the Principles of Evidence, and of the Methods of Scientific Investigation. By John Stuart Mill.]

265 These Remarks were published in 1849, under the title Of Induction, with especial reference to Mr. J. S. Mill's System of Logic.

266 My references are throughout (except when otherwise expressed) to the volume and the page of Mr. Mill's first edition of his Logic.

267 On this subject see an Essay On the Transformation of Hypotheses, given in the Appendix.

268 B. vii. c. iii. sect. 3.

269 B. iii. c. ix. art. 7.

270 B. i. c. iii.

271 B. iii. c. viii.

272Discourse, Art. 192.

273 B. xi. c. xi.

274Phil. b. xiii. c. ix. art. 7.

275 B. xiii. c. viii.

276 Given also in the Phil. Ind. Sc. b. xiii. c. vii. sect. 17.

277Ibid. b. vi. c. iv.

278 See Hist. Ind. Sc. b. xii. note D, in the second edition.

279 There are some points in my doctrines on the subject of the Classificatory Sciences to which Mr. Mill objects, (ii. 314, &c.), but there is nothing which I think it necessary to remark here, except one point. After speaking of Classification of organized beings in general, Mr. Mill notices (ii. 321) as an additional subject, the arrangement of natural groups into a Natural Series; and he says, that "all who have attempted a theory of natural arrangement, including among the rest Mr. Whewell, have stopped short of this: all except M. Comte." On this I have to observe, that I stopped short of, or rather passed by, the doctrine of a Series of organized beings, because I thought it bad and narrow philosophy: and that I sufficiently indicated that I did this. In the History (b. xvi. c. vi.) I have spoken of the doctrine of Circular Progression propounded by Mr. Macleay, and have said, "so far as this view negatives a mere linear progression in nature, which would

place each genus in contact with the preceding and succeeding ones, and so far as it requires us to attend to the more varied and ramified resemblances, there can be no doubt that it is supported by the result of all the attempts to form natural systems." And with regard to the difference between Cuvier and M. de Blainville, to which Mr. Mill refers (ii. 321), I certainly cannot think that M. Comte's suffrage can add any weight to the opinion of either of those great naturalists.

280Hist. Ind. Sc. b. x. note (VA) in the second edition.

281 B. xi. c. v. art. 11.

282 I have given elsewhere (see last chapter) reasons why I cannot assign to M. Comte's Philosophie Positive any great value as a contribution to the philosophy of science. In this judgment I conceive that I am supported by the best philosophers of our time. M. Comte owes, I think, much of the notice which has been given to him to his including, as Mr. Mill does, the science of society and of human nature in his scheme, and to his boldness in dealing with these. He appears to have been received with deference as a mathematician: but Sir John Herschel has shown that a supposed astronomical discovery of his is a mere assumption. I conceive that I have shown that his representation of the history of science is erroneous, both in its details and in its generalities. His distinction of the three stages of sciences, the theological, metaphysical, and positive, is not at all supported by the facts of scientific history. Real discoveries always involve what he calls metaphysics; and the doctrine of final causes in physiology, the main element of science which can properly be called theological, is retained at the end, as well as the beginning of the science, by all except a peculiar school.

283 I have also, in the same place, given the Inductive Pyramid for the science of Optics. These Pyramids are necessarily inverted in their form, in order that, in reading in the ordinary way, we may proceed to the vertex. Phil. Ind. Sc. b. xi. c. vi.

284Cosmos, vol. ii. note 35.

285 The reader will probably recollect that as Induction means the inference of general propositions from particular cases, Deduction means the inference by the application of general propositions to particular cases, and by combining such applications; as when from the most general principles of Geometry or of Mechanics, we prove some less general theorem; for instance, the number of the possible regular solids, or the principle of vis viva.

286 B. vi. c. v.

287 c. vi.

288Hist. b. vi. c. vi. sect. 13.

289Hist. Ind. Sc. b. viii.

290 Reprinted in the Appendix to this volume.

291Phil. Pos. t. iv. p. 264.

292Logic, b. vi. c. 3.

293 Jones, On Rent, 1833.

294Literary Remains, 1859.

295 The substance of this and the next chapter was printed as a communication to the Cambridge Phil. Soc. in 1840.

296 Or in the earlier editions, in the Philosophy of the Inductive Sciences.

297Phil. of Biol. c. v.

298Hist. Ind. Sc. b. ix. c. iii.

299Ibid. b. vii. c. ii.

300 Sir W. Hamilton's Note on the Philosophy of the Unconditioned.

301 Werenfels in Mr. Mansel's Bampton Lectures, lect. ii. Note 15.

302Scholium Generale at the end of the Principia.

303 B. iv. c. i.

304 Reid's Works, Supplementary Dissertation D.

305Hist. Sc. Id. b. iii.

306Hist. Sc. Id. b. vi. c. iii.

307 The remarks contained in this chapter have for the most part been already printed and circulated in a Letter to the Author of Prolegomena Logica, 1852.

308Biographical History of Philosophy, 1846. In a more recent edition the author of this work has modified his expressions, but still employs himself in arguing against Dr. Whewell, in order to overthrow Kant. So far as his arguments affect my philosophy, they are, as I conceive, answered in the various expositions which I have given of that philosophy.

309 B. ii. The Philosophy of the Pure Sciences. Chap. ii. Of the Idea of Space. Chap. iii. Of some peculiarities of the Idea of Space. Chap. vii. Of the Idea of Time. Chap. viii. Of some peculiarities of the Idea of Time.

310Prolegomena Logica, by H. L. Mansel, M.A. 1851.

311Logic, i p. 273, 3rd edit.

312 No. 193, p. 29.

313Prol. Log. p. 123.

314 See Phil. Ind. Sc. b. vi. c. iii.

315 Kant.

316 Republished as The History of Scientific Ideas.

317 Given in the Novum Organon Renovatum.

318Nov. Org. Ren. Aph. cv.

319Hist. Sc. Id. b. ix. c. vi.

320Hist. Ind. Sc. b. xviii. c. vi. sect. 5

321 P. 116. "No amount of human knowledge can be adequate which does not solve the phenomena of these absolute certainties."

322 Prof. Butler, Lect. ix. Second Series, p. 136, appears to think that Plato had sufficient grounds (of a theological kind) for the assumption of such Ideas; but I see no trace of them.

323 I am aware that this translation is different from the common translation. It appears to me to be consistent with the habit of the Greek language. It slightly leans in favour of my view; but I do not conceive that the argument would be perceptibly weaker, if the common interpretation were adopted.

324 In the First Alcibiades, Pythodorus is mentioned as having paid 100 minæ to Zeno for his instructions (119 A).

325 P. 183 e.

326Deip. xi. c. 15, p. 105.

327 Accedit et illud quod naturalis philosophia in iis ipsis viris, qui ei incubuerunt, vacantem et integrum hominem, præsertim his recentioribus temporibus, vix nacta sit; nisi forte quis monachi alicujus in cellula, aut nobilis in villula lucubrantis, exemplum adduxerit; sed facta est demum naturalis philosophia instar transitus cujusdam et pontisternii ad alia. Atque magna ista scientiarum mater ad officia ancillæ detrusa est; quæ medicinæ aut mathematicis operibus ministrat, et rursus quæ adolescentium immatura ingenia lavat et imbuat velut tinctura quadam prima, ut aliam postea felicius et commodius excipiant.

328 μεταξὺ οἰκονομίας καὶ χρεματισμοῦ, between house-keeping and money-getting.

329 τὸ περὶ τοὺς λόγους.

330 The Sciences are to draw the mind from that which grows and perishes to that which really is: μάθημα ψυχῆς ὁλκὸν ἀπὸ τοῦ γιγνομένου ἐπι τὸ ὄν.

331 ἐπὶ θέαν τῆς τῶν ἀριθμῶν φύσεως.

332 τῇ νοήσει αὐτῇ.

333 He adds "and for the sake of war;" this point I have passed by. Plato does not really ascribe much weight to this use of Science, as we see in what he says of Geometry and Astronomy.

334 ἀρθῶς ἔχει ἑξῆς μετὰ δευτέραν αὔξην τρίτην λαμβάνειν, ἔστι δέ που τοῦτο περὶ τὴν τῶν κύβων αὔξην καὶ τὸ βάθους μέτεχον.

335 ἀντίστροφον αὐτοῦ.

336 πρὸς ἐναρμόνιον φορὰν ὦτα παγῆναι.

337 πυκνώματα ἄ ττα.

338 τίνες ξύμφωνοι ἀριθμοὶ, &c.

339 Η καὶ διαλεκτικὸν καλεῖς τὸν λόγον ἑκάστου λαμβάνοντα τῆς οὐσίας; (§ 14).

340 ὥσπερ θριγγὸς τοῖς μαθήμασιν ἡ διαλεκτικὴ ἡμῖν ἐπάνω κεῖσθαι. (§ 14).]

341 Pol. vi. § 19.

342 He adds, "This oraton, this visible world, I will not say has any connexion with ouranon, heaven, that I may not be accused of playing upon words."

343 It is plain that Plato, by Hypotheses, in this place, means the usual foundations of Arithmetic and Geometry; namely, Definitions and Postulates. He says that "the arithmeticians and geometers take as hypotheses (hυποθεμενοι) odd and even, and the three kinds of angles (right, acute, and obtuse); and figures, (as a triangle, a square,) and the like." I say his "hypotheses" are the Definitions and Postulates, not the Axioms: for the Axioms of Arithmetic and Geometry belong to the Higher Faculty, which ascends to First Principles. But this Faculty operates rather in using these axioms than in enunciating them. It knows them implicitly rather than expresses them explicitly.

344 διάνοιαν ἀλλ' οὐ νοῦν.

345 The Diagram, as here described, would be this:

Intelligible World.   Visible World.
Intuition.   Conception.   Things.   Images.
Plato supposes the whole, and each of the two parts, to be divided in the same ratio, in order that the analogy of the division in each case may be represented.

346 The four segments might be as 4: 2: 2: 1; or as 9: 6: 6: 4; or generally, as a: ar: ar: ar2.

347
Hence the mind Reason receives
Intuitive or Discursive.
Milton.
348 τῇ τοῦ διαλέγεσθαι δυνόμει.

349 This term occurs in other parts of Aristotle. See the additional Note.

350 Mr. Owen, to whom I am indebted for the physiological part of this criticism, tells me, "All mammalia have bile, the carnivora in greater proportion than the herbivora: the gall-bladder is a comparatively unimportant accessory to the biliary apparatus; adjusting it to certain modifications of stomach and intestine: there is no relation between natural longevity and bile. Neither has the presence or absence of the gall-bladder any connexion with age. Man and the elephant are perhaps for their size the longest lived animals, and the latest at coming to maturity: one has the gall-bladder, and the other not."

351 Hist. Sc. Ind. b. iii.

352 These remarks were written in 1841. The accompanying Memoir contains a further discussion of this problem.

353 Cartes. Princip. iv. 23.

354 Jac. Bernoulli, Nouvelles Pensées sur le Système de M. Descartes, op. t. i. p. 239 (1686).

355 De la Cause de la Pesanteur (1689), p. 135.

356 Journal des Savans, 1703. Mém. Acad. Par. 1709.

Bulfinger, in 1726 (Acad. Petrop.), conceived that by making a sphere revolve at the same time about two axes at right angles to each other, every particle would describe a great circle; but this is not so.

357 Acad. Par. 1714, Hist. p. 106.

358 Acad. Par. 1733.

359 Acad. Sc. 1709. If we abandon the clear principles of mechanics, the writer says, "toute la lumière que nous pouvons avoir est éteinte, et nous voilà replongés de nouveau dans les anciennes ténèbres du Peripatetisme, dont le Ciel nous veuille preserver!"

It was also objected to the Newtonian system, that it did not account for the remarkable facts, that all the motions of the primary planets, all the motions of the satellites, and all the motions of rotation, including that of the sun, are in the same direction, and nearly in the same plane; facts which have been urged by Laplace as so strongly recommending the Nebular Hypothesis; and that hypothesis is, in truth, a hypothesis of vortices respecting the origin of the system of the world.

360Nouvelle Physique Céleste, Op. t. iii. p. 163.

The deviation of the orbits of the planets from the plane of the sun's equator was of course a difficulty in the system which supposed that they were carried round by the vortices which the sun's rotation caused, or at least rendered evident. Bernoulli's explanation consists in supposing the planets to have a sort of leeway (dérive des vaisseaux) in the stream of the vortex.

361 See Hist. Sc. Ideas, b. iii. c. ix. Art. 7.

362 See Mill's Logic, vol. i. p. 311, 2nd ed.

363 These letters refer to passages in the Translation annexed to this Memoir.

Made in the USA
Middletown, DE
19 January 2019